EARTH-SHELTERED HOUSES

EARTH-SHELTERED HOUSES
An Annotated Bibliography, 1950–1985

Pauline A. Keehn

FOREWORD BY SIDNEY A. BAGGS

WITHDRAWN

McFarland & Company, Inc., Publishers
Jefferson, North Carolina, and London

TH
4819
.E27
K33
1987

Library of Congress Cataloguing-in-Publication Data

Keehn, Pauline A.
Earth-sheltered houses.

Includes indexes.
1. Earth sheltered houses — Bibliography.
2. Earth sheltered houses — Design and construction — Bibliography
I. Title
Z7914.D87K4   1987   [TH4819.E27]   016.69′08   87-42511

ISBN 0-89950-248-2 (acid-free natural paper)

©1987 Pauline A. Keehn. All rights reserved.

Printed in the United States of America

McFarland   Box 611   Jefferson NC 28640

Dedicated to my darling mother
who urged me to
"get a job where you can use
your mind; don't go to work
in the factory."

ACKNOWLEDGMENTS

Thanks are due to the many who helped or took an interest in this work:

The late Donald Gillis, formerly executive director of the American Underground Space Association, for his enthusiasm and good advice and for helping to promote my work;

Raymond Sterling, director of the Underground Space Center, for lending an ear, giving me access to his files, and letting me borrow from his work to arrange this bibliography;

Sydney Baggs at the University of New South Wales for promoting my work;

William Baker of Earth Shelter Living magazine for his hospitality and for giving me access to his Earth Shelter Resource Center in Stillwater, Minnesota;

All at Shields Library who supported me for time off to research and prepare this book, notably Sandra Vella, Kazuko Dailey, Greg Preston and William McCoy;

Gail Schlachter, president of Reference Service Press, for her critique of my work and her detailed advice on publishing matters;

The Interlibrary Loan Division of Shields Library for their uncommon and consistent competence;

Peggy Davis, to whom I am most grateful of all for her help in the final typing of the indexes;

All the correspondents who gave me encouragement.

I also gratefully acknowledge permission from Unisearch Limited, University of New South Wales, Kensington, New South Wales, Australia, to reproduce the abstracts or summaries from the Australasian Proceedings of the First International Earth Sheltered Buildings Conference, and from Oklahoma State University and A&M College, Stillwater, Oklahoma, to reproduce the abstracts, summaries or excerpts from the abstracts or summaries which were published in the Proceedings of the First International Earth Sheltered Buildings Conference, 1983, the Proceedings of the Earth Sheltered Building Design Innovations Conference, 1980, and the Proceedings of the Earth Shelter Performance and Evaluation Conference, 1981. The inclusion of this material will greatly enhance the usefulness of this book to researchers.

TABLE OF CONTENTS

Acknowledgments		vii
Foreword		xiii
Introduction		xv
I.	General/Comprehensive	1
II.	Bibliography	22
III.	Theory/Philosophy	24
IV.	History	32
V.	Vernacular Earth-Integrated Housing	34
VI.	Architectural Design	38
VII.	Construction	53
VIII.	Insulation	80
IX.	Waterproofing/Drainage	83
X.	Heating/Ventilating/Cooling	89
XI.	Energy Consumption/Thermal Performance	93
XII.	Earth Contact Heat Transfer	110
XIII.	Site Considerations	122
XIV.	Landscaping	131
XV.	Costs/Economics	135
XVI.	Indoor Environment/Interior Design	140
XVII.	Psychological Issues/Acceptance	144
XVIII.	Physiological Issues/Health	150
XIX.	Environmental Impact	153
XX.	Surveys	154
XXI.	Urban/Community Issues	158
XXII.	Institutional Issues	163
XXIII.	Public Policy	174
XXIV.	Hazard Mitigation	178
XXV.	Non-Residential Applications	181
XXVI.	Conferences	193
XXVII.	Architects/Builders/Engineers	195
XXVIII.	Regional Applications	203
	Cold Climate	203
	Developing Countries	203
	Hot/Arid Lands	204
	Humid Continental Regions	206

	Australia	207
	China	211
	Korea	212
	Sweden	213
	United States	213
	Eastern U.S.	213
	Midwest U.S.	214
	Northwest U.S.	216
	Southeast U.S.	216
	Southwest U.S.	216
	Western U.S.	218
XXIX.	Case Studies	218
	Australia	218
	Bahamas	223
	Brazil	223
	Canada	223
	China	224
	England	224
	France	225
	Mexico	227
	New Zealand	228
	Norway	228
	Switzerland	228
	United States	228
	Arizona	228
	Arkansas	230
	California	231
	Colorado	235
	Connecticut	238
	Florida	238
	Georgia	240
	Idaho	241
	Illinois	241
	Indiana	243
	Iowa	244
	Kansas	246
	Kentucky	248
	Louisiana	248
	Maryland	249
	Massachusetts	250
	Michigan	251
	Minnesota	253
	Missouri	261
	Montana	264
	Nebraska	264
	Nevada	264
	New Hampshire	265

Table of Contents

New Jersey	266
New Mexico	267
New York	269
North Carolina	271
North Dakota	273
Ohio	273
Oklahoma	275
Oregon	277
Pennsylvania	278
Rhode Island	278
South Carolina	279
South Dakota	279
Tennessee	279
Texas	280
Utah	282
Vermont	283
Virginia	284
Washington State	284
West Virginia	285
Wisconsin	286
Wyoming	289
Location Not Specified	289
Conferences Cited	297
Serials Cited	302
Author Index	311
Geographic Index	323
Subject Index	332

FOREWORD

The concept of seeking shelter and comfort within the protection of the earth began when humans first occupied the cavern and excavated the pit dwelling as shelters from climatic extremes and carnivorous beasts, or as spaces in which to conduct rituals.

Through the millenia, humanity has continued to use spaces within the earth to satisfy the basic needs of comfort, shelter, security and worship. The cavern and pit-dwelling of the past is the lithotecture and earth-covered dwelling of today.

As the caves of our ancestors gave them comfort and protection, so the earth-sheltered building still provides a sense of security and protection. Occupants of present-day earth-covered buildings reduce their need for energy to heat and cool by utilizing the thermal mass of the earth as a heat sink or heat source-- also to modify the effect of climatic extremes. In one form, geotecture even presents a means of obtaining security from catastrophes in times of natural disaster or threats to world peace. It also caters to the need for privacy in a world with increasing populations and urban densities.

It is fascinating to follow the use of underground space for religious worship through the centuries. From caves such as Lascaux, to the underground churches of Europe, to the rock-cut temples of Asia and the many churches of the twentieth century, humanity seems to have had an atavistic need to worship within the cavities of the earth.

Geotecture as applied to the exstruction of lithotecture (space for human use mined into self-supporting rock) or the construction of earth-sheltered buildings (constructions within an excavation completed by a back-filling of earth) presents a tremendous potential for the development of human settlements with minimal impact upon natural systems in this century and the next. For example, in the USSR, Professor Oleg Alimov of the Institute of Automation, Kirghiz Academy of Sciences, Frunze, is working towards the introduction of earth-sheltered housing for the expanding city of Frunze in mountainous Kirghizia, where only 7 percent of the total available land is flat. This means that the conflicting needs of housing and agriculture are to be resolved by the implementation of earth-sheltered housing (in combination with lithotecture) in the foothills of the mountains surrounding Frunze in the next century.

With the passage of the last few decades, the United States movement has burgeoned and become a major force, with its headquarters at the American Underground Space Association (AUSA) at the University of Minnesota. Many thousands of houses had been completed by 1983, when the movement held its First International Conference in Sydney, Australia, formalizing its introduction to that country, where six earth-covered homes were already underway or completed. (Since that time, scores more have been finished.)

Other than extraterrestrial architecture and buildings beneath the sea, geotecture represents the only major significant change in the direction of architecture in this century. It has long needed a comprehensive guide to the information sources, and Pauline Keehn is to be congratulated for her initiative and dedication.

Since 1977, Underground Space (journal of the AUSA) has documented earth-sheltered buildings as well as lithotecture while the journal Geotecture (journal of the Geotecture International Association, GIA, founded in 1983) now emphasizes the international character of the movement. Earth-sheltered associations have been founded in Great Britain, Holland and Australia, and an Earth Building Conference was held in China in 1985. Consequently, the literature is experiencing exponential growth. Up to now, when one attempted research in the modern literature on earth-sheltered housing, it was very clear that the basic "spade work" on cataloguing and referencing (so readily available in other subject areas) had not been undertaken. The student, layman or interested professional found no assistance in the subject headings often found in library catalogues. For example, there was no "earth shelter" or "earth cover" heading, and as recently as the late 1960s, Australian libraries referenced "underground" as "caves"! It required the talents and application of a librarian/researcher with the vital interest and energy of Pauline Keehn to bring order out of the growing chaos.

Having devoted years of research to the production of this guide to the subject, Keehn now presents the reader with authoritative, accurate and comprehensive coverage of the North American as well as the international field. As the first definitive guide to the subject, it represents a basic research and education resource for all those interested in this fascinating "new" (and very ancient) type of shelter.

Dr. Sydney A. Baggs

School of Landscape Architecture, University of New South Wales, Kensington, Australia; founder of Geotecture International.

INTRODUCTION

Earth-integrated homes have been a part of the landscape since Homo sapiens first appeared, but they diminished in number as architecture was developed into an art form. There was a resurgence of interest in earth integration during the OPEC oil crisis in the mid 1970s because of the earth's capacity to moderate temperature. The high cost of fuel gave rise to a need to seek new energy-conserving heating and housing alternatives. Although the oil shortage seems to have subsided temporarily, the earth sheltered housing movement has maintained its growth because in addition to conserving energy, these homes have other attractions: a quieter living environment, protection from natural and man-caused hazards, preservation of the earth's surface affording more value for money spent on land and more land devoted to the plantscape, and an enhanced sense of privacy, an increasingly rare commodity in an overpopulated world. In addition, those who have lived in earth-sheltered homes maintain that they save money in maintenance and living expenses, two reasons being that insurance rates are often lower and, because the outside of an earth-sheltered house is not exposed to the elements, the cost of caring for the structure is lower.

The purpose of this bibliography is to provide access to the literature on earth-sheltered residential structures. No information guide covering a rapidly growing field can hope to be all-inclusive, but an effort has been made to find material on all aspects of earth sheltering published from 1950 through 1985. As a result, the book contains 1,826 English-language titles from both technical and popular literature, the majority covering the period since 1976.

Except in a relatively few cases where it proved impossible, all the entries were checked by the author. The vast majority of the entries are followed by abstracts or annotations. Where these are lacking, it is because the works could not be found and studied, no additional information on them could be located, or because the treatment was at the introductory level and therefore repetitive of what has been covered in many other works.

The 1,826 titles are arranged into twenty-nine broad subject categories, some of which are drawn from a topical outline developed by Dr. Raymond Sterling to arrange the papers of the

Introduction xvi

Second International Earth Sheltered Buildings Conference held in Minneapolis in 1986. Further access to the contents of the book is provided by subject, author, and geographic indexes. For example, the broad subject arrangement provides direct access to information on where earth-sheltered houses are located, but further access is afforded by the geographic index, which indexes locations contained in works cited throughout the book.

A subject index provides access to information on architects, contractors, construction features, architectural design features, building materials, brand names, heating and cooling systems and more.

The author index guides the users to the expertise and views of earth-sheltered housing specialists and aficionados. They include structural engineers, builders, architects, soil scientists, owner-builders, legislators, educators and many others.

Arranging the titles into the various subject categories at times presented a bit of a challenge, as frequently they could be classified equally well under two or three categories. For example, a paper which deals with earth contact heat transfer in a house in Australia gives equal attention to energy consumption. To avoid the necessity of listing citations two or three times under different categories, the other subjects dealt with in the works can be accessed by the detailed subject and geographic indexes.

The rather large General/Comprehensive section (Chapter I) covers both introductory-level works and those more extensive works providing basic information on all aspects of earth-sheltered design and construction. The latter includes those works prepared by the Underground Space Center.

A chronological listing of the conferences and an alphabetical listing of the periodicals (serials) cited as sources in abbreviated form in the bibliography will help in identifying and retrieving the originals of the papers and articles cited.

The only selection criteria were that the subject matter deal with any aspect of the use of subsurface space for residential dwellings--e.g. planning, design, construction, financing, siting, etc., as well as historical, philosophical, sociocultural, and psychological aspects--or that it reveal means and methods that could be used in the construction and design of earth-sheltered homes.

I first became interested in compiling a bibliography on earth sheltering because of a personal interest in innovative housing and energy conservation and because, as a librarian, I knew that there was no organized access to information on this topic. A preliminary bibliography on earth-sheltered housing that I published in 1981 elicited so much interest that I decided a comprehensive bibliography would fill a great need, a decision that was supported by the many experts in this field, whom I subsequently met at conferences and through correspondence. I hope that this bibliography will lead to a further development and acceptance of this form of human habitation.

I. GENERAL/COMPREHENSIVE

1. Advantages of underground explored. St. Paul Pion. Pr., Jan. 26, 1975.

2. Alabama Energy Extension Service. Earth sheltered housing. 6 p.

3. American Underground Space Association. Iowa Chapter. Earth shelter: a positive alternative for housing. 10 p.

4. Anderson, Carol. Earth sheltered housing from the ground up. NAHB Build., Aug. 1, 1980: 44-59.
    Architerra's hillside designs are shown.

5. Answers to questions on geotecture. Geotecture, v. 2, no. 3, 1985: 41-9.

6. Approaching free energy. Emmaus, PA: Rodale Pr., 1980. 117 p.
    The chapter on "Guidelines for going underground" (p. 106-13) briefly discusses site conditions, codes, design, ways of avoiding heat leaks, materials, humidity control and landscaping.

7. Article on increased interest in underground housing. N.Y. Times, Mar. 22, 1979.

8. Baggs, David W. Earth covered low life-cycle-cost housing. Geotecture, v. 1, no. 1, Oct. 1983: 13-6.
    Properly designed and properly functioning earth-contact residences can provide better levels of thermal comfort and lower life-cycle costs than those of above-ground residences. There is a discussion of the advantages and some of the disadvantages of earth contact dwellings, and definitions are given of the various terms applied to earth contact structures. A case study of an earth-covered residence in New South Wales, Australia, is presented and performance results are given. The house is the Hunter Valley Residence in New South Wales.

9. Baggs, Sydney A. Cool comfort underground. Uniken, Mar. 25/Apr. 7, 1978.

10. _____. Living in terraspace. Belle, Jan./Feb. 1978: 94-7.

11. _____. Living underground. Vogue Living, Feb./Apr. 1978: 39-41.

12. _____, Joan C. Baggs and David W. Baggs. 100 most frequently asked questions on earth-covered architecture. Chatswood, NSW, Aust.: BIAD, 1983.

13. _____. Terratecture. Archit. Aust., v. 72, no. 4, July 1983: 60-7.

14. _____. Underground architecture. Aust. House Gard., Dec. 1977: 185-7.

15. _____. Underground architecture. UNSW Q., Aug. 1980.

16. _____. Underground architecture. Planning, S.A., Feb./Mar. 1978: 7-13.

17. _____. Underground earth-integrated architecture. Pts. 1-2. Bldg. Econ., June 1977, Mar. 1978.

18. _____, and David Baggs. Underground, earth sheltered building. Prepared for the Committee of Inquiry into Technological Change in Australia.

19. Bannon-Harwood, Barbara. Earth shelters are here to stay. Concr. Constr., v. 25, no. 9, Sept. 1980: 647-57.
    The underground houses being built today are usually built of concrete and placed in what is commonly referred to as an insulation envelope which enables the thermal mass of the concrete walls, floors, and ceiling to store heat.

20. Barnard, John E. A new life -- underground. Went. Inst. Bull., Oct. 1973.

21. Baum, Gregory T., Andrew J. Boer, and James C. Macintosh, Jr. The earth shelter handbook. Milwaukee, WI: Tech/Data, 1980. 244 p.
    This book discusses siting, design, and construction considerations for many types of earth-sheltered homes including houses which use large earth berms, sod roofs, and those built into earth grades. Many line drawings and photos are included.

3 General/Comprehensive

22. Bethany, Marilyn. Earthy and efficient. N.Y. Times Mag., Oct. 21, 1979: 114.

23. Bligh, Thomas. Building underground. Earth J., v. 6, no. 2, Summer 1976: 29-36.

24. _____. Large scale underground housing projects. Am. Undergr. Assn., Conf., Atlanta, GA, June 1979.

25. _____. An overview of earth-sheltered buildings. Sol. Pass. and Hybr. Cool., DOE Conf., Washington, DC, Feb. 1980.

26. _____. Some technical issues of earth sheltering. U'Bahn Int. Earth Shel. Conf., Granite City, IL, Mar. 1979.

27. Booker, Frank. Why we moved underground. Farmstead, Mar. 1979.

28. Boyer, Lester L. Earth shelter goes international. In Proc., Am. Sol. Energ. Soc., Annu. Mtg., Minneapolis, MN, June 1983.

29. _____. Earth-sheltered housing phenomenon. In Education and industry, a joint endeavor: proc., Am. Soc. of Eng. Educ., 89th Annu. Mtg., Los Angeles, CA, June 21, 1981. v. 2, p. 324-8.

30. _____. Earth-sheltered structures. Annu. R. Energ., v.7, 1982: 201-19.

31. _____. 10 most wanted answers. Earth Shel. Dig. Energ. Rept., no. 3, May/June 1979: 1, 35.

32. Brown, Terry. Down, please. Home Energ. Dig. Wood Q., v. 4, no. 3, Winter 1979: 161-82.

33. Build underground to save energy. Surveyor, v. 154, no. 4567/4568, Dec. 20/27, 1979: 10-1.

34. Burgess, Debora. Living underground. Jefferson City, MO: Missouri Dept. of Nat. Resources, 1980. 15 p.
   This booklet gives general coverage of the basic information, such as: selecting a site, design considerations, design types, heating and cooling, waterproofing, etc.

35. Buried buildings on the rise? Sci. Dig., v. 91, Sept. 1983: 29.

36. Burnett, Ronald A. Earth sheltered living: an introduction. 2nd ed. Rogersville, MO: Dayspring Pr., 1979. 44 p.

37. Cabonne, Pierre. Keeping cave -- the new baroque. Realités, Spec. issue: Styles of living, no. 227, Oct. 1969.

38. Campbell, Stu. The underground house book. Charlotte, VT: Garden Way Pub. Co., 1979.

    This book covers most aspects of building and owning an earth-sheltered home. It discusses the key problems of ventilation, waterproofing, roof structure, and natural lighting. Also, discusses siting, designing, financing, meeting building codes, excavating, and the psychological factors of living close to or under the ground.

39. Capoccia, Stephen. Earth-sheltered comfort. Liv. Alt., v. 2, no. 4, Jan. 1981: 15-6.

40. Carter, Dave. Digging in: earth-sheltered housing for those ready to get started. Martell, NE: Energy Enterprises, 1979. 56 p.

    This book discusses initial planning, how to choose contractors, subcontractors, skilled labor and materials, financing and alternate means, different types of underground house design, such as A-frame, crescent, and dome.

41. _____. The grown man's tunneling guide. Lincoln, NE: Bright Prospects, 1980. 64 p.

    The author discusses the type of underground architecture which, except for exits, does not break the surface. Various kinds of buildings, from tunneled camping shelters to full-sized houses, are discussed.

42. Castles in the earth. Scene: the Dallas Morn. N., Nov. 28, 1976.

43. A computer course on earth-sheltered housing. Undergr. Sp., v. 4, no. 3, Nov./Dec. 1979: 178.

    A five-hour course on earth-sheltered housing on the Control Data PLATO educational system provides information on site selection, structural factors, code compliance, energy use, insulation, waterproofing, and financial considerations.

44. Cooper, B.L. The development and marketing of seminars on underground housing. In Proc., ASEE Coll. Ind. Educ. Conf., Tampa, FL., Jan. 29-Feb. 2, 1979. p. 204-7.

5 General/Comprehensive

45. Cunningham, Kim. Underground architecture: an alternate approach to architecture and energy conservation. Master's thesis. Stillwater, OK: Okla. State Univ., School of Archit., 1977.

46. Data bank attracts attention. Earth Shel. Dig. Energ. Rept., no. 2, Mar./Apr. 1979: 4.
A call for information from builders, architects, etc. on site specifics, construction details, institutional facts, life style, psychology and assessment, etc.

47. Data bank forms are ready. Earth Shel. Dig. Energ. Rept., no. 4, July/Aug. 1979: 31.
Earth Shelter Digest and Energy Report devised a questionnaire to solicit information for and membership in the Earth Shelter Data Bank, information on background, site, construction data, codes, institutional information, lifestyle, assessment, publicity, and additional comments.

48. Data bank started. Earth Shel. Dig. Energ. Rept., no. 1, Jan./Feb. 1979: 5.
The Earth Shelter Data Bank will collect information on existing earth dwellings including information on site orientation, construction data, financing, and code legislation.

49. Dean, Andrea O. Underground housing's first "how to" manual. AIA J., v. 67, no. 13, Nov. 1978: 44-5+.
This is a summary of Earth Sheltered Housing Design prepared by the Underground Space Center.

50. Dean, Tom. Underground buildings are not the complete answer. Workbench, Jan./Feb. 1979: 104-5.

51. Dempewolff, Richard F. Underground housing. Sci. Dig., Nov. 1975: 40-53.
This is a brief review of various existing applications of terratecture: a marriage of surface and subsurface, employing the advantages of both.

52. _____. Your next house could have a grass roof. Pop. Mech., v. 147, no. 3, Mar. 1977: 78-81+.

53. Deppen, D. Guidelines for going underground. New Shel., v. 1, no. 1, Feb. 1980: 74-9.
Two factors to be considered prior to constructing an underground house are site conditions and the location of the water table. The design of the house should be based on the

local climate and site conditions. The common areas of heat loss are discussed, as are alternative designs to reduce heat losses. The roof should be covered with 1.5-2 feet of earth and all slopes should be graded away from the house.

54. _____. Principles for going underground. In <u>Conf. proc., Sol. NW Conf.</u>, Portland, OR, July 14, 1978. p. 26-31.
The following aspects of underground architecture are discussed: land, codes, design, heat leaks, materials, transitions between underground and above ground areas, humidity and landscaping.

55. Diamond, Stuart. Underground life. <u>Omni</u>, v. 4, Nov. 1981: 41.

56. Earth-shelter update. <u>Buildings</u>, v. 74, no. 11, Nov. 1980.

57. <u>Earth sheltered construction: a collection of articles from Concrete Construction magazine</u>. Addison, IL: Concr. Constr. Pub., Inc., World of Concr. Ctr., 1981. 28p.
Eight articles by leaders in the field.

58. Earth-sheltered home tours to be offered. <u>Underline</u>, v. 3, no. 6, Sept./Oct. 1982: 3.
Bus tours of earth sheltered, passive solar homes in Minneapolis and St. Paul are offered by Earth Shel-Tours of St. Paul.

59. Earth-sheltered housing. **Futurist**, v. 16, no. 1, Feb. 1982: 39.

60. Earth-sheltered housing film premiered in Minnesota. <u>Undergr. Sp.</u>, v. 4, no. 5, Mar./Apr. 1980: 321-2.
A 28-minute dramatized documentary, <u>Grass on the roof</u>, was made by the Underground Space Center. It premiered on Dec. 10, 1979.

61. Earth-sheltered -- surprisingly well accepted, but it's technically demanding. <u>Housing</u>, v. 62, no. 3, Sept. 1982: 73.

62. The earth-sheltering idea. <u>Sunset</u>, v. 168, no. 4, Apr. 1982: 120-6.

63. Edelhart, Mike. The good life underground. <u>Omni</u>, Jan. 1980: 50-5.

64. Eggert, Jim. <u>Low cost earth shelters</u>. Harrisburg, PA: Stackpole Books, Inc., 1982. 159 p.

The book is divided into two sections. Pt. 1, Deciding to go underground, discusses the philosophy and possibilities of building a small, inexpensive earth-sheltered home, including information on site selection and planning. Other topics: earth roof versus conventional roof, the pros and cons of various foundation types (pole, concrete block, treated wood, etc.), the theory of underground construction, and some actual experiences of owner/builders. Pt. 2, Building an earth-shelter, gives a detailed description of the building of the author's earth sheltered office.

65. FEMA study finds earth sheltered structures safe, efficient, durable. Underline, v. 4, no. 1, Nov./Dec. 1982: 5.

A Federal Emergency Management Agency study on the energy and safety performance of earth sheltered structures has concluded that well-constructed earth covered homes are exceptionally durable and safe. The 312-page study was conducted by Moreland Associates, Forth Worth, TX; the results are published in Earth-covered buildings: an exploratory analysis for hazard and energy performance.

66. Frank, Robert. Earth-shelter homes: an age-old answer to a new problem. Coeur d'Alene Pr., Mar. 1980: 18-21.

67. Franks, James. Earth shelter building: the reasons for their growth in the USA, and a look at the possible British market. Chart. Quant. Surv., v. 6, no. 1, Aug. 1983: 8-9.

68. Furst, Terry. The complete earth shelter book: introduction.

69. Gangnes, David. On the sunny side . . . earth sheltered homes. Eye of the Falcon, Aug. 1980.

70. Gentle on the land: earth-sheltered homes. Sports Afield, v. 185, Mar. 1981: 71+.

71. Getting down to earth. R. Est. Today, v. 14, May 1981: 16+.

72. Givoni, Baruch. Earth-integrated buildings: an overview. Archit. Sci. R., v. 24, no. 2, June 1981: 42-53.

73. Go underground for the good of our environment? Daily Pac. Build., no. 12, 1973: 4.

74. Going underground. Consum. Res., v. 63, no. 1, Jan. 1980: 11-2.

A brief article giving a generally favorable rating to earth sheltered housing but without much detail.

75. Golany, Gideon S. Earth-sheltered habitat: history, architecture and urban design. New York, NY: Van Nostrand Reinhold, 1983. 240 p.

This book discusses earth sheltering as an alternative housing and settlement design solution especially for climatically-stressed areas. He also applies many of these solutions for housing in nonstressed climates. The many energy-conserving features of earth covered housing are discussed and numerous other aspects of subsurface development are examined, including urban-scale and house-scale design, land use integration, psychological obstacles, historical experience, and others.

76. Gorman, James. The Earth's the ceiling. Sciences, v. 16, no. 2, Apr. 1976: 16-20.

77. _____. Underground architecture. In Underground utilization. T. Stauffer, ed. Kansas City, MO: Univ. of Missouri - Kansas City, Dept. of Geosciences, 1978. v. 3, p. 329-31.

78. Grass on the roof; a new film on earth sheltered housing. St. Paul, MN: Filmart Prod., Inc., Distrib. Dept. C, 199 E. Annapolis St.

This is a dramatized documentary introducing the concepts and techniques of earth sheltering through the eyes of Mortimer, who inherits an earth sheltered house from his Aunt Emma. Emma's ghost takes him on a U.S. tour of earth-sheltered residential and commercial structures via special effects and on-location shooting. Produced and directed by Slavko Nowytski with script by playwright Lance Belville.

79. Green, Bruce H. Underground construction. Alt. Energ., no. 39, Sept./Oct. 1979: 13-5.

Briefly discusses thermal mass, external insulation, earth cover, energy storage, earth-tempered air, and waterproofing as applied to underground housing.

80. _____. Your underground house. In Underground utilization. T. Stauffer, ed. Kansas City, MO: Univ. of Missouri - Kansas City, Dept. of Geosciences, 1978. v. 4, p. 600-7.

This is an introductory article directed to the individual who is considering building an underground house. It describes and illustrates the different types of underground homes and their performance.

81. Green, Larry. Construction going down instead of up. L.A. Times, Sunday, Mar. 9, 1980.

9 General/Comprehensive

82. Green, Terence M. "Dig in" is more than just a catchword. L.A. Times, Mar. 13, 1983, sec. 8: 10.

83. Grondzik, Walter. 101 questions on earth sheltered housing. Stillwater, OK: Okla State Univ., Archit. Ext., 120 Architecture Bldg., 1985. 70 p.
    This book contains answers to questions asked during a 5-1/2 hour teleconference on earth sheltered housing viewed by over 1,000 persons at 30 universities nationwide on March 26, 1983.

84. Harris, Ron. Down to earth. Ford Times, Nov. 1982: 29-31, 47.

85. He joins Mother Earth in new building venture. Wash. Star, May 25, 1979: F8.

86. Herman, L. Vance. The underground house: you can build it. Albuquerque, MN: 620 El Paraiso N.W., 1978. 80 p.

87. High-tech homes -- based on basics. Curr. Hlth., v. 2, no. 9, Dec. 1982: 17-9.

88. Homes under the range. Bost. Mag., v. 74, May 1982: 197+.

89. The house in the hill. Economist, v. 273, Nov. 3, 1979: 38.
    This article discusses the recent interest in earth sheltering in the U.S., including information about the establishment of the Underground Space Center.

90. How would you like to live here? Nat. Geog. World, 49, Sept. 1979: 15-9.

91. Hylton, Joe. Subterranean homes, active/passive solar homes plan book. Portsmouth, OH: Underground Homes, 1980. 130 p.
    The book is divided into two broad sections: solar homes and earth sheltered homes.

92. Interest is building up down under. Buildings, Jan. 1977. 6 p.

93. It's here today . . . the home of the future, embraced by the earth, warmed and lighted by the sun. Workbench, 35, Jan. 1979: 60-1+.

94. Jansson, B. TERRASPACE - a world to explore. Undergr. Sp., v. 1, no. 1, May/June 1976: 9-18.

95. Jones, Edward. The principles of underground. Bascom, OH: Solar Usage Now.

96. Jones, Lloyd S. Thinking down through earth. Nav. Civ. Engr., v. 17, no. 1, Spring 1976: 4-6, 37-9.
This article reviews some of the successful uses that have been made of underground space in industry and, to a lesser extent, in residential applications. John Barnard's Ecology House is used as an example of an underground house which has brought a substantial reduction in energy use.

97. _____. Underground space: another resource. Mil. Engr., v. 69, no. 452, Nov./Dec. 1977: 400-4.
All aspects of underground construction are examined as a means of satisfying the nation's need for land and energy conservation with the minimum of adverse environmental effects. Military uses are stressed, including provision for housing.

98. Keating, Bern. The underground resurfaces. Am. Way, Dec. 1979: 20-4.

99. Kern, Barbara, Ken Kern, Jane Mullan, and Otis Mullan. The earth sheltered owner-built home. North Fork, CA: Mullein Pr./Owner-Builder Pub., 1982. 265 p.
This book surveys many low cost building techniques suitable for the owner-builder, and examines three very different owner-built homes in detail, showing the step-by-step construction sequences. The low cost techniques, costing $30/sq. ft., $15/sq. ft. and $4/sq. ft. are discussed.

100. Kramer, Charlene Kahlor. Interest in underground housing surfaces. Sell./Serv., Jan./Feb. (n.d.).

101. Labs, Kenneth. Building underground: a tempered climate, earth as insulation, and the surface-under-surface interface. In Energy efficient buildings. W. Wagner, ed. New York, NY: Archit. Rec. Books/McGraw-Hill Book Co., 1980.

102. Lane, Charles A. Earth sheltered housing. Log Home Build. Alt. Hous., Feb./Mar. 1981: 24-7.
Questions and answers regarding earth-sheltered housing, excerpted from an essay by the author.

103. _____. An essay -- frequently asked questions on earth sheltered housing. In Residential applications: transcripts of selected presentations; Going Under to Stay on Top,

Minneapolis, MN, Oct. 1977. Minneapolis, MN: Univ. of Minn., Underground Space Ctr., 1979. p. 69-75.

104. _____. An essay -- frequently asked questions on earth sheltered housing. Undergr. Sp., v. 4, no. 3, Nov./Dec. 1979: 143-52.

Brief answers are provided for some of the most frequently asked questions concerning earth-sheltered housing: site selection, structural systems, energy use criteria, heating, ventilation and air conditioning, waterproofing, insulation, and the factors affecting construction costs.

105. _____. Frequently asked questions on earth sheltered housing. Archit. Minn., v. 6, no. 2, Apr. 1980: 31-5.

106. _____. Underground basics. Pop. Sci., v. 221, Nov. 1982: 76-9.

This article discusses the pitfalls to avoid when building underground and some common misconceptions.

107. Langewiesche, Wolfgang. There's a gold mine under your house. House Beaut., v. 92, no. 8, Aug. 1950: 92-4, 133-5.

Basements are re-examined in the light of new information gathered in House Beautiful's Climate Control Project. Since underground temperatures smooth out climatic extremes, basements can be redesigned to create a new kind of room.

108. Lees, A.W. Last word on underground. Pop. Sci., v. 225, Sept. 1984: 120, 122.

This is a continuation of Charles Woods' and William Shurcliff's debate on the pros and cons of earth-sheltered housing.

109. _____. The great underground debate. Pop. Sci., v. 225, Aug. 1984: 102-4.

A debate by earth-shelter designer Charles Woods and William H. Shurcliff, who writes on energy-saving construction. Woods presents the pros, Shurcliff the cons.

110. Linton, Marilyn. Going under to stay on top. Toronto Sun, Tues., Jan. 31, 1978.

111. Living underground. Newsweek, June 5, 1978: 106, 109.
Discusses the boom in underground construction.

112. Lorenz, Ray. Facts about underground homes. Fam. Hand., v. 30, July/Aug. 1980: 44, 46.

This article discusses energy savings, cost of construction, structural strength, financing, designs, and finishing. A diagram shows how an underground home is put together.

113. _____. Underground home. Fam. Hand., v. 30, no. 2, Feb. 1980: 12-5.

114. Low-profile shelter. Mech. Eng., v. 103, no. 8, Aug. 1981: 44-5.

115. McClarin, Jim. Above-ground house exposed. Earth Shel. Dig. Energ. Rept., no. 6, Nov./Dec. 1979: 12.
A witty expose of the conventional, above ground home.

116. McCray, J.W. and S.E. Brubaker. Earth-sheltered housing: the what and the why. Spec. rept. 100. Fayetteville, AR: Univ. of Arkansas, Agric. Exp. Sta., 1982. 20 p. (Agric. pub., A-110. NTIS, PC AO2/MF A01).
This report contains basic information on earth sheltering: benefits; construction-related considerations; financial aspects.

117. McCrone, Susan J. Earth-covered structures are no longer of the future but of the present. Nat. Exp., v. 3, nos. 4, 5, Dec. 1978/Jan. 1979.

118. Machowski, Barb. Go underground. Fam. Hand., v. 33, no. 1, Jan. 1983: 30-1.

119. Marier, Don. Introduction to underground. Alt. Energ., no. 33, Aug. 1978: 4-5.
This article reviews R. Sterling's Earth sheltered housing design and M. Wells' Underground designs, and lists some sources of information.

120. Martindale, David. Earth shelters. New York, NY: E.P. Dutton, 1981. 148 p.
In this highly readable book, the author gives comprehensive coverage of progress in the field: history from the time of cave dwellers; earth-sheltered living in other countries; American history of sod homes and basements; interviews with homeowners and with some of the leaders in the field.

121. _____. New homes revive the ancient art of living underground. Smithsonian, v. 9, no. 11, Feb. 1979: 96-105.
This article describes various underground residences, libraries, etc. in the U.S. and enumerates the disadvantages.

122. Minnesota Masonry Institute. Residential design for the

1980's: earth sheltered space. Minneapolis, MN. (#513).
This is a guide to the technical terms and structural details associated with earth-sheltered housing.

123. Missouri Dept. of Natural Resources. Earth shelter housing. Jefferson City, MO, 1980. 5 p. (Energy Facts).
This booklet answers the questions: What is earth-sheltered housing? What are the advantages? What design restrictions are imposed by an earth-sheltered house? What materials work most effectively? Is insulation necessary? What about drainage and leakage problems? What supplementary heating is required? How much is all this going to cost?

124. Moreland, Frank L. Earth covered habitat - an alternative future. Undergr. Sp., v. 1, no. 4, Aug. 1977: 295-308.
Earth-covered housing is examined from a consumer perspective.

125. _____. Questions frequently asked about earth-covered dwellings. Concr. Constr., v. 23, no. 2, Feb. 1978: 120-4.

126. Neal, Wallace. Human spaces underground - an old/new technology. Constr. Spec., v. 31, no. 1, Jan. 1978: 39-42, 44-50.
This article discusses the techniques of building underground, including energy benefits, types of structures, soil cover, vegetation, heat flow, ventilation, and humidity control.

127. Oddo, Sandra. House-building goes underground. House Gard., v. 153, Sept. 1981: 64+.
This article tells why underground building is gaining popularity around the country.

128. Oehler, Mike. The $50 & up underground house book. Bonners Ferry, ID: Mole Pub. Co., 1978. 112 p.
This is one of the first comprehensive how-to guides for the do-it-yourselfer. The author designs underground homes and has lived underground since 1971. The book is written in a clear and amusing style, and gives many tips on designing, cutting materials and costs up to 90 percent, using solar energy, building into hillsides, etc. The author doesn't like concrete; he has chosen what he calls the "PSP" system (post-shoring-polyethylene) as the structural core of his underground houses.

129. O'Neil, Bill. Earth sheltered housing. Rev. Madison, WI: State of Wisconsin Legislative Council, 1980. 26 p. (Inf. Bull. no. 80-30).

130. Part underground, but still light. South. Liv., v. 19, Oct. 1984: 162+.

131. Patterson, Ann. "House of the future" draws life from design, technological wizardry. Ariz. Repub., Sunday, Feb. 24, 1980.

132. Pittman, S., W. Pittman, and G. Haggard. Earth sheltered passive solar homes. Adobe Today, v. 23, 1979: 16-9+.

133. Portland Cement Association. Design and construction of earth sheltered homes. Skokie, IL: 5420 Old Orchard Rd. (CSO18).
This is a sound/slide presentation developed under the sponsorship of U.S. Dept. of Housing and Urban Development. Running time: 21 min.

134. _____. An overview of earth sheltered construction. June 1979. 9 p.

135. Pringle, Murray T. Cave-dwelling is "in" again. Mpls. Trib., Sunday, Dec. 15, 1974.

136. Questions and answers. Geotecture, v. 2, no. 4, 1985: 11-37.

137. Randall, (Honorable) William J. Space age cave dweller. Cong. Rec., App., v. 109, pt. 10, July 18, 1963: A4569-71.

138. Rawlings, Roger. Why build below? New Shel., v. 3, no. 1, Jan. 1982: 18-22.
Insulated underground houses can be energy efficient, but superinsulated surface houses can be just as efficient and they are both cheaper and easier to build. But there are other reasons to build underground: better security from storms, tornadoes, burglars, and fire. For these reasons, insurance rates are often substantially lower. Underground houses also offer lower maintenance costs, a quiet environment, and preservation of the landscape.

139. Rogers, Patsy. Underground. Wash. Star Sunday Mag., Jan. 1, 1978: 10-2.

140. Roy, Robert L. How to build an underground home. Farmstead, Mar. 1979.

141. Scafe, Gayle R. Underground building: a new form of ar-

chitectural design for the total building market. In The potential of earth-sheltered and underground space: proc., Undergr. Sp. Conf. and Expos., Kansas City, MO: June 8-10, 1981. T.L. Holthusen, ed. Elmsford, NY: Pergamon Pr., 1981. p. 443-50.

Earth-sheltered housing seems to offer a practical and viable approach to solving some of the problems of the building industry. What is needed to make underground building cost-competitive with conventional building is mass production techniques coupled with superior design concepts.

142. Schramm, Donald R. and Gerald Klodt. Underground housing: some questions and answers. Madison, WI: Univ. of Wisc. Ext., 1980. 4 p.

143. Scott, Ray G. How to build your own underground home: a complete guide to planning, designing, building, and living comfortably in a geothermic house. Blue Ridge Summit, PA: TAB Books, 1979. 256 p.

Written by a professional engineer, this book discusses the background of earth shelter and its advantages.

144. _____. The underground home answer book. Blue Ridge Summit, Pa: TAB Books, 1983. 272 p.

Expert advice is given on planning and construction. Also, directions are given for advanced designs incorporating a windmill, geodesic dome, and solar heat.

145. _____. Underground homes: an alternative lifestyle. Blue Ridge Summit, PA: TAB Books, 1981. 400 p.

This book answers questions on designing, building, and living in an underground house, including valuable hints on maintenance, building methods, design, construction, and others.

146. Seitz, Doug. Earth sheltering schools: earth sheltering classes can be taken almost anywhere, including your corner mailbox. Earth Shel. Liv., no. 34, July/Aug. 1984: 10-1.

Courses on earth sheltering are being offered at all levels in all parts of the country. Names and addresses of some sources are given.

147. Sheltered by the earth: living underground, warmed by the sun. Dyn. Yrs., Jan./Feb. 1982: 20-7.

148. Shih, Jason C. Underground architecture. In Architec-

tural research. James C. Snyder, ed. New York, NY: Van Nostrand Reinhold, 1984. p. 242-56.

After giving a brief history, this chapter briefly discusses current research, substantive issues (conservation of resources, structural, material and equipment systems, building habitability, process of design and construction, human security and safety), combining innovation with established practice, and implications for modern architecture.

149. Shurcliff, W. and R. Sterling. Earth-sheltered homes: weighing the advantages. Undergr. Sp., v. 5, no. 4, Jan. 1981: 200-4.

William Shurcliff, a Massachusetts physicist and Ray Sterling, senior editor of Underground Space debate the advantages and disadvantages of earth-sheltered houses on several points: land use, drainage systems, accident risks, isolation from aid if needed, parking, privacy, burglary, site requirements, and others. Both admitted that good planning could overcome some disadvantages and that earth-sheltered housing is appropriate in some but not all locations.

150. _____. Underground houses: some offhand thoughts against them. Earth Shel. Dig. Energ. Rept., no. 11, Sept./Oct. 1980: 27-9.

Some arguments against building underground homes are presented. The author compares an underground house to a superinsulated aboveground house.

151. Simmons, Lon B. Response: cover your roof. Earth Shel. Dig. Energ. Rept., no. 16, July/Aug. 1981: 16-9.

This article discusses the advantages of earth-covered homes over conventional aboveground homes.

152. Smay, V. Elaine. Underground houses - low fuel bills, low maintenance, privacy, security. Pop. Sci., v. 210, no. 4, Apr. 1977: 84-9.

153. Some down-to-earth advantages in underground houses: save on energy costs, and just mow the roof. Chr. Sci. Mon., Sept. 10, 1980: 18, col. 1.

154. Stauffer, Truman, ed. Underground utilization: a reference manual of selected works in eight volumes. Kansas City, MO: Univ. of Missouri - Kansas City, Dept. of Geosciences, 1978. 8 v. (Geog. Publication).

v. 1. Historical perspective. v. 2. Uses for underground space. v. 3. Space construction underground. v. 4. Human response and social acceptance of underground space. v. 5. Advantages in underground space use. v. 6. Regulations and policy in the use of underground space. v. 7. The future of underground development. v. 8. Index.

155. Stephens, D. The underground dwelling - a home for all seasons. Wood Burn. Q. Home Energ. Dig., v. 2, no. 3, Winter 1977: 100-8.

156. Sterling, Raymond L. Current research into the effectiveness of earth sheltered buildings as a passive energy conservation technique. In Proc., 4th Nat. Pass. Sol. Conf., Kansas City, MO, Oct. 3-5, 1979. Newark, DE: Int. Sol. Energ. Soc., Am. Sect., Univ. of Del., 1979. p. 425-8.
   This paper is an overview of current research efforts in earth-sheltered building design, construction, and acceptance.

157. _____. Earth-sheltered, energy independent (ESEI) building design project. Undergr. Sp., v. 1, no. 4, Aug. 1977: 371-2.
   This is a description of a research project conducted between Jan. 1977 and Feb. 1978. The study resulted in the book entitled: Earth Sheltered Housing Design, published by Van Nostrand Reinhold.

158. _____. Earth-sheltered housing: at a threshold. Undergr. Sp., v. 6, no. 1, July/Aug. 1981: 3.
   Earth-sheltered housing is at the threshold of becoming an acceptable housing option in the U.S. Its further success depends on a number of factors: reliable data on their energy efficiency, their suitability for their intended function, and their cost-effectiveness.

159. _____. Earth sheltered housing: a guest editorial. Alt. Energ., no. 33, Aug. 1978: 2.
   Adapted from the author's book, Earth Sheltered Housing Design.

160. _____. Energy and earth sheltering revisited. AIA J., v. 72, no. 1, Jan. 1983: 48-9.
   Earth sheltering is becoming but one design technique to use in combination with others to deal with energy conservation and other problems.

161. _____, Susan R. Nelson, and Martin Jaffe. Planning for underground space. Chicago, IL: Am. Plan. Assn., 1983. 54 p. (Plan. Advis. Serv. Rept., no. 375).

162. Sudjic, Deyan. Hidden depths: underground architecture. Bldg. Des., no. 421, Nov. 10, 1978: 26-7.

163. Swayze, Jay. Underground gardens and homes. Hereford, TX: Geobuilding Systems, 1980. 136 p.
The author relates his experiences as a builder of underground homes for eighteen years. Color sketches of various types of homes and a variety of floor plans are shown. The three basic designs of earth-sheltered homes are discussed with respect to utility savings, security, insurance costs, and benefits to garden plants.

164. Tatz, Vicki. Earth-sheltered homes no longer an "underground" fad. News World, May 1, 1978.

165. They've seen "underground" become respectable. Earth Shel. Dig. Energ. Rept., no. 3, May/June 1979: 38-40.

166. Things are looking up underground (and) Lifeline for the landscape. Bldg. Prog., Mar. 1977.

167. Thompson, Irene. Subterranean living. Ladies' Home J., v. 98, no. 1, Jan. 1981.

168. Thompson, L.K. Below-ground living. Workbench, 35, Mar. 1979: 92.

169. Tollin, Gale. Beneath the surface. Ariz. Repub., Feb. 3, 1980 (and) Wash. Post, Feb. 9, 1980 (and) Wisc. State J., Jan. 27, 1980.

170. Trombley, Stephen and Sydney A. Baggs. Earth sheltered architecture, . . . etc. RIBA J., v. 89, no. 5, May 1982: 67+.

171. Trull, J.R. Solar plus saves a bundle. Mech. Illus., v. 74, June 1978: 64.

172. The 12 technical fact sheets on earth-sheltering commissioned by the Innovative Structures Program in the U.S. Dept. of Energy have been completed and are available to the public. (Brief.) Undergr. Sp., v. 6, no. 4-5, Jan./Apr. 1982: 200.

173. 200 attend Center's film premiere. Underline, v. 2, no. 2, Jan. 1980: 1-2.
The Underground Space Center's new movie Grass on the roof premiered on December 10, 1979.

19 General/Comprehensive

174. Underground Homes. Primer to earth sheltered living. Portsmouth, OH, 1979. 20 p.

175. Underground Homes information manual. Portsmouth, OH. 1 v. looseleaf.
Contents: Plans for the future – a pamphlet of earth sheltered designs; planning your home; structural considerations; waterproofing; insulation; working systems; products; additional sources of information; miscellaneous.

176. Underground house report. Charlotte, VT: Garden Way Pub. Co., 1981?

177. Underground housing seminars are now available. Moth. Earth N., no. 51, May/June 1978: 58.
The seminars are available at Oklahoma State Univ. School of Architecture Extension, since April 1977.

178. Underground movers find safety and savings. Wash. Star, Friday, Sept. 28, 1979.

179. Underground Space Center. Earth sheltered housing design: guidelines, examples and references. Project coordinator: Ray Sterling. New York, NY: Van Nostrand Reinhold, 1979. 318 p.
The "Bible" of the earth-shelter industry used by experts and laymen alike, this book details the vital aspects of earth-sheltered design, construction, and living. Chapters include: site planning, architectural design, energy use, structural design, waterproofing and insulation. It gives an excellent discussion of zoning and building codes and includes numerous photos, charts, diagrams and floor plans.

180. _____. Earth sheltered housing design. Prepared by John Carmody and Raymond Sterling. Rev. ed. New York, NY: Van Nostrand Reinhold, 1985. 350 p.
Every section of this new edition has been rewritten and expanded and some new sections have been added to reflect current trends and give up-to-date information. The chapters cover the history of earth-sheltered design, site and building design, energy use and costs, structural design, waterproofing and insulation, public policy issues and eighteen case studies, ten of them new to this edition. A Bibliography on Earth Contact Heat Transfer is included.

181. _____. Earth sheltered residential design manual. Prepared by Raymond Sterling, William Farnan, John Car-

mody, and Gail Elnicky. New York, NY: Van Nostrand Reinhold, 1982. 251 p.

This technical guide for planning, design, and construction of earth-sheltered housing is intended primarily for use by practicing architects, builders, and developers. It would also be useful to code officials and lending institutions when making decisions concerning financing and construction details. It discusses all of the factors which affect the design and construction of earth-sheltered homes.

182. _____ and Oklahoma State University, Center for Natural Energy Design. Earth sheltered structures fact sheets. Washington, DC: U.S. Dept. of Energy, 1981. 12 fact sheets.

No. 1 Site investigation. No. 2. Planting considerations. No. 3. Waterproofing techniques. No. 4. Waterproofing considerations and materials. No. 5. Insulation principles. No. 6. Insulation materials and placement. No. 7. Daylighting design. No. 8. Indoor air quality. No. 9. Earth coupled cooling techniques. No. 10 Disaster protection. No. 11. Building in expansive clays. No. 12. Passive solar heating.

183. Vadnais, Kathleen. Earth shelter design revival: who's building what, where. In Earth shelter 2: coll. pap., 1st Earth Shel. Hous. Conf. and Exhib., Minneapolis, MN, Apr. 9-11, 1980. Minneapolis, MN: Univ. of Minn., Undergr. Sp. Ctr., 1980.

The author is a journalist interested specifically in earth-sheltered housing.

184. Von Fraunhoffer, Hermann J. The housing alternative. Phoenix, AZ: Concept 2000, 1979. 78 p.

The publisher, Concept 2000, is an architectural group that focuses on energy efficient designs for the Southwest U.S. This booklet is an introduction to earth sheltering and includes some designs.

185. Von Ranson, Jonathan. Taking shelter in the earth. New Roots, (no date): 44-5.

186. Wade, Herb. Building underground: the design and construction handbook for earth sheltered houses. Emmaus, PA: Rodale Pr., 1983. 289 p.

This guide is intended for do-it-yourselfers and for people who want to hire engineers and builders. The well-illustrated text covers: site selection and soil evaluation, basic design options and floor plans, passive solar designs, construction methods and materials, insulation and waterproofing, electrical systems, plumbing, lighting and heating, humidity control, ventilation and natural cooling. Appendices: Estimating heating requirements for underground houses; Manufacturers of waterproofing materials; Bibliography.

187. _____, Jeffrey Cook, Kenneth Labs, and Steve Selkowitz, eds. Passive solar: subdivisions, windows, underground. New York, NY: Am. Sol. Energ. Soc., 1983. 256 p.
Contains eight articles on underground housing, reviewed elsewhere in this bibliography.

188. Wampler, Louis. Underground homes. Rev. ed. Gretna, LA: Pelican Pub. Co., 1980. 121 p.

189. Waterbury, Norman L and Nora E. Villagran. A home for all seasons. Eugene, OR: Utopia Des. & Eng. (no date) 27 p.

190. Weiss, Peter Michael. Earth sheltering: an energy efficient design alternative to housing. Master's thesis. Cornell Univ., 1980. 194 p.

191. Wells, Malcolm. The case for young underground. Learning How, v. 1, no. 1, Oct. 1977.

192. _____. Down with architecture. Printed and distributed by the author, Aug. 1975.

193. _____. The five secrets of earth shelter. The Own. Build., no. 9, Fall 1983: 8-9.
1. Follow local building codes. 2. Structurally sound design. 3. Waterproofing. 4. Insulation. 5. Daylighting and natural ventilation.

194. _____. Mac Wells computes underground bookworms. Earth Shel. Liv., no. 22, July/Aug. 1982: 57.
Statistics computed by Wells and Earth Shelter Living magazine from book and subscription sales indicate that the population in the five largest states, California, New York, Texas, Pennsylvania, and Illinois, have the lowest interest in earth sheltering.

195. _____. Penn's sylvania. Charette, v. 48, no. 1, Jan./Feb. 1968. About underground architecture.

196. White, B.M. Underground housing. Thesis, AB degree. Western Australian Institute of Technology, 1980.

197. Whitford, Graham. They're going down, now. Age, Sept. 8, 1969: 10. About Malcolm Wells' work.

198. Wirtanen, Linda K., ed. Housing alternatives. Portsmouth, OH: Underground Homes. 44 p.
Gives an overview of earth shelter construction and its adaptability to passive solar energy.

199. Wistinghausen, N. Solar groundhouse: the low cost solar home. 45 p.
The author describes how he combined the energy-saving concepts of earth shelter and active/passive solar heating to create a comfortable and affordable dwelling.

200. Wolf, R. Good feeling of living in the earth. Org. Gard. Farm., v. 25, no. 12, Dec. 1978: 58-65.
Earth-sheltered houses combine energy savings and a comfortable lifestyle that leaves more land undisturbed and works with rather than against, nature. Construction and operating costs are lower than those for conventional housing.

201. Wollan, Otis. Owner-built project offers self-reliance. Earth Shel. Liv., no. 27, May/June 1983: 17-21.
The advantages and disadvantages of owner-building an earth-sheltered house are listed.

202. Ziebarth, Allan. A groundswell in earth shelters. Mech. Illus., v. 76, July 1980: 30, 100.

II. BIBLIOGRAPHY

---

203. Akridge, J.M. and C.C. Benton. Bibliography: earth tempering and ground coupling. Atlanta, GA: South. Sol. Energ. Ctr., 1980.

204. Bibliographic Research Library, San Jose, Calif. Back to nature in earth-sheltered dwellings: an introductory bibliography. Monticello, IL: Vance Bibliographies, 1983. 6p. (Architecture Series: Bibliography A-1043).

205. Earth Shelters, Inc. Earth shelters/underground bibliography. Omaha, NE, 1979.

206. Johnson, Terry A. Earth shelter resource guide. Portsmouth, OH: Underground Homes, 1980. 16 p.

23 Bibliography

This guide includes a bibliography of books and periodicals, directories of architects and builders and organizations. Some sources for solar and wind energy information are also included.

207. Jones, LaVerne Koelsch. <u>Earth sheltered construction: a bibliography</u>. Stillwater, OK: Okla. State Univ., Archit. Ext., 1982. 22 p.

208. _____. <u>Underground construction</u>. <u>N.C.P.L. Exchange Bibliography</u> 1443, 1978.

209. Keehn, Pauline A. <u>Earth-sheltered housing: an annotated bibliography and directory</u>. Chicago, IL: Council of Planning Librarians, 1981. <u>CPL Bibliographies</u> no. 43. 61 p.
This bibliography includes more than 200 English-language titles from both technical and popular literature on the various aspects of earth sheltering. The titles included were published between 1950 and 1980, although the majority were published between 1976 and Aug. 1980. Almost all of the citations are annotated and in some cases include information about where the works can be purchased. The directory includes addresses of architects, builders, and others involved in earth-sheltered construction, and the addresses of book sellers of pertinent literature.

210. Labs, Kenneth. <u>Passive earth coupling research bibliography</u>. New Haven, CT: Undercurrent Design Research, 1984. 21 p.
This bibliography is an outgrowth of the list of references cited in <u>Passive earth coupling: the state-of-the-art</u> prepared by Undercurrent for the Dept. of Energy's Solar Thermal Energy Conversion Documentation Project. It contains 249 entries on the following topics: earth coupling as a climate control strategy; problems of undisturbed ground temperature and heat exchange; soil thermal properties; slab-on-grade floors; subgrade walls and floors; simulation of thermal performance; earth-covered roofs; monitoring in the field; building design guidelines; earth-air heat exchangers; and implementation issues. Available from Undercurrent, 147 Livingston St., New Haven, CT 06511.

211. Mansfield, Jerry W. <u>Underground housing is out of sight: selected references</u>. West Lafayette, IN: Purdue Univ., Siegesmund Engineering Library, 1980. 42 p. (<u>Research in Engineering Bibliography Series</u>, no. 1).

212. Moe, C.E. <u>Underground space: a new resource</u>. Monticello, IL: Vance Bibliographies, 1981. 12 p.

This bibliography lists 134 references on the use of underground space and the engineering aspects of underground construction, ranging from food storage to tunnelling technology

213. Niskern, Diana. Earth sheltered buildings: a brief guide to materials in the Library of Congress. Washington, DC: Library of Congress, Sci. and Tech. Div., Sci. Ref. Sect., 1982. 8 p. (LC Science Tracer Bullet, TB 82-3).

214. Stauffer, Truman, Sr. Occupancy and use of underground mined-out space in urban areas: an annotated bibliography. Monticello, IL: Council of Planning Librarians, 1974. (Exchange Bibliography 602).

215. Weaver, Rose S. Bibliography on underground space for residential, commercial and industrial buildings. Monticello, IL: Vance Bibliographies, 1980. 26 p. (Architecture Series: Bibliography A-191).

III. THEORY/PHILOSOPHY

216. Aughenbaugh, N.B. Development of underground space. In Proc., Alt. in Habitat: the Use of Earth Cov. Set., Fort Worth, TX, May 17-19, 1978. F.L. Moreland, ed. Washington, DC: U.S. G.P.O., 1979. v. 2. Earth covered buildings and settlements, p. 152-68.
   Underground space can be developed for housing, storage, industry, utilities, and commercial enterprises. We have the technology to construct stable underground space in most geographic areas but the local topography and geology are the major factors that control site location, type of construction, and the general feasibility and economics for any proposed underground development.

217. Baggs, Sydney A. Design strategies for earth-covered buildings. Kensington, NSW, Aust.: Univ. of New South Wales, Grad. Sch. of the Built. Environ., 1982. 230 p.
   The author presents a taxonomy of the different types of underground space used by man in order to clarify the concept of earth-covered buildings and their place in the context of underground spaces in general. A brief history and the contemporary background of the subject is also given, stressing developments in Australia.

Theory/Philosophy

218. _____, Joan C. Baggs, and David W. Baggs. Explanation of terms used in connection with geotecture. Geotecture, v. 2, no. 3, 1985: 38-40.
Terms: underground, earth-integrated, -covered, -bermed.

219. _____. Taxonomy of underground space. In Earth shelter 2: coll. paper., 1st Earth Shel. Hous. Conf. and Exhib., Minneapolis, MN, April 9-11, 1980. Minneapolis, MN: Univ. of Minn., Undergr. Sp. Ctr., 1980. p. 189-97.
A taxonomy of underground space is outlined.

220. _____. The utilisation of underground space: how, when, where and why. In Proc., Symp. on Des. Strat. for Earth Cov. Bldgs., May 8-9, 1982. S.A. Baggs, ed. Kensington, NSW, Aust.: Univ. of New South Wales, Grad. Sch. of the Built Environ., 1982. p. 1-26.

221. Bennett, David J. Built form: the shape of things to come. Proc., 1st Int. Conf. on Energ. Effic. Bldgs. with Earth Shel. Prot., Sydney, Aust., Aug. 1-6, 1983. L.L. Boyer, ed. Stillwater, OK: Okla. State Univ., Archit. Ext., 1983. p. 179-83.
As we proceed through the post-industrial revolution, we are learning to apply the knowledge developed by our industrial technology to the lessons of pre-industrial architecture. Post-industrial buildings promise to have two characters which will signify them. First, they will assume the form and substance most appropriate to adjusting their external environment and internal purposes. Secondly, they will be capable of transformation at some level. We are already capable of putting in place the mechanical capacity for a building to sense external climatic conditions, analyze their relationship to the response capability of internal environment systems, and activate the systems automatically to bring the two into balance according to predetermined instructions. Solar-integrated earth-sheltered architecture stands as a specific application of the characteristics of post-industrial building. The Civil and Mineral Engineering Building on the Minneapolis Campus of the University of Minnesota exemplifies the generation of a building form conceived to respond to natural forces with a geometry shaped by the physical laws of nature -- the post-industrial principle. The design of the Civil and Mineral Engineering Building was preceded by the design and construction of several other relevant projects. Each of these have addressed similar issues relating to energy utilization and may be considered as antecedent work. --From auth. summary.

222. Bright future is seen in underground development. N.Y. Times, June 12, 1981.

223. Cargo, D.B. Personal change in the conceptual use of land as related to earth-covered housing. In Proc., Alt. in Habitat: the Use of Earth Cov. Set., Fort Worth, TX, May 17-19, 1978. F.L. Moreland, ed. Washington, DC: U.S. G.P.O., 1979. v. 2, Earth covered buildings and settlements, p. 82-93.

A brief history is presented of the concepts and use of open space. Problems of space perception are described. A personal account is presented of the way open space was used by residents of two different communities planned around greenbelts. Some of the land-management restrictions and basic attitudes towards land may need to be changed in earth-covered housing areas.

224. Deppen, Dave. Guest commentary. Energ. Alt., v. 2, no. 4, Winter 1979: 4.

The author formerly worked for Malcolm Wells. He describes underground architecture as a philosophy of building rather than a style or technique.

225. The earth: discussing the basic issues. Prog. Archit., v. 48, no. 4, Apr. 1967: 176-84.

Some architects were asked to respond to the questions: Why are we interested in earthmoving today? Has the rise of the landscape architect focused our attention on earth? Is conservation of the landscape our major concern? How has this view of land affected our image of buildings? Are their interests in earth, earthmoving, and earth forms valid? Should these things be done? What are the justifications? What are the pros and cons concerning underground structures? What are the predictions about the future of earth, earthmoving, and earth forms?

226. Fairhurst, Charles. Beneath the surface. Earth Shel. Dig. Energ. Rept., no. 1, Jan./Feb. 1979: 27.

Reprinted from Underground Space, v. 1, 1978, the author argues for more underground development to be preceded by careful planning.

227. Foster, Eugene L. Social assessment -- a means of evaluating the social and economic interactions between society and underground technology. Undergr. Sp., v. 1, no. 1, May/June 1976: 61-3.

This paper discusses the need to make a social assessment of individual underground projects rather than a continuous promotion of them.

228. Hannula, John Karl. Earth sheltered landscapes: their classification and applicable design principles. <u>Proc., 1st Int. Conf. on Energ. Effic. Bldgs. with Earth Shel. Prot.</u>, Sydney, Aust., Aug. 1-6, 1983. L.L. Boyer, ed. Stillwater, OK: Okla. State Univ., Archit. Ext., 1983. p. 57-60.

During the past decade the development and use of underground space has experienced a strong resurgence because of its energy-conserving qualities, as well as successful construction techniques and technologies which have overcome deterrent problems formerly associated with underground architecture. This development can be accredited to the large amount of research actively funded and encouraged by both the public and private sectors. A quick scan of the research reveals a dearth of information on the aesthetics of underground space, particularly its response to, and integration with the visual landscape. In recognition of this need, the main objective of this paper is to classify and codify the appropriate principles of landscape design as it relates to earth-sheltered structures and their surrounding landscape. --Auth. abstract.

229. Horsbrugh, Patrick. Geospace, geotecture and geopolitan planning: the inevitability of subterranean development. In <u>Underground utilization</u>. T. Stauffer, ed. Kansas City, MO: Univ. of Missouri - Kansas City, Dept. of Geosci., 1978. v. 7, p. 920-9.

230. _____. Geospace: the concept and definition of subterranean accommodation. In <u>Proc. of the Symp. on the Dev. and Util. of Undergr. Sp.</u>, Kansas City, MO, Mar. 5-7, 1975. Washington, DC: Nat. Sci. Found., 1975. p. 147-58.

Geospace implies underground space, and geotecture implies the deliberate creation of conditions of geospace. This paper discusses the need for a professional entity for the design and creation of geospace; classifications of types of geospace (definitions); public use structures better sited underground; urban geotecture; popular acceptance of underground structures; the need for an international medical agency to study the effects of underground living; the need for an inventory of existing geospacial facilities in the U.S.; geospacial legalities; the formation of a non-profit, tax-exempt independent research group on geotectural conditions as the first instrument of geospacial research (an international center for geospace research); geospacial economics; and aesthetic obligations.

231. _____. Geospacial planning. <u>Proc., 1st Int. Conf. on Energ. Effic. Bldgs. with Earth Shel. Prot.</u>, Sydney, Aust.,

Aug. 1-6, 1983. L.L. Boyer, ed. Stillwater, OK: Okla. State Univ., Archit. Ext., 1983. p. 37-42. Also in Geotecture, v. 1, no. 4, July 1984: 5-7.

It is suggested that, under the auspices of the International Sydney Conference, an International Inventory of Geospacial Facilities and Conditions be undertaken with assistance sought from UNESCO. The Conference may also wish to further this endeavor by identifying certain institutions whereat to develop geospacial studies, planning and design programs. A travelling exhibition, illustrating the extent of geospacial investment, ancient and modern, and future potentialities may be justified, and the commissioning of a public opinion poll to determine the popular reaction to the psychological, social, and economic possibilities inherent in geospacial accommodation should be considered. --From auth. abstract.

232. _____. Geotecture, concept, design, construction and economy of geospace -- the creation of subterranean accommodation. Minneapolis, MN: Univ. of Minn., Dept. of Civ. and Min. Eng., 1973.

233. Labs, Kenneth. The architectural use of underground space: issues and applications. Master's thesis. St. Louis, MO: Washington Univ., Sch. of Archit., 1975. 160 p.

This work discusses habitable underground space, health and safety factors, economic logic, technological constraints, and laws discouraging the use of underground space for residences. It also contains a set of notes, references, and appendices which document the state of underground experience up to 1975.

234. _____. Underground design movement of the 1970's: terratecture. Land. Archit., v. 67, May 1977: 244-9.

The origins of modern underground construction can be divided into two categories: circumstantial applications (caused by the immediate circumstances of the building site or building program) and dispositional (buildings designed to be subsurface because architects believe our environment is overurbanized, unnatural, or ugly). There is an emerging vocabulary of architectural-landscape forms and structured spaces pertaining to terratecture (the marriage of building and the natural environment). Several examples of underground designs are given: these include Winston House, Lyme, NH, Geier House, Cincinnati, OH, and the Art Bunker of Philip Johnson in New Canaan, CT.

235. La Nier, Royce. Geotecture: subterranean accommodation

and the architectural potential of earthworks. South Bend, IN: Univ. of Notre Dame, 1970. 72 p.

This book gives the basics of a design discipline that offers an alternative to the proliferation of surface structures. Geotecture is defined as the use of subterranean space for human accommodation. The material used was gathered from various sources and supplemented with interviews and correspondence with experts. Field investigations were carried out in Afghanistan and different parts of the U.S.

236. Lawler, Barry. Returning to the underground: a practical anachronism. Energ. Alt., v. 2, no. 4, Winter 1979: 7, 35.

What is the meaning of the recent renascence in underground construction?

237. Mason, Roy. Underground architecture: what lies ahead may be beneath us. Futurist, v. 10, no. 1, Feb. 1976: 16-20.

This is one of a series of articles devoted to the direction architecture may take in the years ahead. This article discusses the many advantages underground structures have over surface structures, including an unusual ability to conserve energy. Designs for both public and private buildings are shown.

238. Meier, R.L. Catastrophe theory and the acceptance of underground space. Proc., Alt. in Habitat: the Use of Earth Cov. Set., Fort Worth, TX, May 17-19, 1978. F.L. Moreland, ed. Washington, DC: U.S. G.P.O., 1979. v. 2, Earth covered buildings and settlements, p. 141-2.

A method of applying catastrophe theory is proposed that would promote underground housing on the basis of safety, with energy conservation as a secondary benefit. As a suggestion, post-catastrophe publicity could be given to the advantages of underground living.

239. Mendenhall, Norman. Response: let's all work together. Earth Shel. Dig. Energ. Rept., no. 13, Jan./Feb. 1981: 58-9.

This is a pro-earth shelter response to W. Shurcliff's arguments against earth sheltering in Earth Shelter Digest & Energy Report, no. 11.

240. Metz, Don. Architecture and earth shelters. Earth Shel. Dig. Energ. Rept., no. 5, Sept./Oct. 1979: 18.

This is a challenge to architects to define the significance of earth sheltering to architecture.

241. Potential for future building lies down below the ground. Mpls. Trib., Dec. 18, 1977.

Describes the Preusser Home and the Bennett House in Minneapolis.

242. Rollwagen, Mary. Is earth sheltered housing entering the mainstream? Archit. Minn., v. 6, no. 2, Apr. 1980: 29-30.

Although earth-sheltered construction is still regarded by much of the public as untried and unproven, in the central United States at least the pioneering stage is over. The challenge now is to alter our traditional concepts of what "shelter" is and what it looks like.

243. Terman, Max R. Earth sheltered housing: principles in practice. New York, NY: Van Nostrand Reinhold, 1985. 209 p.

This book studies the principles and theories of earth-sheltered housing and how well they have worked in actuality. Focus is primarily on the standard elevational house design which is the most popular and energy efficient for temperate climates. Earth-sheltered homeowners contribute their observations and suggestions for improving methods of design and construction.

244. An underground civilization? Earth Shel. Liv., no. 40, July/Aug. 1985: 8-10. Reprinted from Futurist, Apr. 1985.

This article describes the prospective future development of underground construction and the reasons for it.

245. Warnock, J. Gavin. New frontiers of inner space--underground. Undergr. Sp., v. 3, no. 1, July/Aug. 1978: 1-7.

Underground space is categorized according to stratification (near surface, surface-accessible, deep underground space) and function (according to needs for floor area, volume, insulation, security, etc.). Excavating methods are described and some new uses are suggested.

246. Wells, Malcolm. Absolutely constant incontestably stable architectural value scale. In Proc., Earth Shel. Bldg. Des. Innov., Oklahoma City, OK, Apr. 18, 1980. L.L. Boyer, ed. Stillwater, OK: Okla. State Univ., 1980. p. vi.5-8.

This article discusses a procedure for evaluating conventional surface buildings in relation to ecologically more efficient habitats, the concept of "sky-mining" and enlightened building design strategies, and the advantages and satisfaction to be gained from living in earth-sheltered dwellings. Getting back in tune with nature is stressed.

31 Theory/Philosophy

247. _____. The bright side of going under to stay on top. In Residential applications: transcripts of selected presentations; Going Under to Stay on Top, Minneapolis, MN, Oct. 1977. Minneapolis, MN: Univ. of Minn., Undergr. Sp. Ctr., 1979. p. 9-17.

Wells discusses the growth in underground design, his own realization that we must stop destroying the earth's surface and design earth-integrated buildings which conserve energy and preserve the earth.

248. _____. Gentle architecture. In Buildings and the environment. R. Goodland, ed. Millbrook, NY: Cary Arboretum of the New York Botanical Garden, 1976. p. 45-53.

The author discusses the future of underground architecture and its purpose. He describes his underground suburban office building in Cherry Hill, NJ. He discusses the advantages, adding that underground architecture is expensive.

249. _____. Building without destroying the land. Bldg. Ideas, Sept. 1971: 2-7.

250. _____. No where to go but down. Prog. Archit., v. 46, no. 2, Feb. 1965: 174-9.

Underground structures protect man and preserve nature and the harmony between man and nature.

251. _____. Underground architecture. CoEv. Q., Fall 1976.

Wells tells why he builds underground. He answers some of the most frequently asked underground questions.

252. _____. Why I went underground. Futurist, v. 10, no. 1, Feb. 1976: 21-4.

Wells enumerates the advantages of underground living.

253. Wood, A.M. Muir. Underground space: its contribution to the sustainable society. In The potential of earth-sheltered and underground space: proc., Underground Space Conf. and Expos., Kansas City, MO, June 8-10, 1981. T.L. Holthusen, ed. Elmsford, NY: Pergamon Pr., 1981. p. 11-6.

Economics as presently practiced needs to be reappraised in light of the finite nature of the world's resources with the objective of making better use of subsurface space.

IV. HISTORY

254. Baggs, Sydney. Lithotecture around the world. Geotecture, v. 1, no. 4, July 1984: 31-47.
This is a brief history of troglodyte living in Cappadocia, Turkey, Nottingham, Eng., China, Andalusia, and North America.

255. Cole, R.S. and R. Kennedy. Passive energy in historical Tunisia. In Proc., 5th Nat. Pass. Sol. Conf., Amherst, MA, Oct. 19-26, 1980. Newark, DE: Int. Sol. Energ. Soc., Am. Sec., 1980. p. 704-6.
Different kinds of passive energy strategies were used by the Romans to achieve climate control in the underground houses of Bulla Regia, Tunisia. Three such homes are studied and some of the climate control methods used to achieve an even level of natural daylighting in the homes are described.

256. Croley, Victor A. The frontier dugout. Moth. Earth N., no. 5, Sept. 1970: 38-9.
On the frontier, the first homes were dug into the lee side of low rolling hills, with walls built of sod blocks to a height of seven or eight feet.

257. Going underground. Prog. Archit., v. 48, no. 4, Apr. 1967: 138-51.
This article discusses underground housing in history and in war time: as headquarters and storage for corporations; for use as churches; as nuclear shielding; for underground libraries and art galleries; and as theatres.

258. Hall, Charles L. Architecture of the Anasazi Pueblo culture. N.M. Archit., May/June 1967.
This article discusses the evolution of Anasazi architecture.

259. Heyder, Katherine. Mesa Verde: cliffs formed housing. Earth Shel. Liv., no. 21, May/June 1982: 4-7.
This is the first of a two-part series tracing the history of underground habitation to ancient people. The author lives among the ruins of the cliff dwellers' culture: caves, pithouses, kivas, and multi-storied pueblos.

260. Labs, Kenneth. The architectural underground. Undergr.

Sp., v. 1, No. 1, May/June 1976: 1-8 and no. 2, July/Aug. 1976: 135-56.

Underground space is a resource of great potential benefit which has been exploited in different parts of the world for thousands of years. While some cultures have lived an underground existence, others have yet to realize any of the benefits of subsurface use. This article discusses the use of underground space for human habitation. Pt. 1 deals with the history of the use of underground space. Pt. 2 examines modern underground forms and functions.

261. _____. Over, under, sideways, down. In Passive solar: subdivisions, windows, underground. Ed. by H. Wade and others. Kansas City, MO: Am. Sol. Energ. Soc., Kansas City Chap., 1983. p. 167-70.

The author reviews some of the recent important events in the history of underground building.

262. _____. The use of earth covered buildings through history. In Proc., Alt. in Energ. Conserv.: the Use of Earth Cov. Bldgs., Fort Worth, TX, July 9-12, 1975. Washington, DC: U.S. G.P.O., 1976. p. 7-19.

This is a brief review of the historical development of earth-sheltered housing and suggests a basic taxonomy of terratectural structures.

263. McFadden, Charles B. Mankind marches on: back to the cave. Mpls. Trib., Nov. 21, 1976.

264. Morgan, William. Florida's earth architecture. Fla. Archit., May/June 1975: p. FA/6-FA/12.

This article discusses the design conceptions of pre-Europeans and some of the more recent earth architecture in Florida.

265. _____. Sense of place. Proc.: Archit., no. 21, Jan. 1981: 120-5.

This article discusses the earth architecture of prehistoric and pre-European North America, giving examples of reshaping of site soil and other earth materials to form structures. A few examples from contemporary U.S. architecture are shown.

266. Rudofsky, Bernard. Troglodytes: putting architecture underground. Horizon, v. 9, no. 2, Spring 1967: 28-39.

This is an historical examination of caves as dwelling places.

267. Vadnais, Kathleen. Future includes more earth sheltering. Proc. of the 6th Nat. Pass. Sol. Conf., Portland, OR, Sept. 8-12, 1981. p. 730-3. (Progress in passive solar energy, v. 6).
The author predicts that if present trends continue, earth sheltering will be included in half the new construction in the next 20 years.

268. Wampler, M.S. Expression of earth sheltered architecture. Earth shelter 2: coll. pap., Earth Shel. Hous. Conf. and Exhib., Minneapolis, MN, Apr. 9-11, 1980. Minneapolis, MN: Univ. of Minn., Undergr. Sp. Ctr., 1980. p. 94-100.
Earth-sheltered design is discussed as a form of architectural expression, both historical and contemporary. The design of an earth-covered church in Fort Smith, AR, is briefly discussed.

269. Wells, Malcolm. "Gentle" architecture catches on. Earth Shel. Dig. Energ. Rept., no. 9, May/June 1980: 18-9.
The growth in interest in underground architecture since 1964 is discussed.

270. _____. What your home will be like in fifty years. Mainlines, Sept. 1974.

271. Wilcox, R. Peter. Monticello: a passive solar pioneer. Earth Shel. Liv., no. 19, Jan./Feb. 1982: 55-7, 60.
Thomas Jefferson's homes is analyzed as an example of solar architecture. "All-weather" passages extend totally underground connecting the ends of the house with the earth-sheltered wings which are buried and on grade but have exposed fronts.

V. VERNACULAR EARTH-INTEGRATED HOUSING

---

272. Andreadaki-Chronaki, Eleni. Vernacular architecture of Greece: earth-sheltered buildings of Santorini. In Proc., 1st Int. Conf. on Energ. Effic. Bldgs. with Earth Shel. Prot., Sydney, Aust., Aug. 1-6, 1983. L.L. Boyer, ed. Stillwater, OK: Okla. State Univ., Archit. Ext., 1983. p. 25-9. Also in Geotecture, v. 1, no. 4, July 1984: 12-4.
Local volcanic materials have been used to build communities with subsurface or semi-subsurface earth dwellings with vaulted roofs. These buildings have all the advantages of modern

earth-sheltered housing. A problem which remains unsolved is excessive relative humidity especially in the innermost subsurface rooms.

273. Baker, D. Rock dwellings in Worcestershire and Staffordshire. Sub. Brit., 3, 1976: 9-10.

274. Bourdier, Jean-Paul and Trinh T. Minh-Ha. Koumbili: semi-sunken dwellings in Upper Volta. Afr. Arts, v. 16, no. 4, Aug. 1983: 40-5, 88.
Lowering the floor level is a common practice among the Gurunsi people of Upper Volta. Compounds have flat roof mud structures with floors 50-80 cm. below grade. There are underground systems of corridors by which occupants of the compounds can communicate.

275. Bowen, A. Energy design of vernacular earth shelters throughout the world. Proc., Earth Shel. Perf. and Eval., 2nd Nat. Tech. Conf., Tulsa, OK, Oct. 16-17, 1981. Stillwater, OK: Okla. State Univ., Archit. Ext., 1981. p. 19-38.
Indigenous earthen and earth-integrated buildings in temperate and equatorial climates are analyzed. Notable historical developments are identified and recent attempts at earth integration recorded.

276. Carmody, John and Douglas Derr. The use of underground space in the People's Republic of China. Undergr. Sp., v. 7, no. 1, July/Aug. 1982: 7-11, 14-5.
The underground has been used for a variety of purposes during China's long history. The indigenous atrium-style house architecture in the self-supporting loess soil of Henan Province is of special interest.

277. Cole, Robert S. Underground dwellings in southern Tunisia. In Passive cooling: proc. of the Int. Pass. and Hybr. Cool. Conf., Miami Beach, FL, Nov. 6-16, 1981. Newark, DE: Int. Sol. Energ. Soc., Am. Sec., 1981.
The underground Berber dwellings in the village of Matmata were studied during the spring of 1980 and the summer of 1981. Temperature and solar measurements and room orientation and dimensional measurements were made in several dwellings.

278. Crosbie, Michael J. Vernacular underground villages of Iberia. AIA J., v. 72, no. 1, Jan. 1983: 70-3.
Photographs by Norman F. Carver.

279. Engelken, Ruth. Underground in Tunisia. Moth. Earth N., no. 66, Nov./Dec. 1980: 155.

Wealthy Romans built underground summer homes in Bulla Regia during the early years of the Christian era in the coastal area of Tunisia. Three basic floor plans are described. These ruins are well-preserved. The Berbers have also built underground homes in the hills of the great desert in southern Tunisia, 3,000 in the town of Matmata alone. There are two underground hotels.

280. Fanchiotti, A., E. Dimitriadou, J. Mirtsios, and F. Moumtzidou. The earth-sheltered dwellings of Santorini, Greece. Proc. of the 2nd Int. Conf. on Pass. and Low Energ. Archit., Crete, Greece, June 28-July 1, 1983. Oxford: Pergamon Pr., 1983. p. 225-32.

The thermal performance of the earth-sheltered dwellings on the island of Santorini in Greece is reported.

281. Flint, Benny. Troglodytic and semi-troglodytic dwellings of the Göreme Valley, Anatolia, Turkey. In Passive cooling: proc. of the Int. Pass. and Hybr. Cool. Conf., Miami Beach, FL, Nov. 6-16, 1981. Newark, DE: Int. Sol. Energ. Soc., Am. Sec. 1981. p. 183-7.

These dwellings are rocks hollowed out so as to provide several apartments, with large entrance doors and windows providing well-lighted rooms. They have been inhabited for centuries.

282. Goldfinger, Myron. Subterranean village. Arts Archit., v. 84, no. 6, June 1967: 24-6.

Matmata, Tunisia is a village of artificial caves built around large man-made craters in dry sandstone.

283. Kennedy, Richard J. Historical passive examples of sun-facing hill towns, cliff dwellings, and underground villages of the Mediterranean. Proc., 5th Nat. Pass. Sol. Conf. Amherst, MA, Oct. 19-26, 1980. Newark, DE: Int. Sol. Energ. Soc., Am. Sec., 1980. p. 27-30.

The underground houses of the Roman town of Bulla Regia and the Berber town of Matmata and other villages in Tunisia were compared with regard to energy performance. Unique energy conservation strategies were observed, as well as unusual construction and water collection methods.

284. _____ and Robert S. Cole. Passive-solar: lessons from the past. Undergr. Sp., v. 6, no. 1, July/Aug. 1981: 24-8.

Two sections, Passive-solar design in ancient hill towns and underground villages of the Mediterranean area by Kennedy, and Keeping cool in the desert: a study of ancient underground villages in Tunisia by Cole, reveal ancient energy-efficient building techniques used in constructing Roman houses and present-day Berber homes.

285. Machowski, Barb. Dugouts pioneer earth sheltering. Earth Shel. Dig. Energ. Rept., no. 16, July/Aug. 1981: 44-7.
This article discusses the sod-houses and dugouts used by the American pioneers in the Midwest and the various terms used to describe them.

286. Mulligan, Helen C. Environmental characteristics of the vernacular underground dwelling. In Proc. of the 2nd Int. Conf. on Pass. and Low Energ. Archit., Crete, June 28-July 1, 1983. Oxford, Eng.: Pergamon Pr., 1983. p. 217-24.
This paper discusses a technique for capturing solar energy by exploiting the fabric of a structure and also discusses the use of the earth itself as a collector and storage medium directly utilized by positioning the building underground. Case studies of three dwellings are presented. Some proposals are made for renovating and upgrading existing rock-cut housing in the Mediterranean region.

287. _____. The low-input dwelling: energy requirements in the vernacular use of under space. In Proc., 1st Int. Conf. on Energ. Effic. Bldgs. with Earth Shel. Prot., Sydney, Aust., Aug. 1-6, 1983. L.L. Boyer, ed. Stillwater, OK: Okla. State Univ., Archit. Ext., 1983. p. 19-23. Also in Geotecture, v. 1, no. 4, July 1984: 8-11.
This paper examines a number of historical examples of earth-sheltered dwellings in order to investigate how their typical forms and materials may determine their environmental performance and thus what factors have been most influential in their adoption. The use of a microcomputer programme is described to predict internal temperatures given meteorological data and some knowledge of the thermal properties of the surrounding rock. --Auth. abstract.

288. _____. Subterranean dwellings: a survey of vernacular forms. Dissertation submitted for the second Diploma Examination in Architecture, Easter term, 1981. Cambridge, Eng.: Univ. of Cambridge, Fac. of Archit. and Hist. of Art.

289. Schurer, Gerhard. Historical earth covered building in South Australia. Geotecture, v. 1, no. 4, July 1984: 19-20.
A description is given of the underearth dwellings in Burra,

South Australia made and used by the copper miners in the nineteenth century.

290. Tour of troglodyte dwellings to be offered in August. Underline, v. 6, no. 1, Oct./Dec. 1984: 5.
The Science Museum of Minnesota is sponsoring the 20-day tour to Turkey, Spain, France, and Tunisia in August 1985.

VI. ARCHITECTURAL DESIGN

---

291. Anderson, Philip B. 15 (fifteen) architect designed earth sheltered houses. Willmar, MN: Genesis Two, Nov. 1980. 18 p.
The objective of this booklet is to introduce the home buyer, contractor, or prospective home builder to some simple house plans designed to retain solar energy. Brief advice is given on locating a suitable site.

292. The architecture of cut and fill. Prog. Archit., v. 48, no. 4, Apr. 1967: 160-2.
This article discusses contemporary applications of the classic use of terraces, mounds, and pyramidal forms in architecture, and the way cut and fill projects are approached by the developer, the engineer, and the architect.

293. Baggs, David W. Award winner in NSW Building Society Design Competition. Bldg. Econ., June 1980: 34-6.

294. Barnard, John E., Jr. The Cape Cod cottage and the earth sheltered/passive solar home. Archit. Minn., v. 6, no. 2, Apr. 1980: 49-50.
A Cape Cod cottage is compared to a side hill south-facing linear earth-sheltered home utilizing passive solar. The advantages of the earth-sheltered house are enumerated. It is less expensive to build and less costly on an annual basis and also requires 60 percent less nonrenewable fossil fuels.

295. Bligh, Thomas P. Alternatives in building design -- the underground option. In Alt. Energ. Sources Conf.: Tech. and Appl. for Minn., Minneapolis, MN, Apr. 1976. Minn. Energ. Agcy.

296. _____. Design manual, earth-sheltered buildings. Contractor: Setter, Leach and Lindstrom, Inc., Minneapolis. Dept. of the Navy, Naval Facil. Eng. Com., 1983.

39 Architectural Design

297. _____, R. Sterling, and C. Fairhurst. Earth-sheltered energy-independent (ESEI) building design project -- residential design study. Int. Prog. Rept. to Minn. Energ. Agcy., 1977. 106 p.

298. Boyer, Lester L. Prize-winning underground designs from Oklahoma State. Earth Shel. Dig. Energ. Rept., no. 3, May/June 1979: 4-7.
There was a design competition in a graduate class at OSU. Awards were given by the Tulsa and Oklahoma City chapters of the Illuminating Engineering Society.

299. _____, W. Grondzik, and A. Orr. Design and analysis of subterranean structures: seminar workbook. Stillwater, OK: Okla. State Univ., Archit. Ext., 1977.

300. Brent Anderson Associates, Inc. Earth integrated residential designs: perspective/floor plans. Bloomington, MN, 1985.
Sixty-five modular floor plan designs and matching perspectives, traditional to modern in appearance, are presented. Also included are 42 complete architectural construction drawing sets of earth-sheltered and earth-bermed/superinsulated house plans, ranging from 1,080-4,695 sq. ft.

301. Building to duck underground. Pop. Sci., Mar. 1954: 171.
This retractable house would rest on roller-mounted concrete slabs. In the event of an air raid, the slabs would be rolled out from under the house permitting the house to be lowered into the ground by a hydraulic elevator. The concrete floor would then slide over the shelter. A patent on this design was granted to W. Rowles, Santa Monica, CA.

302. Chalmers, Larry S. and Jeremy A. Jones. Homes in the earth. San Francisco, CA: Chronicle Books, 1980. 112 p. (Design Concept Associates book.)
Brief descriptions of 40 designs are presented and the reasons for their development are suggested. The plans are for: diagonal roof, west-view home, north-view home, snail plan, second story entry, patio home, pavilion home, atrium home, and others.

303. Design brings architect special attention. Earth Shel. Dig. Energ. Rept., no. 4, July/Aug. 1979: 44-5.
Michael McGuire of Stillwater, MN is originator of the "tube" design for earth-sheltered homes.

304. Design constraints lead to award. Earth Shel. Dig. Energ. Rept., no. 7, Jan./Feb. 1980: 4-6.

Berg and Associates, Inc., Plymouth, MN was awarded a $12,000 design and build grant by the U.S Dept. of Housing and Urban Development in Cycle 5 of the Residential Solar Heating and Cooling Demonstration Program in 1979. There were requirements for a three-bedroom home. Principal design features and construction techniques included: passive solar space heating, passive cooling methods, active solar domestic hot water system, earth-sheltered construction, movable night glazing insulation system, total envelope exterior insulation system, basic building shell of reinforced unit masonry, basic structure with significant time lag/thermal inertia effect, water conserving bath and toilet fixtures.

305. Designer's portfolio. Earth Shel. Liv., no. 31, Jan./Feb. 1984: 32.

A sketch and floor plan are shown for a 1,144 sq. ft. earth-sheltered home designed by Richard Webster of Asheville, NC.

306. Designer's portfolio. Earth Shel. Liv., no. 32, Mar./Apr. 1984: 36.

Sketches and plans are shown of a house designed by Philip B. Anderson of Willmar, MN.

307. Designer's portfolio. Earth Shel. Liv., no. 33, May/June 1984: 34.

Drawing and floor plan are presented of a 1,284 sq. ft. earth-covered home designed by Suntel Design Associates of Lake Oswego, OR.

308. Designer's portfolio. Earth Shel. Liv., no. 34, July/Aug. 1984: 41.

A sketch and floor plan are presented for a design by Geoff Blackbeard of Earth Shelter Developments of Canada.

309. Designer's portfolio. Earth Shel. Liv., no. 35, Sept./Oct. 1984: 35.

A sketch and a floor plan are presented for an earth-sheltered house designed by Joe Hylton, Norman, OK.

310. Designer's portfolio. Earth Shel. Liv., no. 36, Nov./Dec. 1984: 35.

Richard Sibley of the Martin Organization in Atlanta, GA, designed this earth-sheltered home.

311. Designer's portfolio. Earth Shel. Liv., no. 37, Jan./Feb. 1985: 14.

Richard Engan of Willmar, MN, designed this earth-sheltered house.

312. Designer's portfolio. <u>Earth Shel. Liv.</u>, no. 38, Mar./Apr. 1985: 18.
Johnathan Majid designed this four-bedroom home.

313. Designer's portfolio. <u>Earth Shel. Liv.</u>, no. 39, May/June 1985: 15.
Architect Robert Stirling Morris of Pawtucket, RI, designed this earth-sheltered home.

314. Designer's portfolio. <u>Earth Shel. Liv.</u>, no. 40, July/Aug. 1985: 20.
Fleckenstein Associates Architects of Rochester, NY, designed this earth shelter. Special features: cool air is forced through ducting in the concrete slab floor, warmed and regulated thermostatically by dampers. Windows have ultraviolet light reduction coatings.

315. Designer's portfolio. <u>Earth Shel. Liv.</u>, no. 41, Sept./Oct. 1985: 11.
The architect G. Walker Hagens of Carrboro, NC, designed an earth shelter that incorporates a unique heating system.

316. Dynamic Integration, Fairlee, VT. The natural architecture of the earthen home. In <u>Proc., 4th Nat. Pass. Sol. Conf.</u>, Kansas City, MO, Oct. 3-5, 1979. Newark, DE: Int. Sol. Energ. Soc., Am. Sect., 1979. p. 759.
The author designed a semibermed masonry structure integrated with an air-envelope system which passively distributes warm air and cool air, effectively regulating the temperature, achieving 62 to 72 degrees in all climates.

317. Earth Integrated Technics, Inc. <u>Earth sheltered plans for better living</u>. Stillwater, MN: WEBCO, 1982? 44 p. (An Earth Shelter Living book).
Contains 30 house designs.

318. Earth-sheltered design wins award in Australia. <u>Undergr. Sp.</u>, v. 5, no. 2, Sept./Oct. 1980: 70.
The NSW Building Society gave a design award to David Baggs for his home in an earth mound.

319. Earth sheltered house built for HUD. <u>Underline</u>, v. 2, no. 3, Mar./Apr. 1981:2, 4.
A model of an earth-sheltered house designed by Ellison Design and Construction was displayed at a convention of the

National Association of Home Builders in Las Vegas in Jan. 1981.

320. Earth-sheltered housing. Washington, DC: U.S. G.P.O., 1980. 141 p.
Discusses design ideas ranging from three-sides-banked to all-underground atrium layouts, the advantages and disadvantages of earth-sheltered construction, and extensive information on building codes, zoning, and financing.

321. Earth sheltering settles in city. Earth Shel. Dig. Energ. Rept., no. 10, July/Aug. 1980: 12-4.
An earth-sheltered condominium development is proposed and described. Site plans are shown. This project took second place in the Underground Space Center's 1980 design competition.

322. Edelhart, Mike. The handbook of earth shelter design. Garden City, NY: Doubleday, 1982. 256 p.
There are floor plans and photographs of atrium homes, hillside homes, suburban designs, and desert houses and information about the leading earth-shelter architects. There is also a discussion of the advantages and disadvantages of earth sheltering, the commercial applications of earth sheltering, and information on soil, air, water, structure, insulation, and cost.

323. Ellison Design and Construction. Prototype designs. 10 p.
Designs for one-level earth-sheltered homes are shown.

324. Emilio Ambasz. Prog. Archit., v. 61, Jan. 1980: 84-5.
An architectural design for an underground weekend retreat in Spain is shown.

325. Frenette, Edward R. Earth sheltering: the form of energy and the energy of form. T.L. Holthusen, ed. Elmsford, NY: Pergamon Pr., 1981. 256 p.
This work contains the best entries in the 1981 design awards program on earth-sheltered buildings sponsored by the American Underground Space Association. The winners were chosen from student and professional entries in four categories: single-family residential, multi-family residential, nonresidential, and research. Architectural details are presented, including construction plans, floor plans, landscaping ideas, and photos of the 50 examples. The three research examples include a regional analysis of ground and above-ground climate, biotechnical earth-support systems, and evaluation of free-span earth-sheltered structures and their method of production.

326. _____. Earth sheltering: the form of energy and the energy of form. Undergr. Sp., v. 6, no. 6, May/June 1982: 370-95.

Some of the designs entered in the 1981 AUA Design Competition are presented.

327. Friedman, Jonathan Block. A user-built incremental earth-sheltered solar dwelling. In Proc., 1st Int. Conf. on Energ. Effic. Bldgs. with Earth Shel. Prot., Sydney, Aust., Aug. 1-6, 1983. L.L. Boyer, ed. Stillwater, OK: Okla. State Univ., Archit. Ext., 1983. p. 387-92.

A method is outlined and detailed architectural development is presented which may transform the current environment in suburbia in industrial nations into a quiet energy-efficient, life-affirming landscape of loftiness and depth. A simple system of cut and fill which creates protected spaces to the sunward side and an insulating hill to the shadow side can grow incrementally into a home for 30 people and four generations or more. The retaining wall may be extended towards the sunrise as a remote collecting Trombe wall that enlarges as the volume of the house grows. A development of various sizes of these solar-heated and power producing "Homes for Generations" may actually increase the density of suburbia from about 17 persons per hectare at present to over 25 per hectare (6,500 per sq. mi.), an increase of almost 50 percent. Such homes could be built and modified as needed by the inhabitants. The plans can apply to almost any site including the Moon, where a breathable atmosphere can be generated by the vegetation that is encouraged to flourish on the moist and shady insulating hillside. --From auth. abstract.

328. Furst, Terry. Back to nature earth shelter designs.

329. Haupert, David. Underground housing is coming on strong. Bet. Homes. Gard., v. 57, no. 9, Sept. 1979: 97-105, 180.

Four styles are described: chamber (walls are windowless), atrium (walls open onto subgrade courtyard), elevational (one wall is exposed), and penetrational (portions of two or more walls are exposed).

330. Hawkins, Donald. Design had to be practical, attractive. Earth Shel. Liv., no. 35, Sept./Oct. 1984: 14-5.

The owners wanted an earth-sheltered house which was conventional in appearance. It was designed but not built.

331. High-tech houses. Pop. Sci., v. 218, no. 5, May 1981: 87-111.

Reports are given on homes designed to conserve energy

and to keep the initial building costs down. Included are super-insulated homes, a thermally-layered house, passive solar homes, earth-sheltered houses, and procedures for building high technology houses.

332. Holland, E. A fancy for earth sheltering. Sol. Age, v. 4, no. 10, Oct. 1979: 34-5.
Several earth-sheltered housing designs by a New Hampshire architect are described. One house plan may be adapted to a southeast, southwest, or south slope.

333. Hylton, Joe. Design development process for subterranean homes. In Proc., 1st Int. Conf. on Energ. Effic. Bldgs. with Earth Shel. Prot., Sydney, Aust., Aug. 1-6, 1983. L.L. Boyer, ed. Stillwater, OK: Okla. State Univ., Archit. Ext., 1983. p. 203-9.
To enable us to live in harmony with any environment, we must understand the basic factors existing in a particular environment and how they may change our existence. In a subterranean environment, the form of the structure is determined by the site, landscaping, and building materials.

334. _____. Earth sheltered and solar homes: a book of plans. Stillwater, MN: Earth Shelter Resource Center, 1985?

335. Isaacson, Paul. Paul Isaacson's underground house plans.
Complete plans are given for an energy-efficient, subterranean, 2,000 sq. ft. dwelling topped by two clear plastic geodesic domes that serve as a food-producing greenhouse and a solar energy heat source. The plans have been approved for presentation to the VA, mortgage institutions, and zoning boards.

336. Kliewer, Tim. Underground envelope is a natural heat pump. Pop. Sci., v. 221, Oct. 1982: 49-50.
The author thought putting an envelope house underground would solve problems associated with both kinds of houses. He says the design works well.

337. Lees, Al. Earth-bermed L-shape. Pop. Sci., v. 220, no. 5, May 1982: 130.
This split-level house is set within a pedestal of earth that is sloped to drain away moisture.

338. _____. Earth-bermed wood foundation. Pop. Sci., v. 222, no. 4, Apr. 1983: 112-3.
This design is Charles Woods' first all-wood, earth sheltered, passive-solar, superinsulated, double-wall house. Its fully bermed walls are made of pressure-treated lumber and plywood.

339. ──────. Earth-sheltered atrium. Pop. Sci., v. 221, Sept. 1982: 116-7.

Charles Woods designed this 2,060 sq. ft. house with direct gain passive solar features and exterior walls almost fully earth-bermed.

340. ──────. Earth-sheltered heat trap. Pop. Sci., v. 219, Sept. 1981: 78-9.

Charles Woods has designed an earth-sheltered house with four skylighted bedrooms. This 1,850 sq. ft. house has walls and floor of reinforced concrete for strength and thermal mass. The south wall and roof are post-plank-and-beam construction. Surfaces in earth-contact are waterproofed either with the Bentonize spray process or with butyl rubber.

341. ──────. Earth-sheltered solar. Pop. Sci., v. 222, Jan. 1983: 76+.

This is a design for a house whose lower floor is L-shaped and below grade. It was designed by Ken Gephart of Home Building Plan Service, Portland, OR.

342. ──────. Earth-sheltered sun trap. Pop. Sci., June 1983: 105.

Most windows of this house face south. It is fully earth-bermed on three sides.

343. ──────. Earth-sheltered two-story. Pop. Sci., v. 218, no. 6, June 1981: 94-5.

A design is shown for an earth-sheltered passive solar home with a Plenwood heating system. Foundation walls are built of All-Weather Wood Foundation. The house was designed by Ken Gephart of Home Building Plan Service, Portland, OR.

344. ──────. Hermit's cabin. Pop. Sci., v. 225, no. 2, Aug. 1984: 94-5.

This is a design for a 600+ sq. ft. cabin fully earth bermed on three sides and featuring a six ft. in diameter masonry silo at the back wall that serves as a light shaft.

345. ──────. Secret shelter. Pop. Sci., v. 226, Mar. 1985: 90.

This design is by William T. Farnan. Only the front of the house is exposed.

346. Lowing, Arnold E. Earthquake, pt. 3: architectural detailing. Earth Shel. Liv., no. 25, Jan./Feb. 1983: 34-5.

Many architectural details, such as parapets, face brick, patio covers, and roof overhangs, can be subject to considerable movement and displacement during an earthquake and could prove to be dangerous to occupants.

347. McGroarty, Bryan. Waterproofing: design to work. Earth Shel. Dig. Energ. Rept., no. 12, Nov./Dec. 1980: 23-6.

This article discusses the usual waterproofing errors made in the three design categories: the extravagant design, the nonfunctional design, and the irrelevant design.

348. Metz, Don. Aesthetics of the underground building. In Earth shelter 2: coll. pap., 1st Earth Shel. Hous. Conf. and Exhib., Minneapolis, MN, Apr. 9-11, 1980. Minneapolis, MN: Univ. of Minn., Undergr. Sp. Ctr., 1980. p. 18-21.

The basics of architecture (form, space, light) as they are manipulated in earth-sheltered design are discussed.

349. _____. The latest, not the last word in underground house design. Sol. Age, v. 4, no. 10, Oct. 1979: 36-9.

Design and thermal considerations for underground houses are discussed. Large loads of earth on top of a structure are thought to provide good temperature moderation, but the costs for additional structural strength to support the weight become prohibitive. However, the earth cover needs to be deep enough to support vegetation. Waterproofing must be installed beneath the insulation and bentonite, bituthene, or sure-seal elastomeric membrane are suitable materials. Condensation problems are reviewed. Reinforced concrete is commonly used for structural members of underground houses. Concrete block is often used for exterior walls and pressure-treated lumber and plywood have been used below grade.

350. _____. Superhouse. Charlotte, VT: Garden Way Pub., 1981. 150 p.

The author discusses the pros and cons of earth shelters, double envelope houses, and superinsulated designs for energy efficient housing. Then he describes the process of designing a "superhouse."

351. Miller, Thomas R. Aesthetics should be considered. Earth Shel. Liv., no. 20, Mar./Apr. 1982: 58-9.

This article discusses those design principles which affect the design and construction of earth-sheltered houses.

352. Minnesota announces energy winners. Earth Shel. Dig. Energ. Rept., no. 12, Nov./Dec. 1980: 52-3.

The Minnesota Housing Finance Agency financed a design competition calling for Minnesota builders to submit designs for homes with a maximum thermal integrity factor (TIF) of 3, limited in size and price, to be sold in a lottery at seven percent interest.

353. Minnesota Masonry Institute. Earth sheltered housing: the dawning of a new era. Minneapolis, MN. (#514.)
The reasons to design an earth-sheltered house are discussed.

354. Natural Spaces. Earthatecture: designs for earth sheltered homes. North Branch, MN, 1982. 29 p.

355. Newman, Jerry O., L.C. Godbey, and Martin Davis. Design considerations for below-grade housing. Adapted by Larry W. Turner and Robert L. Fehr. Lexington, KY: Univ. of Kentucky, Coop. Ext. Serv. 4 p. (Energy Fact Sheet.)

356. _____. Design considerations for below-grade-level houses. In Pap., Wint. Mtg., Am. Soc. of Agric. Engrs., Chicago, IL, Dec. 18-20, 1978. St. Joseph, MO: ASAE, 1978. Pap. 78-4551.
The subsurface environment provides a potential alternative housing possibility, but several functional, structural, and psychological features must be satisfied if quality underground housing is to be achieved. The design considerations for underground housing are well-known, but conventional building practices often do not meet the necessary criteria. Potential design considerations are identified in this paper, and the merits of several choices are discussed.

357. Ohanian, Richard. Earth homes.
An earth-shelter plan book.

358. Oklahoma State University, Architectural Extension. Earth sheltered condominiums booklet. L.L. Boyer, ed. Stillwater, OK, 1980. 30 p.
This booklet is based on a design competition held at OSU. It features descriptions and illustrations of designs for various sites. Design features such as natural lighting and solar heating are also discussed.

359. _____. An earth sheltered guest house. L.L. Boyer, ed. Stillwater, OK, 1979. 28 p.
This booklet resulted from a competition among graduate students at OSU to design a 1,000 sq. ft. earth-sheltered guest house to complement an existing three-bedroom house in a rural area.

360. Passive solar plus. Moth. Earth N., no. 82, July/Aug. 1983: 124-5. A design by Charles G. Woods.

361. Peterson, Forrest. Bank to finance winners. Earth Shel. Dig. Energ. Rept., no. 4, July/Aug. 1979: 28-30.

An Earth-Sheltered Housing Design Competition was sponsored by the Underground Space Center in Mar. 1979. Financing for design fees, land, and construction was offered by the Northwestern Bank of Minneapolis. The winners are named.

362. Powell, Evelyn J. Design considerations for the elderly and handicapped. In Proc., Alt. in Habitat: the Use of Earth Cov. Set., Conf., Fort Worth, TX, May 17-19, 1978. F.L. Moreland, ed. Washington, DC: U.S. Dept. of Energy, 1979. 2 v. v. 2, Earth covered buildings and settlements, p. 149-51.

Earth-covered homes that are designed to meet the needs of the elderly and handicapped would be an economical and practical way of providing appropriate housing without removing these special groups from the neighborhood. A plan is suggested for developing mini-condominiums in established neighborhoods as a way to virtually eliminate many handicap problems aggravated by conventional architecture.

363. Preliminary design information for underground space. Minneapolis, MN: Univ. of Minn., Dept. of Civ. and Min. Eng., Aug. 1975.

364. Preservation of landscape. Prog. Archit., v. 48, no. 4, Apr. 1967: 150.

This article discusses an underground subdivision proposal for a 56-acre community to be built near Southampton, Long Island, NY. The architect is Richard D. Kaplan.

365. Quarmby, Arthur. Earth shelters as architecture. In Proc., 1st Int. Conf. on Energ. Effic. Bldgs. with Earth Shel. Prot., Sydney, Aust., Aug. 1-6, 1983. L.L. Boyer, ed. Stillwater, OK: Okla. State Univ., Archit. Ext., 1983. p. 167-72.

Earth-sheltered architecture is different. It is a reverse of the normal situation in which the exterior form of the structure makes the greatest impact. In adopting an earth-sheltered form, the designer is normally setting out to minimize the external effect. Indeed, it is often his aim to blend his building into the landscape, and to do this he not only sinks the structure wholly or partially into the ground but also uses elements of the natural landscape both living and inert to assist in the concealment. If the end result is to be classifiable as architecture, then a corresponding increase in the internal effect is necessary. An interior which simply recreates the rooms of a normal above-grade building is disappointingly inadequate and a waste of the stunning contrast between exterior and interior which can be achieved with this form of construction. This paper intends to show examples of the emergence of the architectural form of earth-sheltered construction and points the way towards its further development. --Auth. abstract.

366. Reynoldson, George. Let's reach for the sun: 30 original solar and earth sheltered home designs. Rev. ed. Sedona, AZ: Space/Time Designs, 1981. 143 p.

Thirty house designs are presented and details for obtaining them are included. The houses feature heavy mass walls, greenhouses, and direct gain passive heat assistance, as well as active solar heating systems.

367. Rose, Michael A.H. Design for 20 interconnected hillside subgrade dwellings. In Proc., 1st Int. Conf. on Energ. Effic. Bldgs. with Earth Shel. Prot., Sydney, Aust., Aug. 1-6, 1983. L.L. Boyer, ed. Stillwater, OK: Okla. State Univ., Archit. Ext., 1983. p. 104-8.

Concrete time-sharing vacation units were designed for a chalk downland slope in the Sussex Downs on England's south coast. Interior layout and design, services, construction, daylighting (with modelling data), are discussed.

368. Rylander, Rod. Appropriate technology in earth-sheltered construction. In Proc., 1st Int. Conf. on Energ. Effic. Bldgs. with Earth Shel. Prot., Sydney, Aust., Aug. 1-6, 1983. L.L. Boyer, ed. Stillwater, OK: Okla. State Univ., Archit. Ext., 1983. p. 367-9.

Appropriate technology is used to eliminate or reduce some of the problems encountered in earth-sheltered construction. One method is the creation of a vertical crawl space (VCS) whose design, construction, use and advantages are discussed.

369. _____. Roof extends over extra space. Earth Shel. Liv., no. 25, Jan./Feb. 1983: 10-1.

Rylander's vertical crawl space alleviates soil pressure and adds to the house's function. Most of these VCS homes have been constructed in north and central Texas.

370. _____. Vertical crawl space developed. Earth Shel. Dig. Energ. Rept., no. 12, Nov./Dec. 1980: 8-9.

The author's innovative design feature does not require strong walls and roof to withstand earth pressures and eliminates the need for backfilling.

371. Scalise, James W., ed. Terratecture: the environmental benefits of earth integrating architectural design techniques. Tempe, AZ: Ariz. State Univ., Coll. of Archit., May 1974.

This is a workbook by 16 architectural students in the College of Architecture, Arizona State University.

372. Simmons, Lon B. Passive solar earth sheltered housing. High Ridge, MO: Simmons and Sun, Inc., Solar-Earth Consultants, Inc., Dec. 1980. 36 p.
Contains 21 floor plans.

373. Smay, V. Elaine. Solar-earth retreat. Pop. Sci., v. 223, Sept. 1983: 120+.

This is the fifth earth-sheltered design Charles Woods has done for Popular Science.

374. A solar house buried partly underground investigates architectonic implications of solar heating, along with a definition of exterior and interior private space. Prog. Archit., v. 58, no. 1, Jan. 1977: 59.

A design which received a citation in the 24th Awards Program. The first floor is buried under a berm which is partially carved out to create a protected courtyard. Natural light enters the living room through a skylight which penetrates the second floor. The architects were Chimacoff/Peterson.

375. Sterling, Ray. Step by step how to . . . using examples of Midwest projects. In Residential applications: transcripts of selected presentations, Going Under to Stay on Top, Minneapolis, MN, Oct. 1977. Minneapolis, MN: Univ. of Minn., Underground Space Center, 1979. p. 29-42.

This paper discusses the processes in deciding which type of house to design and shows the variety of designs and the effect the design has on layout of space within the house and on the structural considerations. There are also comments on the materials used in construction, especially the waterproofing.

376. Swayze, Julian H. Underground building. U.S. Patent Office, 3,227,061, patented Jan. 4, 1966.

This underground structure, designed as living quarters for the atomic age, has many features intended to ease the fear of being underground.

377. Terra-Dome Corp. Underground design for twenty-first century living. Independence, MO, 1980. 100 p.
This is a collection of articles on: design, an underground

51 Architectural Design

house in the Northwest, Terra-Dome House, planning and building, floor plans and exterior house designs, financing the underground home, and the art of scrounging materials.

378. Tingerthal, Mary. Myths and realities: a response. In <u>Residential applications: transcripts of selected presentations, Going Under to Stay on Top</u>, Minneapolis, MN, Oct. 1977. Minneapolis, MN: Univ. of Minn., Undergr. Sp. Ctr., 1979. p. 155-9.

The author is coordinator of the Minnesota Housing Finance Agency's Earth-Sheltered Demonstration Program which sponsored an earth-sheltered house design competition and contributed some financing for construction of the homes. The Program obtained data on energy use, market acceptance, construction, and psychological impact.

379. Underground Homes. <u>Plans for the future</u>. Portsmouth, OH. 44 p.

These plans are full color artists' renditions of 26 underground home designs, including floor plans, sketches, and descriptions of several different kinds of earth-sheltered homes, i.e. hillside, earth-bermed, totally below grade level, etc., and a discussion of the most desirable sites and climates for each type.

380. Underground Space Center. <u>Earth sheltered homes: plans and designs</u>. By Donna Ahrens, Tom Ellison, and Ray Sterling. New York, NY: Van Nostrand Reinhold, 1981. 125 p.

This book contains 23 designs for homes in the U.S. and Europe with photos, floor plans, details, and energy data.

381. Vadnais, Kathleen. Early franchise network continues. Earth Shel. Liv., no. 21, May/June 1982: 30-5.

Davis Caves dealers modify their plans and specifications to create custom designs. The designs shown are in Armington, IL; Laura, IL; Suffolk, VA; Beulah, CO; Montgomery City, MO; Mounds, IL; Stanwood, IA; Fenton, MO; Jesup, IA; Metamora, IL; and Aledo, IL.

382. _____. Earth shelter design types. In <u>Conf. proc., Energex '82, a Forum on Energy Self-Reliance: Conservation, Production and Consumption</u>, Regina, Saskatchewan, Aug. 23-29, 1982, Fred A. Curtis, ed. Winnipeg, Can.: Sol. Energ. Soc. of Can., 1982. p. 786-90.

383. Villis, Peter and Richard Tossani. Earth sheltered houses South Australia. <u>Geotecture</u>, v. 2, no. 3, 1985: 20-7.

The authors, who are architects, present the philosophy behind their earth-sheltered design practices, discuss the technical features which they incorporate into their earth-covered building designs, and give brief descriptions of four existing earth-sheltered homes which they designed.

384. Von Fraunhoffer, Herman. Original creations. Phoenix, AZ: Concept 2000, 13825 North 7th St., Suite F.
A book of designs.

385. Vosbeck, R.R. Womb or tomb: the designer's role in the energy crisis. In Potential of earth-sheltered and underground space: today's resource for tomorrow's space and energy viability: Undergr. Sp. Conf. and Expos., Kansas City, MO, June 8-10, 1981. T.L. Holthusen, ed. Elmsford, NY: Pergamon Pr., 1981. p. 17-21.
Specific projects are cited which have achieved award-winning status because of their superior design.

386. Wells, Malcolm. Underground designs. Cherry Hill, NJ: The Author, 1977. 87 p.
This was one of the first books on underground design, some built, some not. The last part of the book has tips on waterproofing, insulating, and landscaping. It contains much information on Wells' experience with underground design and ideas for businesses, offices, public works, and homes.

387. _____ and Sam Glenn-Wells. Underground plans book - 1. 1st Print. Brewster, MA: The Authors, P. O. Box 1149, 1980. 44 p.
This book was produced to meet the needs of those who want to design and build their own earth-sheltered houses. The authors set forth two caveats: that the publication is meant to be only a generator of ideas and that the designs apply only to cooler climates. Eight designs are included. Each design shows floor plans, cross sections, views from several sides and includes general comments. Both conventional and unique construction and design methods are used.

388. Woods, Charles G. The complete earth-sheltered house book. New York, NY: Van Nostrand Reinhold, 1984. 144 p.
The design and working drawings of a prototype award-winning modular home are included. This design can be adapted in size, room arrangement, construction, and appearance.

389. _____. Natural architecture: 35 earth-sheltered house designs. Stillwater, MN: WEBCO Pub. Co., Inc., 1982? (Earth Shelter Living book).

Woods draws upon the theories of Louis Sullivan and F.L. Wright concerning organic architecture and applies them to earth-sheltered designs, from small inexpensive cabins to rambling mansions, utilizing all the major building methods and materials.

390. _____. Natural architecture: 40 earth sheltered house designs. Rev. ed. New York, NY: Van Nostrand Reinhold, 1984. 145 p.
This edition has added five new designs and a complete set of working drawings.

391. Wright, R and S. Wright. Detailing the earth sheltered building. Earth shelter 2: coll. pap., 1st Earth Shel. Hous. Conf. and Exhib., Minneapolis, MN, Apr. 9-11, 1980. Minneapolis, MN: Univ. of Minn., Underground Space Ctr., 1980. p. 1-4.
The paper discusses all design aspects of earth-sheltered building with examples.

392. Wukasch, Eugene. The integrated-design process of the passive environmentally-designed structure. In Proc., 1st Int. Conf. on Energ. Effic. Bldgs. with Earth Shel. Prot., Sydney, Aust., Aug. 1-6, 1983. L.L. Boyer, ed. Stillwater, OK: Okla. State Univ., Archit. Ext., 1983. p. 187-90.
This article discusses the problems of integrating art and technology harmoniously in the ecologically sound structural design.

VII. CONSTRUCTION

---

393. Air-inflated forms cause high hopes: re-usable inflatable forms reduce building costs. Earth Shel. Liv., no. 32, Apr./May 1984: 16-9.
This new construction method can be used in both residential and commercial applications, and it is economical. The first home built using this method is in Owasso, OK.

394. Anderson, Brent. Earth integrated residential designs: earth bermed, earth sheltered, superinsulated; construction plans available for selected designs. Stillwater, OK: Earth Shel. Resource Ctr., 1985?

395. _____. Earth sheltering: a growing market for concrete constructors. <u>Concr. Constr.</u>, v. 27, no. 1, Jan. 1982: 73-7.

396. Andre, John and Larry G. Pleimann. Earth sheltered concrete domes using a geodesic formwork. In <u>Proc., Earth Shel. Bldg. Des. Innov.</u>, Oklahoma City, OK, Apr. 18, 1980. L.L. Boyer, ed. Stillwater, OK: Okla. State Univ., 1980. p. VII. 47-50.

An earth-sheltered structure being built in northwest Arkansas is a thin concrete dome sprayed on a triangular panel geodesic dome formwork. Polyurethane insulation was sprayed on the concrete dome after proper curing. A central skylight provides daylighting and ventilation. It is operable for different ventilation rates and as a secondary means of exit. A southerly exposed greenhouse on the southwest side of the dome provides additional winter solar heating.

397. Arches are his signature: builder uses arches to put personal stamp on his homes. <u>Earth Shel. Liv.</u>, no. 34, July/Aug. 1984: 22-3.

An earth-covered home builder in Cambridge, MN, makes arches his trademark. Forms hold up the bricks and blocks until dry.

398. Architect details: cuts roof costs. <u>Earth Shel. Dig. Energ. Rept.</u>, no. 15, May/June 1981: 8-11.

Architect Angus MacDonald has used three low-cost roof systems in three earth-sheltered houses he has built: log roof, a steel truss roof, a cast-in-place concrete slab.

399. Armco Atlantic, Inc. introduces new precast concrete wall panel. <u>Earth Shel. Liv.</u>, no. 40, July/Aug. 1985: 18-9.

CW-100 is a hardwall structural system using 53 percent less concrete owing to a proprietary ribbed design in its precast concrete panel. Write Armco Atlantic, Inc., P.O. Box 465622, Cincinnati, OH 45246-5622.

400. Baggs, David W. Practical aspects of materials and construction for earth-covered buildings. In <u>Proc., Symp. on Des. Strat. for Earth Cov. Bldgs.</u>, May 8-9, 1982. S.A. Baggs, ed. Kensington, NSW, Aust.: Univ. of New South Wales, Grad. Sch. of the Built Env., 1982. p. 211-20.

401. Bailey, Brian. Berming can mean a basement, too. <u>Earth Shel. Liv.</u>, no. 35, Sept./Oct. 1984: 13.

Two methods of putting basements in earth-bermed homes are discussed.

402. Bargabus, Dave and Darrell Laubach. Covered vs. conventional roofs: what's best? Earth Shel. Dig. Energ. Rept., no. 10, July/Aug. 1980: 26-8.

The authors built a modified earth-shelter structure with a conventional truss roof without any soil cover. The house is notched into the hill on the east, west, and north sides up to ceiling level. The roof is exposed, and the attic is heavily insulated. The roof structure provides two advantages: the construction of it was achieved by unsophisticated work crews, and it was low-cost.

403. Behr, Richard A., E.W. Kiesling, J.E. Fossum, and R.S. Childress. Design program: improved structural systems for earth sheltered housing. Lubbock, TX: Texas Tech Univ. Pr., 1981.

This work examines the use of domes for earth-sheltered housing. Because of their high structural efficiency, they could be used to reduce the price differential between above-ground and earth-covered housing.

404. _____ and _____. Estimated cost of earth-covered arch and dome shells. Undergr. Sp., v. 9, no. 1, 1985: 45-50.

Costs of earth-covered arch and dome construction were found to be very competitive with costs of conventional flat roof construction.

405. _____, _____, and G. Boubel. Thin shell roof systems and construction techniques for earth-sheltered housing. In Proc., Earth Shel. Bldg. Des. Innov., Oklahoma City, OK, Apr. 18, 1980. L.L. Boyer, ed. Stillwater, OK: Okla. State Univ., 1980. p. VIII. 19-27.

Various thin shell design concepts, including arches, domes, free-form, and sandwich panels are discussed. Their economic benefits and concept marketability are explored. Construction details are given for a house in Muleshoe, TX, utilizing the soil as formwork together with a trenching technique.

406. Bennett, Randy. Precast panels have appeal. Earth Shel. Liv., no. 28, July/Aug. 1983: 31-3.

Precast concrete panels in a prefabricated building system are discussed. Advantages: they can be erected in cold weather in a short time, and they have less of a moisture load after completion than poured-in-place concrete.

407. The big pour. Earth Shel. Liv., no. 33, May/June 1984: 4-6.

Deco Homes in Bladensburg, MD, formed the shell for its

model earth-covered home with a single pour of 126 yards of concrete in 12 hours.

408. Bohn, C. The underground tube home. <u>Home Energ. Dig. Wood. Q.</u>, v. 3, no. 2, Fall 1978: 156-64.

409. Brann, Donald R. <u>How to build a low cost house above or below ground</u>. Rev. ed. Briarcliff Manor, NY: Easi-Bild. 226 p.

This is a guide to building a one-story house over a full basement or a more economical earth-sheltered "foundation house."

410. Brown, James J. and Terry A. Johnson. <u>Structural considerations for earth-sheltered homes</u>. Portsmouth, OH: Underground Homes.

This book discusses loading, reinforcing steel, walls, retaining walls, roof sections, etc.

411. Build underground with wood. <u>Fam. Hand.</u>, v. 33, Mar. 1983: 128.

412. Building standards on the way. <u>Earth Shel. Dig. Energ. Rept.</u>, no. 11, Sept./Oct. 1980: 60-1.

Civil and mechanical engineer William Kneeland thinks that the only thing retarding the development of earth-sheltered housing is the lack of standardized information to guide building contractors.

413. Calvert, Terri. Solartron prefabricated earth-sheltered homes. <u>Moth. Earth N.</u>, no. 57, May/June 1979: 157-9.

The concept: building an earth-sheltered dwelling from preformed, fiberglass-reinforced plywood panels, a development of Ralph Bullock at American Solartron Corp. This company now has several hundred designs and floor plans available, including blueprints for hotels and office buildings. They are located in Centralia, IL.

414. Carter, David. <u>Build it underground: a guide for the self-builder and building professional</u>. Morganville, NJ: Sterling Pub. Co., 1982. 208 p.

This guide presents a wide range of both built and unbuilt earth-sheltered designs and construction techniques stressing the use of indigenous materials.

415. Concrete can be sprayed. <u>Earth Shel. Liv.</u>, no. 20, Mar./Apr. 1982: 20-2.

This article discusses the past and present uses of shotcrete (sprayed concrete).

416. Concrete shells reinforced with curved steel plates support earth sheltered home. <u>Concr. Constr.</u>, v. 27, no. 1, Jan. 1982: 43.

David Stearns has built a superinsulated earth-sheltered home in Hudsonville, MI, using concrete and expanded metal plates.

417. <u>Constructing earth sheltered housing with concrete.</u> Washington, DC: Dept. of Hous. and Urb. Dev.

418. Construction details for earth-sheltering. <u>Concr. Constr.</u>, v. 27, no. 6, June 1982: 521-3.

Drawings show details of walls, roof structures, and parapets with insulation, waterproofing, and drainage systems.

419. Cook, G. Robert and Gerald E. Allen. Earth, energy, architecture and steel culvert construction. In <u>Proc., Earth Shel. Bldg. Des. Innov.</u>, Oklahoma City, OK, Apr. 18, 1980. L.L. Boyer, ed. Stillwater, OK: Okla. State Univ., 1980. p. VII. 39-44.

The design for an office-residence complex (Terratech Center) is presented in detail. It is constructed of two pre-engineered steel vaults, parallel-placed, and connected by an atrium. The building contains the office of Control Data/Terra Tech Divisions, Criteria, Inc. and an apartment for Criteria's president and family.

420. Cottrell, Richard. Building systems: an energy analysis. In <u>Proc., 1st Int. Conf. on Energ. Effic. Bldgs. with Earth Shel. Prot.</u>, Sydney, Aust., Aug. 1-6, 1983. L.L. Boyer, ed. Stillwater, OK: Okla. State Univ., Archit. Ext., 1983. p. 191-5.

This paper presents an overview of the systems and procedures used successfully to reduce energy use and maximize habitability of residential and commercial earth-sheltered structures across the United States. --From auth. abstract.

421. Daniel, James I. and Brad Burnside. Design information for concrete arch system. <u>Concr. Constr.</u>, v. 27, no. 7, July 1982: 581-5.

This system, which combines concrete with modular steel sheets, is useful for earth shelters or cut and cover construction.

422. Darvas, R.M. Structural problems in earth-covered buildings. In <u>Proc., Alt. in Habitat: the Use of Earth Cov. Set., Conf.,</u> Fort Worth, TX, May 17-19, 1978. F.L. Moreland, ed. Washington, DC: U.S. Dept. of Energy, 1979. v. 1, <u>Earth covered buildings</u>, p. 70-3.

This paper discusses the unusual forces which create stresses on earth-sheltered structures, weatherproofing and waterproofing, and the construction problems encountered when installing them.

423. Davy, James. Earth-sheltered roof systems. <u>Earth Shel. Bldgs. - Tech. Pap.</u>, TP-IIB, 1983.

424. Dick, Chester J., Jr. Add mixture, not water. <u>Earth Shel. Dig. Energ. Rept.</u>, no. 17, Sept./Oct. 1981: 23.

Cracks and leaks in concrete can be eliminated by not using excessive water.

425. Dome offers option. <u>Earth Shel. Dig. Energ. Rept.</u>, no. 9, May/June 1980: 23.

This dome is bermed on all sides but the south side.

426. Duncan, James M. Earth pressures on structures due to fault movement. <u>ASCE Proc.</u>, v. 99, SM 12, no. 10237, Dec. 1973.

If a buried structure is not strong enough to withstand the earth pressure loads induced by fault movements, it will be ripped apart by the movements. Therefore, when a buried structure is being designed, the earth pressure loads caused by faulting must be known. This work discusses the characteristics of these earth pressure loads and considers two kinds of finite element analyses used to calculate their magnitudes.

427. _____ and Guy Lefebvre. Earth pressures on structures due to fault movement. <u>J. Soil Mech. Found. Div., ASCE</u>, Dec. 1973: 1153-63.

428. Earth Habitats. <u>Earth habitats</u>. Dallas, TX, 1980. 40 p.

This book presents a modular design and construction system which reduces construction costs and offers a functionally efficient home that eliminates the need for hallways. There are floor plans for 12 variations of the design.

429. An earth-integrated housing concept for difficult-to-build sites. <u>Concr. Constr.</u>, v. 25, no. 9, Sept. 1980: 688-90.

Using the method developed by Architerra, Inc., the earth itself is sculpted to form individual building sites. Terraces are shaped and stabilized by precast concrete panels forming side walls and curving rear walls of the housing units.

59 Construction

430. Earth Systems, Inc. <u>Tomorrow's home today</u>. 49 p.
   Domes combined with earth-sheltering are shown in house plans. There is also information on financing, waterproofing, performance, construction, materials, costs, etc.

431. The Earth Systems kit house. <u>Moth. Earth N.</u>, no. 85, Jan./Feb. 1984: 68-9.
   The Earth Systems kit house has a pre-engineered dome shape (oval, half, or "true" dome) and is composed of an integral steel framing network covered with a shell of concrete eliminating seams and joints and comes in four sizes. Most are two-story units. The cost of the kit is $10,000-$15,000.

432. Energy-saving system shapes, stabilizes land. <u>Multi-hous. N.</u>, July 1980.
   The architectural firm Architerra, Inc. has created a design system for building earth-sheltered homes into steep hillsides. Created by Henri Vidal, architect and engineer, the system utilizes an arcuate shell design and an associated technology called Reinforced Earth by which a hillside land parcel is sloped and stabilized forming curved walls.

433. Erb, Ellsworth R., III. Construction details for small-scale earth-sheltered buildings. <u>Earth Shel. Bldgs. - Tech. Pap.</u>, TP-IIID, 1983.

434. Factory-built hand-assembled: building an earth-shelter can be as easy as building with blocks -- or putting together factory built kits. <u>Earth Shel. Liv.</u>, no. 36, Nov./Dec. 1984: 26-8.
   Integrated Building Systems, Inc. is marketing a panelized wood earth-shelter system called Wood-Tech^{TM} which they think will reduce construction costs.

435. Factory system approved with HUD bulletin. <u>Earth Shel. Dig. Energ. Rept.</u>, no. 10, July/Aug. 1980: 50-1.
   American Solartron's prefabricated earth shelter with fiberglass panels is the first to receive an FHA-HUD Engineering Bulletin (#998) complete with testing reports and approval for potential federal financial support because of the Company's quality control. The system of interlocking wood panels sealed in fiberglass can be erected in one day. Specifications are given.

436. Feduniw, Leon O. Floor systems for energy-efficient houses in the southwest arid regions of the United States. <u>Earth Shel. Bldgs. - Tech. Pap.</u>, TP-IC, 1983.

437. Firbank, James J. Low-technology, earth-shelter, construction system utilizing "Triform." In Proc., 1st Int. Conf. on Energ. Effic. Bldgs. with Earth Shel. Prot., Sydney, Aust., Aug. 1-6, 1983. L.L. Boyer, ed. Stillwater, OK: Okla. State Univ., Archit. Ext., 1983. p. 381-5.

The design and construction of earth-covered dwellings has long been restricted by the low strengths achievable using existing low-technology materials, the problems of groundwater ingress and the subsequent development of mould, and the question of fire control and control of related toxic gases. This paper introduces a new range of building materials based on a new co-polymer binder known as Triform. The various potential applications of these Triform-based materials are discussed together with preliminary laboratory test results, with specific reference to their relevance to the design and construction of low technology, earth-sheltered construction.

438. Flathau, W.J. and J.P. Balsara. Soil-structure interaction - an overview. Proc., Alt. in Habitat: the Use of Earth Cov. Set., Conf., Fort Worth, TX, May 17-19, 1978. F.L. Moreland, ed. Washington, DC: U.S. Dept. of Energy, 1979. v. 1, Earth covered buildings, p. 13-33.

Because the surrounding soil is a significant part of the load carrying capability of a structural system, with proper design and selection of geometry, soil cover can substantially increase the load carrying capacity of the structure. The long-span elements of the structure need not be designed to accept the full dead load of the overlying soil.

439. Foam house: another option. Earth Shel. Liv., no. 28, July/Aug. 1983: 34-5.

A conventional house built of lightweight blocks of expanded polystyrene anchored to a standard foundation using reinforcing steel bars can be heated for less than $100 a year. It requires more air conditioning in warm weather than would an earth-sheltered home.

440. Green, Bruce Hamilton. Basic principles of underground house construction. In Underground utilization. T. Stauffer, ed. Kansas City, MO: Univ. of Missouri - Kansas City, Dept. of Geosci., 1978. v. 4, p. 608-13.

This article is limited to the main design principles in underground construction, those which prevent water leakage and thermal failure.

441. _____ and D.A. Summers. On-site building materials using UMR water jet technology. In The potential of earth-sheltered and underground space: proc., Undergr. Space Conf. and Expos., Kansas City, MO, June 8-10, 1981. T.L. Holthusen, ed. Elmsford, NY: Pergamon Pr., 1981. p. 259-65.

A mass of "waste" rock is generated by the creation of underground space. An energy savings can be achieved by cutting this mass of rock into blocks for use as on-site building materials. High pressure water jets are advocated as a means of cutting the blocks as they are energy economical.

442. Hassall, David N.H. Fixed inclined louvres for solar control to facades and atria of earth-sheltered buildings. Proc., 1st Int. Conf. on Energ. Effic. Bldgs. with Earth Shel. Prot., Sydney, Aust., Aug. 1-6, 1983. L.L. Boyer, ed. Stillwater, OK: Okla. State Univ., Archit. Ext., 1983. p. 125-9.

Louvres can be designed to be fitted "diagonally" across the outside of fenestration for the purpose of solar control. Angles and dimensions can be designed so that the device does not have to be adjusted, i.e., it operates as a completely "passive" device in blocking out summer sun and admitting winter sun while at the same time admitting light from the sky. There is a unique solution for each window depending on its slope, aspect, and latitude. Examples of fixed inclined louvres designed for vertical and sloping facades and atria roofs of earth-sheltered buildings are given. The system has advantages of lower cost, increased reliability, and added building security. --Auth. abstract.

443. Haupert, David. Earth-sheltered housing. Bet. Homes Gard., v. 59, Sept. 1981: 44+.

This article describes two earth-sheltered houses using two different construction methods: concrete with post and beam and poured into place post tensioned concrete.

444. How to make a two rowlock Roman arch. Earth Shel. Liv., no. 34, July/Aug. 1984: 24.

445. Hull, M. Earth shelters by inflation-formed thin-shell domes. In Earth Shelter 2: coll. pap., Earth Shel. Hous. Conf. and Exhib., Minneapolis, MN, Apr. 9-11, 1980. Minneapolis, MN: Univ. of Minn., Undergr. Sp. Ctr., 1980.

This paper deals with a patented method for inflatable-form moulding of thin-shell concrete domes for earth-sheltered construction. Advantages: the inflatable form is lightweight; the form can be erected by two people; it is reusable; the cost is low; it is adaptable to a wide range of structure sizes and shapes.

446. Hurst, Homer T. Economical underground house structures. In <u>Papers, Am. Soc. of Agric. Engrs., Winter Mtg.</u>, New Orleans, LA, Dec. 11-14, 1979. St. Joseph, MO: ASAE, 1979. Pap. 79-4559.

This paper discusses the recent developments of the All-Weather Wood Foundation System and some alternatives. Four exterior wall designs are discussed: two All-Weather Wood Foundation Systems, an alternate with framing, and an experimental design with 28 percent less total material cost than the first two.

447. Impson, Loren C. Ferrocement earth-sheltered housing projects. In <u>The potential of earth-sheltered and underground space: proc., Undergr. Sp. Conf. and Expos.</u>, Kansas City, Mo, June 8-10, 1981. T.L. Holthusen, ed. Elmsford, NY: Pergamon Pr., 1981. p. 373-77.

The use of ferrocement to build simple earth-sheltered houses is discussed.

448. _____. Ferrocement: a technique for passive solar earth sheltered structures. <u>Proc., Int. Sol. Energ. Soc., Am. Sec., Annu. Mtg.</u>, 1982.

The ferrocement construction system has been used since 1847. It utilizes commonly available materials and permits more design possibilities than any other widely used technique. Also discussed are insulation methods and the air flow characteristics of domes.

449. Inflate, spray, cover dome. <u>Earth Shel. Dig. Energ. Rept.</u>, no. 9, May/June 1980: 20.

Tecton Corp. manufactures a dome which could be earth-covered.

450. An innovative approach to installed skylights. <u>Earth Shel. Liv.</u>, no. 40, July/Aug. 1985: 16.

Skyflex is a lightweight, three-piece, leak-proof, flexible shaft which automatically adjusts to roof pitch and height. The reflective interior funnels light into the room below.

451. Japan presents versatile pod. <u>Earth Shel. Dig. Energ. Rept.</u>, no. 14, Mar./Apr. 1981: 10-11.

Gel-coated, fiberglass reinforced plastic pods in two sizes, 60 sq. ft. and 25 sq. ft., can be joined together in any combination to be used as earth-sheltered homes. The manufacturer is Taisei Construction Company of Tokyo.

452. Japanese firm markets portable "pod houses" as disaster shelters. <u>Undergr. Sp.</u>, v. 4, no. 5, Mar./Apr. 1980: 320.

A multi-purpose, portable, pod-shaped house is being marketed in Japan by the Taisei Construction Company as a shelter from disasters. They are also used as holiday homes. They can be transported to remote areas by helicopter or truck, can be used as homes, communications bases or emergency medical centers.

453. Jensen, Harley R. Conserve with zero lot lines. Earth Shel. Dig. Energ. Rept., no. 13, Jan./Feb. 1981: 8-10.
If the walls of two homes are joined over the common lot line between them, the amount of exterior wall that is exposed is reduced. If two earth-sheltered homes are joined in this way, that wall will be a "warm wall" as opposed to the 55-degree earth-bermed walls. This will further help to conserve energy.

454. Johnson, Terry A. 105 Earth shelter building tips. Portsmouth, OH: Underground Homes. 21 p.

455. Joints in concrete slabs. Earth Shel. Dig. Energ. Rept., no. 5, Sept./Oct. 1979: 30.
The what, why, and how of joints in concrete slabs.

456. Kimber, Wayne. Wood used successfully. Earth Shel. Dig. Energ. Rept., no. 16, July/Aug. 1981: 20-21.
This article discusses the use of wood treated with Chromated Copper Arsenate (CCA).

457. Kistler, Eugene C. Quantification of internal loads in earth sheltered residences. Earth Shel. Bldgs. - Tech. Pap., TP-IIE, 1983.

458. Klodt, Gerald. Earth sheltered housing. Reston, VA: Reston Pub. Co., 1985. 296 p.
This book covers the essential technical details of earth-sheltered house construction and presents economical construction methods that stress the energy conserving features of terratecture. Readers are encouraged to analyze each problem and select an energy efficient design. Special features include: calculations for evaluating energy efficiency, details on site analysis, and an advanced method for determining heat loss through the earth for any structure in any area of the U.S.

459. Klump, E.H. Excavation technology. In Proc., Alt. in Energ. Conserv.: the Use of Earth Cov. Bldgs., Fort Worth, TX, July 9-12, 1975. Washington, DC: U.S. G.P.O., 1976. p. 263-68.
Briefly discusses a few excavation techniques.

460. Langley, John B. Application of the BERNOLD system to barrel shell earth-sheltered architecture. In <u>The potential of earth-sheltered and underground space: proc., Undergr. Sp. Conf. and Expos.</u>, Kansas City, MO, June 8-10, 1981. T.L. Holthusen, ed. Elmsford, NY: Pergamon Pr., 1981. p. 277-96.

    The BERNOLD plate system was designed for mining, tunneling, and culverts. This study devises an application of the system for concrete barrel shell earth-sheltered architecture. First the nomenclature, product, process, and design detail parameters are identified. This is done by applying the BERNOLD plate to a particular prototype project. It is concluded that the system as presently manufactured can lessen the need for time and skilled labor in earth-sheltered construction.

461. _____. The barrel shell -- structural rethinking in earth-sheltered design. <u>Undergr. Sp.</u>, v. 5, no. 2, Sept./Oct. 1980: 92-101.

    Concrete barrel shell structures used in earth-sheltered construction offer both economic and functional advantages. This paper discusses the basic technology and costs related to barrel shell construction. The construction of Ward House, a barrel shell home in central Florida, is described.

462. _____. Earth covered barrel shell structures. In <u>Proc., Earth Shel. Bldg. Des. Innov.</u>, Oklahoma City, OK, April 18, 1980. L.L. Boyer, ed. Stillwater, OK: Okla. State Univ., 1980. p. VII. 5-15.

    Details are given of the economic and functional advantages and challenges of the concrete barrel shell structure. Ward House, a shell house in central Florida, is described.

463. Lash, David Michael. <u>Opportunities and limitations for the use of precast concrete in earth-sheltered housing</u>. Master's thesis. Mass. Inst. of Tech., Dept. of Civ. Eng., June 1981.

464. Laufer, A. Economic comparison of prefabricated box and on-site reinforced concrete casting construction methods. <u>Undergr. Sp.</u>, v. 9, no. 1, 1985: 41-4.

    A comparison is made of construction time and cost, and labor requirements for the construction methods discussed and a cost sensitivity analysis is presented. The construction methods are box-type prefabricated modules and conventional on-site reinforced concrete casting.

465. Loker, Rex. Use of wood foundations in earth-sheltered buildings. <u>Earth Shel. Bldgs. -- Tech. Pap.</u>, TP-ID, 1983.

466. Lowing, Arnold N. and Kenneth J. Griffith. Earthquake considerations for earth-sheltered residential buildings. In <u>Proc., 1st Int. Conf. on Energ. Effic. Bldgs. with Earth Shel. Prot.</u>, Sydney, Aust., Aug. 1-6, 1983. L.L. Boyer, ed. Stillwater, OK: Okla. State Univ., Archit. Ext., 1983. p. 141-5.

The structural behavior and performance of earth-shelter residential buildings subjected to an earthquake are examined in broadscope concepts adequate to provide engineering and construction principles necessary to ensure personal safety and reduction of property damage. Earthquake-resistant engineering design principles, based upon equivalent static force lateral loading requirements and probable failure modes, are presented to assist the reader in incorporating the necessary structural provisions. Non-structural elements, architectural features, and service utility provisions are discussed in an effort to illustrate the inherent dangers of component elements and to provide guidelines for proper construction and installation practices. --Auth. abstract.

467. _____. Earthquake considerations for earth-sheltered residential buildings. <u>Undergr. Sp.</u>, v. 8, no. 3, 1984: 169-73.

This paper addresses the basic engineering provisions and general concepts necessary to achieve structural stability in the event of an earthquake. Only lateral ground motion is considered in formulating design requirements. Measures against landslides, soil liquification, consolidation, and fault rupture are not studied.

468. _____. Earthquakes, pt. 1: building in seismic zones. <u>Earth Shel. Liv.</u>, no. 23, Sept./Oct. 1982: 13-4, 50.

A guide for incorporating earthquake resistant construction techniques in earth-sheltered residential buildings. The primary example used is an open-front bermed house.

469. _____. <u>Structural behavior of residential earth shelter buildings and earthquake resistant construction techniques</u>. Santa Rosa, CA, 2165 Mt. Olive Drive. 29 p.

This work examines the problem of structural behavior of earth shelter residential buildings independent of seismic zones. It gives earthquake resistant construction techniques using static engineering principles and conventional design and construction methods.

470. Lunde, Martin R. Precast concrete walls for earth-sheltered construction. <u>Earth Shel 2: coll. pap., Earth Shel.</u>

Hous. Conf. and Exhib., Minneapolis, MN, Apr. 9-11, 1980.
Minneapolis, MN: Univ. of Minn., Undergr. Sp. Ctr., 1980.
Results of an analysis of wall structural systems point to the use of precast concrete walls for residential below-grade wall construction rather than reinforced concrete block, wood, and cast-in-place concrete construction techniques.

471. _____. Precast would make good walls. Earth Shel. Dig. Energ. Rept., no. 2, Mar./Apr. 1979: 16-7.

Precast concrete wall panels may help promote underground housing by offsetting some costs that don't occur in conventional housing.

472. Lunstrum, Kurt. Precast dome buried. Earth Shel. Dig. Energ. Rept., no. 12, Nov./Dec. 1980: 10-1.

The author, a contractor, has developed a low-cost (less than $10 per sq. ft.) dome module which can be manufactured by most precast concrete companies, transported and erected with little labor.

473. McDonald, James E. and Tony C. Liu. Concrete for earth-covered structures. In Proc., Alt. in Habitat: the Use of Earth Cov. Set., Conf., Fort Worth, TX, May 17-19, 1978. F.L. Moreland, ed. Washington, DC: U.S. Dept. of Energy, 1979. v. 1, Earth covered buildings, p. 74-91.

This paper discusses the composition of concrete, its permeability to water, the effect of the aggregate in concrete, the effect of cement paste, the effect of admixtures, the effect of placing and curing, and concrete coatings to prevent leakage. Specialized concretes with potential application in earth-covered structures are discussed briefly: polymer-impregnated concrete, polymer concrete, ferro-cement, fiber-reinforced concrete.

474. McGrath, D.J. Builders go underground. Venture, v. 4, no. 1, Jan. 1982: 48-51.

In 1981, 1,000 new earth-sheltered houses brought the total in the U.S. to about 5,000. Some earth-sheltered building techniques are discussed.

475. Metz, Don. Heavy loads. New Shel., v. 3, no. 1, Jan. 1982: 33-5.

This article presents a summary of current subsurface construction practices. The three basic structural systems for underground houses are described: precast, pretensioned concrete plank roofs, poured-in-place concrete roofs, and heavy-timber roofs.

67 Construction

476. Mini fact: footings. Earth Shel. Liv., no. 21, May/June 1982: 18-9.

477. Mini fact: lateral pressure. Earth Shel. Liv., no. 20, Mar./Apr. 1982: 19.
Lateral soil loads on walls are measured in the same way as water pressure: it increases with depth. And it also depends on the type of soil the structure is built in.

478. Mini fact: structural loads. Earth Shel. Liv., no. 19, Jan./Feb. 1982: 19.
This article briefly discusses the structural load carried by one story and two story earth-sheltered homes.

479. Minke, Gernot. Earth sheltered buildings utilizing tamped earth and plant stabilized earth as building materials. Proc., 1st Int. Conf. on Energ. Effic. Bldgs. with Earth Shel. Prot., Sydney, Aust., Aug. 1-6, 1983. L.L. Boyer, ed. Stillwater, OK: Okla. State Univ., Archit. Ext., 1983. p. 377-80.
Two elemented rammed earth wall construction techniques were developed at the University of Kassel and successfully tested in Germany and Latin America. The traditional rammed earth technique was deeply refined so that the erection time could be reduced by 50 percent and linear shrinkage was only 0.4 percent instead of two percent. This was reached by utilizing a self-moving vibrating press which runs in a climbing form work. A very efficient new construction technique to produce wall and dome structures was found further by using a simple extrusion device. This extruder produces loam profiles which can be used as building elements without any formwork or mortar. A new system for inclinated grass and earth roofs was developed which reduces the heat flow up to 50-80 percent utilizing a layer of 16-20 cm. of earth and expanded clay which is covered by a layer of a special grass vegetation. --Auth. abstract.

480. Minnesota Masonry Institute. Earth sheltered housing with concrete masonry. Minneapolis, MN. (#227).
This is an introductory discussion of the basic terminology and concepts of earth sheltering with concrete masonry.

481. Misra, Prem K. Earth-covered homes: the application of precast portals and low profile arches in suburbs of New South Wales. In Australasian proc., 1st Int. Conf. on Energy. Effic. Bldgs. with Earth Shel. Prot., Sydney, Aust., Aug. 1-6, 1983. S.A. Baggs, ed. Kensington, NSW, Aust.: Unisearch, Ltd., 1983. p. E26-30.

Three methods of earth-covered home construction, namely cast in-situ concrete method, precast portal unit method and low-profile arch shell method were studied. Study revealed that low-profile, arch method was the cheapest construction method when compared with the other two methods. This method of construction also provides better plan layout flexibility when compared with precast, portal method, and construction is only one-third of the cost of cast in-situ method. The drawbacks of low profile arch method are that it requires substantial capital outlay for the fabrication of special formwork, and the resultant curved internal shape may be objectionable to some potential buyers. --Auth. abstract.

482. A modular earth-sheltered system with domed roofs. Concr. Constr., v. 25, no. 9, Sept. 1980: 684-6.

The modular earth-sheltered dome-roofed homes developed by Gayle R. Scafe of Terra-Dome, Inc., Independence, MO, were designed to appeal to the conventional building market. The modules can be joined in any number and direction to create any size and shape structure and connected by 16-foot wide arches.

483. Mott, Larry. Structural, reinforcing are combined. Earth Shel. Dig. Energ. Rept., no. 16, July/Aug. 1981: 8-9, 43.

The Enviromass System consists of the application of shotcrete-sprayed concrete layers to an expanded polystyrene core, objective - to improve the thermal and structural performance of reinforced concrete.

484. Nelson, James. Tilt-up done on site. Earth Shel. Dig. Energ. Rept., no. 18, Nov./Dec. 1981: 6-9.

The tilt-up system involves using a finished concrete floor as a form for concrete slabs which are poured laying flat on the floor and then tilted up to positions as walls or roofs.

485. Newman, J.O. and R.E. Harrison. Panelized wood foundations for earth-embanked walls. Am. Soc. Agric. Engrs., Summer Mtg., Orlando, FL, June 21-24, 1981. (Unpublished?)

This paper evaluates the potential of a wood foundation system with standardized panel designs for use in earth-embanked houses and in basements. Discusses design, materials, structural testing, and installation.

486. Norton, Willard S. Concrete work for earth-sheltered buildings. Concr. Constr., v. 25, no. 9, Sept. 1980: 659-64.

Some of the topics discussed: requirements for concrete

and steel; post-tensioning; precast roof slabs; uniform foundation support; adequate waterproofing and drainage; placing and protecting the steel; structurally adequate retaining walls; adequacy of concrete curing; stripping requirements (forms for concrete); backfilling.

487. _____. Concrete work for earth sheltered buildings. Earth Shel. Dig. Energ. Rept., no. 14, Mar./Apr. 1981: 21-3.

This paper discusses the concrete mix required for earth-sheltered structures, post-tensioning operations, concrete precast slabs for use in earth-sheltered structures, and concrete floor slabs.

488. _____. Structural design for poured concrete earth contact structures. In Passive solar: subdivisions, windows, underground. Ed. by H. Wade and others. Kansas City, MO: Am. Sol. Energ. Soc., Kansas City Chap. -- Missouri Sol. Energ. Assn., 1983. p. 224-30.

This chapter details the author's experiences in using poured reinforced concrete for earth-contact structures.

489. _____. Use concrete correctly. Earth Shel. Dig. Energ. Rept., no. 15, May/June 1981: 23.

An engineer tells how to use concrete in earth shelters.

490. Now -- mail order earth shelters: company will send kits, and representative anywhere. Earth Shel. Liv., no. 31, Jan./Feb. 1984: 18-20.

This earth-sheltered dome kit is marketed by Earth Systems, Inc. of Durango, CO.

491. Noziska, Howard. Blocks are a natural choice. Earth Shel. Dig. Energ. Rept., no. 2, Mar./Apr. 1979: 18.

Concrete block is used in underground homes because of its being inert to water, readily adaptable to any wall length, fireproof, and energy efficient.

492. Oehler, Mike. The folly of overbuilding: cheap does not have to mean the quality is poor. Earth Shel. Liv., no. 29, Sept./Oct. 1983: 8-10.

Most earth-sheltered homes are overbuilt so very expensively. The author uses no floor or wall insulation, no concrete slab or wood floor, and always uses sloped roofs to work with nature instead of conquering it and thereby keeping his building costs very low.

493. Ohanian, R. Shelterra Earth Homes structural shell and other general observations. In Earth shelter 2: coll. pap., 1st Earth Shel. Hous. Conf. and Exhib., Minneapolis, MN, April 9-11, 1980. Minneapolis, MN: Univ. of Minn., Undergr. Sp. Ctr., 1980.

Shelterra Homes have precast roofs and poured wall systems. Costs for the shell are $18.50 to $23.50, finishing cost $16.50 to $20.50, for a total of about $40 sq. ft.

494. Oliver, Gordon. Precast concrete manufacturer promotes earth sheltered housing. Earth Shel. Dig. Energ. Rept., no. 6, Nov./Dec. 1979: 8.

Western Industries, Cadillac, MI, maker of precast roof and floor systems, has been supplying earth-sheltered construction projects since 1978.

495. Pearcey, Dale and Gene Pearcey. Thin-shell dome kit buried. Earth Shel. Dig. Energ. Rept., no. 8, Mar./Apr. 1980: 4-7.

Earth Systems of Phoenix, AZ, offers a mass produced thin shell concrete dome kit that contains the major structural and forming components in a design with a flexible floor plan. The base can be up to 20 ft. below grade permitting excavated dirt to cover the top half of the dome.

496. Pendergast, Robert E. Calculate for soil pressure. Earth Shel. Dig. Energ. Rept., no. 11, Sept./Oct. 1980: 4-5.

Little has been written about lateral earth pressure on below-grade walls. The design values usually used to calculate lateral pressure may be too low which could result in a collapsed wall. The type of soil, soil properties, soil conditions, and wall design are key factors in constructing an earth-sheltered wall. A professional subsurface investigation to determine the site's soil properties is recommended.

497. Planning footings for earth-sheltered construction. Concr. Constr., v. 27, no. 6, June 1982: 499-504.

This article discusses the types of footings used in earth-sheltered buildings, evaluating the loads to be supported, the factors affecting the width of the footing, and calculating footing reinforcement.

498. Portland Cement Association. Constructing earth sheltered housing with concrete. By R.E. Spears. Skokie, IL: PCA, 1981?

Discusses the design and construction of an earth-sheltered house using cast-in-place concrete, precast concrete, and concrete masonry. Details of concrete construction currently used are shown to be applicable using reasonable care in building an earth-sheltered home.

499. _____. Earth integrated building construction. Skokie, IL: PCA, 1978. 24 p. (PCA Concrete Report CRO56.01B).
This report discusses the use of concrete in earth-sheltered construction. It provides background information on earth sheltering and several examples of projects both planned and completed. It includes construction details for a single family house and provides a short bibliography.

500. Precast gives glimpse of future. Earth Shel. Dig. Energy Rept., no. 17, Sept./Oct. 1981: 46-7.
David Lash of the Mass. Inst. of Tech. discusses the contents of and research for his thesis Opportunities and limitations for the use of precast concrete in earth sheltered housing.

501. Precast panels form earth-sheltered homes. Concr. Constr., v. 27, no. 6, June 1982: 507-8.
Describes a six-year-old patented multipurpose precast panel system used in earth-sheltered and above-ground construction.

502. Precast shell is quick, low cost. Earth Shel. Liv., no. 23, Sept./Oct. 1982: 38-41.
The precast, modular shells called C/Shells were developed by Richard Sibley and Richard Seedorf in Atlanta. The C/Shell system has no interior bearing walls permitting flexible floor plans. These shells can be built in about a month by owner-builders.

503. Precast voids serve purpose. Earth Shel. Dig. Energ. Rept., no. 16, July/Aug. 1981: 10-1, 57.
Waffle-Crete precast panels have been used to construct a townhouse project where the living area is underground.

504. Prefabricated wood system marketed. Earth Shel. Dig. Energ. Rept., no. 14, Mar./Apr. 1981: 34-6.
Everstrong, Inc. built its earth-sheltered office in Redwood Falls, MN, using their prefabricated wood system, erected without footings. The roof is 100 percent covered with 12 to 18 inches of earth. The east and west walls are 67 percent covered. The floor is set on risers forming an underfloor plenum over a storage bed.

505. Quigley, Donald W. and James M. Duncan. Earth pressures on shallow buried structures. In Proc., Alt. in Habitat: the Use of Earth Cov. Set., Conf., Fort Worth, TX, May 17-19, 1978. F.L. Moreland, ed. Washington, DC: U.S. Dept. of Energy, 1979. v. 1, Earth covered buildings, p. 34-4.

This review shows that the factors which determine the earth pressures on shallow buried structures are fairly simple and well understood. When soil type, groundwater conditions, structure movements and surface loads are determined, then by using simple theories and field data, earth pressure can be estimated which will lead to safe and economical designs for buried structures at sites available for their use. Also, the identification of sites where their use is unsuitable will result.

506. Retrofit with a planter box. Earth Shel. Liv., no. 27, May/June 1983: 10-1.

Earth shelter retrofit consists of putting earth around the walls of an existing conventional structure. Everstrong Marketing introduced an earth-berming "planter box" at the 1983 Minneapolis Home & Garden Show.

507. Riewerts, John L. Surface bonding strengthens earth shelters. Earth Shel. Dig. Energ. Rept., no. 11, Sept./Oct. 1980: 56.

Surface bonding cement is a mixture of plasticizers, waterproofing agents, portland cement, and special alkali-resistant glass fibers. When mixed with water and applied to both sides of stacked concrete masonry blocks, it creates an exceptionally strong wall.

508. Rollwagen, Mary, Susan Taylor, and T. Lance Holthusen. The consumer's guide to earth sheltered housing. New York, NY: Van Nostrand Reinhold, 1984. 160 p.

Intended for the layperson who plans to have an earth-sheltered house built, this step-by-step manual guides the prospective homebuilder through the processes of planning, designing, and construction. The assistance of a professional earth-sheltered builder and architect is strongly recommended. Appendixes offer a short bibliography, a five-page directory of designers and builders, and a glossary.

509. Roy, Robert L. How to build an underground home. Alt. Energ., no. 39, Sept./Oct. 1979: 16-9.

This article discusses surface bonding -- the application of a special cement-based material to both the exterior and interior surfaces of a wall of concrete blocks laid up without mortar after the first course. It's also an excellent waterproofing agent. Block and mortar walls with surface bonding, plank and beam roofing, and costs are also discussed.

510. _____. The temporary earth shelter: when building it yourself, start small and learn as you go. Earth Shel. Liv., no. 36, Nov./Dec. 1984: 16-9.

Try out new techniques by building a small earth shelter first, e.g. a tool shed, a root cellar, etc. Rough plans are given.

511. _____. Underground houses: how to build a low-cost home. New York, NY: Sterling Pub. Co., 1979. 128 p.

This book describes the construction of a low-cost wood, post and beam earth-sheltered home. This one-story, 900 sq. ft. log-end house has earth-bermed walls made of block-bonded masonry blocks, and the roof is covered with one foot of soil and sod. Many of the building materials were salvaged to keep costs down.

512. Rush, Richard. Technics: reinforced concrete: underground architecture. Prog. Archit., v. 59, no. 5, May 1978: 108-9.

513. Saving energy with concrete: earth-sheltered construction. Concr. Constr., v. 28, no. 7, July 1983: 537-9.

514. Scafe, Gayle and John C. Scafe. Twenty-first century homes. 3rd ed. rev. Independence, MO: Terra-Dome Corp., 1979. 72 p.

This book describes the Terra Dome modular form system of building underground homes.

515. _____. Underground building: a new form of architectural design using a modular forming system. In Forming economical concrete buildings: proc. of an Int. Conf., Lincolnshire, IL, Nov. 8-10, 1982. p. 24/1-20.

This paper discusses a modular forming system for cast-in-place concrete buildings developed by the Terra-Dome Corp. This system fulfills the requirements of mass production. Various applications for its use are discussed.

516. Schlosser, François. Reinforced earth. Paris, France: Min. de l'Equipement, Lab. Central des Ponts et Chaussées, 1976. 23 p. (Note d'Information Technique).

The technique and material known as Reinforced Earth was invented by Henri Vidal in 1966. It is protected by his patents both in France and abroad, and its development and the processes used in practical application are the property of the Reinforced Earth Company (La Terre Armée, S.A.). This document deals with the principles, technology, structural design, practical procedures, and civil engineering applications of Reinforced Earth. In English, translated from French.

517. Scott, Norman L. Do your earth-sheltered homework. Concr. Constr., v. 27, no. 6, June 1982: 493-6.
This article describes the unique problems presented by earth-sheltered construction.

518. Setting up a fiberglass house. Earth Shel. Dig. Energ. Rept., no. 10, July/Aug. 1980: 48-50.
Steps are given for constructing an American Solartron fiberglass panel home from excavation to the spreading of the roof cover.

519. Shih, Jason. Literature review on the structural optimization for the possible application of earth covered buildings. In Proc., Alt. in Habitat: the Use of Earth Cov. Set., Fort Worth, TX, May 17-19, 1978. F.L. Moreland, ed. Washington, DC: U.S. G.P.O., 1979. v. 1, Earth covered buildings, p. 115-22.
Although earlier investigations have presented the optimum design approach for determining structures in many fields of mechanics, contributions toward optimizing building structures suitable for human occupation have been few. For reasons of economy, the optimum design of underground structures is considered to be a very worthwhile study.

520. _____. The optimization of earth-covered shell structures. In Proc., Alt. in Habitat: the Use of Earth Cov. Set., Conf., Fort Worth, TX, May 17-19, 1978. F.L. Moreland, ed. Washington, DC: U.S. G.P.O., 1979. v. 1, Earth covered buildings, p. 92-114.
The shape and thickness of an earth-covered shell must be determined for loads corresponding to the two different depths so that the resulting stresses in the shell are constant and compressive throughout. However, this process is rather complex because the shape of the shell, the earth load exerted on it, and the variable thickness distribution are unknowns. Therefore, the problem is not manageable for a case of plastic deformation and for shells with bending.

521. _____. Simplified design procedure of underground shells. Undergr. Sp., v. 4, no. 1, July/Aug. 1979: 45-9.
This article analyzes the factors involved in the design of earth-covered shells, including calculations for both shallow and deep depths. Maximum values are given for the earth load. The shape of the shell and the variable thickness distribution are discussed. Tables show the results obtained.

522. Shoring system pops up. Earth Shel. Dig. Energ. Rept., no. 12, Nov./Dec. 1980: 39.

The Ho-Vert shoring system, invented by John L. Gober, to hold up the framing for a concrete roof, consists of connected sections that pop up when in place.

523. Simmons, Lon B. Earth contact building: accent on post-tensioning of concrete. In Passive solar: subdivisions, windows, underground. Ed. by H. Wade and others. Kansas City, MO: Am. Sol. Energ. Soc., Kansas City Chap. -- Missouri Sol. Energ. Assn., 1983. p. 245-9.

This article was previously published in Earth Shelter Digest and Energy Report. It describes the manufacture of post-tensioned concrete, whose advantages the author lists: it uses less steel and concrete than reinforced concrete; a savings is also realized in waterproofing houses built with post-tensioned concrete because it is less likely to leak. Other underground passive solar house construction techniques are described.

524. _____. Post-tensioning: it makes sense for earth-sheltered homes. Concr. Constr., v. 26, no. 2, Feb. 1981: 105-9.

Post-tensioning the entire building prevents cracking, helps prevent leaks and saves concrete, steel, and waterproofing.

525. _____. Success with residential post-tensioning. Earth Shel. Dig. Energ. Rept., no. 4, July/Aug. 1979: 23-7.

526. Slater, Donald E. Backfill properly to prevent damage. Earth Shel. Liv., no. 22, July/Aug. 1982: 50-1.

527. Smay, V. Elaine. Domes, arches, and cylinders square off against the box in earth-sheltered housing. Pop. Sci., v. 218, no. 5, May 1981: 108-11.

Curved walls and roofs can be used to good advantage in earth-sheltered housing since they are better at resisting the immense weight of the soil and the lateral pressure against its walls. This can result in saving both materials and labor and maximum volume with minimum of wall area. Designs utilizing modular domes, cylinders with see-through roofs, culvert pipes, and spray-on domes are discussed and shown.

528. Spirited group tests elliptical dome. Earth Shel. Dig. Energ. Rept., no. 5, Sept./Oct. 1979: 14, 41.

Geosphere, Inc. built an earth-sheltered house for the Minnesota Renaissance Festival grounds.

529. Stafford, Lannon. Conduit did it: highway conduit makes earth covered warehouse. Earth Shel. Liv., no. 37, Jan./Feb. 1985: 16-7.

This owner-builder selected a highway conduit as the structural material for an underground warehouse near Phoenix, AZ.

530. Stall, James P. Corrugated steel plate structures for earth-sheltered buildings. Earth Shel. Bldgs. - Tech. Pap., TP-IF, 1983.

531. Steel culverts actively promoted. Earth Shel. Liv., no. 24, Nov./Dec. 1982: 12.
Lane Metal Products have prepared two earth-sheltered design floor plans utilizing high strength low-profile box culverts.

532. Sterling, Raymond L. and M. Tingerthal. Construction problems in the Minnesota Demonstration Program. In The potential of earth-sheltered and underground space: proc., Undergr. Sp. Conf. and Expos., Kansas City, MO, June 8-10, 1981. T. L. Holthusen, ed. Elmsford, NY: Pergamon Pr., 1981. p. 311-9.
Building costs and construction problems experienced in earth-sheltered construction are described using as an example the construction of seven projects completed under the Minnesota Solar/Earth-Sheltered Demonstration Housing Program.

533. _____. Structural systems for earth sheltered housing. In Proc., Alt. in Habitat: the Use of Earth Cov. Set., Conf., Fort Worth, TX, May 17-19, 1978. F.L. Moreland, ed. Washington, DC: U.S. G.P.O., 1979. v. 1, Earth Covered buildings, p. 60-9. Also in Undergr. Sp., v. 3, no. 2, Sept./Oct. 1978: 75-81.
This paper summarizes briefly the major considerations affecting the selection and design of structural systems for earth sheltered housing and how well existing structural systems satisfy these considerations. The potential of the various structural systems is examined and promising research areas are identified.

534. Sullivan, M. Steel reinforced concrete shell structures: forming techniques, structural design, and earth sheltered applications. In Earth shelter 2: coll. pap., 1st Earth Shel. Hous. Conf. and Exhib., Minneapolis, MN, Apr. 9-11, 1980. Minneapolis, MN: Univ. of Minn., Undergr. Sp. Ctr., 1980.
Construction of a 6.1 m. in diameter ellipsoid made of steel reinforced concrete is described. It was covered by no less than 20 cm. of earth and sod on top and no more than 1.5 m. on the side.

535. Surface bonding coats dry stack. Earth Shel. Liv., no. 19, Jan./Feb. 1982: 17-8.

In surface-bonded construction, concrete masonry blocks are first dry stacked into walls without mortar between them. Then both sides of the walls are coated with a thin (1/16 to 1/8 in.) layer of cement mortar reinforced with glass fibers. The advantages of surface bonding are discussed and the construction technique is detailed.

536. System keeps earth shelter builder busy. Earth Shel. Liv., no. 41, Sept./Oct. 1985: 19.

A sandwich wall system used by Wood Brothers Concrete Construction Co. of Gallatin, MO, has performed well in earth-sheltered homes and exceeded the requirements for animal confinement buildings in the rural area they serve. Extruded polystyrene is sandwiched between two layers of concrete creating a durable economical wall that is easy to finish.

537. Tait, David B. Rammed earth construction: its potential for use in earth-sheltered buildings. Earth Shel. Bldgs.-- Tech. Pap., TP-IIIH, 1983.

538. Texas University at Arlington. Clearinghouse for Earth Covered Settlements. Fact sheet on earth sheltered construction.

539. Thin shell earth-sheltered structures: shotcrete and foam insulation shaped over inflated balloon form. Concr. Constr., v. 27, no. 6, June 1982: 511-3.

This article briefly describes the construction of this type of dome when used for earth-sheltered houses.

540. Towson, Peter G. and Manfred R. Hausmann. Geotextiles for earth shelters. Undergr. Sp., v. 8, no. 3, 1984: 174-6.

This article discusses the types and properties of geotextiles, their functions, materials to reinforce soil structures, geotextiles for formwork, and their future applications.

541. _____ and _____. Geotextiles for earth structures. In Proc., 1st Int. Conf. on Energ. Effic. Bldgs. with Earth Shel. Prot., Sydney, Aust., Aug. 1-6, 1983. L.L. Boyer, ed. Stillwater, OK: Okla. State Univ., Archit. Ext., 1983. p. 363-6. Also in Geotecture, v. 1, no. 3, Apr. 1984: 8-11.

Synthetic fabrics and membranes are used increasingly in geotechnical engineering. Replacing traditional graded material, they can act as separators of different soil types, or as drainage and filter layers. Using textiles as reinforcements, layered earth retaining walls can be formed. This technique can be extended to structural elements such as beams and columns. Conceptual applications of geotextiles are investigated and the relevant mechanical properties are discussed. —Auth. abstract.

542. Traylor, Everett. Build a model home as you wait. <u>Earth Shel. Dig. Energ. Rept.</u>, no. 14, Mar./Apr. 1981: 55-6.
   While awaiting early retirement, build a model retirement earth-sheltered home. Model building techniques and materials are described.

543. True, D.G. Economical structural and footing considerations for buried structures. In <u>Proc., Alt. in Habitat: the Use of Earth Cov. Set., Conf.</u>, Fort Worth, TX, May 17-19, 1978. F.L. Moreland, ed. Washington, DC: U.S. G.P.O., 1979. v. 1, <u>Earth covered buildings</u>, p. 45-59.
   The special objectives sought are energy conservation and environmental compatibility. Considerable variation in economy may be realized depending upon the materials, structural configuration, and details selected. This variation is the subject of the paper. The study deals with the conditions imposed, soil-structure interaction, available materials and feasible configurations. It concludes with eight recommendations for economical construction.

544. Understanding structural loads. <u>Earth Shel. Liv.</u>, no. 39, May/June 1985: 20-1.

545. Vadnais, Kathleen. City subdivision developer "rides waves." <u>Earth Shel. Liv.</u>, no. 19, Jan./Feb. 1982: 4-6.
   A Kansas City, KS, developer plans to build 24 earth-sheltered homes using arches and domes.

546. _____. Engineer prefers one-pour houses. <u>Earth Shel. Dig. Energ. Rept.</u>, no. 3, May/June 1979: 12-5.
   Willard Norton builds houses of concrete reinforced with mild steel.

547. _____. Newest arch is wood. <u>Earth Shel. Liv.</u>, no. 26, Mar./Apr. 1983: 15-7.
   "Arch-Tech" curved panels are manufactured by Integrated Building Systems, Grand Haven, MI. The preservative used in the wood is chromated copper arsenate.

548. _____. Old arch, new material combined. <u>Earth Shel. Dig. Energ. Rept.</u>, no. 17, Sept./Oct. 1981: 6-7.
   Bernold metal sheets are formed into a clear span arch re-

quiring no internal supports then sprayed with five inches of concrete.

549. _____. Precast considered cost effective. Earth Shel. Dig. Energ. Rept., no. 6, Nov./Dec. 1979: 6-10.
Precast concrete panels are slowly gaining popularity in earth-sheltered construction. But some manufacturers are reluctant to get involved in one-residence projects, which they say are not cost effective.

550. _____. Products could be useful. Earth Shel. Dig. Energ. Rept., no. 15, May/June 1981: 54-6.
Products are finding new uses in earth-sheltered residential construction: i.e. Bernold sheets; Thermocurve (insulation in the form of molded expanded polystyrene totally enclosed in poured concrete walls); Aglite (shale burned at 2,200 degrees F. to a weight of 25-30 lbs. per cu. ft.) used for backfilling.

551. _____. Warranty backs earth shelter. Earth Shel. Liv., no. 19, Jan./Feb. 1982: 12-3.
Over 500 builders belong to the Housing Warranty Corporation (HWC, Indianapolis, IN) warranty program. Heritage International (Salt Lake City, UT) offers an earth shelter prefabricated wood panel house system through an affiliate, Everstrong, Inc. (Redwood Falls, MN), which is the first earth-sheltered house system to come with a warranty.

552. _____. Windows: look for quality. Earth Shel. Liv., no. 21, May/June 1982: 8-11.
Describes different window systems.

553. Vaile, Buck and Janitye Vaile. Designing, building, and living in underground homes. In Passive solar: subdivisions, windows, underground. Ed. by Herb Wade and others. Kansas City, MO: Am. Sol. Energ. Soc., Kansas City Chap. -- Missouri Sol. Energ. Assn., 1983. p. 250-6.
The authors relate their experiences in building "solar earth" houses, including their mistakes.

554. Villagran, Nora. Domes form room clusters. Earth Shel. Liv., no. 21, May/June 1982: 20-2.
Thin shell concrete is sprayed onto an inflated form that is recycled to become part of the waterproofing. Every room is a dome connected by arched hallways.

555. When designing passive solar for masonry . . . Earth Shel. Liv., no. 39, May/June 1985: 13-4.

Guidelines are given for designing passive solar into concrete masonry structures based on suggestions from the National Concrete Masonry Association.

556. Wukasch, Eugene. Proposed: an earth-covered dome development. Earth Shel. Liv., May/June 1985: 7-10.

VIII. INSULATION

557. Anderson, Brent. Selecting insulation: know the facts before selecting your insulation. Earth Shel. Liv., no. 33, May/June 1984: 7-11.
Extruded polystyrene for insulation is recommended for earth-sheltered structures.

558. Baggs, David W. A review of insulation materials for Australian earth-covered buildings. In Proc., 1st Int. Conf. on Energ. Effic. Bldgs. with Earth Shel. Prot., Sydney, Aust., Aug. 1-6, 1983. L.L. Boyer, ed. Stillwater, OK: Okla. State Univ., Archit. Ext., 1983. p. 255-8.
Inappropriate utilization of an unsuitable insulation material can result in a serious and permanent increase in the energy consumption of an earth-covered building with a corresponding reduction in occupant comfort conditions. Consequently, when designing an energy-efficient, earth-covered building, it is necessary to understand when insulation should or should not be incorporated and what materials can be used. The use of insulation is considered in the climatic context of the Australian continent. Commercially available insulation materials are then compared and results are given in terms of their suitability for use in subsoil conditions. --Auth. abstract.

559. Bligh, Thomas P. Insulation techniques in earth-sheltered buildings for minimizing winter heat loss and maximizing summer cooling. In Passive cooling: proc., Int. Pass. and Hybr. Cool. Conf., Miami Beach, FL, Nov. 6-16, 1981. Newark, DE: Int. Sol. Energ. Soc., Am. Sec., 1981.

560. _____, Paul Shipp, and George Meixel. Where to insulate earth protected buildings and existing basements. In Proc., Alt. in Habitat: the Use of Earth Cov. Set., Fort Worth, TX, May 17-19, 1978. F.L. Moreland, ed. Washington, DC: U.S. G.P.O., 1979. v. 1, Earth covered buildings, p. 251-72.

The contribution of window, wall, and roof insulation is evaluated as well as weather-related factors. The comparative data are based on above ground and underground houses in Minneapolis during summer and winter. Design plans and net-energy calculations are made for several combinations of insulating materials.

561. _____, G.D. Meixel, and P.H. Shipp. Where to insulate earth-sheltered buildings and existing basements. In Thermal performance of the exterior envelopes of buildings, DOE/ASHRAE Conf., Orlando, FL, Dec. 1979.

562. _____. Where to insulate underground buildings. Am. Undergr. Assn., Annu. Mtg., Toronto, Can., Oct. 1978.

563. Brown, James J. and Terry A. Johnson. Earth shelters and insulation: guidelines for planning your home. Portsmouth, OH: Underground Homes. 27 p.
This booklet discusses the methods of insulating earth shelters and the special insulation needs of windows, doors, fireplaces, and wingwalls. There is a listing of manufacturers and their products and a bibliography.

564. Choice and installation of insulation. Concr. Constr., v. 25, no. 9, Sept. 1980: 665-7.
Tables show the characteristics desirable in insulation for earth-sheltered buildings and the relative efficiency and cost of useful insulating materials. Extruded polystyrene is usually the best choice for external application due to its high R-value per dollar, and because it is less absorptive of water than polystyrene bead board or polyurethane. Inside application of insulation should be avoided.

565. Choices in underground insulation. Sol. Age, v. 8, Mar. 1983: 16+.

566. Insulating glazing brightens earth-sheltered building. Plant Energ. Mgmt., v. 5, Nov./Dec. 1981: 31-2.
An office and residential complex combines earth-sheltering and solar energy. The core of the complex, a 1,600 sq. ft. atrium, is glazed with a double-skinned acrylic sheet providing an insulating value comparable to a 5/8" thick insulating glass unit.

567. Insulation: puddle rebuttal. More questions. Same answer. Earth Shel. Liv., no. 28, July/Aug. 1983: 4-5.
A forum for discussion by readers.

568. Langa, Frederic S. A new technique for underground homes. New Shel., v. 4, no. 7, Sept. 1983: 98-100.

A prototype insulation system was installed on an earth-covered geodesic dome in Missoula, Montana. By day and during summer, the earth "bubble" surrounding the dome is charged with free ambient warmth. By night and during winter, the stored heat returns to warm the house. John Hait, the creator of the system, thinks it will result in essentially zero fuel consumption even in severe climates.

569. Meixel, George D., Paul H. Shipp, and Thomas P. Bligh. The impact of insulation placement on the seasonal heat loss through basement and earth-sheltered walls. Undergr. Sp., v. 5, no. 1, July/Aug. 1980: 41-7.

The article demonstrates that placing insulation horizontally outside the earth contact wall results in good winter performance, reduces the possibility of foundation damage, and allows the underground wall to lose heat to the soil during the summer.

570. Severson, J.L. Thermal performance of various insulations in below-earth-grade perimeter application. Presented at DOE-ORN/ASTM Conf., Clearwater Beach, FL, Dec. 8-11, 1981.

571. Skorusa, Mike. Technique is in the groove: innovative insulation treatment permits access to space between insulation and waterproofing. Earth Shel. Liv., no. 35, Sept./Oct. 1984: 34.

572. Space age insulation. Earth Shel. Liv., no. 40, July/Aug. 1985: 15.

Foil-Ray^{TM} insulation is made of polyethylene bubbles with aluminum foil bonded to both sides. It is ¼" thick. Write: Energy Saver Imports, Inc., 2150 W. 6th Ave., Box 387, Broomfield, CO 80020.

573. Vadnais, Kathleen. FTC disclosure standards to help clarify insulation values. Earth Shel. Dig. Energ. Rept., no. 7, Jan./Feb. 1980: 14-5.

Labels would disclose the dimensions and area that could be covered by the insulation, an explanation of R-value, and the need for proper insulation.

574. _____. Insulation should retain R-value. Earth Shel. Liv., no. 19, Jan./Feb. 1982: 7-9.

This article tells how to decide what is the most efficient

insulation for an earth-sheltered home and how to shop for it. Methods of testing by private enterprise and the ASTM are discussed.

575. _____. Truths may be buried with insulation. Earth Shel. Dig. Energ. Rept., no. 18, Nov./Dec. 1981: 10-2.
Questions to be asked when looking for the best insulation for an underground house.

IX. WATERPROOFING/DRAINAGE

576. Advanced Waterproofing, Inc. "Negative side" spraying. Earth Shel. Liv., no. 23, Sept./Oct. 1982: 15-6.

577. Anderson, Brent. Consider all sources of moisture. Earth Shel. Liv., no. 38, Mar./Apr. 1985: 19.
Successful waterproofing requires a knowledge of all the basic sources of moisture: surface runoff, water table and capillary draw, underground streams or lakes, broken water or sewage lines, perched water tables, and water vapor migration. The three lines of defense against water are: proper site planning and landscaping, backfilling and drainage techniques, a protective barrier system.

578. _____. Judging waterproofing products. Earth Shel. Liv., no. 30, Nov./Dec. 1983: 34-5.
This is an excerpt from Underground waterproofing by the author. It discusses the life of the product and its warranty, its ease of application, its leak-localizing capability, its resealability, its resistance to chemicals, its compatibility with other materials, and its cost.

579. _____. Underground waterproofing. Stillwater, MN: WEBCO Pub., Inc., 1983. 66 p.
This book analyzes problems, products and systems, and contains over 35 waterproofing detail drawings of various systems. Intended for architects, engineers, contractors and potential earth-sheltered homeowners. It is divided into three parts: the first part gives a general review of waterproofing treatments, sources of moisture and methods of control, waterproofing products, and provides 12 general guidelines to use in the waterproofing design and construction of an earth-sheltered building. The second part shows the sequence of waterproofing design and application technique through various modes of con-

struction. The third part gives technical information useful in evaluating generic waterproofing components and their performance.

580. _____. Waterproofing concrete begins early. Earth Shel. Liv., no. 37, Jan./Feb. 1985: 29.
For good waterproofing, concrete must be poured and cured properly.

581. Angel, Craig. Drainage schemes for earth-sheltered houses in the Sonoran Desert region of the southwest United States. Earth Shel. Bldgs. - Tech. Pap., TP-IIIA, 1983.

582. Baggs, Sydney, Joan C. Baggs, and David W. Baggs. Waterproofing issues. Geotecture, v. 2, no. 1, Jan. 1985: 36-8.
Brief descriptions are given of the best-known generic types of waterproofing systems and materials.

583. Bannon-Harwood, Barbara. Experiences and preferences of of earth-shelter builders. Concr. Constr., v. 25, no. 9, Sept. 1980: 676.
There is no one waterproofing method preferred by builders over others. A survey of builders revealed the types of waterproofing used: polyethylene-coated rubberized asphalt, asphalt coating with bentonite, spray-on bentonite, vinyl single-ply membrane in addition to regular waterproofing just beneath the final dirt layer.

584. Basement waterproofing: a product review. New Shel., v. 2, no. 4, Apr. 1981: 38-48.
This article evaluates the best buys in 22 waterproofing agents and discusses ways of correcting leakage through basement walls.

585. Brown, James and Terry A. Johnson. Earth shelter waterproofing: the guide to total moisture control. Portsmouth, OH: Underground Homes, 1980. 40 p.
Includes 36 illustrations and photos and a reference guide of 32 manufacturers/suppliers of water proofing materials.

586. Burns, Donna M. An analysis and control of water vapor problems in the interiors of earth-integrated buildings. Earth Shel. Bldgs. - Tech. Pap., TP-IA, 1983.

587. Drainage: options are growing. Earth Shel. Liv., no. 27, May/June 1983: 34-5.
Gives choices in waterproofing materials.

588. Effective Building Projects, Inc. Earth sheltered structures: waterproofing instruction manual utilizing Bentonize C-R-80-T, Bentonize C-R-80-S, Bentonize C-R-80-S4, Waterstop-plus. Cleveland, OH, 1982. 52 p.
The Bentonize system incorporates products made from bentonite, a clay formed from volcanic ash which has permanent waterproofing characteristics. Waterstop-plus is a chemical joint sealer.

589. Eller, Kenneth R. Evaluation and selection of waterproofing for cast-in-place concrete structured earth-sheltered buildings. Earth Shel. Bldgs. - Tech. Pap., TP-IIIC, 1983.

590. Fitz-Hugh, Sarah. The war against water. New Shel., v. 3, no. 1, Jan. 1982: 30-2.
This is a survey of waterproofings for underground homes. It also deals with site selection, planning, drainage, and backfilling techniques. The ideal waterproofing system is described.

591. Flecknoe-Brown, A.E. New developments in drainage of subground structures. Geotecture, v. 1, no. 3, Apr. 1984: 12-5.
Prefabricated drain systems are discussed.

592. Getting into it: drainage system is different. Earth Shel. Liv., no. 22, July/Aug. 1982: 19.
The Eljen Drainage System has features which direct water away from the structure, into the drainpipe, and prevent fine soil from entering the pipe.

593. Gruber, K.A. Leak-free roof for underground garage. Archit. Rec., v. 140, Dec. 1966: 163-4.
A butyl rubber membrane over a waffle slab roof deck waterproofs the roof of an underground garage at an apartment development designed by I.M. Pei & Partners.

594. Hammes, Jeffrey L. Soil drains: a swale idea. Earth Shel. Liv., no. 24, Nov./Dec. 1982: 16-7.
Draining water away from a house using a gully or trench is an important aspect of waterproofing.

595. Lane, Charles A. Waterproofing earth-sheltered houses. Fine Homebldg., no. 2, Apr./May 1981: 35-7.

596. _____. Waterproofing methods and products: an ESL special: a consultant takes a look at waterproofing. Earth Shel. Liv., no. 32, Mar./Apr. 1984: 23-7.

597. Lowing, Arnold N. Earthquakes. Pt. 2. Earth Shel. Liv., no. 24, Nov./Dec. 1982: 23-4, 29.

This article discusses the effects on waterproofing systems in earth-sheltered homes which might be subject to earthquakes. It also discusses how retaining walls may fail and the values and disadvantages of berms.

598. McGroarty, Bryan. Moisture control. In Residential applications: transcripts of selected presentations: Going Under to Stay on Top, Minneapolis, MN, Oct. 1977. Minneapolis, MN: Univ. of Minn., Undergr. Space Ctr., 1979. p. 77-80.
A waterproofing expert discusses the difference between waterproofing and dampproofing and gives advice on how to apply the materials and what to use.

599. _____. Waterproofing: do your homework. Earth Shel. Dig. Energ. Rept., no. 13, Jan./Feb. 1981: 23-7.
Ask 14 questions before making a decision regarding the type of waterproofing to use.

600. _____. Waterproofing: evaluation backed by experience. Earth Shel. Dig. Energ. Rept., no. 11, Sept./Oct. 1980: 23-6.
The many products and materials which have been used for waterproofing are arranged into eight categories, and their negative and positive features are discussed.

601. _____. Waterproofing: sort through the myths. Earth Shel. Dig. Energ. Rept., no. 10, July/Aug. 1980: 10-1.
Moisture control specifications called dampproofing were set down by the VA, FHA, and HUD. Dampproofing products are those which will prevent moisture in the soil from penetrating a structure but will not prevent the entrance of water. Myths associated with waterproofing include: sloping an earth-sheltered roof prevents leaks, a loose laid sheet can be used on an earth-sheltered roof just as on a conventional roof, most leaks occur at the junction of the wall with the footing, because there's more water pressure there. Using a concrete additive, penetrant, sealant, etc. will make the concrete waterproof. They can even be applied to the inside of the wall.

602. Metz, D. Keeping dry underground. Sol. Age, v. 7, no. 5, May 1982: 24-31.
Serious waterproofing problems are discussed, i.e. poor application, wrong roofing materials used, punctures, flashing failures, shrinking-swelling due to thermal cycling, and decomposition.

603. Moore, Gordon L. Water and vapor control in earth contact

87 Waterproofing/Drainage

homes. Columbia, MO: Univ. of Missouri, Columbia Ext. Div. 3 p. (Eng. Sci. and Tech. Guide, 5521).

604. Ohanian, Richard. Before you waterproof - detail! Earth Shel. Dig. Energ. Rept., no. 5, Sept./Oct. 1979: 20:1.
Proven architectural detailing to prevent the entrance of moisture should precede waterproofing.

605. Products aim to keep structures warm and dry. Earth Shel. Liv., no. 37, Jan./Feb. 1985: 27.
Owens-Corning Fiberglass offers Tuff-N-Dri, a spray-applied polymeric material, as a waterproof membrane, and Warm-N-Dri, a fiberglass foundation insulation.

606. Randall, Frank A., Jr. Construction recommendations for moisture control. Concr. Constr., v. 25, no. 9, Sept. 1980: 675-7.
This article is excerpted from the text of Earth-integrated building construction, Concrete report CRO56.01B, Portland Cement Association, Skokie, IL. Recommendations given: obtain the assistance of a designer and engineer familiar with the area of the building site; avoid building in a location with a high water table; determine soil conditions before building; design to control surface water; provide for proper excavation and backfill; provide proper and adequate waterproofing; and relieve water pressure against outside walls.

607. Seitz, Doug. Drain system alternative. Earth Shel. Liv., no. 38, Mar./Apr. 1985: 16-7.
This article discusses a prefabricated in-plane drainage system which eliminates stress on waterproofing. It consists of a filter fabric cover which permits water to pass through but keeps soil out and a three-dimensional drainage core which transmits the water to the base and thence to the drainage system. Its several advantages are described and manufacturers are listed.

608. Selde, Vernon. Protection down under: the waterproofing of earth-sheltered structures. Constr. Spec., Mar. 1981: 44-9.
The characteristics of the five most-used waterproofing products (asphalt and pitch, bituthene liquid polyurethanes, butyl, EPDM membranes, and bentonite), and their methods of application and cost are discussed.

609. Skorusa, Mike. Getting into it: pull the plug on water problems. Earth Shel Liv., no. 28, July/Aug. 1983: 12-3.

Vertical pipes are connected under the insulation to exhaust air and prevent moisture buildup.

610. Steiner, Robert M. Waterproofing of earth-sheltered buildings. Earth Shel. Bldgs. - Tech. Pap., TP-IG, 1983.

611. Subgrade waterproofing. Bldg. Res., v. 1, no. 6, Nov./Dec. 1964: 37-47.
  Contains short articles on: structural considerations in subgrade waterproofing, soil considerations, an open forum discussion, materials and systems, writing and enforcement of specifications.

612. Szigethy, Les. Leaking roof fixed by owner. Earth Shel. Liv., no. 22, July/Aug. 1982: 40-2.

613. Vadnais, Kathleen. Waterproofing comes into its own: oil shortage gives earth sheltering a boost. Earth Shel. Dig. Energ. Rept., no. 1, Jan./Feb. 1979: 6-7.
  Bryan McGroarty was the first to successfully use bentonite in waterproofing products.

614. _____. Waterproofing: learn the complete system. Earth Shel. Liv., no. 20, Mar./Apr. 1982: 8-10, 60.
  Planning for waterproofing should begin before construction, in fact it should be kept in mind when looking for the site. Topics discussed: siting, structure, products (bentonite, liquid applied membranes, roll goods, sheets), dealing with companies, installation, drainage, warranties.

615. Viceps, Karlis. Plan for leaks. Earth Shel. Liv., no. 23, Sept./Oct. 1982: 16-7.

616. Von Fraunhoffer, H.J. Waterproofing the earth sheltered building. In Western SUN 1980 Sol. Update Conf., Salt Lake City, UT, Sept. 24, 1980. p. 65-71.

617. White, George. Waterproofing materials for the earth-shelter contractor. Concr. Constr., v. 25, no. 9, Sept. 1980: 669-72.
  Gives details on types of waterproofing materials: bentonite, composite sheet membranes, synthetic rubber sheet membranes, liquid-applied membranes, cementitious coatings.

X. HEATING/VENTILATING/COOLING

618. Ahmed, Syed Faruq and Steven R. Barnes. Passive ventilation of an underground bath house by the use of solar chimney. In Proc., 5th Nat. Pass. Sol. Conf., Amherst, MA, Oct. 19-26, 1980. Newark, DE: Int. Sol. Energ. Soc., Am. Sec., 1980. p. 752-6.
The bathhouse is not heated or cooled and is meant to be used in the summer only. The ventilation rate provided by the absorption of solar energy on the inside surface of a tall chimney is predicted using a mathematical model. The solar chimney also provides for some of the lighting needs of the bathhouse.

619. Air conditioning is easier underground. Heat. Vent. Engr. J. Air Cond., Jan. 1963.

620. Balcomb, J. Douglas. Storing heat in concrete masonry. Earth Shel. Liv., no. 26, Mar./Apr. 1983: 40-4.
This article discusses the specific numbers that indicate how much heat can be stored in particular masonry units in direct gain applications and describes how heat storage can be enhanced by filling the cores of the units with sand or grout.

621. Becklian, Barbara. Homemade system pipes in savings. Earth Shel. Dig. Energ. Rept., no. 9, May/June 1980: 6-7.
A system consisting of a windcatcher and earth pipes helps to heat and cool an earth-sheltered home in Dalton, MN.

622. Boeing Co. Solar project description for Colorado Sunworks: single family residence, Longmont, Colorado. Contract AB01-76CS31020. Seattle, WA, 1981. 74 p.
A passive solar energy system for space heating and domestic hot water preheating is described. The house utilizes earth berms on the north, east, and west sides of the house, a one-foot covering of earth on the roof, and an entry vestibule to conserve energy.

623. Cunningham, Gregory W. An investigation into the use of cooling by non-mechanically-induced convection and evaporation for earth-sheltered building applications in arid regions. Earth Shel. Bldgs. - Tech. Pap., TP-IB, 1983.

624. Direct-vent furnaces: direct-vent furnaces are economi-

cal, efficient, and small enough for earth shelters. Earth Shel. Liv., no. 37, Jan./Feb. 1985: 20-1.

625. Empty chamber provides heat. Earth Shel. Dig. Energ. Rept., no. 18, Nov./Dec. 1981: 16-7.
   The underfloor plenum is a system to distribute conditioned air throughout the living area of a house using a tightly sealed underfloor area. It can provide both radiant and convective heat. The information in this article was reprinted from Underfloor plenum manual prepared by the NAHB Research Foundation, Inc., Rockville, MD.

626. Forwood, Bruce. Natural ventilation for passive solar buildings. In Proc., 1st Int. Conf. on Energ. Effic. Bldgs. with Earth Shel. Prot., Sydney, Aust., Aug. 1-6, 1983. L.L. Boyer, ed. Stillwater, OK: Okla. State Univ., Archit. Ext., 1983. p. 227-9.
   This paper explores the functions of natural ventilation in buildings, with particular reference to earth-integrated structures and examines techniques for predicting energy transfer rates due to natural ventilation. --Auth. abstract.

627. Green, Bruce and Richard Anderson. A convective chimney rock bin energy storage retaining wall for the underground house. In Proc., 1st Int. Conf. on Energ. Effic. Bldgs. with Earth Shel. Prot., Sydney, Aust., Aug. 1-6, 1983. L.L. Boyer, ed. Stillwater, OK: Okla. State Univ., Archit. Ext., 1983. p. 115-8.
   There are many benefits to adding heat storage to the retaining walls of the home: the auxiliary heating requirements become minimal; the retaining walls are a requirement for the earth-sheltered home, and this is a reasonably inexpensive addition to them; the view from the earth-covered home can be retained by using this energy storage system in the place of Trombe walls; finally, the structural integrity of both the home and retaining walls can be improved. --Auth. abstract.

628. Hylton, Joe. Wind towers tested. Earth Shel. Dig. Energ. Rept., no. 11, Sept./Oct. 1980: 8-10.
   Wind towers can be used to provide natural ventilation in earth-sheltered homes.

629. Johnson, Terry A. Heating, ventilating, and air conditioning for earth sheltered homes. Portsmouth, OH: Underground Homes. 31 p.

630. Kneeland, William F. State-of-the-art cooling by loca-

tion. Earth Shel. Dig. Energ. Rept., no. 15, May/June 1981: 24-5.
This article discusses the cooling techniques needed to provide cool indoor comfort levels, dependent on surrounding ground temperatures.

631. Labs, Kenneth. Human comfort and underground climate control. Undergr. Sp., v. 7, no. 2, Sept./Oct. 1982: 115-23.
Considers comfort variables and outlines 16 hypothetical control strategies.

632. Lane, Charles A. Ventilation for air-tight houses. Earth Shel. Liv., no. 38, Mar./Apr. 1985: 22-5.
Controlled ventilation techniques have to be devised to solve the problem of lower quality indoor air in earth sheltered and other air-tight houses.

633. Lees, Al. Thermally layered retreat. Pop. Sci., v. 218, no. 5, May 1981: 92-3.
Thermosiphoning ensures comfort throughout this multi-level house designed by architect Alfredo De Vido.

634. Movement in the air-to-air heat exchanger field. Alt. Energ., no. 53, Jan./Feb. 1982: 28.
Gives a source list for air-to-air heat exchangers.

635. Newman, J.O. Solar heating and earth insulation for economical houses. Int. J. Hous. Sci. Appl., v. 6, no. 3, 1982: 195-207.
Site-built warm air solar systems have been developed by the Rural Housing Research Unit. Several earth-bermed structures have been built. This article describes design considerations, construction, and results.

636. Olson, Myron. Gaining thermostatic control of our home. Earth Shel. Dig. Energ. Rept., no. 2, Mar./Apr. 1979: 19.
Electric radiant panels radiate heat into the floors. They need separate thermostats in each room to help regulate heat variations.

637. Orlowski, Henry. Thermal chimneys and natural ventilation. In Proc., Alt. in Habitat: the Use of Earth Cov. Set., Fort Worth, TX, May 17-19, 1978. F.L. Moreland, ed. Washington, DC: U.S. G.P.O., 1979. v. 1, Earth covered buildings, p. 220-5.
The placement, construction, design, and use of thermal chimneys to enhance natural ventilation in earth-sheltered houses is discussed.

638. Pfister, Peter. Integrating energy efficient alternatives. In <u>Residential applications: transcripts of selected presentations: Going Under to Stay on Top</u>, Minneapolis, MN, Oct. 1977. Minneapolis, MN: Univ. of Minn., Undergr. Space Ctr., 1979. p. 81-95.

This paper discusses the earth-sheltered house as a passive solar system. It presents some calculations that indicate the impact of passive solar techniques on earth-sheltered houses in terms of annual heating load.

639. Photovoltaics: another dimension added. <u>Earth Shel. Liv.</u>, no. 25, Jan./Feb. 1983: 15-7.

Solar Design Associates, Inc., Lincoln, MA, designs homes with PV arrays including a 2,350 sq. ft. home in southeastern Massachusetts.

640. Strong, Steven J. and Robert J. Osten, Jr. Two earth sheltered passive solar residences with photovoltaic electricity. In <u>Proc., 5th Nat. Pass. Sol. Conf.</u>, Amherst, MA, Oct. 19-26, 1980. Newark, DE: Int. Sol. Energ. Soc., Am. Sec., 1980. p. 1111-3.

The design and construction of two earth-sheltered passive solar residences are described and the design and installation of the photovoltaic array are discussed.

641. Vadnais, Kathleen. Fresh air can be tempered. <u>Earth Shel. Liv.</u>, no. 22, July/Aug. 1982: 8-9.

Heat exchangers bring in fresh air without losing warmth.

642. Wade, Herb. Integrating passive solar heating and passive cooling into earth sheltered residences. In <u>Proc., 1st Int. Conf. on Energ. Effic. Bldgs. with Earth Shel. Prot.</u>, Sydney, Aust., Aug. 1-6, 1983. L.L. Boyer, ed. Stillwater, OK: Okla. State Univ., Archit. Ext., 1983. p. 97.

Passive cooling and passive solar heating are concepts well-matched to earth-sheltered dwellings. The primary design error in implementing passive conditioning is to provide an excessive amount of these elements, and care must be taken not to oversize the various systems that can be implemented. These systems are discussed along with suggestions for integrating passive cooling and heating into earth-integrated dwellings. --Auth. abstract.

643. Williams, Monty. Heat exchanger uses water efficiently. <u>Earth Shel. Dig. Energ. Rept</u>, no. 10, July/Aug. 1980: 40-1.

One way to take advantage of the relatively constant temperatures below the earth's surface is through a heat pump that uses groundwater as its heat source. Because efficiency and economy depend on a free and reliable groundwater source with a flow rate of four to twelve gal. per min., rural areas are most suitable for this type of system.

XI. ENERGY CONSUMPTION/ THERMAL PERFORMANCE

644. Baggs, David W. Thermal properties, processes and passive design relating to solar, earth-covered buildings. In Proc., Symp. on Des. Strat. for Earth Cov. Bldg., May 8-9, 1982. S.A. Baggs, ed. Kensington, NSW, Aust.: Univ. of NSW, Grad. Sch. of the Built Env., 1982. p. 222-30.

645. Baggs, Joan C. Management of earth-covered houses for energy efficiency. In Proc., 1st Int. Conf. on Energ. Effic. Bldgs. with Earth Shel. Prot., Sydney, Aust., Aug. 1-6, 1983. L.L. Boyer, ed. Stillwater, OK: Okla. State Univ., Archit. Ext., 1983. p. 317-20.

Incorrect thermal management by occupants of an earth-covered house can negate the various passive solar, energy efficiency strategies incorporated into the design of that building. The fact that completed buildings will be judged on the comfort conditions prevailing after occupation is of particular concern to those involved in the design and construction of such houses in Australia. These reduced comfort conditions would not necessarily reflect the degree of care taken by the professional team. They could be the fault of the owner, not the building. A brief background to the problem is given, together with observations made during interviews with both U.S. and Australian homeowners experienced in the underground lifestyle. Guidelines are presented for the use of occupants of earth-covered dwellings which, if followed, would enable them to achieve the level of comfort conditions required. --Auth. abstract.

646. Benedict, Fredric A. Huddling together in Mother Earth. In Solar architecture: proc., 4th Aspen Energy Forum, May 27-29, 1977. Workshop on Solar Energy Applications. Ann Arbor, MI: Ann Arbor Science Publishers, 1978. p. 29-39.

The advantages of earth-integrated architecture are discussed. The author concludes that to conserve energy in the future, Americans must reduce commuting by auto from suburbs into metropolitan areas. By living in reasonably-sized enclaves, he believes society will be able to curtail the extremely wasteful auto-oriented energy policy.

647. Bice, Thomas Neal. Energy analysis of earth sheltered dwellings. Master's thesis, archit. eng. Stillwater, OK: Oklahoma State Univ., 1980. 178 p.

648. _____, L.L. Boyer, and W.T. Grondzik. Energy performance characteristics of selected earth sheltered residences. In Earth shelter 2: coll. pap., 1st Earth Shel. Hous. Conf. and Exhib., Minneapolis, MN, Apr. 9-11, 1980. Minneapolis, MN: Univ. of Minn., Undergr. Space Ctr., 1980. p. 33-42.
 The earth-sheltered residences are in Oklahoma. The metered energy usage of each residence is presented for a full year on a monthly basis. This metered energy consumption is compared to a currently accepted energy conservation standard.

649. Bligh, Thomas P. Building underground. Bldg. Syst. Des., v. 73, no. 5, Oct./Nov. 1976: 1-22.
 Energy consumption, heat flow losses and U values of above and below-ground structures in Minneapolis and St. Paul are compared. This article is extracted from a paper presented at the Conference on Alternatives in Energy Conservation: the Use of Earth Covered Buildings, Fort Worth, TX, July 9-12, 1975.

650. _____ and E.W. Grald. A complete energy balance of an earth-sheltered house. U.S. DOE Sol. Pass. Div. Rept., DOE/DE-AC03-80SF11508, June 1983. 73 p.

651. _____ and Richard Hamburger. Conservation of energy by use of underground space. In Legal, economic and energy considerations in the use of underground space. Washington, DC: Nat. Acad. of Sci., 1974. p. 103-17.

652. _____. Economic myths and realities: energy and money. In Residential applications: transcripts of selected presentations, Going Under to Stay on Top, Minneapolis, MN, Oct. 1977. Minneapolis, MN: Univ. of Minn., Undergr. Space Ctr., 1979. p. 19-28.
 This paper discusses the depletion of fossil fuels and the energy performance of underground buildings.

653. _____, P. Shipp, and G. Meixel. Energy comparisons and where to insulate earth-sheltered buildings and basements. Energy, v. 5, no. 5, May 1980: 451-65.

Earth-sheltered structures use much less energy than conventional designs. This is shown by a computer study of single and two-story residences. Different types of insulation are discussed for windows and for roofs, walls, and floors of earth-sheltered houses and for basements of conventional buildings.

654. _____. Energy conservation by building underground. Undergr. Sp., v. 1, no. 1, May/June 1976: 19-33.
Underground and earth-covered structures present an opportunity for saving energy, reducing building costs, and preserving the land. Designs are presented for earth-covered houses with solar heating systems and various other energy conservation features. Examples are given of high density underground developments with figures on the amount of space used and the energy saving.

655. _____. Energy conservation by earth sheltering houses. Am. Undergr. Assn. Annu. Mtg. and Undergr. Hous. Conf. Kansas City, MO, Mar. 1979.

656. _____. Energy implications of underground domestic and commercial buildings. In Residential applications: transcripts of selected presentations, Going Under to Stay on Top, Minneapolis, MN, Oct. 1977. Minneapolis, MN: Univ. of Minn., Undergr. Sp. Ctr., 1979.

657. _____ and G. Meixel. Energy performance of earth-sheltered buildings in both hot and cold climates. In Proc., 3rd Int. Conf. on Alt. Energ. Sources, Miami Beach, FL, Dec. 1980. Washington, DC: Hemisphere Pub. Corp., 1983.

658. _____ and K.K. Replogle. A method for performing an energy balance on a building applied to an earth sheltered house in Massachusetts. Cambridge, MA: Mass. Inst. of Techn., 1982. 88 p. (Energ. Effic. Bldgs. and Syst. Rept., no. 10).

659. _____ and B.H. Knoth. A thermal study of an earth-sheltered residence: instrumentation, data processing techniques, soil temperature and heat flux data. U.S. DOE Sol. Pass. Div. Rept., DOE/DE-AC03-80SF11508, Dec. 1982. 395 p.

660. Boyer, L.L. and W.T. Grondzik. Energy performance of earth covered dwellings in the U.S. In Proc., 1st Int. Conf. on Energ. Effic. Bldgs. with Earth Shel. Prot., Sydney, Aust., Aug. 1-6, 1983. L.L. Boyer, ed. Stillwater, OK: Okla. State Univ., Archit Ext., 1983. p. 295-8.

In a large region of the United States, reaching from the Canadian border to south Texas, interest in earth-covered dwellings led to the construction of well over 1,000 such homes in the late 1970s. This interest and construction activity is being maintained through the early 1980s in spite of a general decline in the economic position of the building industry as a whole. Studies have shown this particular interest and activity in earth sheltering to be directly related to the primary issue of energy conservation. Sizable energy savings are, in fact, being realized by owners of current generation earth shelters. For example, total household energy consumption for all-electric earth-covered dwellings in Oklahoma was found to average 35 to 40 percent below usage in comparable aboveground homes. Research studies at Oklahoma State University indicate that these savings could be more than doubled if well-considered dwelling construction and lifestyle adjustments were jointly implemented. --From auth. abstract.

661. _____, W.T. Grondzik, and T.N. Bice. Energy usage in earth covered dwellings in Oklahoma. In Proc., Earth Shel. Bldg. Des. Innov., Nat. Tech. Conf., Oklahoma City, OK, Apr. 18, 1980. L.L. Boyer, ed. Stillwater, OK: Okla. State Univ., 1980. p. IV. 19-31. Also in Undergr. Sp., v. 5, no. 4, Jan./Feb. 1981: 227-36.

Some earth-covered dwellings in Oklahoma were analyzed with regard to energy consumption. The study considered predicted energy consumption calculated using standard methods, a compilation of actual metered energy usage, and derivation of expected energy requirements for a comparable structure meeting current energy conservation standards. The values predicted compare well with metered usage except for the midwinter months.

662. _____ and _____. Human comfort and energy conservation in earth sheltered buildings. Stillwater, OK: Okla. State Univ., Archit. Ext., 1980.

663. "Cave" homes save energy. Moneysworth, v. 9, Sept. 1979: 5.

664. Comparative energy use for earth sheltered, aboveground houses. Underline, v. 4, no. 1, Nov./Dec. 1982: 4.

A table shows energy consumption for five earth sheltered and one aboveground house for June and July 1982.

665. Comparative energy use for earth sheltered, aboveground houses. Underline, v. 4, no. 2, Jan./Mar. 1983: 5.

A table shows energy consumption for five earth sheltered and one aboveground house for Aug. through Nov. 1982.

666. Davies, Gary R. Thermal analysis of earth covered buildings. In Proc., 4th Nat. Pass. Sol. Conf., Kansas City, MO, Oct. 3-5, 1979. G. Franta, ed. Newark, DE: Int. Sol. Energ. Soc., Am. Sec., Univ. of Del., 1979. p. 744-8.

Transient heat transfer from earth-covered buildings was predicted by using a detailed finite difference model that allows user input of structure geometry, thermal parameters, and random indoor and outdoor temperature profiles.

667. Dike, G.A. and L.F. Kinney. Superior energy performance at very low construction costs: design principles of six superinsulated, earth-coupled houses that really work. In Proc., 7th Nat. Pass. Sol. Conf., Knoxville, TN, 1982. Newark, DE: Am. Sol. Energ. Soc., Univ. of Del., 1982. p. 865-70.

668. The down-to-earth way to beat the energy problem. Med. Econ., Oct. 22, 1978: 150-1.

669. Drucker, E.E. and J. T. Haines. A study of thermal environment in underground survival shelters using an electronic analog computer. ASHRAE Trans., v. 70, no. 1857, 1965.

This paper gives the results of a detailed study of an underground concrete shelter designed for 50 people. The objective of the study was to predict the thermal environment of the shelter as a function of ventilation rate, physical properties of the earth and air conditioning.

670. Earth sheltered performance data show house operating efficiently. Underline, v. 1, no. 5, July/Aug. 1980: 2.

The first six months of energy use of an earth-sheltered home in suburban Minneapolis was monitored.

671. Emery, A.F., D.R. Heerwagen, and C.J. Kippenhan. Earth sheltered passive solar structures: occupant comfort and energy use. In Proc., Earth Shel. Bldg. Des. Innov., Nat. Tech. Conf., Oklahoma City, OK, Apr. 18, 1980. L.L. Boyer, ed. Stillwater, OK: Okla. State Univ., 1980. p. IV. 35-40.

The thermal performance of an earth-sheltered passive solar structure was studied by numerical simulation using the finite difference program UWENSOL. There is a correlation between the economical use of energy and the embedding of

672. _____, _____, _____, and G.B. Varey. Numerical procedures for the simulation of thermal environments in earth-covered structures. In Proc. of the Conf. on Alt. in Habitat: the Use of Earth Cov. Set., Fort Worth, TX, May 17-19, 1978. F.L. Moreland, ed. Washington, DC: U.S. Dept. of Energy, 1979. v. 1, Earth covered buildings: technical notes, p. 139-70.

It is known that earth-covered structures are capable of reducing large annual and diurnal air temperature variations and the effects of strong variations in insolation. However, practical use of these buildings depends upon the capacity to predict their thermal response, since such unusual living spaces require modification of the usual conditioning and lighting and control systems. Simultaneously, it is known that a full three-dimensional thermal analysis may be necessary because of the large envelope thickness. This paper shows that under normal weather conditions, a simple one-dimensional thermal analysis can be carried out. The energy analyzer, UWENSOL, is used to compare a conventional and two earth-covered structures during summer and winter seasons. The difference in the thermal response and the savings in energy consumption connected with the earth-covered structures are discussed.

673. Evans, R.S. A thermal model of an underground house. MSEE thesis. Rapid City, SD: South Dakota School of Mines and Technology, 1980.

674. _____, R.D. McNeil, and L.D. Feisel. Validation of a lumped parameter thermal model for earth shelters. Conf. proc., Earth Shel. Perf. and Eval., 2nd Nat. Tech. Conf., Tulsa, OK, Oct. 16-17, 1981. Stillwater, OK: Okla. State Univ., Archit. Ext., 1981. p. 193-202.

A thermal model based on the analogy to a leakage-free, non-inductive tansmission line is presented. Validation was achieved using a computer transient analysis from actual recorded earth shelter temperature data.

675. Fairhurst, Charles. Energy, conservation, and the underground. Undergr. Sp., v. 1, no. 2, July/Aug. 1976: iii.

Energy conservation must be made the first priority of the United States according to this editorial. The 1976 plan (ERDA-76-1) gives top priority to energy conservation. A chart is included with the projected energy requirements for the year

2000. The plan identified building conservation as having the highest potential for energy savings at between 2.0 and 2.8 million barrels of oil per day by 1985. Underground buildings are not likely to become the mainstay of future housing mainly because of the lack of technology. The American Underground Association was established on June 15, 1976, to promote underground architecture. The author was elected president of the Association.

676. _____. Going under to stay on top. Undergr. Sp., v. 1, no. 2, July/Aug. 1976: 71-86.
This paper reviews some of the possibilities of combining energy sufficiency and environmental quality through the use of the underground.

677. Feisel, L.D., R.D. McNeil, and R.J. Schmitz. Energy conservation by underground construction for a residential building. In Proc., 3rd Nat. Conf. and Exhib. on Tech. for Energ. Conserv., Tucson, AZ, Jan. 22, 1979. Silver Spring, MD: Information Transfer, Inc., 1979. p. 589-94.
This paper presents an analysis of a new earth-sheltered house, outlines the instrumentation system installed in it, and one that is proposed, and presents some preliminary results.

678. Goldberg, Louis F. A comparative experimental evaluation of five earth-sheltered houses. Undergr. Sp., v. 8, no. 1, 1984: 36-43.
Six of the eight houses which were built under the Solar/Earth-Sheltered Housing Demonstration Program were monitored to determine their energy performance. The houses' details are shown in a table. Results show that, in general, the earth-sheltered and superinsulated, above-grade houses monitored offer comparable energy conservation potentials. However, when occupant's lifestyle is factored out, the results seem to indicate that earth-sheltered housing potentially offers superior performance in absolute terms.

679. _____ and R.L. Sterling. Energy performance aspects of five houses in the Minnesota Housing Finance Agency's Earth-Sheltered Housing Demonstration Program. American Society of Civil Engineers, Conference, 1982.

680. _____. An experimental passive solar performance assessment of an earth-sheltered house. In Proc., Annu. Mtg., Am. Sol. Energ. Soc., June 1983. 24 p.
This paper delineates a simple mathematical model describing the performance of energy efficient housing.

681. _____. Factoring lifestyle into energy study: second part of series discusses analytic methods and results. Earth Shel. Liv., no. 31, Jan./Feb. 1984: 8-10.

This article gives an overview of the experimental data analysis methodology used in and discusses the results of an earth-sheltered housing energy performance monitoring program. The results show that superinsulated and earth-sheltered housing have better energy performance than above-grade housing in the Minnesota winters. However, occupant lifestyle was important in gauging overall energy performance.

682. _____ and C.A. Lane. A preliminary, experimental, energy performance assessment of five houses in the MHFA earth-sheltered housing demonstration program. In The potential of earth-sheltered and underground space: proc., Undergr. Sp. Conf. and Expos., Kansas City, MO, June 8-10, 1981. T.L. Holthusen, ed. Elmsford, NY: Pergamon Pr., 1981. p. 321-49.

Five earth-sheltered houses in Minnesota were studied during the period June 1980 to Feb. 1981 for net electrical energy consumptions, component load distributions, and heating efficiency comparisons. By studying the results, the earth-sheltered housing concept can be assessed, and the efficacy of the Total Gaseous Internal Energy as a quantitative earth-sheltered housing comparative indicator can be demonstrated.

683. _____. Underground Space Center: monitoring program. Earth Shel. Liv., no. 29, Sept./Oct. 1983: 33-5.

Some earth sheltered and above-grade solar heated houses in Minnesota were monitored to gather data on energy performance. Results are presented.

684. Grondzik, W.T., L.L. Boyer, and J.W. Zang. Analysis of utility billings for 55 earth-shelter projects. In Conf. proc., Earth Shel. Perf. and Eval., 2nd Nat. Tech. Conf., Tulsa, OK, Oct. 16-17, 1981. Stillwater, OK: Okla. State Univ., Archit. Ext., 1981. p. 175-84.

Utility billings for some all-electric earth-sheltered earth homes in the south central U.S. were analyzed and compared with above-ground homes in the same areas. Geographical similarities and differences were discussed.

685. _____. Energy conservation is earth-sheltered structures. Am. Soc. of Agric. Eng., Annu. Mtg., Orlando, FL, June 1981.

686. _____, T.L. Johnston, and L.L. Boyer. Monitoring of earth sheltered residences in Oklahoma. Proj. rept. for Control Data Corp., Stillwater, OK: Okla. State Univ., 1981.

687. _____ and L.L. Boyer. Performance evaluation of earth sheltered housing in Oklahoma. In Proc. of the Annu. Mtg., Am. Sec., Int. Sol. Energ. Soc., Phoenix, AZ, June 2, 1980. p. 729-33.
This paper discusses passive cooling, passive heating, and the overall performance of earth-sheltered houses in Oklahoma, stressing the importance of using an integrated systems design approach in earth-sheltered architecture.

688. Hanna, A.M. and N. Evans. Limitations of underground building as an energy alternative. In Proc., 7th UMR-DNR Conf. on Energ., Univ. of Missouri-Rolla, 1980. Rolla, MO: Univ. of Missouri-Rolla, 1980. p. 191-7.
The limitations and the potential energy-saving processes of earth-sheltered construction are discussed, emphasizing the soil properties, construction techniques, and structural design which may reduce energy savings.

689. House performs according to design objectives. Earth Shel. Dig. Energ. Rept., no. 9, May/June 1980: 43, 55.
Architect Richard Webster discusses the thermal performance of the prototype 1,900 sq. ft. earth shelter he designed.

690. Hutchinson, M., M. Fagerson, and C. Nelson. Measured thermal performance and the cost of conservation for a group of energy efficient Minnesota homes. Proc., ACEEE (Am. Coun. for an Energ. Effic. Econ.) Conf., Santa Cruz, CA, Aug. 1982.

691. Hylton, Joe. Contrasts in energy design and performance for passive solar vs. earth sheltered homes. In Conf. proc., Earth Shel. Pef. and Eval., 2nd Nat. Tech. Conf., Tulsa, OK, Oct. 16-17, 1981. Stillwater, OK: Okla. State Univ., Archit. Ext., 1981. p. 141-50.
Energy design considerations for earth-sheltered homes were contrasted with those of above-ground passive solar-heated homes. Energy performance was documented using utility billings.

692. Jones, C.D. Analysis of the thermal performance of earth covered roofs based upon a formulated interactive computer design aid. M.S. thesis, archit. eng. Stillwater, OK: Okla. State Univ., May 1983.

693. Kimber, Wayne. Energy and humidity performance of "Total Wood" earth sheltered homes. In Proc., 1st Int. Conf. on Energ. Effic. Bldgs. with Earth Shel. Prot., Sydney, Aust., Aug. 1-6, 1983. L.L. Boyer, ed. Stillwater, OK: Okla. State Univ., Archit. Ext., 1983. p. 299-303.
The performance of Everstrong Marketing's "Total Wood" earth-sheltered system in three structures in Redwood Falls, MN, is discussed: a retail store, an office building, and a residence. --Auth. abstract.

694. _____ and Rod W. Belsheim. The viability of the wood plenum compared to thermal mass. Conf. proc., Earth Shel. Perf. and Eval., 2nd Nat. Tech. Conf., Tulsa, OK, Oct. 16-17, 1981. Stillwater, OK: Okla. State Univ., Archit. Ext., 1981. p. 91-9.
Thermally massive structures using poured concrete construction were contrasted with total wood earth-covered structures employing underfloor plenums with rock storage, and the results were evaluated.

695. Konarske, Jim. Housing alternatives. Southgate, MI: Cave Enterprises, 1979. 47 p.
Earth sheltering is discussed from the viewpoint of energy savings.

696. Kubota, H. and N. Miley. Thermal analysis of a passive solar earth sheltered home. In Conf. proc., Earth Shel. Perf. and Eval., 2nd Nat. Tech. Conf., Tulsa, OK, Oct. 16-17, 1981. Stillwater, OK: Okla State Univ., Archit. Ext., 1981. p. 127-40.
More than a year of performance data on a two-story earth-sheltered passive solar home was employed to describe interior and exterior temperature and humidity fluctuations and air infiltration rates. A detailed thermal heat balance was also developed.

697. LaVigne, A.B. and M.A. Schuldt. Thermal performance of an earth-sheltered passive solar residence. In Proc., 6th Nat. Pass. Sol. Conf., Portland, OR, Sept. 8-12, 1981. (Prog. in Pass. Sol. Energ., v. 6) p. 54-8.
Results are given of the measured thermal performance of a direct gain, passive solar residence in the Pacific Northwest.

698. Lunde, Martin R. Effects of internal mass. Earth Shel. Dig. Energ. Rept., no. 16, July/Aug. 1981: 23-5.
This is the second part of a three-part series comparing earth covered and earth bermed/thermal roof structures.

699. Machowski, Barb and Kathleen Vadnais. Building test berm spec market. Earth Shel. Liv., no. 20, Mar./Apr. 1982: 14-8.

Builders are responding to the public's need for energy efficient housing. One evidence is the more frequent use of berming. Bermed houses are more easily marketed than fully covered houses. Other energy conservation features are discussed.

700. _____. Utility answers energy questions. Earth Shel. Liv., no. 19, Jan./Feb. 1982: 58.

Utility customers in Minnesota, North Dakota, South Dakota, and Wisconsin can dial their phones and hear a four-minute taped mini-lecture about earth sheltering, a part of the Northern States Power's energy tape library, "Ask NSP."

701. McCreath, D.R. and D.E. Mitchell. Build underground and conserve energy: fact or fiction. Eng. J., v. 6, no. 2, Apr. 1978: 14-6.

702. Monitoring system defined. Earth Shel. Dig. Energ. Rept., no. 9, May/June 1980: 34-5.

This article describes an instrumentation system to provide data on the thermal performance of an earth-sheltered house in Rapid City, SD.

703. Moore, Gordon L. Natural forces should be trapped. Earth Shel. Dig. Energ. Rept., no. 5, Sept./Oct. 1979: 22.

The author discusses maintaining a near constant comfortable temperature in a concrete earth-contact home.

704. Oklahoma State University. School of Architecture. Human comfort and energy conservation in earth sheltered buildings. Stillwater, OK. 100+ p.

The workbook in a three-ring binder includes papers on comfort parameters, comfort evaluations, energy and moisture, heat loss calculations, cooling load analysis, the earth environment, subterrannean analysis, HVAC systems design, energy performance, daylighting, passive solar, and thermal design of interiors.

705. Peterson, Roger A. Energy budgets of super-insulated versus earth-sheltered housing in Minnesota. Paper submitted as coursework for architectural design. Minneapolis, MN: Univ. of Minn., 1980.

706. Poulos, J.F.J. Thermal performance of underground structures: the development of the decremented average ground temperature method for estimating the thermal performance of underground walls. M.A. thesis, architecture. Atlanta, GA: Ga. Inst. of Tech., 1982. 112 p.

707. Puri, V.M. and P. Ranganathan. Design curves for soil bermed structure. In Solar engineering: ASME Sol. Energ. Conf., Albuquerque, NM, Apr. 26, 1982. W.D. Turner, ed. New York, NY: Am. Soc. of Mech. Eng., 1982. p. 237-43.
 This study encompassed several key parameters: ambient temperature, indoor temperature, ground temperature, and wall height and grade level distance covered with soil. The design curves were applied to an average Midwest domestic residence in order to determine the best berm profile based on cumulative annual energy savings. Results showed that about two-thirds annual energy savings can be obtained with a single optimal passive design feature.

708. Raman, K. Analytic method for performance modelling of passive solar systems. In Proc., Annu. Mtg., Am. Sec., Int. Sol. Energ. Soc., 1982. p. 679-84.
 The effects of earth sheltering are illustrated by quantitative results in an example. The storage effectiveness of massive building elements and some other subjects are discussed.

709. Report evaluates potential for earth sheltered housing. Underline, v. 3, no. 5, July/Aug. 1982: 1-2, 4.
 The 52-page report is Earth-sheltered housing, an evaluation of energy-conservation potential, prepared by R.L. Wendt under the Dept. of Energy's Innovative Structures Program at Oak Ridge National Laboratory. It states that earth-sheltered homes are capable of very good energy performance, but they are likely to cost ten to 35 percent more than conventional, above-ground homes.

710. Ribot, Jesse C., Arthur H. Rosenfeld, Francoise Flouquet, and Wolfgang Luhrsen. Monitored low-energy houses in North America and Europe: a compilation and economic analysis. Undergr. Sp., v. 8, no. 3, 1984: 156-63.
 This study compares the thermal and economic performance of superinsulated, passive solar, active solar, and earth sheltered dwellings, as well as many which combine these techniques throughout North America and Europe. Data on submetered energy consumption, inside and outside temperature, number of occupants, and the associated costs of the conservation measures were used. The only cost effective measures demonstrated in the data sample were superinsu-

lation and superinsulation in combination with moderate south glass area.

711. Ruppel, Dennis L. Potential heating and cooling savings utilizing earth sheltering: an analytical evaluation. Earth Shel. Bldgs. - Tech. Pap., TP-IIIG, 1983.

712. Samuel, Barbara. Owners concur. Earth Shel. Liv., no. 28, July/Aug. 1983: 44-5.
Thermal performance of three earth-sheltered homes during 1981-83 winters.

713. Shapira, H.B., S.E. Brite, and M.B. Yost. Up and down: energy and cost comparison. In Proc., Annu. Mtg., Am. Sec., Int. Sol. Energ. Soc., Philadelphia, PA, May 26, 1981. p. 931-5.
Oak Ridge National Laboratory is conducting a study to compare the cost and energy performance of equal aboveground and earth-sheltered homes in five cities selected to represent five regions of the U.S.

714. Shen, L.S. and J.W. Ramsey. A simplified thermal analysis of earth sheltered buildings using a Fourier-series boundary method. ASHRAE Trans., v. 89, pt. 1, 1983: 438-48.
A thermal analysis program is described which is capable of simulating slab-on-grade, berm, basement, and earth-covered building configurations.

715. Shipp, P.H. Thermal characteristics of large earth-sheltered structures. Ph.D. Thesis. Minneapolis, MN: Univ. of Minn., 1979.

716. Simmons, Lon B. The sun shines at the bottom. Earth Shel. Dig. Energ. Rept., no. 5, Sept./Oct. 1979: 4-6.
Discusses earth sheltering's role in alleviating the energy shortage.

717. Speltz, J.J. and G.D. Meixel, Jr. Computer simulation of the thermal performance of earth covered roofs. In The potential of earth-sheltered and underground space: proc., Undergr. Sp. Conf. and Expos., Kansas City, MO, June 8-10, 1981. T.L. Holthusen, ed. Elmsford, NY: Pergamon Pr., 1981. p. 91-108.
A computer model of the one-dimensional heat flow through earth-covered roofs is developed and is used to examine thermal performance for winter heating and summer cooling periods. Details of the model are given. The computer model is applied

to the assessment of heat flow through ordinary roof structures and also through more complicated earth-covered roofs during summer cooling periods, and the results are presented.

718. _____. Sensitivity of earth sheltered building thermal performance to inside radiation exchange. In <u>Proc., 1st Int. Conf. on Energ. Effic. Bldgs. with Earth Shel. Prot.</u>, Sydney, Aust., Aug. 1-6, 1983. L.L. Boyer, ed. Stillwater, OK: Okla. State Univ., Archit. Ext., 1983. p. 337-43.

Digital computer thermal analysis methodologies are developed and utilized to determine the effect of neglecting inside-surface radiation coupling on the prediction of inside surface temperatures and air temperature and on heating or cooling loads. Computations are based on utilizing a transient two-dimensional finite difference computer model which is coupled to a complete internal heat balance of the building's inside surface temperatures and air temperature. Studies are performed for three building types with varying levels of earth-sheltering.

719. _____ and P. Haves. Thermal benefits and cost effectiveness of earth berming. In <u>Proc., Annu. Mtg., Am. Sec., Int. Sol. Energ. Soc., 5th Nat. Pass. Sol. Conf.</u>, Amherst, MA, Oct. 19-26, 1980. Newark, DE: Int. Sol. Energ. Soc., Am. Sec., 1980. p. 337-41.

Some of the advantages of earth-sheltered buildings are enumerated. Results of a comparison of earth-sheltered structures with a house with perimeter insulation and a house with neither earth sheltering or insulation show that the major savings from an earth-sheltered house is obtained in colder climates. Earth berming substantially reduces the cost of the foundation because the frost line is raised.

720. Stanford, Greg. Thermal environment of the lithotectural dugouts of White Cliffs, Australia. In <u>Proc., 1st Int. Conf. on Energ. Effic. Bldgs. with Earth Shel. Prot.</u>, Sydney, Aust., Aug. 1-6, 1983. L.L. Boyer, ed. Stillwater, OK: Okla. State Univ., Archit. Ext., 1983. p. 265-9. Also in <u>Geotecture</u>, v. 1, no. 4, July 1984: 26-30.

In various case studies of lithotecture in White Cliffs, NSW, exterior environment heat patterns are traced through to the interior environment and analysed. Temperatures are plotted on plan and graph to illustrate the earth's thermal damping effect with depth and distance, from the external environment through to the deep dugout environment. Thermal components that are graphically represented in these studies include: M.R.T. (black bulk/air speed) humidity, ambient environmental temperature

and interior surface temperatures of dugouts. Results are interpreted and conclusions drawn concerning dugout performance. Questionnaire responses are used to support test findings.
--Auth. abstract.

721. _____. Thermal environment of the White Cliffs lithotectural dugouts. Undergr. Sp., v. 8, no. 3, 1984: 150-5.

This work examines atmospheric thermal data from eight randomly selected lithotectural dugouts in White Cliffs, NSW, Aust. situated in claystone rock deposits with a shallow clay soil cover. Different elements of the thermal environment were measured at various locations ranging from far external environment to deep internal environment. The results were graphed to show thermal patterns and the influence earth cover has on achieving comfort levels.

722. Sterling, Ray. State of the art. In Residential applications: transcripts of selected presentations, Going Under to Stay on Top, Minneapolis, MN, Oct. 1977. Minneapolis, MN: Univ. of Minn., Undergr. Sp. Ctr., 1979. p. 97-9.

The author discusses data that has been collected on energy use of existing earth-sheltered homes.

723. Stewart, Donald R. Energy performance of an earth-sheltered active solar house. In Proc., Earth Shel. Bldg. Des. Innov., Nat. Tech. Conf., Oklahoma City, OK, Apr. 18, 1980. L.L. Boyer, ed. Stillwater, OK: Okla. State Univ., 1980. p. IV. 11-5.

An active solar earth-covered house in Wichita was monitored for almost two years. Its energy performance was studied to determine the relative contributions of solar conditioning, earth tempering, and utility usage. A description of the house, the systems, and construction conditions are given. The energy consumption of five different house types near Wichita compared.

724. Sunearth house efficiency monitored. Earth Shel. Dig. Energ. Rept., no. 1, Jan./Feb. 1979: 15-7.

This earth-sheltered house in Boulder, CO, built by Sunworks, is being monitored by IBM to track total energy flow and climate performance in and around the house for five years. The results will be published monthly by the Nat. Bur. of Stand.

725. Terman, Max R. Energy performance of an earth-sheltered home with Trombe walls. Undergr. Sp., v. 6, no. 3, Nov./Dec. 1981: 180-5.

A passive solar, earth-sheltered home in central Kansas

was monitored over a 17-month period for temperature, relative humidity, and energy use. Interior temperatures varied diurnally from a low of 62 degrees F in winter to a high of 87 degrees F in summer. It used 30 percent less electricity than a conventional surface home of similar size. It is estimated that at least 80 percent of heating needs were met by passive solar and earth-sheltering strategies.

726. _____. Performance data for a passive solar earth sheltered home. In Conf. proc., Earth Shel. Perf. and Eval., 2nd Nat. Tech. Conf., Tulsa, OK, Oct. 16-17, 1981. Stillwater, OK: Okla State Univ., 1981. p. 275-83.

Measurements of temperature, moisture, and energy are reviewed throughout an annual cycle for this earth shelter incorporating a Trombe wall.

727. "Thermal roof" is introduced. Earth Shel. Dig. Energ. Rept., no. 14, Mar./Apr. 1981: 27-9.

The earth-bermed house with a thermal roof costs less than an earth-covered house and both seem to require the same amount of energy to heat.

728. USC completes research on earth sheltered houses' energy performance. Underline, v. 5, no. 2, 1984: 1-3, 5.

A five-year study was completed of the energy performance of houses on the Solar/Earth-Sheltered Housing Demonstration Program of the Minnesota Housing Finance Agency. It was designed to develop a data acquisitions system, a system to process the large volume of data produced, and analytical tools capable of yielding performance parameters. Eight two and three-bedroom houses were built. Five are earth sheltered. Results of the study are shown.

729. Van der Meer, Wybe J. Underground and earth covered housing deserves consideration--energy savings of 67 percent compared with conventional construction with increased FHA insulation requirements. In Proc., IAHS Int. Symp. on Hous. Prob., Atlanta, GA, 1976. Parvis F. Rad, ed. Coral Gables, FL: Int. Assn. for Hous. Sci., 1976. v. 2, p. 1137-49.

A hypothetical underground residence in the Midwest (Chicago) was analyzed to determine the possible magnitude of energy savings for environmental control. The factors reducing heat loss from underground structures are discussed, as are the estimated dollar value of savings in energy costs, energy use in lighting, materials and economic considerations, psychological considerations of underground housing, building code and lending agency restrictions or limitations, synergistic mechanical systems, and the non-energy-related advantages of underground housing.

730. Varde, K.S. Study of energy usage in underground dwellings. In Changing energy use futures, Int. Conf. on Energ. Use Mgmt., Los Angeles, CA, Oct. 22, 1979. New York, NY: Pergamon Pr., 1979. v. 3, p. 1317-27.

An underground dwelling is analyzed for heating requirements. The analysis shows that up to 70 percent of the energy needed for space heating in above-grade homes can be saved in below-grade homes.

731. Wendt, R.L. Earth-sheltered housing: an evaluation of energy-conservation potential. Oak Ridge, TN: Oak Ridge Nat. Lab., Apr. 1982. 49 p. (NTIS, PC A05/MF A01).

This report presents the findings of the projects carried out under the U.S. Dept. of Energy's Innovative Structures Program during its evaluation of the energy conservation potential of earth-sheltered homes. The major conclusions of the studies are presented: earth-sheltered structures are capable of very good energy performance; earth-sheltered houses perform significantly better in some climatic regions than in others.

732. _____. The energy conservation potential of earth-sheltered housing. Undergr. Sp., v. 7, no. 6, May/June 1983: 372-80.

This paper is derived from the author's Earth-sheltered housing: an evaluation of energy-conservation potential, produced for the Innovative Structures Program at Oak Ridge National Laboratory. It raises questions about the future of earth-sheltered housing in the U.S.

733. Wigington, Fred J. and Roger Kness. Earth shelter/greenhouse integration assessments. In Conf. proc., Earth Shel. Perf. and Eval., 2nd Nat. Tech. Conf., Tulsa, OK, Oct. 16-17, 1981. Stillwater, OK: Okla. State Univ., Archit. Ext., 1981. p. 115-23.

Performance is estimated and compared with selected operational data for a hillside project dominated by a greenhouse facade. Balanced design treatments for both heating and cooling seasons are developed.

734. You can control energy use. Earth Shel. Dig. Energ. Rept., no. 6, Nov./Dec. 1979: 37-8.

XII. EARTH CONTACT HEAT TRANSFER

735. Akridge, James M. A decremented average ground temperature method for estimating the thermal performance of underground houses. In <u>Passive cooling; proc. of the Int. Pass. and Hybr. Cool. Conf.</u>, Miami Beach, FL, Nov. 6-16, 1981. Newark, DE: Int. Sol. Energ. Soc., Am. Sec., 1981. p. 141-5.

The methods usually used to estimate thermal performance (Average ground temperature method, the Underground degree day method, and the Ground as an insulator method) have ignored the effect the structure has on the ground temperatures. This has led to an underestimation of the thermal performance during the heating season and an overestimation of the performance during the cooling season. This paper describes a method which takes into account the effect of the structure on ground temperatures. It allows the determination of the effect of insulation, soil properties, depth, and time of the structure's performance.

736. _____. Indirect earth cooling techniques. In <u>Proc., Earth Integr. for Cool. Sem., Okla. State Univ., 1981.</u>

737. Bircher, Tad L. The thermal performance of ground-coupled desert buildings. In <u>Progress in passive solar energy; proc. of the 6th Nat. Pass. Sol. Conf.</u>, Portland, OR, Sept. 8-12, 1981. p. 266-70.

The results of a computer simulation study of ground-coupled structures in desert areas are presented.

738. Blick, E.F. Simple method for determining heat flow through earth covered roofs. In <u>Proc., Earth Shel. Bldg. Des. Innov., Nat. Tech. Conf.</u>, Oklahoma City, OK, Apr. 18, 1980. L.L. Boyer, ed. Stillwater, OK: Okla. State Univ., 1980. p. III. 19-23.

Below the first six to eight inches of soil, the temperature profiles of an earth-covered roof are nearly linear. An equation is developed to be used to predict the heat loss through earth-covered roofs in winter and predict heat gain in summer.

739. Bligh, T.P. Building heat transfer. In <u>Thermal properties of soil and earth contact heat transfer: Ctr. for Bldg. Tech. Conf.</u>, Nat. Bur. of Stand., Mar. 1983.

740. _____ and G.D. Meixel. Cooling potential of earth coupled buildings. Sol. Pass. and Hybr. Cool. DOE Conf., Washington, DC, Feb. 1980.

741. _____ and B.H. Knoth. Data from one, two and three dimensional temperature fields in the soil surrounding an earth-sheltered house. And discussion. ASHRAE Trans., v. 89, pt. 1, 1983: 395-404.
Data show that extended roof insulation obstructs heat flow to the ground surface in the winter but permits heat to flow to the cool soil depths in the summer.

742. _____ and G.D. Meixel. Earth contact systems: final report. U.S. DOE DE-ACO-80SF11508, Nov. 1983. 335 p.

743. _____, B.H. Knoth, E. Smith, and D. Apthorp. Earth contact systems: soil temperature and thermal conductivity data, heat flux data, and meter calibration. Pass. and Hybr. Energ. Conf., DOE, Washington, DC, Sept. 1982.

744. _____, E.R.G. Eckert, and E. Pfender. Energy exchange between earth-sheltered structures and the surrounding ground. Midwest Energ. Conf., Chicago, IL, Nov. 1978.

745. _____. Experimental procedures for In situ monitoring of temperature, heat flow, soil thermal properties, and all weather conditions on an earth coupled structure. DOE Sol. Pass. and Hybr. Cool. Update Conf., Oakland, CA, Jan. 1981.

746. _____ and T. Willard. A finite element model with phase change for predicting heat transfer from earth-contact buildings. Rept. to Consolidated Edison Co., NY, Sept. 1983. 155 p.

747. _____. Heat transfer from earth contact buildings. Am. Undergr. Assn. Annu. Mtg. and Conf., June 1981.

748. Carmody, J., G. Meixel, and T.P. Bligh. Preliminary design guidelines for earth contact buildings. U.S. DOE Pass. Cool. Prog. Rept., DE-AC03-80SF11508, Mar. 1983. 101 p.

749. Colliver, D.G., R.L. Fehr, and B.F. Parker. Comparison of heating requirements for underground vs. earth bermed houses. ASAE Trans., v. 25, no. 6, Nov./Dec. 1982: 1701-7, 1710.
The heat transferred and stored in the soil and the resultant

heat fluxes for the ceilings, walls, and floors are estimated for underground and earth-bermed structures using a two-dimensional finite difference technique. Based on the weather conditions at Lexington, KY, the calculated heat fluxes are shown for the earth-bermed and the underground structures at different soil cover depths and for varying insulation thicknesses.

750. Cristy, G.A. Computer simulation of heating and cooling of ventilation air for a passive solar house. In Proc., 3rd Nat. Pass. Sol. Conf., San Jose, CA, Jan. 11, 1979. Newark, DE: Int. Sol. Energ. Soc., Am. Sec., 1979. p. 457-64.

The temperature of ventilation air in a semi-buried passive solar house was moderated using a rock bed installed outside the insulation of the three buried walls of the house. The soil outside the rock bed is covered with insulation permitting the soil to augment the thermal mass of the rock bed. The ventilation air will be warmed in winter by passing through the rock bed before entering the house. This cools the rock bed and the soil next to it. In the summer, the intake air will be cooled by passing over the cooled rock bed.

751. Davis, William B. Earth temperature: its effect on underground residences. In Proc., Alt. in Habitat: the Use of Earth Cov. Set., Conf., Fort Worth, TX, May 17-19, 1978. F.L. Moreland, ed. Washington, DC: U.S. Dept. of Energy, 1979. v. 1, p. 205-9.

Results of independent verification of the potential energy savings from an underground structure covered with eight to ten feet of soil are presented. This type of structure can reduce the amount of air conditioning required in the summer by 80 percent and the amount of heating required in winter by 80 to 85 percent.

752. Dirr, T. Typical building loads: earth-contact systems contract. Task 1.3. Oct. 1980-Dec. 1981. Minneapolis, MN: Architectural Alliance. 154 p.

In an effort to develop more accurate procedures for predicting thermal performance of earth-contact construction, the hand-calculation methods presently used have been reviewed and typical heating and cooling loads calculated for a typical earth-contact residence in six locations: Phoenix, Fresno, Miami, Minneapolis, Kansas City, and Albuquerque.

753. Dupont, William C. Cool tubes for energy-conscious buildings: the use of terrestrial heat exchangers for cooling. Earth Shel. Bldgs. - Tech. Pap., TP-IIIB, 1983.

754. Earth pipes played to perfection. Earth Shel. Dig. Energ. Rept., no. 4, July/Aug. 1979: 20-2.

Lord's Power Co., Nora Springs, IA, has developed Terra Therm system for heating and cooling: a series of pipes trenched or driven through the ground about ten feet down through which air or liquid is run from the pipes to the structure and then used directly or through a heat exchanger.

755. Eckert, E.R.G. Ground used as energy source, energy sink, or for energy storage. Energy, v. 1, no. 3, Sept. 1976: 315-23.

The energy required to maintain a structure at constant temperature can be reduced by burying it in the ground or locating it below the ground surface. The potential of this idea is explored using simple relations for unsteady heat conduction. The earth also serves as a heat storage medium for annual storage in an underground building when temperature fluctuations of a few degrees are tolerated in the building and when the heat flux into the ground is the dominating heat loss.

756. Elifrits, C. Dale and A.D.S. Gillies. Earth pipes: preconditioning house air. Pt. 1. Earth Shel. Liv., no. 29, Sept./Oct. 1983: 6-7; Pt. 2. Ibid., no. 30, Nov./Dec. 1983: 26-7.

Discusses the use of earth pipes to draw fresh air into buildings to passively heat, cool, and ventilate.

757. Gillies, A.D.S., C.D. Elifrits, and N.B. Aughenbaugh. An analysis of air heating during flow through ground passages. In Proc., 1st Int. Conf. on Energ. Effic. Bldgs. with Earth Shel. Prot., Sydney, Aust., Aug. 1-6, 1983. L.L. Boyer, ed. Stillwater, OK: Okla. State Univ., Archit. Ext., 1983. p. 43-8.

During a ten-day period of below freezing temperatures, air was circulated through an underground tunnel. Under constant air flow rate, rock and air temperatures were observed every four hours at instrumented stations along the tunnel from the portal intake to the exhaust outlet. Tunnel ice formation and the depth of rock temperature cooling in from the tunnel surface were also recorded. The data were analyzed to establish the heat flow energy transfer characteristics between the circulating air and the rock. The day-to-day surface climatic changes were recorded and correlated to the air and rock temperatures within the tunnel. Comparisons were made with theory developed for use in hot underground mining conditions at depth and a general equation formulated to describe the thermodynamic behaviour of the system. From this empirical base, suitable designs are proposed for ground tubes or tunnels to temper winter air for home heating. The authors propose incorporating a heat pump unit as an energy transfer stage between below ground warmed air and the home heating system. System dimensions are proposed and compared for homes in three climatic areas of the U.S. and for various soil and rock subsurface ground conditions. The comparisons are based on both open flow below ground passages and closed loop air flow paths. From the results of the study, the home owner should be able to design a ground passage air tempering system with sizing appropriate to location and environment. --Auth. abstract.

758. Givoni, B. Modifying the ambient temperature of underground buildings. In Proc., Alt. in Habitat: the Use of Earth Cov. Set. Conf., Fort Worth, TX, May 17-19, 1978. v. 1, Earth covered buildings: technical notes, p. 123-38.
Thermal conductivity, which is affected by water content and heat capacity in combination determine the earth's Thermal Time Constant (TTC) and its point of temperature stabilization. When underground buildings are occupied, they generate heat. The heat flows to the surrounding soil by conduction and convective heat transfer, and the structures are ventilated. Some options are suggested for raising or lowering the level of stabilization so that comfortable temperatures are achieved in any season.

759. Grondzik, Walter, Lester L. Boyer, and Timothy L. Johnston. Earth coupled cooling techniques. In Progress in passive solar energy: proc. of the 6th Nat. Pass. Sol. Conf., Portland, OR, Sept. 8-12, 1981. p. 837-41.
A review is presented of the benefits to expect from passive earth contact cooling techniques. Design recommendations for earth-sheltered structures to incorporate earth-coupled cooling strategies are also presented.

760. _____, Daniel K. Fitzgerald, and Siva Kumar Haran. Seasonal variations in soil temperatures surrounding two occupied earth-sheltered residences. In Passive and low energy alternatives: proc. of the 1st Int. PLEA Conf., Bermuda, Sept. 13-15, 1982. New York, NY: Pergamon Pr., 1982. p. 7:20-26.
Information is presented concerning the seasonal variations in soil temperature and interior surface temperatures of two occupied earth-sheltered homes in Oklahoma.

761. _____, Lester L. Boyer, and Timothy L. Johnston. Variations in earth covered roof temperature profiles. In Passive cooling: proc. of the Int. Pass. and Hybr. Cool. Conf., Miami Beach, FL, No. 6-16, 1981. Newark, DE: Int. Sol. Energ. Soc., Am. Sec., 1981. p. 146-50.

Two occupied earth-sheltered dwellings were monitored to compare their earth-covered roof performance during summer conditions. The influence of vegetation on roof performance is discussed, and earth contact cooling from earth-backed wall surfaces is documented.

762. Hait, John. Controlling your solar heat: storing solar heat depends on size and location of windows. Earth Shel. Liv., no. 33, May/June 1984: 12-3.

Earth is the best substance for storing heat but heat must be absorbed slowly if it is to be stored for long periods. Windows admitting solar heat should be moderately sized, and the house should have adjustable shading devices to limit solar gain.

763. _____. Passive annual heat storage. Moth. Earth N., no. 91, Jan./Feb. 1985: 146-8.

By placing a "cap" over an earth-sheltered home that extends beyond its walls, the heat that the home radiates into the earth is captured and returns to the interior of the home in the winter. The same principles can be applied for cooling homes in hot climates.

764. _____ and the Rocky Mountain Research Center. Passive annual heat storage: improving the design of earth shelters. Missoula, MT: Rocky Mountain Research Center, 1983? 152 p.

Contents: Improving the earth shelter; passive annual heat storage; why water washes away the heat; water, water everywhere, so control it; the insulation/watershed umbrella; what goes up (convective heat flow); earth tube ventilation; hot and cold running radiant (radiant heat flow); adjusting the earth's constant temperature; the earth-shelter pioneer; design guidelines; conversion tables; bibliography.

765. _____. Umbrella modifies soil temperature. Earth Shel. Liv., no. 27, May/June 1983: 8-9.

A process is described called passive annual heat storage whereby heat is passively collected, stored, and retrieved over the entire year.

766. Hanna, A.M., R.J. Raman, and S.A. Hanna. Building underground as energy alternative. Int. J. Hous. Sci. Appl., v. 4, no. 5, 1980: 395-9.

Although thermally efficient, earth-sheltered construction is subject to some limitations. Soil conditions could reduce thermal efficiency and costs could be increased to the point that a conventional house would be preferable.

767. Holmes, William Whittaker. "Subcalc": an automated earth-cooling design procedure for passive solar earth-sheltered structures. In Passive cooling: proc. of the Int. Pass. and Hybr. Cool. Conf., Miami Beach, FL, Nov. 6-16, 1981. Newark, DE: Int. Sol. Energ. Soc., Am. Sec., 1981. p. 151-5.

"Subcalc" is an automated month-by-month structure-to-earth heat loss algorithm appropriate for computing the earth components of total structure heat flows in summer or winter. The operation of the program is described, and an example calculation is given for an actual earth sheltered, passive solar dwelling.

768. Hourmanesh, Mo, Ray Hourmanesh, and Donald B. Elmer. Earth air heat exchanger system. In Proc., 2nd Nat. Pass. Sol. Conf., Philadelphia, PA, Mar. 16-18, 1978. Newark, DE: Int. Sol. Energ. Soc., Am. Sec., 1978. p. 146-9.

This paper shows how the ability of the earth as an energy storage (heat source/sink) system can be effectively utilized in the modeling of passive energy systems. The earth's properties as universal principles and thermophysical properties of the soil as climatic parameters can be integrated by means of a passive energy system (earth-air heat exchanger) to provide comfort conditioning within dwelling spaces.

769. Katz, Martin A. Heat flows through underground walls and floors: analysis and implications for insulation placement in earth-sheltered buildings. Earth Shel. Bldgs. - Tech. Pap., TP-IIIE, 1983.

770. Kimura, K., M. Shukuya, and S. Tanabe. Estimation of annual heat loss and heat gain from earth-contact floors and walls with insulation in temperate climate regions. In Proc., 1st Int. Conf. on Energ. Effic. Bldgs. with Earth Shel. Prot., Sydney, Aust., Aug.1-6, 1983. L.L. Boyer, ed. Stillwater, OK: Okla. State Univ., Archit. Ext., 1983. p. 331-5.

Results are given of calculations of the heat loss and heat gain from earth-contact floors and walls with insulation using two-dimensional heat conduction within the soil. It is shown that heat loss through a wall down to two m. deep in the soil was 30 percent less than an exterior wall facing the ambient air in all seasons except summer. The heat loss through the wall from ground level to one m. deep was found to be so large that insulation of this portion of the wall might be important. —Auth. abstract.

771. Kuehn, T.H. Temperature and heat flow measurements from an insulated concrete bermed wall and adjacent floor. J. of Sol. Energ. Eng., v. 104, 1982: 15-22.

772. Labs, Kenneth and K. Harrington. Comparison of ground and above-ground climates for identifying appropriate cooling strategies. In Proc., 5th Nat. Pass. Sol. Conf., Amherst, PA, Oct. 19-26, 1980. Newark, DE: Int. Sol. Energ. Soc., Am. Sec., 1980.

The value of earth-tempering techniques in six regions of the U.S. were assessed using a mathematical model of undisturbed ground temperature. Earth tempering is evaluated with relation to other passive cooling strategies. It is found that ground-cooling methods are of most value in temperate and arid areas but of limited value in warm, humid zones where they may even present obstacles to natural ventilation.

773. _____. Direct-coupled ground cooling: issues and opportunities. In Passive cooling; proc. of the Int. Pass. and Hybr. Cool. Conf., Miami Beach, FL, Nov. 6-16, 1981. Newark, DE: Int. Sol. Energ. Soc., Am. Sec., 1981. p. 131-5.

Some regional ground and dew-point temperatures are presented as indicators of ground-cooling potential and of the relative probability of condensation occurrence in the region. The identification of different methods of ground-temperature modification to increase the cooling power of the ground is stressed.

774. _____. Earth tempering as a passive design strategy. In Proc., Earth Shel. Bldg. Des Innov., Oklahoma City, OK, Apr. 18, 1980. L.L. Boyer, ed. Stillwater, OK: Okla. State Univ., 1980.

Basic climate control strategies, such as insulation, thermal mass, natural ventilation, passive solar heating, and evaporative cooling, are available to the architect. Earth-tempering design practices can provide the same benefits as many of these, but may be in conflict with some. This depends on local climatic factors and the type of design used. A method is presented for analyzing local climate by determining the relative priority of the basic climate control strategies. Computer analyzed example data are shown for four geographical regions of the U.S.

775. _____. Earth tempering practices in overheated condi-

tions. Pt. 1, Architectural and regional issues in application. In <u>Passive cooling: proc. of the Int. Pass. and Hybr. Cool. Conf.</u>, Miami Beach, FL, Nov. 6-16, 1981. Newark, DE: Int. Sol. Energ. Soc., Am. Sec., 1981. p. 773-81.

Historical examples are presented to reveal that earth-cooling techniques are better suited to arid than to humid overheated areas. Earth-cooling techniques are most effective in temperate climates with hot summers, as compared to tropical, hot climates.

776. _____ and K. Harrington. Investigations into ground climate as an alternative thermal building environment. In <u>Earth shelter 2: coll. pap., 1st Earth Shel. Hous. Conf. and Exhib.</u>, Minneapolis, MN, Apr. 9-11, 1980. Minneapolis, MN: Univ. of Minn., Undergr. Sp. Ctr., 1980.

The paper discusses a mathematical model for estimating the temperature of a selected vertical profile in the soil under undisturbed thermal conditions. Some suggested uses: installation of earth pipes and determination of degree day assignments to different soil profiles.

777. _____. Underground building climate. <u>Sol. Age</u>, v. 4, no. 10, Oct. 1979: 44-5, 47-50.

Methods for calculating and evaluating the thermal properties of the ground are presented. The calculations are used to evaluate the thermal parameters affecting underground buildings.

778. Lane, C.A. <u>A simplified method for estimating the envelope heat transfer characteristics for small earth sheltered buildings</u>. Rept. to the Control Data Corp. (Unpublished).

779. Langley, John. Remember thermal breaks. <u>Earth Shel. Dig. Energ. Rept.</u>, no. 12, Nov./Dec. 1980: 19.

A thermal break reduces the amount of heat flow from and to the house. This brief excerpt is from <u>Sun belt earth sheltered architecture</u> by Langley and Gay.

780. Lunde, Martin R. Efficiency compared: earth covered and thermal roof. <u>Earth Shel. Dig. Energ. Rept.</u>, no. 15, May/June 1981: 26-9.

This article compares the advantages and disadvantages of a house with a thermal roof and bermed walls vs. an earth-covered home. Tables show results of heat loss comparison, roof loss comparison at +72 degrees F. indoors, and the internal mass comparison.

781. MacArthur, J.W. Analytical methods for predicting heat flow in earth-contact systems. Roseville, MN: Honeywell, Inc., Tech. Strategy Ctr., June 1981. 126 p. (DOE/SF/11508--T2; AC03-80SF11508).

782. Meixel, G.D., Jr., T.P. Bligh, B.H. Knoth, and E.A. Smith. Earth contact systems. U.S. Dept. of Energy Pass. and Hybr. Sol. Energ. Prog. Update, Feb. 1982. p. 6.39-6.42. (CONF-810832).
A multi-dimensional heat conduction and moisture migration model for earth-contact systems for buildings is developed. Existing energy transport models are listed. Experimental computer model validation and soil temperature measurements are discussed.

783. Moore, Gordon L. ISOlation, INSUlation, INSOlation -- earth contact as heat transfer. In Passive solar: subdivisions, windows, underground. Ed. by H. Wade and others. Kansas City, MO: Am. Sol. Energ. Soc., Kansas City Chap., 1983. p. 219-23.
The author argues that the earth mass around an earth-integrated structure serves as a heat recycler feeding warmth into the living space during cold weather, warmth which had entered the earth cover from the structure.

784. Moulds, Matthew. Calculating heat loss, II. Earth Shel. Liv., no. 32, Mar./Apr. 1984: 20-2.
The author calculated heat loss through a typical earth-sheltered building.

785. Newberry, James R. Active earth coupling. Earth Shel. Bldgs. -- Tech. Pap., TP-IE, 1983.

786. Newman, Jerry O. Seasonal variation in heat transfer through earth embanked wall. In Proc., 4th Nat. Pass. Sol. Conf., Kansas City, MO, Oct. 3-5, 1979. Newark, DE: Int. Sol. Energ. Soc., Am. Sec., 1979. p. 739-43.
Earth-embanked walls reduce heat loss from homes by more than 60 percent.

787. _____ and L.C. Godbey. Soil temperatures adjacent to earth shelter. In Papers, Winter Meeting, Am. Soc. of Agric. Eng., New Orleans, LA, Dec. 11-14, 1979. St. Joseph, MO: ASAE, 1979.
A study was conducted to measure the seasonal variation in temperatures of soil adjacent to an underground structure, and the influence of house temperatures on the energy balance. A solar-earth house near Easley, NC, is described.

788. Pick, E. Operation characteristics of a utility-free dwelling in Kansas. In Proc., Earth Shel. Bldg. Des. Innov., Oklahoma City, OK, Apr. 18, 1980. L.L. Boyer, ed. Stillwater, OK: Okla. State Univ., 1980. p. IV. 5-8.

Subterranean temperature modification is a new technology employed to alter subgrade wall temperatures to enhance the heating and cooling requirements of a structure.

789. Raff, S.J. Ground temperature control. Undergr. Sp., v. 3, no. 1, July/Aug. 1978: 35-44.

The energy required to maintain human comfort in underground space depends on the temperature of the surrounding earth. This, in turn, depends on the four mechanisms by which heat is lost or gained by the earth: insolation, evaporation, long wavelength radiation to the sky, and conduction to the air. Each of these factors is examined in relation to their effects on ground temperature.

790. Reindl, Wilhelm. Getting into it. Earth Shel. Dig. Energ. Rept., no. 7, Jan./Feb. 1980: 16-7.

Questions and answers: explanation of heat transfer; concrete reinforcing calculations.

791. Roy, Robert L. Earth roof thickness: the tradeoff. Earth Shel. Dig. Energ. Rept., no. 13, Jan./Feb. 1981: 16-19.

Earth is not completely without insulative value, but the greatest value per inch is in the three or four inches which is the part of the earth cover aerated by root systems and not greatly compacted. The vegetation cover also supplies additional insulation. Therefore, putting more than up to one foot of soil on the roof is not cost effective because a stronger and more expensive structure must be built to support the thicker earth cover.

792. Speltz, J. A numerical simulation of transient heat flow in earth sheltered building for seven selected U.S. cities. M.S. thesis. Trinity University, 1980.

793. Sterling, Ray and George Meixel. Review of underground heat transfer research. In Conf. proc., Earth Shel. Perf. and Eval., 2nd Nat. Tech. Conf., Tulsa, OK, Oct. 16-17, 1981. Stillwater, OK: Okla. State Univ., Archit. Ext., 1981. p. 67-79.

A review of methods of analysis of heat flow in earth-contact systems is presented, including the status and future program of heat transfer research at the Underground Space Center.

794. Strayer, Richard D. Cost effective solar heated earth structures and earth/air tunnels. In Proc., 4th Nat. Pass. Sol. Conf., Kansas City, MO, Oct. 3-5, 1979. Newark, DE: Int. Sol. Energ. Soc., Am. Sec., 1979. p. 420-4.

This paper discusses ways of attaining cost effective solar heated earth-protected structures which exceed 97 percent energy savings for heating and cooling.

795. Szydlowski, R.F. Analysis of transient heat loss in earth-sheltered structures. M.S. thesis. Ames, IA: Iowa State Univ., 1980.

796. _____ and Thomas H. Kuehn. Analysis of transient heat loss in earth-sheltered structures. Undergr. Sp., v. 5, no. 4, Jan./Feb. 1981: 237-46.

Heat loss in several earth-sheltered structures is found using a computer-generated mathematical model. The computer program is compared with data taken from a monitored conventional residence basement. The model takes into account various kinds of below grade configurations, variable soil properties, and different types, thicknesses, and locations of insulation. Heat gain and loss through the exterior of the building versus location and time of year are given as functions of construction materials, insulation, and soil geometry. The program was used to analyze the thermal impact of varying levels of interior and exterior insulation on conventional basements, earth-bermed walls, and earth-covered structures, but only results for the earth-covered structures are presented in this paper. An economic analysis indicates the cost effectiveness of the insulation levels under consideration.

797. _____. An earth sheltered building research facility at Ames Laboratory. In Conf. proc., Earth Shel. Perf. and Eval., 2nd Nat. Tech Conf., Tulsa, OK, Oct. 16-17, 1981. Stillwater, OK: Okla. State Univ., Archit. Ext., 1981. p. 185-92.

A variable experimental building has been constructed to validate thermal models designed to accommodate numerous earth shelter configurations. Preliminary test facility results are compared to modeled energy performance predictions.

798. _____ and T.H. Kuehn. Transient analysis of heat loss in earth bermed structures. In Proc., 5th Nat. Pass. Sol. Conf., Amherst, MA, Oct. 19-26, 1980. Newark, DE: Int. Sol. Energ. Soc., Am. Sec., 1980.

To obtain more information on the thermal response of earth-bermed structures, a transient two-dimensional model was developed which, because it can accommodate numerous earth-sheltered configurations under various boundary and soil conditions, allows accelerated study of systems which are transient in nature due to their thermal properties.

799. Underground solar heat storage for homes is being facilitated by the use of hollow foundation piles in a Swedish experiment by Hagconsult-AB. (Brief.) Undergr. Sp., v. 6, no. 4-5, Jan./Apr. 1982: 201.

XIII. SITE CONSIDERATIONS

800. Allan, Jerry. Responding to space and creating environments. In Residential applications: transcripts of selected presentations, Going Under to Stay on Top, Minneapolis, MN, Oct. 1977. Minneapolis, MN: Univ. of Minn., Undergr. Sp. Ctr., 1979. p. 43-51.
This paper deals with siting considerations and planning the earth-sheltered house to blend with its environment and to respond to the owner's needs and lifestyle. A worksheet asks questions about wants, problems, space, and functions.

801. Allen, Peter C. Designing the site: design doesn't stop at front door. Earth Shel. Liv., no. 32, Mar./Apr. 1984: 38-9.
In site design, the good and bad qualities of the site should be inventoried as these features dictate the form and orientation of the house. The key to energy efficient design is to design a structure so that the natural features of the site are utilized to best advantage.

802. Anderson, Brent. Determining your thermal strategy: where your house is located can be extremely important to your design and materials selection. Earth Shel. Liv., no. 35, Sept./Oct. 1984: 22-5.

803. _____. Investigating soils. Archit. Minn., v. 6, no. 2, Apr. 1980: 39-41.
To avoid overdesigning an earth-sheltered house and adding to construction costs, a soils analysis should be performed. The various parameters to be analyzed and costs are discussed.

804. _____. Save money--investigate your soils. Earth Shel. Dig. Energ. Rept., no. 8, Mar./Apr. 1980: 15-7.
This is a brief discussion of the weight that different soil types can bear and its relationship to structural design.

805. Baggs, Sydney A. A design aid for assessing the suitability of soils at earth-covered building sites. In Proc., 1st Int. Conf. on Energ. Effic. Bldgs. with Earth Shel. Prot., Sydney, Aust., Aug. 1-6, 1983. L.L. Boyer, ed. Stillwater, OK: Okla. State Univ., Archit. Ext., 1983. p. 323-9.

The soil enveloping an earth-covered building not only functions as a plant support medium but also to damp amplitude in the ground temperature wave and induce a phase shift which correlates with increase in depth below ground surface. The resultant phase lag interval, referred to as "time lag," may be used as a design strategy to improve the energy efficiency of this building type. In considering the suitability of a potential site, it is desirable to determine (preferably from one site visit) what conditions of soil will optimise its thermal capacity as well as its capability of establishing and supporting vigorous plant growth. A diagram is presented to enable designers of earth-covered buildings to conduct an on-site assessment of whether the soil(s) in question will: (a) effectively optimise phase shift in the ground temperature wave; (b) minimise the quantity of introduced water needed to establish and sustain potential plant growth to the roof of a proposed earth-covered building; and (c) require any introduced water at all after the early establishment stage. --Auth. abstract.

806. _____. Ground temperatures assessed. Uniken, Mar. 25/Apr. 7, 1982.

807. _____. A mathematical equation for the prediction of periodic ground temperatures at various depths relevant to the design of earth covered housing. In Proc., Symp. on Des. Strat. for Earth Cov. Bldgs., Kensington, NSW, Aust., 1982. S.A. Baggs, ed. Kensington, NSW, Aust.: Univ. of NSW, Grad. Sch. of the Built. Env., 1982. p. 134-64.

808. _____, J.C. Baggs, and D.W. Baggs. Selecting a site. Geotecture, v. 2, no. 1, Jan. 1985: 39-44.

Attributes of the five typical earth-covered house sites are given.

809. Basic soil considerations for earth-sheltered construction. Concr. Constr., v. 27, no. 6, June 1982: 485-91, 536-41.

This article discusses the composition and classification of soils, the ability of soils to moderate temperature, its bearing capacity, settlement, lateral soil pressure, backfilling, soil swelling, frost action, and soil borings.

810. Brown, G.Z. and Barbara-Jo Novitski. Climate responsive earth-sheltered buildings. Undergr. Sp., v. 5, no. 5, Mar./Apr. 1981: 299-305.

A method is discussed for analyzing climate conditions in terms of architectural response required for thermal comfort. It is found that earth-sheltered buildings can be especially responsive to climate through proper architectural and site treatment.

811. Costello, Michael James. Geologic, hydrologic, and architectural aspects of reclaiming a sand and gravel mine into earth sheltered housing. M.S. thesis. University of Minnesota, 1980. 179 p.

812. _____. Reclaiming minelands for earth-sheltered housing. Undergr. Sp., v. 5, no. 5, Mar./Apr. 1981: 279-86.

By reclaiming sand and gravel mines for earth-sheltered housing developments, costs can be reduced and societal benefits increased. Sites with a southern aspect, well-drained soils, and with short, steep slopes are desirable. A plan is presented for mining a mineral deposit and later reclaiming it for earth sheltered housing. A design is presented for a specific gravel deposit in Lakeville, MN.

813. DeBord, David Douglas and Thomas R. Dunbar. Earth-sheltered landscapes: site considerations for earth-sheltered houses. New York, NY: Van Nostrand Reinhold, 1985. 126 p.

This is a guide to landscape design for earth-sheltered housing. It stresses the identification and use of environmental and design criteria to select the proper site and to adapt sites for existing earth-sheltered buildings. The six chapters discuss vegetation, land, sun and wind, and their effects in different environments, soil type, slope, orientation, plant varieties, zoning, and analyzes the relative energy costs and conserving characteristics of different materials and structures. There are many case studies.

814. Elifrits, C. Dale and Nolan B. Aughenbaugh. Geotechnical aspects of site selection and evaluation for earth sheltered-type housing. In The potential of earth-sheltered and underground space: proc., Undergr. Sp. Conf. and Expos., Kansas City, MO, June 8-10, 1981. T.L. Holthusen, ed. Elmsford, NY: Pergamon Pr., 1981. p. 297-309.

An earth-contact house is influenced more by its geological environment than a conventional house. There is a discussion of the various methods of site selection and evaluation with particular attention given to foundation materials, excavation at the site, accessibility, use of passive solar energy, drainage, seepage, and construction planning. There is a checklist for site comparison and evaluation from a geotechnical standpoint.

815. Hammes, Jeffrey L. Soil mottling: spot water before you build. Earth Shel. Dig. Energ. Rept., no. 13, Jan./Feb. 1981: 20-1.

You can tell if water has saturated soil within the last 50 years if the soil is mottled, i.e. if there are red, yellow, and gray flecks, spots, or streaks in different locations and amounts.

816. Hannula, J.K. Integrating site locational criteria for underground housing. In Earth shelter 2: coll. pap., 1st Earth Shel. Hous. Conf. and Exhib., Minneapolis, MN, Apr. 9-11, 1980. Minneapolis, MN: Univ. of Minn., Undergr. Sp. Ctr., 1980. p. 55-63.

Site location criteria include: orientation, vegetation, soil, depth to bedrock and to water table, weight, and utility factors.

817. Hodgkinson, Allan. Art of construction: groundwater. Archit. J., v. 173, no. 12, Mar. 25, 1981: 557-9.

Design considerations and groundwater problems that may occur during construction are indicated. There is a discussion of site investigation and unpredictability, groundwater basics, effect of water on bearing capacity of the soil, foundation design and construction problems.

818. Hylton, J. Underground-solar house wind-tunnel test. In Proc., Alt. in Habitat: the Use of Earth Cov. Set., Conf., Fort Worth, TX, May 17-19, 1978. F.L. Moreland, ed. Washington, DC: U.S. Dept. of Energy, 1979. v. 1, Earth covered buildings, p. 195-204.

Wind tunnel tests indicate that under prevailing southerly breezes, it would be possible to obtain a naturally cool air flow through the house via air entering the north bedroom windows.

819. Jones, D. Earl. The expansive soil problem. Undergr. Sp., v. 3, no. 5, Mar./Apr. 1979: 221-6.

This article provides a general overview and quantification of the expansive soils problem, because soil expansion is horizontal and vertical beneath structures, resulting in structural damage widespread throughout the U.S.

820. Klepper, M.R. Underground space: an unappraised natural resource: some geologic and hydrologic considerations. In

Underground utilization. T. Stauffer, ed. Kansas City, MO: Univ. of Missouri - Kansas City, Dept. of Geosciences, 1978. v. 1, p. 31-3.

This paper by a geologist briefly outlines some of the characteristics of subspace, the types of interactions between surface and subsurface systems, and impediments to the use of the underground.

821. Kusuda, Tamami. The effect of ground cover on earth temperature. In Proc., Alt. in Energy Conserv.: the Use of Earth Cov. Bldgs., Fort Worth, TX, July 9-12, 1975. F.L. Moreland, ed. Washington, DC: U.S. G.P.O., 1976. p. 279-303.

An earth temperature study was conducted on the grounds of the National Bureau of Standards in a program sponsored by the Office of Civil Defense to improve existing thermal design information relating to the type of surface, solar radiation, and weather conditions. The results showed that the surface temperature becomes lower than the ambient air temperature during clear summer nights except for a black asphalt surface; the temperature in the earth is affected by the nature of the ground surface; the diurnal temperature wave did not penetrate beyond the two-foot depth, but the annual wave penetrated to the 30-foot depth.

822. Labs, Kenneth. Exploitation of ground climate for energy efficient building design. In Proc., 3rd Int. Conf. on Alt. Energy Sources, Miami Beach, FL, Dec. 1980. Washington, DC: Hemisphere Pub. Corp., 1983. p. 19-37.

Earth sheltering as it relates to climate control strategies is explored. A method of weather data analysis is shown as are the results of analysis of four U.S. cities. A model for predicting ground temperature at any depth or over any profile range is presented. Tables showing the ground temperature of those four cities are also included to give a complementary view of the climate above and below ground.

823. _____. Living up to underground design. Sol. Age, v. 7, no. 8, Aug. 1982: 34-8.

This article considers the effect of climate on the design of earth-sheltered homes. Climate control strategies are discussed in relation to conduction, convection, radiation, and evaporation for both summer and winter applications. Applications of earth-sheltered design are discussed for three areas of the country: southeastern areas with high humidity and limited heating demand; southwestern regions with dry climate but high ground temperatures; northern regions where heating and heat conservation are most important.

824. _____. Planning for underground housing. In Underground utilization. T. Stauffer, ed. Kansas City, MO: Univ. of Missouri - Kansas City, Dept. of Geosciences, 1978. v. 4, p. 553-61.

This article examines site-planning issues in the design of terratectural housing and the planning which may be needed to facilitate and encourage underground design.

825. _____. Regional analysis of ground and above-ground climate. Undergr. Sp., v. 6, no. 6, May/June 1982: 397-422.

This report won the 1981 AUA Design Competition research award. Pt. 1, Regional suitability of earth-tempering practices, and Pt. 2, Bioclimatic data, are presented here. It was found that the regional suitability of subsurface construction as a climate control technique varies geographically. While the subsurface by itself almost always provides a thermal advantage, it can compromise the effectiveness of other climate control techniques. This report also contains reviews of above and below-ground climate mapping schemes related to human comfort and architectural design and a detailed description of a theoretical model of ground temperature, heat flow, and heat storage in the ground. Passive climate control strategies are presented in a discussion of the building bioclimatic analysis procedure which has been used in a computer analysis of 30 years of weather data for each of 29 locations in the United States.

826. _____. Regional analysis of ground and above-ground climate. Conclusion. (Pt. 3). Undergr. Sp., v. 7, no. 1, July/Aug. 1982: 37-65.

This article surveys the state of the art of describing climate zones for building design and reviews the literature of ground climate related to design. The discussion focuses on climatography and architecture, the data base for ground climatography, and heat transfer in soil.

827. _____. The underground advantage: climate of soils. In Proc., 4th Nat. Pass. Sol. Conf., Kansas City, MO, Oct. 3-5, 1979. G. Franta, ed. Newark, DE: Int. Sol. Energ. Soc., Am. Sec., 1979. Also in Passive solar: subdivisions, windows, underground. Ed. by H. Wade and others. Kansas City, MO: Am. Sol. Energ. Soc., Kansas City Chap., 1983. p. 171-97.

This is a review of the fundamentals of soil climate as presented in a selected group of 64 references to be used in the design of underground structures, earth pipes, etc., the performance of which is affected by the thermal environment of soils.

828. Lane, Charles A. When designing, consider the local climate. Pt. 1. Earth Shel. Liv., no. 35, Sept./Oct. 1984: 10-2; Pt. 2. Ibid., no. 36, Nov./Dec. 1984: 22-5.

This work attempts to describe the local climatic factors designers should consider when assessing the optimum earth-sheltered design for a given climate. Examples of five U.S. cities are used: St. Paul, MN; Seattle, WA; Indianapolis, IN; Atlanta, GA; and Phoenix, AZ.

829. Langley, John B. and Michel R. Elias. A graphic means of selecting the required average depth of earth shelter coverage. In Passive cooling: proc. of the Int. Pass. and Hybr. Cool. Conf., Miami Beach, FL, Nov. 6-16, 1981. Newark, DE: Int. Sol Energ. Soc., Am. Sec., 1981. p. 156-60.

This paper describes a graphic mathematical procedure for developing an annual subsoil temperature curve from N.O.A.A.-published air temperature data adjusted by short-term graphic analysis of site specific data.

830. Lesiuk, Stephen and Paul Pholeros. Soil stratification techniques for underground buildings. In Proc., 1st Int. Conf. on Energ. Effic. Bldgs. with Earth Shel. Prot., Sydney, Aust., Aug. 1-6, 1983. L.L. Boyer, ed. Stillwater, OK: Okla. State Univ., Archit. Ext., 1983. p. 83-7.

The soil media surrounding an earth-sheltered structure can be broadly divided into continuous, or homogeneous profiles and discontinuous, or heterogeneous profiles. The flux of heat, both into and emanating from earth-sheltered buildings, can be markedly altered and the energy regime controlled by employing stratified soil conditions with different thermal and moisture-retention characteristics to produce total soil profiles. A variety of discontinuous soil profiles are experimentally examined in different combinations with the results being compared with homogeneous soil profiles. --Auth. abstract.

831. Lytton, Robert. Soil and water considerations. In Proc., Alt. in Energ. Conserv.: the Use of Earth Cov. Set. Conf., Fort Worth, TX, July 9-12, 1975. F.L. Moreland, ed. Washington, DC: U.S. G.P.O., 1976. p. 257-62.

The ideal geotechnical conditions for earth-covered and below-grade buildings are: diggable soils, flat slopes, bedrock below soils, seismically quiet, low water table, arable land. Appendices give methods of measuring diggability of soils and some brief admonitions.

832. Mini fact: soil testing. Earth Shel. Dig. Energ. Rept., no. 18, Nov./Dec. 1981: 21.

Soil borings when tested can indicate a site's bearing capacity, lateral pressure, water table, and swell potential.

833. Salomone, Lawrence A. Procedures used to predict the thermal behavior of soils. In Proc., 1st Int. Conf. on Energ. Effic. Bldgs. with Earth Shel. Prot., Sydney, Aust., Aug. 1-6, 1983. L.L. Boyer, ed. Stillwater, OK: Okla. State Univ., Archit. Ext., 1983. p. 49-53.

The thermal conductivity of soils can vary in time and space because of changes in moisture content, density and/or soil type. Nevertheless, a majority of existing computer models of the energy exchange between earth-contact structures and the surrounding soil do not account for the variation in soil thermal conductivity. Constant values of soil thermal properties are often used in these computer models. To achieve better agreement between measured temperature fields and heat fluxes and those predicted by computer models, incorporation of the variation in soil thermal conductivity into the computer models will be necessary. The Geotechnical Engineering Group at the National Bureau of Standards is studying the thermal behavior of soils to understand better the soil characteristics which affect soil thermal behavior and to develop low cost, simple tests for assessing the thermal conductivity of soils. This paper discusses the factors that were found to affect significantly the thermal resistivity (the reciprocal of thermal conductivity) of soils and presents an approach for establishing the values of soil thermal resistivity to be used when evaluating the energy exchange between earth-contact structures and the surrounding soil. --Auth. abstract.

834. Shick, Wayne L. Proper building orientation can save you energy. Earth Shel. Dig. Energ. Rept., no. 2, Mar./Apr. 1979: 38-9.

A home with property shading, superinsulation, and with south orientation of windows will have the least energy need for heating and cooling.

835. Site soil stability: points to consider before selecting a site for geotecture. Geotecture, v. 1, no. 3, Apr. 1984: 19-23.

Earth movements are defined in relation to the altered environment of an earth-sheltered site.

836. Slater, Donald E. Expansive soils: how they affect earth shelters. Earth Shel. Liv., no. 34, July/Aug. 1984: 4-5.

When designing homes to deal with expansive soil problems, special attention should be given to foundation design, soil treatment, and moisture treatment.

837. _____. Soils affect design. Earth Shel. Liv., no. 20, Mar./
Apr. 1982: 57.
A brief article on analyzing soils to find those most suitable for earth-sheltered construction.

838. _____. Why water is such a problem: understanding the ways of water now may help you avoid problems later. Earth Shel. Liv., no. 33, May/June 1984: 16-8.
Describes the action of groundwater in relation to an earth-sheltered structure.

839. Sterling, Ray. Site considerations for earth-sheltered structures. Concr. Constr., v. 25, no. 9, Sept. 1980: 653-7.
This article is excerpted from the first chapter of Earth Sheltered Housing Design by the author. Site considerations are topography, soil and groundwater conditions, lot size, and location of adjacent structures. The grouping of window and door openings and the direction which they face can be referred to as the orientation of the structure on the site. Determinants of orientation are sun, wind, and outside views. Proper orientation can produce significant energy savings.

840. Study assesses earth sheltered potential for different climates. Underline, v. 3, no. 3, Mar./Apr. 1982: 1-2, 4.
The study Regional analysis of ground and above-ground climate by Kenneth Labs for the DOE's Innovative Structures Program, is a 237 p. report providing data on estimated ground temperatures in many U.S. regions. It offers tentative conclusions about the suitability of earth sheltering from an energy conservation standpoint for various climatic regions.

841. Study examines regional suitability of earth-sheltering. Undergr. Sp., v. 6, no. 2, Sept./Oct. 1981: 78-81.
The Regional analysis of ground and above-ground climate by K. Labs attempts to synthesize ground temperature from atmospheric data.

842. Thorsen, G.W. and R.L. Rue. High bank instead of high rise. In Earth shelter 2: coll. pap., 1st Earth Shel. Hous. Conf. and Exhib., Minneapolis, MN, Apr. 9-11, 1980.
Minneapolis, MN: Univ. of Minn., Undergr. Sp. Ctr., 1980.
An alternative is proposed for conventional residential development on steep slopes. The special features of the residential complex discussed are: utilization of slopes of 35 degrees or greater; earth sheltering of the building; standardization of the units.

843. Undercurrent Design Research, New Haven, CT. <u>Regional analysis of ground and above-ground climate.</u> Oak Ridge, TN: Oak Ridge Nat. Lab., Dec. 1981. 199 p. (NTIS, PC E08/MF A01).
Report prepared under Contract W-7405-ENG-26. The applicability of underground construction as a climate control technique is examined with regard to: a bioclimatic analysis of long-term weather data for 29 locations in the U.S. to determine appropriate above-ground climate control techniques; a data base of synthesized ground temperatures for the coterminous U.S.; and monthly dew-point ground temperature comparisons for identifying the relative likelihood of condensation from one region to another. It was found that the applicability of earth tempering varies geographically; but the subsurface almost always provides a thermal advantage when compared to above-ground climatic data.

844. White, Bret Milford. A guide to soil investigation and analysis for earth-sheltered buildings. In <u>Australian proc., 1st Int. Conf. on Energ. Effic. Bldgs. with Earth Shel. Prot.</u>, Sydney, Aust., Aug. 1-6, 1983. S.A. Baggs, ed. Kensington, NSW, Aust.: Unisearch, Ltd., 1983.
A guide to soil investigation and analysis for earth-covered housing. The techniques of soil analysis are examined and their implications to design an earth-sheltered building on a domestic scale. Relevant soil investigations and tests available are discussed and appropriate design implications are analyzed. It was found that the microenvironment of soil imposes certain constraints on the design of an earth-covered building. It is imperative that the soil be investigated and tested to ascertain these constraints. --Auth. abstract.

845. Wuelpern, Thomas D. Undisturbed ground climate of the USA: implications for earth sheltered buildings. <u>Earth Shel. Bldgs. -- Tech. Pap.</u>, TP-IIIM, 1983.

XIV. LANDSCAPING

846. Appleton, Bonnie L., Landscaping for earth shelters. <u>Earth Shel. Liv.</u>, no. 37, Jan./Feb. 1985: 7-8.
Landscaping problems include: is soil depth adequate to accept vegetation, and will it retain adequate moisture; what plants will be suitable; how can vegetation hide structural outcroppings from the house such as antennas, chimneys, vents, etc.

847. Baggs, David W. Earth-covered buildings: the true landscaped architecture. <u>Landscape</u>, Autumn 1983: 3-9.

848. Baggs, Sydney A. Effects of vegetation on earth cooling potential. In <u>Conf. proc., Earth Shel. Perf. and Eval.</u>, 2nd Nat. Tech. Conf., Tulsa, OK, Oct. 16-17, 1981. Stillwater, OK: Okla. State Univ., Archit. Ext., 1981. p. 81-90.
   The effect of moisture content, vegetation shading, evapotranspiration effects, etc. on the annual range of soil climate temperatures is presented by a simple ground-temperature equation which has been modified for Australian conditions.

849. _____. Landscape considerations in the energy-effectiveness design of roof gardens for earth-covered buildings. In <u>Australian proc., 1st Int. Conf. on Energ. Effic. Bldgs. with Earth Shel. Prot.</u>, Sydney, Aust., Aug. 1-6, 1983. S.A. Baggs, ed. Kensington, NSW, Aust.: Unisearch, Ltd., 1983. p. C21-31.
   Landscape visual quality and the thermal energy-efficiency of an earth-covered building are often jeopardised by the incorrect installation and maintenance of its roof garden. Procedures are given to ensure the establishment and continuity of growth of plants to such a garden and guidelines are suggested for the analysis and correction of problems in plant growth to roof gardens. --Auth. abstract.

850. Friedberg, M. Paul. Roofscape. <u>Archit. Eng.</u>, Sept. 1969.
   This article details the problems encountered when landscaping roofs.

851. Garcia-Chavez, Jose R. and Marshall Thomas. Vegetation for earth-sheltered buildings: the use of plants as roof cover to provide passive cooling in hot arid climates. <u>Earth Shel. Bldgs. -- Tech. Pa.</u>, TP-IID, 1983.

852. Garland, Steven R. Designing irrigation systems on and around earth-sheltered buildings. In <u>Australian proc., 1st Int. Conf. on Energ. Effic. Bldgs. with Earth Shel. Prot.</u>, Sydney, Aust., Aug. 1-6, 1983. S.A. Baggs, ed. Kensington, NSW, Aust.: Unisearch, Ltd., 1983. p. C32-38.
   The problems and establishment of irrigation system requirements are analysed. The limitations of climate, site, soil, and desired plant material are discussed. Appropriate systems for variable situations are given. Indications are that an automatic trickle irrigation system with temporal control and climatic feedback circuits can provide a cheap, durable, and reliable solution to most of the problems of irrigation on, and around, earth-sheltered buildings. --Auth. abstract.

853. Gordon, Ann. Plantings provide landscaping harmony. Earth Shel. Dig. Energ. Rept., no. 9, May/June 1980: 10-11.
This article is excerpted from a paper the author presented at the Earth-Sheltered Building Design Innovations Conference.

854. _____. Rooftop plantings for earth covered buildings in temperate climates. In Proc., Earth Shel. Bldg. Des. Innov., Oklahoma City, OK, Apr. 18, 1980. L.L. Boyer, ed. Stillwater, OK: Okla. State Univ., 1980. p. III. 13-16.
This paper discusses the design of rooftop plantings, the types of plants to be used and the management of a roofscape. Some uses to be made of the area are suggested.

855. Gray, Donald H. Living walls retain steep slopes. Earth Shel. Liv., no. 20, Mar./Apr. 1982: 4-7.
Plants and structural grids stabilize slopes by controlling erosion.

856. Hagstrom, Jim V. Landscape architecture. Earth Shel. Dig. Energ. Rept., no. 1, Jan./Feb. 1979: 32.
This article defines landscape architecture, tries to correct some misconceptions, and discusses the role of the landscape architect.

857. Kis, Babette. Grow native prairie plants. Earth Shel. Dig. Energ. Rept., no. 9, May/June 1980: 12.
Instead of a lawn on the roof, the author suggests using plants suited to dry areas.

858. Kramer, Ann. A woman's viewpoint. Earth Shel. Liv., no. 20, Mar./Apr. 1982: 48-9.
Factors to keep in mind when you're planning the landscaping of your earth-sheltered home are discussed. Names several ground covers which can be used on slopes and roof covers.

859. Lesiuk, Stephen. Landscaping for energy conservation. In Australian proc., 1st Int. Conf. on Energ. Effic. Bldgs. with Earth Shel. Prot., Sydney, Aust., Aug. 1-6, 1983. S.A. Baggs, ed. Kensington, NSW, Aust.: Unisearch, Ltd., 1983. p. C45-50a.
Vegetation can alter the energy requirements of buildings (both in summer and winter) by modifying the solar regime at the building or ground surface and modifying the energy balance of the building system. In both instances, the degree and extent of modification is dependent upon canopy influences, i.e. the morphological and physiological characteristics of the plant canopy. This paper initially establishes the state of the

art then reviews a theoretical and experimental analysis of the impact of vegetation on building energetics, with particular reference to earth-covered buildings. --Auth. abstract.

860. Lu, John C.M. Soil makeup and related plant growth for roofs of earth-sheltered buildings. Earth Shel. Bldgs. -- Tech. Pap., TP-IIIF.

861. Otto, Lorrie. Healing with a natural yard. Earth Shel. Dig. Energ. Rept., no. 9, May/June 1980: 12-3.
 This article suggests landscaping with a wide variety of wild native plants. This reduces or eliminates the need for fertilizers and chemicals for insect and plant control.

862. Precast blocks form flexible walls. Earth Shel. Liv., no. 20, Mar./Apr. 1982: 6-7.
 A precast concrete block invented by a German landscape architect, called "Loffelstein," has a concave surface on top which can be filled with dirt and planted with vegetation.

863. Schiler, Marc. Landscape for energy efficiency. Earth Shel. Liv., no. 20, Mar./Apr. 1982: 45-7.
 The author discusses the landscaping strategies appropriate for earth sheltered and energy-efficient housing for solar control and wind deflection.

864. Weiss, Piera Millicent Antonia. Landscape design and underground houses: an examination of underground houses to determine issues that affect and influence landscape design. M.L.A. thesis. Cornell Univ., Jan. 1980. 117 p.

865. Wimble, E. Douglas. The need for embankment and berm stabilization in the construction and landscape establishment of erosion control vegetation for earth-covered buildings. In Australian proc., 1st Int. Conf. on Energ. Effic. Bldgs. with Earth Shel. Prot., Sydney, Aust., Aug. 1-6, 1983. S.A. Baggs, ed. Kensington, NSW, Aust.: Unisearch, Ltd., 1983. p. C63-66. Also in Geotecture, v. 1, no. 3, Apr. 1984: 16-8.
 In many developments where civil earthworks are concerned as in large earth-covered building projects, proper erosion control measures are often ignored due to cost. Though the need for such procedures is obvious, it is generally at the end of the project that somebody realizes the need for erosion control. By that time, it is too late to change what is already done and such measures must be tailored to the finished job

instead of being part of the initial plan. Many considerations must be examined at the planning stage to ensure the success of the job. The type of soil to be used must be tested and analyzed, planning of slope areas and topography, climatic conditions carefully considered, and the appropriate seed and fertilizer chosen before the final specification can be written. This paper will outline a particular approach to this type of project, inclusive of the methods of seeding to be used for erosion control measures on the project. --Auth. abstract.

866. Wirth, Thomas E. Landscape architecture above buildings. Undergr. Sp., v. 1, no. 4, Aug. 1977: 333-46.
This article discusses the structure, waterproofing, planting materials, mechanical systems, cost and coordination which influence the landscaping of rooftops. Some examples of large, urban commercial buildings are presented.

867. Wylie, Jim. Gardening in earth shelters. Earth Shel. Liv., no. 27, May/June 1983: 28-30.

XV. COSTS/ECONOMICS

868. Behr, Richard A. and Ernst W. Kiesling. Economics of shell structures for earth sheltered buildings. In Proc., 1st Int. Conf. on Energ. Effic. Bldgs. with Earth Shel. Prot., Sydney, Aust., Aug. 1-6, 1983. L.L. Boyer, ed. Stillwater, OK: Okla. State Univ., Archit. Ext., 1983. p. 353-6.
Construction costs of thin shell barrel arches and domes are compared with those of more commonly used flat roof concepts. Despite the innovative nature of thin shell concrete construction, the structural shell costs per unit of net living area for curvilinear shell structures are found to be very competitive with those of a more conventional flat roof structural system commonly used for earth-sheltered housing. --Auth. abstract.

869. _____. Life cycle costs evaluation of flat site earth shelter design. In Conf. proc., Earth Shel. Perf. and Eval., 2nd Nat. Tech. Conf., Tulsa, OK, Oct. 16-17, 1981. Stillwater, OK: Okla. State Univ., Archit. Ext., 1981. p. 285-96.
A flat site earth-shelter design developed for HUD is compared with a similar conventional house on a life cycle cost analysis basis. Construction cost and energy performance estimates are studied.

870. Bligh, T.P. Low cost multiple earth-sheltered housing. Am. Undergr. Space Assn., Annu. Mtg., Minneapolis, MN, April 1980.

871. Boubel, Gary A. Life cycle cost analysis for earth sheltered houses. M.S. thesis. Lubbock, TX: Texas Tech Univ., Civil Engineering Dept., May 1980.

872. Bregg, Gary. Cost overruns analyzed by do-it-yourselfers. Earth Shel. Liv., no. 23, Sept./Oct. 1982: 42-5.
Several mistakes during construction led to lost time and cost overruns turning an estimated nine-month job to cost $30,000 into a three-year job costing $125,000.

873. Bressler, Gary. Builder was forced up. Earth Shel. Dig. Energ. Rept., no. 2, Mar./Apr. 1979: 14-5.
Builder had to make changes including uncovering the roof to bring down costs and obtain adequate financing.

874. Brown, James J. and Terry A. Johnson. The step by step cost estimation guide for earth shelter construction. Portsmouth, OH: Underground Homes, 1980. 24 p.
This guide is intended for use by designers and builders. Materials and services needed for earth-sheltered construction are listed.

875. Buying an existing earth-sheltered home. Moth. Earth N., no. 83, Sept./Oct. 1983: 84-5.
This is a chapter excerpted from The consumer's guide to earth sheltered housing by Mary Rollwagen, Susan Taylor, and T.L. Holthusen. It tells what to look for when inspecting earth-sheltered homes: structural soundness and waterproofing, interior signs of leakage, exterior signs of leakage, condition of heating and cooling systems, compliance with building codes, and questioning the current owner. It lists NAMIC conditions for insuring an earth-sheltered home.

876. De Courcy Hinds, Michael. The economics of building down. N.Y. Times, Mar. 22, 1979.

877. Earth shelters for low and mid-incomes. Earth Shel. Liv., no. 30, Nov./Dec. 1983: 18-9.
A plan to make earth-sheltered developments financially available to low and middle-income buyers entails a bond issue.

878. Emery, A.F., D.R. Heerwagen, C.J. Kippenhan, and B.R. Johnson. Conventional versus earth-sheltered housing: a

comparative study of construction and operating costs for three cities. In Conf. proc., Earth Shel. Perf. and Eval., 2nd Nat. Tech. Conf., Tulsa, OK, Oct. 16-17, 1981. Stillwater, OK: Okla. State Univ., Archit. Ext., 1981. p. 163-74.

Annual cooling and heating requirements for similar houses in Seattle, Minneapolis, and Amarillo are calculated with computer simulations. Total cost-effective comparisons are then developed, including total construction cost and long-term operating expenses.

879. Feisel, Lyle L. Economic and design considerations for an underground house. Rapid City, SD: South Dakota School of Mines and Technology, Div. of Eng., 1979. 32 p.

A report submitted to the South Dakota Housing Development Authority.

880. Guy, Homer L. Economic comparison of passively conditioned underground houses. Master's thesis. Oklahoma State Univ., Stillwater. Wright-Patterson AFB, OH: A.F. Inst. of Tech., May 1981. 143 p. (NTIS PC A07/MF A01).

Underground housing types are compared based on the premise that using average climatic conditions of temperature and insulation and average conditions of usage and habitation, each of the underground types would be designed to provide thermal conditions in the statistical comfort range. Appendices contain the calculations for thermal comfort for each underground type and a comparison of the cost to provide equivalent thermal comfort based on a 20-year life cycle with all costs paid at the beginning of the life cycle.

881. Harrison, Lloyd, Jr. Is it time to go underground? Nav. Civ. Engr., v. 14, no. 3, Fall 1973: 28-9.

This article discusses the non-economic and economic factors to be considered when reviewing an underground house proposal.

882. Homeowners save lettuce by living under the grass. Moneysworth, v. 10, July 1980: 8.

883. Lane, Charles A. Report amounts to "statistical witchcraft." Earth Shel. Liv., no. 34, July/Aug. 1984: 2-3.

The author disagrees with an Oak Ridge Nat. Lab. report which concluded that earth-covered homes cost more to build than above-ground homes, and that the additional cost would not be repaid by energy savings over the life of a 30-year mortgage. The study's research methods are questioned.

884. Langley, John B. Earth shelter income: use your earth shelter to educate the public and to make the mortgage payments. Earth Shel. Liv., no. 36, Nov./Dec. 1984: 13-5.

885. Lunde, Martin R. Thermal and covered roof costs compared. Earth Shel. Dig. Energ. Rept., no. 18, Nov./Dec. 1981: 18-20.
Actual construction costs of earth-covered/earth-bermed houses are compared with earth-bermed/thermal-roofed houses.

886. Machowski, Barb. Builders report healthy spec market. Earth Shel. Dig. Energ. Rept., no. 17, Sept./Oct. 1981: 15-7.
The earth-sheltered spec homes sold relatively well in all price ranges during the recession in comparison with conventional homes.

887. McWilliams, Donald B. and Stephen M. Findley. A life cycle cost comparison between a conventional and an earth-covered home. In Alt. in Habitat: the Use of Earth Cov. Set., Conf., Fort Worth, TX, May 17-19, 1978. F.L. Moreland, ed. Washington, DC: U.S. Dept. of Energy, 1979. v. 2, Earth covered buildings and settlements, p. 94-107.
The comparison was made to see if the energy and maintenance savings of underground housing are enough to justify the higher initial cost. All other costs are assumed to be the same. It is found that home buyers interested in a long-term payoff will find the earth-sheltered home has an economic advantage. But many buyers are more interested in short-term marketability.

888. Meyer, William T. Energy economics and building design. New York, NY: McGraw-Hill, 1983. 341 p.
Chapter 9, Heating and cooling savings with the thermal mass, presents methods for estimating yearly energy savings when an earth covering is part of the design approach.

889. Roy, R.L. Owner-builder and the underground: building a low-cost home. In Earth shelter 2: coll. pap., 1st Earth Shel. Hous. Conf. and Exhib., Minneapolis, MN, Apr. 9-11, 1980. Minneapolis, MN: Univ. of Minn., Undergr. Sp. Ctr., 1980. p. 64-71.
The author dispels myths about the lack of proven technology and the high cost of earth-sheltered structures.

890. Schmitt, Greg and Ron Eikens. Appraisal concepts include solar. Earth Shel. Liv., no. 23, Sept./Oct. 1982: 46.

Briefly discusses the steps in appraising the value of an earth-sheltered home using the "present value" method and the "capitalization" method.

891. Secrist, Don. Economics of homes that are in-ground passive solar vs. above-ground all-electric vs. above-ground active solar. In Solar diversification: proc., Int. Sol. Energ. Soc., Am. Sec., Annu. Mtg., Denver, CO, Aug. 28, 1978. Newark, DE: ISES, 1978. v. 2, p. 238-44.

Studies of a solar-earth home in Columbus, OH, and several other solar-earth homes showed that a 2,038 sq. ft. home can be heated in Columbus for about one cord of wood and can be cooled and humidity controlled for the cost of running a 1/6 h.p. fan part time. There is an active solar hot water system, and the maintenance and insurance costs are also reduced resulting in a total savings amounting to 22 percent of the mortgage on an above-ground electric home of equal quality.

892. Selling earth sheltered homes. In Earth shelter 2: coll. pap., 1st Earth Shel. Hous. Conf. and Exhib., Minneapolis, MN, Apr. 9-11, 1980. Minneapolis, MN: Univ. of Minn., Undergr. Sp. Ctr., 1980. p. 187-88.

This paper describes efforts to market 12 earth-covered townhouses in Minnesota. Their special features are discussed.

893. Shapira, Hanna B., George A. Christy, Steve E. Brite, and Michael B. Yost. Cost and energy comparison study of above and below-ground dwellings. Undergr. Sp., v. 7, no. 6, May/June 1983: 362-71.

This paper is based on an initial-cost vs. operating-cost study of earth sheltered and conventional above-grade houses in five cities in different regions of the U.S.: Minneapolis/St. Paul, Boston, Salt Lake City, Knoxville, and Houston. It is concluded that above-ground and earth-sheltered houses of the same size and quality built on equal lots will not cost the same. The construction cost of the earth-sheltered house is more than that of the surface structure.

894. Solomon, Nancy. Are earth shelters going under? Sci. Dig., v. 92, no. 10, Oct. 1984: 32.

Although there are about 6,000 earth-sheltered houses in the U.S. today, a recent report by the Oak Ridge National Laboratory states that earth-sheltered homes are not cost effective. Using computer models and 1981 figures, life-cycle costs were analyzed for well-insulated, above-ground homes and below-ground designs over a 30-year period. Focusing mainly on energy performance, the above-ground house was found to be more cost effective. Other positive factors such as noise reduction, land preservation, and hazard protection were not taken into account.

895. Sterling, Raymond L. and J. Carmody. The future potential of earth-sheltered structures: cost, acceptability and planning considerations. In Proc., 3rd Int. Conf. on Alt. Energ. Sources, Miami Beach, FL, Dec. 1980. Washington, DC: Hemisphere Pub. Corp., 1983. v. 7, p. 3-18.

The authors believe the greatest construction potential is in earth-sheltered developments which can replicate homes and thereby cut costs.

896. Study shows lower energy and construction costs from earth-sheltering. Undergr. Sp., v. 5, no. 4, Jan./Feb. 1981: 197-8.

Using computer models, a U.S. Navy study found construction costs for half and fully-bermed structures were less than those for above-ground buildings. The study confirmed that such structures have reduced heating and cooling loads.

897. Vadnais, Kathleen. "Affordable housing" costs industry changes. Earth Shel. Liv., no. 22, July/Aug. 1982: 11-4.

The need for low-cost housing is leading to houses that are more compact and efficient and in many cases attached to other houses.

898. Woodrum, Dave. Earth cover expense is balanced. Earth Shel. Liv., no. 24, Nov./Dec. 1982: 10-1, 17.

The author tells how he brought down the cost of the earth-sheltered roofs he constructed to a finish cost of from $29.50/sq. ft. to $33.25/sq. ft. providing customers with a balance of initial cost, energy efficiency, and custom design achieving a roof that costs only 10-15 percent more than the roof of a conventional house.

XVI. INDOOR ENVIRONMENT/ INTERIOR DESIGN

899. Bennett, David J. and David A. Eijadi. Solar optics: light as energy, energy as light. Undergr. Sp., v. 4, no. 6, May/June 1980: 349-354.

Solar optics is a technique for illuminating interior spaces with natural light. It uses a heliostat to track the sun and lenses and mirrors to direct the light to remote interior spaces. It is more efficient than converting solar radiation into electricity. It offers energy savings by transmitting light through a small aperture instead of through a large window.

900. Boyer, Lester L., Walter T. Grondzik, and T.L. Johnston. Comfort analysis of earth shelter interiors. In Conf. proc., Earth Shel. Perf. and Eval., 2nd Nat. Tech. Conf., Tulsa, OK, Oct. 16-17, 1981. Stillwater, OK: Okla. State Univ., Archit. Ext., 1981. p. 205-216.
A procedure is presented for analyzing spatial, thermal, lighting, and acoustic habitability parameters in earth shelters. Simplified design index charts are used.

901. _____ and _____. Comfort assessment in earth-covered dwellings. In Proc., 1st Int. Conf. on Energ. Effic. Bldgs. with Earth Shel. Prot., Sydney, Aust., Aug. 1-6, 1983. L.L. Boyer, ed. Stillwater, OK: Okla. State Univ., Archit. Ext., 1983. p. 245-249.
The recent worldwide interest in earth-sheltered buildings has tended to focus on energy concerns, while occupant comfort benefits have often been overlooked or misconstrued. In fact, a host of traditional habitation parameters should be re-examined for this unconventional housing context to more fully understand overall occupant satisfaction. In order to obtain an effective solution with respect to comfort and energy, a sensitive systems design approach is essential. Key energy design parameters include effective thermal mass, earth-contact potential, interiors and spatial design impacts, and systems coordination considerations among others. For example, items as diverse as insulation, wall finishes, waterproofing, and room locations may all have an impact on earth-cooling potential and thermal storage optimization. With regard to occupant satisfaction, the personal discomfort typically associated with many conservation schemes need not be associated with earth-sheltered designs, which in many cases represent exemplary contemporary habitats. —Auth. abstract.

902. _____. Daylighting designs presented. Earth Shel. Dig. Energ. Rept., no. 18, Nov./Dec. 1981: 13-5.
This article presents some problems and design solutions for improving daylighting in earth-sheltered structures.

903. _____ and Timothy L. Johnston. Organization of interior spaces for earth cooling. In Passive cooling: proc., Int. Pass. and Hybr. Cool. Conf., Miami Beach, FL, Nov. 6-16, 1981. Newark, DE: Int. Sol. Energ. Soc., Am. Sec., 1981. p. 121-5.

This paper presents some of the results of a research project at Oklahoma State University to develop technical design data for earth-shelter interior engineering.

904. _____. Subterranean designs need daylighting. Earth Shel. Dig. Energ. Rept., no. 4, July/Aug. 1979: 32-4.

905. Clark, Rod. Conceptual solution to three nagging code problems. Earth Shel. Dig. Energ. Rept., no. 6, Nov./Dec. 1979: 40-2.
The author proposes an energy well design to solve the problem of windowless interior rooms which combines a solution to code problems, energy gains, and cost effectiveness. A slit, two and a half to three feet wide, runs the entire length of the back part of the house to admit light and heat and permit ventilation.

906. Collins, J.B. and C.G.H. Plant. Preferred luminance distribution in windowless spaces. Light. Res. Tech., v. 3, 1970: 174-85.

907. Dalton, Ann P. Colors, texture add up to spaciousness, comfort. Earth Shel. Liv., no. 39, May/June 1985: 4-6.
The author decorated the interior of an earth-sheltered house.

908. Duffy, Brian J. Infiltration rates and indoor air quality of earth sheltered buildings. Earth Shel. Bldgs. -- Tech. Pap., TP-IIC, 1983.

909. Kearney, Robert P. Preventing the subterranean home blues. Undergr. Sp., v. 6, no. 3, Nov./Dec. 1981: 171-3.
An ersatz natural environment is not necessary in an underground home. Through the use of color and light an unoppressive atmosphere can be created.

910. Langfeldt, Steffen. Life in a 20th century cave. Res. Int., no. 3, Jan. 1978: 70-1.
An underground recreation area was designed and built as an experiment. It is an extension to an existing surface dwelling. Features include an advanced system of climate control, a pool and beach, exercising equipment and game equipment, refreshment area, sauna and shower and sun lamp, underfloor heating, special lighting system to simulate natural daylight.

911. Machowski, Barb. Sunlight piped underground. Earth Shel. Liv., no. 21, May/June 1981: 47-8.

Maurice Daniel is a Washington, DC, inventor/physicist whose lighting system collects sunlight and transmits it along fiber-optic wires to a special fabric on a room's ceiling which emits a soft, uniform light.

912. McKown, Cora and Evelyn Davis. Interior design of earth shelters - high market impact. In Proc., 1st Int. Conf. on Energ. Effic. Bldgs. with Earth Shel. Prot., Sydney, Aust., Aug. 1-6, 1983. L.L. Boyer, ed. Stillwater, OK: Okla. State Univ., Archit. Ext., 1983. p. 251-4.

Discusses the importance of interior design and decoration when marketing an earth-sheltered home.

913. Mink, John Woodward. The potential of utilizing beamed daylighting in earth-sheltered housing design. Earth Shel. Bldgs. -- Tech. Pap., TP-IIF, 1983.

914. Raetzman, Ron and Menelaos Triantafillou. Need for an interdisciplinary approach to the design of earth-sheltered environments: the role of the interior designer. In The potential of earth-sheltered and underground space: proc., Undergr. Sp. Conf. and Expos., Kansas City, MO, June 8-10, 1981. T.L. Holthusen, ed. Elmsford, NY: Pergamon Pr., 1981. p. 179-85.

The increased livability of earth-sheltered housing will lead to its greater acceptance by the public. For this reason interior designers are challenged and need to participate in all design-planning decisions.

915. Simmons, John D. and Martin A. Davis. Light distribution in below-grade houses. Am. Soc. of Agric. Eng., Annu. Mtg., Orlando, FL, June 21-24, 1981.

The amount of natural light in four different types of earth-sheltered houses is discussed. Studies are presented on the effect of design on the levels of natural light.

916. _____, J.O. Newman, L.C. Godbey, and M.A. Davis. Light distribution in three earth-embanked houses. In Proc., Earth Shel. Bldg. Des. Innov., Nat. Tech. Conf., Oklahoma City, OK, Apr. 18, 1980. L.L. Boyer, ed. Stillwater, OK: Okla. State Univ., 1980. p. VI. 11-7.

Three earth-covered houses with southern exposure were studied to determine the amount and distribution of natural light throughout. Results showed that the house designed for maximum energy conservation did not meet the standards set for sufficient natural light. The second house was in partial compliance, and the third house, built last, met or even exceeded the standards for natural light in all rooms.

917. Thomas, Craig R. Preventing condensation problems in earth-sheltered buildings. Earth Shel. Bldgs. -- Tech. Pap., TP-IIIJ, 1983.

918. Vadnais, Kathleen. Solar optics brings sun, view to interiors. Earth Shel. Dig. Energ. Rept., no. 6, Nov./Dec. 1979: 30-3.
There are two aspects of solar optics which could be utilized in underground development: sunlight transmission from the surface to a building's windowless interior and three-D image transmission by means of remote view optics. Light transmission is being studied by Dr. Michael Duguay of Bell Labs, NJ.

919. Veen, James C. Skylights lighten home, not billfold. Earth Shel. Liv., no. 34, July/Aug. 1984: 38-40.
Skylights are a cost-effective device for earth-sheltered homes. Their characteristics and virtues are discussed.

920. Wells, Malcolm. North light admitted. Earth Shel. Dig. Energ. Rept., no. 18, Nov./Dec. 1981: 14-5.
The author has developed a periscope solution to the problem of installing northside windows in south facing earth-covered houses.

921. Wilcox, Joe Stephen. Daylighting of earth-sheltered structures. Earth Shel. Bldgs. -- Tech. Pap., TP-IH, 1983.

XVII. PSYCHOLOGICAL ISSUES/ ACCEPTANCE

922. Baggs, Kate L. Psychological factors influencing attitude to earth covered dwellings and the underground lifestyle. In Australasian proc., 1st Int. Conf. on Energ. Effic. Bldgs. with Earth Shel. Prot., Sydney, Aust., Aug. 1-6, 1983. S.A. Baggs, ed. Kensington, NSW, Aust., Unisearch, Ltd., 1983. p. A15-9. Also in Geotecture, v. 2, no. 4, 1985: 39-46.
There appear to be certain difficulties confronting those wishing to market earth-covered homes. On the one hand, when some people are confronted with the concept for the first time, they become enthusiastic right from the start. At the other end of the scale, there are others who, without knowing anything about the concept, vehemently reject it. In between, there are those initially rejecting the idea, who change their attitude

when shown color photographs of existing earth-covered buildings. Normative influences on such attitudes are discussed and the user-image of earth-covered dwellers considered. As individuals' preconceived ideas or stereotypes about earth-covered housing will influence their acceptance or rejection of the concept, these are also investigated. Recommendations are made to guide those interested in marketing earth-covered buildings. --Auth. abstract.

923. Baggs, Sydney A. Attitude of Coober Pedians towards living in earth covered housing. In Proc., Symp. on Des. Strat. for Earth Cov. Bldgs., May 8-9, 1982. S.A. Baggs, ed. Kensington, NSW, Aust.: Univ. of New South Wales, Grad. Sch. of the Built Environ., 1982. p. 27-133.

924. _____. Attitude to living underground in the arid region of Australia. Int. Conf. on Environ. Psych., Univ. of Surrey, Guildford, Eng., July 16-20, 1979.

925. Barker, Joel. New paradigms of energy policy and mandates for the built environment of the future. In Residential applications: transcripts of selected presentations, Going Under to Stay on Top, Minneapolis, MN, Oct. 1977. Minneapolis, MN: Univ. of Minn., Undergr. Sp. Ctr., 1979. p. 55-67.
  The author, a noted futurist, avers that acceptance of earth-sheltered housing will be affected by stressing the similarities of earth sheltering to conventional housing and convincing people that it will help bring about a better future.

926. Bechtel, Robert B. Psychological aspects of earth covered buildings. In Proc., Alt. in Habitat: the Use of Earth Cov. Set., Conf., Fort Worth, TX, May 17-19, 1978. F.L. Moreland, ed. Washington, DC: U.S. Dept. of Energ., 1979. v. 2, Earth covered buildings and settlements, p. 71-7.
  The literature indicates a need for more research on the problems of image and life style. Many of the negative impressions of underground living can be changed by education. If attention is given to the life-style needs of resident groups by age, occupation, culture, and other categories, building specifications can be made that will be acceptable.

927. Bell, J.L. Consumer attitudes toward an earth-insulated solar house and a solar greenhouse residence. Master's thesis. Stillwater, OK: Okla. State Univ., Hous. Des. and and Cons. Res., July 1979.

928. Collins, Belinda Lowenhaupt. Review of the psychological reaction to windows. In Underground utilization. T. Stauffer, ed. Kansas City, MO: Univ. of Missouri - Kansas City, Dept. of Geosciences, 1978. v. 4, p. 532-40.

Review of the literature indicated that acceptance of a windowless space is governed by the character of the space itself. This paper is an extended summary of NBS Bldg. Sci. Ser., Pub. 70.

929. _____. Windows and people: a literature survey; psychological reaction to environments with and without windows. Gaithersburg, MD: Nat. Bur. of Stand., June 1975. 88 p.

The response of subjects to a variety of windowless situations revealed that although attitudes toward windowless space are often somewhat unfavorable, the most adverse reaction occurs in a small, restricted and essentially static environment. This indicates that a window functions as a means of introducing a dynamic, active quality to an interior environment. Windows also enhance the basic character of the room so that the presence of a window may cause a room to seem more spacious. The optimum size and shape of a window for fulfilling these functions is discussed.

930. Conference participants assess community attitudes. Earth Shel. Dig. Energ. Rept., no. 4, July/Aug. 1979: 42-3.

Approximately 1,500 participants at two conferences sponsored by the Underground Space Center were asked to assess the attitudes toward earth sheltering in their communities.

931. Cook, Marcia J. Factors associated with the decision to live in an earth sheltered house. Master's thesis. Stillwater, OK: Okla. State Univ., 1981.

932. Curry, Marianne. Profile of a community's attitude towards earth sheltered housing. In Residential applications: transcripts of selected presentations, Going Under to Stay on Top, Minneapolis, MN, Oct. 1977. Minneapolis, MN: Univ. of Minn., Undergr. Sp. Ctr., 1979. p. 125-7.

One of the biggest hurdles to acceptance is public resistance and sometimes professional resistance of architects. Other obstacles are mentioned, e.g. the groundhog image, fear of conservation as bringing a lower quality of life, health problems related to the construction materials, and others.

933. Grendell, Eric A. Grounders are pioneers. Earth Shel. Dig. Energ. Rept., no. 12, Nov./Dec. 1980: 13.

The author, an engineer who consults on the building of earth-sheltered homes, reveals the characteristics of the "grounders."

934. Grondzik, Walter T. Earth sheltered housing: perceptions vs. performance. In Passive and lower energy alternatives I: proc., 1st Int. PLEA Conf., Bermuda, Sept. 13-15, 1982. New York, NY: Pergamon Pr., 1982. p. 7/13-9.

Misinformation and misperceptions lead to a lack of acceptance of earth-sheltered housing as an energy-saving alternative. Several of the more common misperceptions and misunderstandings are discussed.

935. Hollon, Steven D., Philip C. Kendall, Steven Norsted, and David Watson. Psychological responses to earth-sheltered, multilevel, and above-ground structures with or without windows. Undergr. Sp., v. 5, no. 3, Nov./Dec. 1980: 171-8.

Employees in structures that are underground, below ground in multilevel structures, above ground without windows and above ground with windows were studied with regard to their psychological reactions to these working conditions. It was found that workers in underground locations had a negative psychological bias toward their job setting.

936. Hughey, Joseph B. and Robert L. Tye. Psychological reaction to working underground: a study of attitudes, beliefs, and evaluations. Kansas City, MO: Univ. of Missouri - Kansas City, Ctr. for Undergr. Sp. Stud., 1983. 21 p.

This research was conducted by members of the Dept. of Psychology of the University of Missouri and funded by a grant from the Underground Developers Association and conducted in conjunction with the University of Missouri--Kansas City Center for Underground Space Studies. It summarizes the results of a survey conducted with 312 persons working underground in Kansas City who were surveyed about their views of the underground environment. Results showed that a positive overall evaluation of working underground also encompassed opinions concerning its advantages and disadvantages.

937. Ingersoll, John. 12 subterranean pioneers report: it's great to live underground. Pop. Mech., v. 153, no. 5, May 1980: 114-7+.

Twelve families were queried about their satisfaction with their underground homes. There were few complaints. Most prefer them to their former above-ground homes.

938. Johnson, Richard F. Assessment of attitudes and educational needs for residential contractors in the states of Wisconsin and Minnesota to transfer from typical above grade residential construction to earth sheltered house construction. Menomonie, WI: Univ. of Wisc. - Stout, Grad. Coll., 1978. 48 p.

A research paper submitted to complete the plan B requirements for 190-735, Problems in Industrial Education.

939. Kendall, P.C., S.D. Hollon, D. Watson, and S. Norsted. Psychological sets regarding underground housing, working and recreational environments. Unpublished ms. Minneapolis, MN: Univ. of Minn.

940. Kramer, Ann. Country living changes ways. Earth Shel. Dig. Energ. Rept., no. 17, Sept./Oct. 1981: 20-1.

The joys of country living in an earth-sheltered home are related.

941. _____. Living in a fishbowl. Earth Shel. Dig. Energ. Rept., no. 14, Mar./Apr. 1981: 49-50.

The inconveniences of putting your earth-sheltered house on display are discussed.

942. Living below ground can be elevating. Earth Shel. Dig. Energ. Rept., no. 1, Jan./Feb. 1979: 28-9.

A light-hearted discussion of below-ground living.

943. McKown, Cora and K.K. Stewart. Consumer acceptance as a research technique. In Proc., 1st Int. Conf. on Energ. Effic. Bldgs. with Earth Shel. Prot., Sydney, Aust., Aug. 1-6, 1983. L.L. Boyer, ed. Stillwater, OK: Okla. State Univ., Archit. Ext., 1983. p. 223-6.

A consumer acceptance survey for an underground home is discussed. It is concluded that such a survey is not meant to replace other evaluation methods but provides a structure to earlier "open house" type surveys.

944. _____. Consumer evaluation of an earth sheltered dwelling. In Passive cooling: proc., Int. Pass. and Hybr. Cool. Conf., Miami Beach, FL, Nov. 6-16, 1981. Newark, DE: Int. Sol. Energ. Soc., Am. Sec., 1981. p. 501-5.

Although the initial consumer response to the words "earth sheltered" and "underground" are often negative, most earth-sheltered houses do not deserve the reputation. People are interested in earth-sheltered homes because of their advantages: enery efficiency, protection, escape from air and noise pollution, and land conservation. More examples of earth-sheltered houses are needed to help overcome negative stereotypes.

945. Paulus, Paul B. On the psychology of earth covered buildings. Undergr. Sp., v. 1, no. 2, July/Aug. 1976: 127-30.
Earth covering and low noise levels have a positive effect. Being underground and windowless provoke negative reactions. More research is suggested.

946. Peterman, Jeffrey D. Revenge of the earth-shelterers! Earth Shel. Liv., no. 39, May/June 1985: 11.
A story about how to get rid of a boorish guest by feeding him "dirt."

947. Routh, Barbara. A study of human response to attitude statements about use and occupancy of underground space: a preliminary report. In Underground utilization. T. Stauffer, ed. Kansas City, MO: Univ. of Missouri - Kansas City, Dept. of Geosciences, 1978. v. 4, p. 541-5.
This report is based on a survey made by the author to determine the attitudes of people to the use and occupany of underground space. The survey consisted of interviews in which 20 interviewees were asked to respond to 30 carefully selected attitude statements. Photographs, viewed after responses were completed, served to change the attitudes of some of the participants.

948. Seybert, Jeffrey A. Psychological factors and future expansion of underground space utilization. In Underground utilization. T. Stauffer, ed. Kansas City, MO: Univ. of Missouri - Kansas City, Dept. of Geosciences, 1978. v. 7, p. 1018-19.

949. Stewart, Kay K., Cora McKown, and Jerry Newman. Attitudes of visitors to an earth sheltered solar house. Hous. Soc., v. 8, no. 2, 1981.

950. Volkman, Nancy. User perceptions of underground houses and its implications for site planning. Master's project, Master of Landscape Architecture. Univ. of Ill. - Urbana-Champaign, 1980. 60 p.

951. Who wants earth sheltering. Earth Shel. Dig. Energ. Rept., no. 1, Jan./Feb. 1979: 11.
A study by Gary Solomonson and Associates, Minneapolis, identifies the kinds of people who are most interested in earth-sheltered housing.

952. Winter, Ruth D. Consumer evaluation of an earth insulated solar house. Master's thesis. Stillwater, OK: Okla. State Univ., Hous. Des. and Cons. Res., May 1980.

953. Wunderlich, Elizabeth. Psychology and underground development. In Underground utilization. T. Stauffer, ed. Kansas City, MO: Univ. of Missouri-Kansas City, Dept. of Geosciences, 1978. v. 4. p. 526-9.
    Present research in the psychological aspects of subspace development indicates a fear of closed spaces working against acceptance of underground living. Acceptance of subspace as a working-place is much greater than acceptance as a home environment.

XVIII. PHYSIOLOGICAL ISSUES

954. Baggs, Sydney A., M.W. Carter, and V.A. Leach. Radon daughters and the health of geospace users. In Australasian proc., 1st Int. Conf. on Energ. Effic. Bldgs. with Earth Shel. Prot., Sydney, Aust., Aug. 1-6, 1983. S.A. Baggs, ed. Kensington, NSW, Aust.: Unisearch, Ltd., 1983. p. B18-27.
    Designers of geotecture in Australia are entering a new phase in which energy conservation design strategies are being applied in the development of living environments that rely, in part, for their thermal energy-efficiency upon a reduction in the number of interior, air-exchange cycles. However, questions must be asked concerning the potential effect of such strategies upon the health of occupants. One aspect of this question, viz, the incidence of Radon-222 and the potentially carcinogenous effects of Radon Daughters is considered in and around living environments and in the context of (a) the relationship between Radon Daughter exposure and risk estimates; and (b) the literature on the subject. Alpha and gamma radiation monitoring will be the subject of the first stage of a programme currently being implemented by the architect co-author in occupied Australian earth-covered homes (terratecture) and the dugouts (lithotecture) of White Cliffs, NSW, and Coober Pedy, SA. —Auth. abstract.

955. Landa, Edward R. Radon concentrations in the indoor air of earth sheltered buildings in Colorado. In Proc., 1st Int. Conf. on Energ. Effic. Bldgs. with Earth Shel. Prot., Sydney, Aust., Aug. 1-6, 1983. L.L. Boyer, ed. Stillwater, OK: Okla. State Univ., Archit. Ext., 1983. p. 275-9.

151 Physiological Issues

Radon concentration in the indoor air of six residential and three non-residential earth-sheltered buildings in eastern Colorado were monitored quarterly using passive, integrating detectors. Average radon concentrations during the three-month sampling periods generally ranged from about one to nine pCi/L, although one building, a poorly ventilated storage bunker, had concentrations as high as 39 pCi/L. These radon concentrations are somewhat greater than typically reported for conventional buildings (generally around one pCi/L), but are of the same order of magnitude as radon concentrations reported for energy efficient, non-earth sheltered buildings. Radium contents and radon emanation coefficients of soils at the building sites and radon concentrations in water supplies are discussed. —Auth. abstract.

956. _____. Radon in earth-sheltered structures. Undergr. Sp., v. 8, no. 4, 1984: 264-9.

This is an expanded version of a paper published in the Proceedings of the Sydney Conference on Earth Sheltered Buildings, Aug. 1-6, 1984. It describes a study of the radon concentration in indoor air of six residential and three non-residential earth-sheltered buildings in Colorado over a nine-month period using passive, integrating detectors. The radon concentrations were found to be greater than those reported for conventional buildings (about one pCi/L) but about the same as the concentrations reported for non-earth sheltered energy-efficient buildings.

957. Lord, David. Interior environmental quality in earth shelters. In Conf. proc., Earth Shel. Perf. and Eval., 2nd Nat. Tech. Conf., Tulsa, OK, Oct. 16-17, 1981. Stillwater, OK: Okla. State Univ., Archit. Ext., 1981. p. 231-41.

The nature of indoor environmental pollutants in airtight buildings were identified from sampling, monitoring, and modeling results.

958. May, H. Ionizing radiation levels in energy conserving structures. In Earth shelter 2: coll. pap., 1st Earth Shel. Hous. Conf. and Exhib., Minneapolis, MN, Apr. 9-11, 1980. Minneapolis, MN: Univ. of Minn., Undergr. Sp. Ctr., 1980. p. 215-36. Also in Undergr. Sp., v. 5, no. 6, May/June 1981: 384-91.

The physical principles that govern emission of radon to the atmosphere are summarized, and the factors that contribute to radon buildup and concentration in structures are discussed. Data on the health effects of long-term exposure to low levels of radon are examined. There are limited data on earth-sheltered structures, but what there is suggests that radon levels in well-constructed earth-contact homes are not much higher than those reported for above-ground homes.

959. Nero, Anthony V. Radon in energy-efficient earth-sheltered structures. In <u>Proc., 1st Int. Conf. on Energ. Effic. Bldgs. with Earth Shel. Prot.</u>, Sydney, Aust., Aug. 1-6, 1983. L.L. Boyer, ed. Stillwater, OK: Okla. State Univ., Archit. Ext., 1983. p. 281-5.

Earth-sheltered structures have a still unmeasured potential for having radon entry rates higher than than for other structures. Radon as an indoor pollutant is discussed. The few data available indicate that radon concentrations in earth-sheltered dwellings are higher than average, but conventional housing in the same area show similarly high levels.

960. Oswald, Richard A. Tight house can seal in pollution. <u>Earth Shel. Liv.</u>, no. 27, May/June 1983: 36-7.

This article tells how radon adds to indoor pollution. Terradex Corp. has learned through testing that indoor radon levels are related more to the surrounding soil, rock, and mineral conditions than to the structural design or the materials in a structure.

961. Rand, George. Psychological and physiological ecology of indoor environments. In <u>The potential of earth-sheltered and underground space: proc., Undergr. Sp. Conf. and Expos.</u>, Kansas City, MO, June 8-10, 1981. T.L. Holthusen, ed. Elmsford, NY: Pergamon Pr., 1981. p. 413-20.

Indoor air pollution in earth-sheltered houses is examined. A review of the literature is given, and studies of the negative effects of modern buildings are summarized.

962. _____. Thinking ecologically about indoor environments. <u>Undergr. Sp.</u>, v. 6, no. 2, Sept./Oct. 1981: 105-8.

This paper discusses the possibility of indoor air pollution in underground and other energy-efficient structures. This problem requires special attention by engineers and architects in order to insure a safe, healthy, and comfortable habitation.

963. Scientist researches radon effects. <u>Earth Shel. Dig. Energ. Rept.</u>, no. 10, July/Aug. 1980: 19-20.

The concern about the danger of radiation from radon gas in earth shelters is legitimate. Radon, a radioactive gas, results from the decay of the parent element radium which is found everywhere in soil and many building materials, most sources of natural gas which often do not decay during pipeline transmission, and deep well water which is released when showers are run. Sealing and waterproofing precautions are desirable in preventing entry of radon; measures to ensure adequate drainage, such as tiling around walls and use of proper backfill materials are beneficial. Instrument readings were made of six earth-sheltered homes and six conventional homes.

964. Special house aids recovery: house frees woman from toxic indoor pollution. Earth Shel. Liv., no. 31, Jan./Feb. 1984: 6-7.

Living in an earth-sheltered home containing no synthetic materials cured the allergy-problems of this Minnesota woman.

XIX. ENVIRONMENTAL IMPACT

965. Carleton, Joseph G. An environmentalist's views on underground construction. In Underground utilization. T. Stauffer, ed. Kansas City, MO: Univ. of Missouri - Kansas City, Dept. of Geosci., 1978. v. 6, p. 894-9.

966. Foute, Steven J. and Douglas B. Cargo. Earth covered housing: hydrologic and pollution considerations. In Proc., Alt. in Habitat: the Use of Earth Cov. Set., Fort Worth, TX, May 17-19, 1978. Frank L. Moreland, ed. Washington, DC: U.S. Dept. of Energy, 1979. v. 2, p. 108-24.

The pollutants discussed are five-day biochemical oxygen demand, total suspended solids, total nitrogen, and total phosphorus. This study showed that the kind of pollutants do not change in the transition to earth-sheltered homes; only magnitudinal differences are noticed.

967. La Nier, Royce. Assessing environmental impact of earth-covered buildings. Undergr. Sp., v. 1, no. 4, Aug. 1977: 309-15.

Some negative impacts of excavating for earth-covered buildings (such as increased stream sediment loads and filling methods with excavated materials) can be expected, but there is no way to measure the magnitude of the change without more study. Reductions in energy utilization may be the most promising aspect of earth-sheltered urban development.

968. Terman, Max R. Get attuned to nature. Earth Shel. Dig. Energ. Rept., no. 8, Mar./Apr. 1980: 34-5.

An argument for maintaining a healthy ecological balance by living underground.

XX. SURVEYS

969. Baggs, Sydney A. Underground housing: new life-styles in an Australian settlement. J. Soc. Pol. Econ. Stud., v. 6, no. 2, Summer 1981: 177-205.
   Dugout residents in Coober Pedy, SA, were surveyed to discover their attitudes and experiences concerning the underground homes.

970. Boyer, Lester L. Earth-shelter trends in the south central plains. In The potential of earth-sheltered and underground space: proc., Undergr. Sp. Conf. and Expos., Kansas City, MO, June 8-10, 1981. T.L. Holthusen, ed. Elmsford, NY: Pergamon Pr., 1981. p. 135-48.
   Detailed questionnaires, telephone conversations, and visits were used to survey earth-sheltered homes in a nine-state region of the south central U.S. Energy and habitability aspects of earth-shelter living were the chief interests of the survey. The results of the survey indicate that the residents are satisfied with the structural safety, thermal comfort, and acoustical ambiance, but some residents are less satisfied with the site design, thermal radiation control, daylighting, and energy design and performance of their homes. However, owners think they have achieved substantial savings by living in an earth-sheltered home.

971. _____, Walter T. Grondzik, and D.K. Fitzgerald. Earth sheltered housing performance: a summary report. In Proc., Annu. Mtg., Int. Sol. Energ. Soc., Am. Sec., Philadelphia, PA, May 26, 1981. v. 4.2, p. 1084-8.
   Extended questionnaires and telephone interviews were used to determine earth-sheltered house occupant responses to this new dwelling concept. Passive energy design and habitability are the chief subjects of interest at Oklahoma State University. Results of the survey showed that occupants are generally satisfied with the structural safety, thermal comfort, and acoustic ambiance of their homes but have reservations about site design, privacy of family members, daylighting and energy design, and performance. However, owners still think they have achieved substantial savings as compared with their previous homes.

972. _____, Margaret J. Weber, and Walter T. Grondzik. Energy and habitability aspects of earth sheltered housing in Oklahoma. Project report, Presidential Challenge Grant

Program. Stillwater, OK: Okla. State Univ., Sch. of Archit. and Dept. of Hous. Des. and Cons. Resources, 1980. 88 p.

Results are presented of a survey conducted by a detailed questionnaire, on-site interviews, and extended telephone calls. Energy savings were the primary incentive for building earth-sheltered houses, but 30 percent felt energy consumption was higher than expected. In general, comfort and habitability were not sacrificed to achieve energy savings.

973. _____, _____, and _____. Passive energy design and habitability aspects of earth-sheltered housing in Oklahoma. Undergr. Sp., v. 4, no. 6, May/June 1980: 333-9.

The residents of earth-sheltered houses in Oklahoma were polled by means of a detailed questionnaire during the first phase of a long-range funded project. The preliminary results of the energy and habitability factors are presented here. The results indicate that the majority of the respondents consider their energy savings expectations were reached, but more than 40 percent think that energy consumption was higher than expected.

974. Grondzik, W.T. and L.L. Boyer. Oklahoma earth shelters: a state-of-the-art review. In Earth shelter 2: coll. pap., 1st Earth Shel. Hous. Conf. and Exhib., Minneapolis, MN, Apr. 9-11, 1980. Minneapolis, MN: Univ. of Minn., Undergr. Sp. Ctr., 1980. p. 43-54.

More than 80 earth-sheltered residences in Oklahoma were identified and investigated using a detailed questionnaire procedure which focused on three main concerns: building construction parameters, occupant attitudes and evaluations, and energy utilization. Responses regarding earth-shelter living were overwhelmingly positive.

975. Johnson, Richard F. Contractors and earth-sheltered housing. Undergr. Sp., v. 3, no. 6, May/June 1979: 285-91.

A survey of residential contractors in Minnesota and Wisconsin indicated that 16 percent would require formal training in order to acquire the knowledge of earth-sheltered construction techniques. Many contractors remained skeptical of the market's acceptance.

976. McKown, Cora and Kay Stewart. Consumer attitudes concerning construction features of an earth-sheltered dwelling. Undergr. Sp., v. 4, no. 5, Mar./Apr. 1980: 293-5.

Consumer responses to construction features of earth-sheltered houses were studied. Results showed that female respondents favored the addition of more light into the houses and males favored building more deeply underground or covering the roof with more earth to increase insulating values.

977. _____. Earth sheltered dwellings in Texas: identification and survey. In Passive and low energy alternatives I: proc., 1st Int. PLEA Conf., Bermuda, Sept. 13-15, 1982. New York, NY: Pergamon Pr., 1982. p. 7/27-31.
   The survey showed that earth-sheltered homeowners are highly satisfied with their homes. About half of those surveyed participated in the construction of their homes.

978. Preliminary survey research completed. Earth Shel. Dig. Energ. Rept., no. 7, Jan./Feb. 1980: 33-4.
   Oklahoma State's survey of 70 earth-shelter structures revealed that the 34 participants ranked energy savings as the most positive feature of their homes. Topics in the survey included: insulation, thermal mass, special energy systems, energy consumption, thermal and lighting comfort, and various consumer attitudes.

979. Rivers, W. Joel, Bob Helm, William D. Warde, and Walter T. Grondzik. Analysis of earth sheltered dwellings in the south central United States. In Passive cooling: proc. of the Int. Pass. and Hybr. Cool. Conf., Miami Beach, FL, Nov. 6-16, 1981. Newark, DE: Int. Sol. Energ. Soc., Am. Sec., 1981. p. 126-30.
   A 1980 survey of earth-sheltered houses in eight states followed an earlier survey of similar houses in Oklahoma. The survey evaluated data collected from 92 owners of earth-sheltered houses and 87 non-owners who were prospective earth-sheltered house owners. The owners reported a high degree of satisfaction with their homes' performance and economy of construction and operation.

980. _____, W.D. Warde, and B. Helm. A comparison of assessments by above-ground and earth-shelter occupants. In Conf. proc., Earth Shel. Perf. and Eval., 2nd Nat. Tech. Conf., Tulsa, OK, Oct. 16-17, 1981. Stillwater, OK: Okla. State Univ., Archit. Ext., 1981. p. 243-57.
   Questionnaire results from a nine-state region dealing with occupancy factors in earth shelters are compared to the viewpoints of present occupants and those for prospective occupants. Specific sub-regional occupancy traits were also identified.

981. Scalise, James W. A survey of earth sheltered housing in the Arizona-Sonoran Desert. In Proc., 1st Int. Conf. on

Energ. Effic. Bldgs. with Earth Shel. Prot., Sydney, Aust., Aug. 1-6, 1983. L.L. Boyer, ed. Stillwater, OK: Okla. State Univ., Archit, Ext., 1983. p. 69-74.

In late 1980, an investigation into the location and quantification of earth-sheltered desert housing was undertaken as a research project funded by the Control Data Corp. of Minneapolis, MN. Entitled Reduce existing data and compilation of additional data on earth sheltered housing in the Arizona-Sonoran Desert, this investigation sought to fill a void in the information available about the nature and extent of earth-sheltered residential construction in arid regions. During the four months of the initial investigation, 27 sites were located and documented. Subsequently, an additional 16 residential sites were located and added to the original list. The detailed documentation has been condensed and presented here as a synopsis of this research investigation. --Auth. abstract.

982. Stanford, Greg. Occupant evaluation of down under in the White Cliffs community. In Conf. proc., Earth Shel. Perf. and Eval., 2nd Nat. Tech. Conf., Tulsa, OK, Oct. 16-17, 1981. Stillwater, OK: Okla. State Univ., Archit. Ext., 1981. p. 217-29.

An environmental and behavioral assessment of this dugout town in Australia was made by means of on-site visits, test instrument results, and questionnaire responses.

983. Stewart, Kay, Cora McKown, and Carolyn Peck. Consumer attitudes concerning an earth-sheltered house. Undergr. Sp., v. 4, no. 1, July/Aug. 1979: 11-15.

Visitors to an earth-sheltered residence in March 1978 responded positively to their experience with underground living. Nearly 80 percent said they would consider living in an earth-sheltered house. Those with the greatest interest in earth-sheltered living were males between the ages of 25-34 and 55-64.

984. _____ and _____. Consumer evaluation of an earth sheltered solar residence. In Proc., Earth Shel. Bldg. Des. Innov., Nat. Tech. Conf., Oklahoma City, OK, Apr. 18, 1980. L.L. Boyer, ed. Stillwater, OK: Okla. State Univ., 1980. p. VI. 31-5.

Consumer evaluation data were collected during openhouse tours of a house partially embanked with earth on three sides. The design features evaluated were size, spatial arrangement, lighting, privacy, access, expected maintenance costs, and energy efficiency. Results indicated that there is a considerable consumer interest in earth-sheltered living.

985. Tremblay, Kenneth R., Jr. and Anne L. Sweaney. Attitudes studied. Earth Shel. Liv., no. 38, Mar./Apr. 1985: 20.

The Southern Regional Housing Research Project conducted a survey to find out why more people don't live in earth-sheltered houses.

986. Underground Space Center. Earth sheltered house opinions survey. By Roger G. Aiken. Minneapolis, MN, Dec. 1979. 211 p.

A survey of opinions and viewpoints on earth-sheltered houses was carried out in the areas of codes and zoning, financing, housing design, construction, and use. The reason for the survey, the design of the questionnaire, computer analysis techniques, and the telephone interview technique used are described. This study was commissioned by the U.S. Dept. of Housing and Urban Development to identify barriers to the large-scale construction of earth-sheltered houses and was carried out in the 18-month period from Summer 1978 to Fall 1979.

987. Weber, Margaret J., L.L. Boyer, and W.T. Grondzik. Implications for habitability design and energy savings in earth-sheltered housing. In Proc., Earth Shel. Bldg. Des. Innov. Nat. Tech. Conf., Oklahoma City, OK, Apr. 18, 1980. L.L. Boyer, ed. Stillwater, OK: Okla. State Univ., 1980. p. VI. 21-7.

More than 50 earth-sheltered houses in Oklahoma were studied by means of questionnaires, on-site interviews, and telephone calls. Energy conservation was found to be the main incentive for building earth-sheltered houses. This was achieved without sacrificing comfort and habitability.

XXI. URBAN/COMMUNITY ISSUES

---

988. Aughenbaugh, N.B. and John D. Rockaway. Go underground for low cost housing. Proc., IAHS Int. Symp. on Hous. Prob., Atlanta, GA, 1976. Parvis F. Rad, ed. Coral Gables, FL: Int. Assn. for Hous. Sci., 1976. v. 2, p. 1229-44.

The authors propose an alternative to high-rise surface apartments for low-income residents in urban areas: underground housing wherever geologic considerations are favorable. Present-day use of underground space for large-scale developments in urban areas is discussed, as are the advantages of underground use, environmental and planning considerations.

989. Berman, Jean. Profile of a community's attitude towards earth-sheltered housing. In Residential applications: transcripts of selected presentations, Going Under to Stay on Top, Minneapolis, MN, Oct. 1977. Minneapolis, MN: Univ. of Minn., Undergr. Sp. Ctr., 1979. p. 123-4.

The author discusses the immediate prospect for acceptance of earth-sheltered housing in St. Paul, MN, and the factors affecting acceptance, i.e. small lot-size requirement, possibility of southern exposure for passive solar design.

990. Carmody, John C. and Raymond L. Sterling. A comparison of the community planning implications for passive solar, earth sheltered and conventional highly insulated housing developments. In Passive and low energy alternatives I: proc., 1st Int. PLEA Conf., Bermuda, Sept. 13-15, 1982. New York, NY: Pergamon Pr., 1982. p. 7/1-12.

The different types of energy-efficient houses vary in their need for solar exposure. There is a discussion of the effect of full solar exposure on maximum densities of earth sheltered and solar developments and the effect of ground slope angles on the densities that can be achieved.

991. Davidoff, Linda. Social issues in community planning for earth covered shelter. In Proc., Alt. in Habitat: the Use of Earth Cov. Set., Fort Worth, TX, May 17-19, 1978. F.L. Moreland, ed. Washington, DC: U.S. Dept. of Energy, 1979. v. 2, p. 17-24.

Exclusionary zoning issues are obstacles to the development of earth-covered settlements. Presenting the possibility of a broader range of housing choices is a way to interest citizens and public officials in earth-sheltered housing as an energy-conservation method and a way to enhance the urban environment. Four benefits are suggested: high population density without apparent crowding of units; separation of pedestrian from vehicular traffic; life-cycle cost reduction; less apparent status differentiation among units.

992. Harrison, Lloyd. Should the city be interested in an underground subdivision? In Underground utilization. T. Stauffer, ed. Kansas City, MO: Univ. of Missouri - Kansas City, Dept. of Geosci., 1978. v. 6, p. 860-2.

This paper discusses the various considerations a city administrator should develop in viewing a proposal for an underground subdivision. Energy savings of up to 72 percent could be significant in easing the energy crisis in the cities. This type of subdivision would be particularly applicable to zoning around airports because of the protection it affords from accidents, the decrease of the effect of aircraft noise, and the reduction of distracting lights of the aircraft at night. Landscape preservation is another consideration.

993. Hauser, Leroy. Profile of a community's attitude towards earth sheltered housing. In Residential applications: transcripts of selected presentations, Going Under to Stay on Top, Minneapolis, MN, Oct. 1977. Minneapolis, MN: Univ. of Minn., Undergr. Sp. Ctr., 1979. p. 121-2.
The author is a building inspector who briefly addresses: community attitudes, lender attitudes, and taxing.

994. Jacobs, Sol. Profile of our community attitudes towards earth sheltered housing. In Residential applications: transcripts of selected presentations, Going Under to Stay on Top, Minneapolis, MN, Oct. 1977. Minneapolis, MN: Univ. of Minn., Undergr. Sp. Ctr., 1979. p. 117-9.
This paper discusses earth-sheltered housing in relation to building and zoning codes.

995. Labs, K.B. Performance of earth-covered development: planning issues. In Proc., Alt. in Habitat: the Use of Earth Cov. Set., Conf., Fort Worth, TX, May 17-19, 1978. F.L. Moreland, ed. Washington, DC: U.S. Dept. of Energy, 1979. v. 2, p. 125-40.
Construction must be carefully planned to achieve the goals of energy conservation and reducing the environmental impacts of housing. Site planning needs to take into account the effects on stormwater runoff, aesthetic and cultural values, ambient temperatures, and compatible land-roof uses without assuming that subsurface construction will automatically be beneficial.

996. Mason, R. Projections on the future of underground development. In Proc., Alt. in Habitat: the Use of Earth Cov. Set., Conf., Fort Worth, TX, May 17-19, 1978. F.L. Moreland, ed. Washington, DC: U.S. Dept. of Energy, 1979. v. 2, Earth covered buildings and settlements, p. 169-73.
The future of earth-sheltered developments depends on the future of population growth, the capacity of urban areas to remain viable, and the development of new technologies, materials, and energy sources. Some recent developments in building systems, such as cellular structures and container structures, are discussed, and some future possibilities are suggested.

997. Miller, J.R. City Hall's response to a proposed subterranean dwelling. In Proc., Alt. in Habitat: the Use of Earth Cov. Set., Conf., Fort Worth, TX, May 17-19,

1978. F.L. Moreland, ed. Washington, DC: U.S. Dept. of Energy, 1979. v. 2, Earth covered buildings and settlements, p. 12-6.

The author briefly describes the response of Los Alamos City Hall to his request for permission to construct a home in a canyon wall. He describes the site and the plans for construction.

998. Moreland, Frank. An alternative to suburbia. In Proc., Alt. in Energ. Conserv.: the Use of Earth Cov. Bldgs., Conf., Fort Worth, TX, July 9-12, 1975. F.L. Moreland, ed. Washington, DC: U.S. G.P.O., 1976. p. 183-208.

Earth-covered neighborhoods are considered from a consumer perspective as an alternative to conventional suburbs. The format for the considerations are two: decision matrices representing the considerations of a typical consumer in 1972 and a consumer in the 1980 period.

999. _____. Earth sheltered housing. In Desert housing: balancing experience and technology for dwelling in hot arid zones. Kenneth N. Clark and Patricia Paylore, eds. Tucson, AZ: Univ. of Arizona Pr., 1980. p. 253-69.

This article discusses the benefits of using earth-covered dwellings in urban development.

1000. _____. Notes on earth covered settlements. In Proc., Alt. in Habitat: the Use of Earth Cov. Set., Conf., Fort Worth, TX, May 17-19, 1978. F.L. Moreland, ed. Washington, DC: U.S. Dept. of Energy, 1979. v. 2, Earth covered buildings and settlements, p. 278-355.

Earth-covered neighborhoods are proposed for Fort Worth, TX. Alternative housing studies which study the costs of housing designs and bus transportation at different population densities suggest that earth-sheltered houses at medium density have many environmental, health, and cost advantages. Some variations are shown for patio houses and a hill village.

1001. Nelson, George. The hidden city. Archit. Plus., v. 2, Nov./Dec. 1974: 70-7.

The author, an industrial designer and architect, proposes to make cities less boring by making them less visible.

1002. Rockaway, John D. and N.B. Aughenbaugh. Go underground for low-cost housing. In Underground utilization. T. Stauffer, ed. Kansas City, MO: Univ. of Missouri - Kansas City, Dept. of Geosci., 1978. v. 4, p. 614-8.

The authors propose an alternative to high-rise surface

apartments; they recommend going underground for low-cost urban housing wherever geologic conditions are favorable. This will result in double use of the land. Figures show how a compartmentalized mine, utilizing room and pillar extraction methods, could be converted into an apartment complex.

1003. Stauffer, T., Sr. Perspectives of planned two-tiered use of space in Kansas City, Norway and Sweden. In <u>The potential of earth-sheltered and underground space: proc., Undergr. Sp. Conf. and Expos.</u>, Kansas City, MO, June 8-10, 1981. T.L. Holthusen, ed. Elmsford, NY: Pergamon Pr., 1981. p. 421-32.

The subsurface is being used for additional space in congested areas. A comparison is made between the use of two tiers of space in Kansas City and in Scandinavia.

1004. Thorsen, Gerald W. and Roger L. Rue. High bank instead of high rise - an earth sheltered approach to medium-density housing. <u>Undergr. Sp.</u>, v. 5, no. 3, Nov./Dec. 1980: 149-51.

The authors recommend that stable slopes in urban areas could be developed for earth-sheltered housing, leaving the flat lands for agricultural uses.

1005. Underground Space Center. <u>Earth sheltered community design: energy efficient residential development.</u> By Raymond Sterling, John Carmody and Gail Elnicky. New York, NY: Van Nostrand Reinhold, 1981. 270 p.

This work examines the aspects of community design which should be considered when planning earth-sheltered projects: these include site selection, soil data, topography, orientation, climate, roads and utilities, site design, density, marketability, etc. It discusses earth-sheltered developments in relation to above-ground developments to facilitate comparison. It also studies actual and proposed earth-sheltered communities with the purpose of reinforcing the suitability of the design guidelines presented.

1006. Uttley, James P. <u>The emergence of earth sheltered and underground space technologies in creating alternative urban environments.</u> A report presented for Urban and Regional Studies 667, Star Paper. Mankato, MN: Mankato State Univ., Mar. 1978. 30 p.

1007. Vadnais, Kathleen. Vistas opening for urban earth shelters. <u>Earth Shel. Dig. Energ. Rept.</u>, no. 5, Sept./Oct. 1979: 7-9+.

This is a report on the progress toward urban earth-sheltered development, specifically in Fort Worth and St. Paul.

XXII. INSTITUTIONAL ISSUES

1008. Adams, Larry. Money hard to come by for "gentle architecture." Earth Shel. Dig. Energ. Rept., no. 2, Mar./Apr. 1979: 10.
A Letter to the Editor telling about financing problems.

1009. American Underground Space Association. Borrower's guide. Minneapolis, MN.
This booklet gives details on financing an innovative energy-conserving home: where to start; how to prepare; what you need; when to seek help; why to keep trying.

1010. _____. Earth-sheltered home financing: an introduction for lenders and appraisers. Minneapolis, MN.
Gives a brief description of earth sheltering and suggestions for underwriting and appraisal.

1011. Appraisers are critical to your loan. Earth Shel. Dig. Energ. Rept., no. 2, Mar./Apr. 1979: 11.

1012. Atchison, Tom. Financing earth sheltered housing. In Residential applications: transcripts of selected presentations, Going Under to Stay on Top, Minneapolis, MN, Oct. 1977. Minneapolis, MN: Univ. of Minn., Undergr. Sp. Ctr., 1979. p. 141-2.
Financing is the most serious impediment to the development of earth-sheltered housing.

1013. Browne, F.R. Role of the real estate developer in the future of the underground industry. In Potential of earth-sheltered and underground space: proc., Undergr. Sp. Conf. and Expos., Kansas City, MO, June 8-10, 1981. T.L. Holthusen, ed. Elmsford, NY: Pergamon Pr., 1981. p. 395-9.
The five elements in the development of underground real estate are location (land identification and control), defining the product (the building), identifying the user, financing the project, and the property management function. These are the elements needed for the meaningful growth of the underground space industry.

1014. Code change followed up. Earth Shel. Dig. Energ. Rept., no. 5, Sept./Oct. 1979: 22.
Discusses a change in the building code (Building Officials and Code Administrators International) in Subsection 609.4 on emergency escape.

1015. Codes, zoning and financing: impediments to earth sheltered construction. Concr. Constr., v. 27, no. 6, June 1982: 515-9; v. 27, no. 7, July 1982: 589-91.
The information in these articles comes from Earth sheltered housing: code, zoning, and financing issues by the Underground Space Center, published April 1980.

1016. Comments on the finance of earth-covered dwellings. In Proc., Alt. in Habitat: the Use of Earth Cov. Set., Conf., Fort Worth, TX, May 17-19, 1978. F.L. Moreland, ed. Washington, DC: U.S. Dept. of Energ., 1979. v. 2, Earth covered buildings and settlements, p. 54-70.
Six specialists discuss the problems of financing earth-covered homes and the larger problem of introducing technological innovation into traditional value systems. They also discussed the problems of the utility's role in pricing and risk sharing, future energy costs, the present true costs of energy conservation, obstacles to innovation, and financing options for earth-sheltered structures.

1017. De Saventhem, E.M. Insuring risks underground -- some general considerations. Undergr. Sp., v. 2, no. 1, Sept. 1977: 19-25.
This paper discusses how insurers' attitudes vary when considering different kinds of underground construction, mainly large-scale commercial structures.

1018. Donovan, Hamester and Rattien, Inc. Financing barriers to the earth-sheltered/underground building market: a policy analysis. Washington, DC, Nov. 1979. (Unpublished).

1019. The ESL interview: Gene Ihrke, Creative Financing, Incorporated. Earth Shel. Liv., no. 37, Jan./Feb. 1985: 9-11.
The interviewee finances manufactured earth-sheltered homes.

1020. Fischer, Hank. Critical concerns related to financing earth sheltered housing. In Residential applications: transcripts of selected presentations, Going Under to Stay on Top, Minneapolis, MN, Oct. 1977. Minneapolis,

MN, Oct. 1977. Minneapolis, MN: Univ. of Minn., Undergr. Sp. Ctr., 1979. p. 165-7.

The author is an authority in the field of finance. He discusses what earth-sheltered housing pioneers will have to do to obtain financing to build their earth-sheltered houses.

1021. Green, Melvyn. Building codes and underground buildings. In Proc., Alt. in Habitat: the Use of Earth Cov. Set., Conf., Fort Worth, TX, May 17-19, 1978. F.L. Moreland, ed. Washington, DC: U.S. Dept. of Energy, 1979. v. 2, Earth covered buildings and settlements, p. 27-9.

Building codes may present problems in the development of earth sheltering. They are criticized by many for restricting innovative and less costly construction methods. Underground structures will be affected by the codes governing health and hygiene, fire and life safety, structural stability, and accident prevention. The chief concern is over egress in case of danger.

1022. The Hanover Insurance Company, Worcester, Massachusetts, is offering reduced homeowner's insurance rates for customers whose homes are built of approved earth-sheltered construction. Undergr. Sp., v. 6, no. 4-5, Jan./Apr. 1982: 200.

1023. Hanzal-Kashi, Amy. Determinants of loan officers' attitudes toward financing earth sheltered dwellings. Master's thesis. Univ. of Nebraska, 1983.

1024. _____ and E. Raedene Combs. Loan officers' perceptions concerning earth-sheltered housing: risk, complexity, and advantage. Undergr. Sp., v. 8, no. 3, 1984: 191-5.

The study found that loan officers would require more stringent terms and a larger down-payment for an earth-sheltered home than for a conventional home.

1025. Higgs, Forrest S. Integrating earth covered housing into existing energy efficiency code structures. In Proc., Alt. in Habitat: the Use of Earth Cov. Set., Conf., Fort Worth, TX, May 17-19, 1978. F.L. Moreland, ed. Washington, DC: U.S. Dept. of Energy, 1979. v. 2, Earth covered buildings and settlements, p. 44-53.

The emerging building codes aimed at energy efficiency in buildings specify energy consumption per unit of floor area for specific generic types of construction. But these codes are only as flexible as the mechanisms specified for design evaluation. These mechanisms which are automated, prescriptive, or hand-calculation-oriented, are developed for conventional construction practice. They give little response to atypical approaches like passive systems or earth-covered structures. By exploring the problems related with the development of thermal models for high mass construction, the author hopes it can be led from its present state to a form easily usable within existing building codes.

1026. Isakson, H.R. Institutional constraints on the marketing and financing of earth-covered settlements. In <u>Proc., Alt. in Habitat: the Use of Earth Cov. Set., Conf.</u>, Fort Worth, TX, May 17-19, 1978. F.L. Moreland, ed. Washington, DC: U.S. Dept. of Energy, 1979. v. 2, <u>Earth covered buildings and settlements</u>, p. 7-11.
Constraints the real estate market will encounter in marketing earth-covered homes are: utility pricing, which disguises the savings value of earth-covered settlements; an emphasis on front-end costs, which distort life-cycle costs; excessive optimism that technology will find a way to avoid life style changes; academic and business specialization in preference to multidisciplinary approaches; inadequate information; and a reluctance to finance unproven earth-covered structures. However, building performance standards and public awareness will provide strong incentives to finance earth-sheltered houses.

1027. Kahn, Terry. Private development opportunities in earth covered buildings. In <u>Proc., Alt. in Energ. Conserv.: the Use of Earth Cov. Bldgs., Conf.</u>, Fort Worth, TX, July 9-12, 1975. F.L. Moreland, ed. Washington, DC: U.S. G.P.O., 1976. p. 239-42.
Some practical variables encountered by the private developer of earth-sheltered structures are addressed. Three topics are discussed: land use controls adaptable to subsurface development, ownership of subsurface development, and the unknown factors encountered by subsurface developers.

1028. Korell, Mark L. Financing earth sheltered housing: issues and opportunities. In <u>Residential applications: transcripts of selected presentations, Going Under to Stay on Top</u>, Minneapolis, MN, Oct. 1977. Minneapolis, MN: Univ. of Minn., Undergr. Sp. Ctr., 1979. p. 143-9. Also in <u>Undergr. Sp.</u>, v. 3, no. 6, May/June 1979: 297-301.
Issues include the special risk factors for financial institutions (such as borrower default and building codes), legislation and regulation, research, and demonstration homes. Opportunities for future action to encourage further support include market experience, examination of current coding standards

167 Institutional Issues

for overrestrictiveness, and insufficient guidance for earth-sheltered applications.

1029. Labs, Kenneth. Underground development, zoning, and you. Earth Shel. Dig. Energ. Rept., no. 4, July/Aug. 1979: 4-7.
Zoning in Minnesota, Kansas, and Pennsylvania.

1030. Loans there - if you flick the chip off your shoulder. Earth Shel. Dig. Energ. Rept., no. 5, Sept./Oct. 1979: 10-1.
The Head of Midwest Savings and Loan in Minneapolis/St. Paul discusses getting long-term financing to buy an earth-sheltered home. Lending regulations relating to earth shelters are presented.

1031. McGough, Kenis. The housing industry goes underground. Calif. R. Est., v. 60, no. 11, Nov. 1980: 6-9.
This article cites advantages and problems, one of which is financing, because lenders still know virtually nothing about the resale market for underground homes. Scarcity of contractors is another disadvantage. Also, construction costs are higher by 10 to 30 percent. Several different buildings are described.

1032. Manson, Dean A. Equity requirements of earth covered buildings and instruments of remedy. In Proc., Alt. in Energ. Conserv.: the Use of Earth Cov. Bldgs., Conf., Fort Worth, TX, July 9-12, 1975. F.L. Moreland, ed. Washington, DC: U.S. G.P.O., 1976. Also in Undergr. Sp., v. 1, no. 2, July/Aug. 1976: 123-6.
Underground home financing is attempted at the primary mortgage market level and should be at the secondary mortgage market level.

1033. Mason, Susan. Mortgage finance for alternative housing. Earth Shel. Dig. Energ. Rept., no. 6, Nov./Dec. 1979: 26-7.
This article details the concerns expressed by home mortgage lenders when dealing with requests to finance innovative housing, including earth-sheltered homes: i.e. potential marketability, present and future property values, technical performance, etc.

1034. MHFA housing program underway. Underline, v. 2, no. 1, Nov./Dec. 1980: 2.
The Minnesota Housing Finance Agency offered financing to 38 residential builders to construct 165 energy efficient

moderately-priced housing units, 81 of which were to be earth bermed or earth covered.

1035. Minnesota's answer to NASA. RIBA J., v. 89, no. 5, May 1982: 36.
A discussion of the Underground Space Center and earth-sheltered architectural development in the U.S.

1036. Mosena, David R. Planners and the underground: editorial. Undergr. Sp., v. 4, no. 5, Mar./Apr. 1980: iii-iv.
The development of underground space is entering a new era in which it is receiving more widespread attention and more serious recognition as a valuable resource and development option. The greatest surge of interest has been in the housing field. Planners and public officials will have to inform themselves about underground resources and will have to break down institutional barriers to underground space use. Most of all, planners and public officials will have to be receptive to new ideas.

1037. Muller, C.A. and R.A. Taylor. No cause for apprehension about costs of insuring earth-sheltered homes. Undergr. Sp., v. 5, no. 1, July/Aug. 1980: 28-30.
Insurance costs for earth sheltered and above-ground houses were compared. The results suggest that well-constructed earth-sheltered homes will probably command lower insurance costs, because analysis of insurable hazards indicates that underground buildings are less vulnerable to natural hazards with the possible exception of earth movements.

1038. _____. Risk and insurance. In Potential of earth-sheltered and underground space: proc., Undergr. Sp. Conf. and Expos., Kansas City, MO, June 8, 1981. T.L. Holthusen, ed. Elmsford, NY: Pergamon Pr., 1981. p. 467-73.
This is a report on the insurance aspects of underground projects emphasizing avoiding and minimizing hazards and their importance to all concerned with the details of developing an effective insurance program. A research project is discussed which is designing a Comprehensive Underground Space Insurance Policy (CUSIP).

1039. National Association of Mutual Insurance Companies. Underwriting considerations for earth-sheltered homes. Indianapolis, IN: Sept. 1981. 5 p. (NAMIC Energ. Bull.).
Provides guidelines, highlights areas of concern and furnishes a survey form to use in gathering information needed to underwrite an earth-sheltered home.

1040. Perkins, Jerry. Codes slow down progress. Earth Shel. Dig. Energ. Rept., no. 10, July/Aug. 1980: 21-3.

Earth-sheltering projects meet legal obstacles in Iowa and Illinois.

1041. Raab, Richard. Building codes and zoning ordinances affecting earth-sheltered home construction in New York State. Undergr. Sp., v. 7, no. 2, Sept./Oct. 1982: 110-4.

There are many legal limitations to building an earth-covered home in urban New York State. Building codes must be met that were devised for conventional housing, and conservative and exclusionary zoning ordinances must also be dealt with.

1042. Rivard, Mike. How to borrow the money to build your earth-sheltered home. Earth Shel. Dig. Energ. Rept., no. 2, Mar./Apr. 1979: 8-9.

This article sets forth strategies for developing and financing your home.

1043. Schmidt, Mark. Code study clarifies needed changes. Earth Shel. Dig. Energ. Rept., no. 9, May/June 1980: 36.

The Underground Space Center, under contract from the Dept. of Housing and Urban Development, made a survey to determine the need for changes to building and zoning codes affecting earth-sheltered homes.

1044. Schneider, Dick. Discussion: financing. In Residential applications: transcripts of selected presentations, Going Under to Stay on Top, Minneapolis, MN, Oct. 1977. Minneapolis, MN: Univ. of Minn., Undergr. Sp. Ctr., 1979. p. 151-3.

Lenders will not be on the cutting edge of earth-sheltered acceptance. The changes will come from the marketplace and the demand created by consumers. That will make lenders willing to extend financing. The author also thinks that energy-efficient housing will be a factor in the future, and lenders will finance projects which will be reproduced.

1045. Scott, D.M. Earth shelter experience of codes, zoning ordinances, financing. In Proc., West. SUN 1980 Sol. Update Conf., Salt Lake City, UT, Sept. 24, 1980. p. 73-9.

The subjects discussed are fire egress, ventilation, natural light, structural design, energy, waterproofing, guard rails, financing, and incentives.

1046. Solar and earth-sheltered home insurance rates cut 10 percent. Sol. Age, v. 6, no. 11, Nov. 1981: 71.

The Hanover Insurance Co., Worcester, MA, is offering a ten percent discount to owners of solar heated and earth-sheltered homes in Connecticut, Georgia, Illinois, Massachusetts, Missouri, New York, Alabama, Indiana, Maine, New Hampshire, Pennsylvania, Rhode Island, South Carolina, and Virginia with a dozen more states awaiting approval from state insurance commissions.

1047. Solomonson, Gary. Specific experiences and projects. In Residential applications: transcripts of selected presentations, Going Under to Stay on Top, Minneapolis, MN, Oct. 1977. Minneapolis, MN: Univ. of Minn., Undergr. Sp. Ctr., 1979. p. 169-71.

The author is involved in market research and feasibility studies in the housing market. He offers suggestions about marketing homes and tells what he's found out about consumer value formation.

1048. Sterling, R.L. Cost and code study of underground buildings: a report to the Minnesota Energy Agency. Undergr. Sp., v. 4, no. 3, Nov. 1979: 119-36.

This report covers public policy issues (building code restrictions, taxation, insurance) and residential construction costs (cost breakdowns, general factors affecting costs, and life cycle costs). It also deals with regulatory and insurance issues (building codes, fire protection, insurance provisions) and construction costs for large underground buildings. Several recommendations are made.

1049. Swenson, Gregory S. Zoning ordinances as obstacles to earth sheltered housing: a Minnesota perspective. Undergr. Sp., v. 3, no. 4, Jan./Feb. 1979: 165-74.

Each obstacle is described and its effect on earth-sheltered housing development is examined. Methods of overcoming the obstacles are suggested. Some examples: required minimum lot and floor area and excessive setbacks, required minimum height, and prohibition of living below grade. It is concluded that state legislation is necessary in order to encourage potential earth-sheltered home builders by clarifying the conditions under which they can build.

1050. Tarlock, A. Dan. Legal aspects of the use of the underground. In Legal, economic and energy consideration in the use of underground space. Washington, DC: Nat. Acad. Sci., 1974. Also in Underground utilization. T. Stauffer, ed. Kansas City, MO: Univ. of Missouri, Dept. of Geosci., 1978. v. 6, p. 826-30.

The legal aspects of the use of the underground, and the ownership of underground space are discussed. The need for incentives and restrictions on underground space use are explored.

1051. _____. Property rights considerations. In Proc., Alt. in Energ. Conserv.: the Use of Earth Cov. Bldgs., Fort Worth, TX, July 9-12, 1975. Washington, DC: U.S. G.P.O., 1976. p. 233-8.

The author addresses the problem of how the law should structure a system of property right assignments to encourage the use of subspace.

1052. Thomas, William A. Ownership of subterranean space. Undergr. Sp., v. 3, no. 4, Jan./Feb. 1979: 155-63. Also in Underground utilization. T. Stauffer, ed. Kansas City, MO: Univ. of Missouri, Dept. of Geosci., 1978. p. 801-7.

Ownership of land in the U.S. and in other nations is usually interpreted to include ownership from the surface to the center of the earth. This wedge can, in turn, be divided into several strata each with a separate owner. Or, one entity might own only the minerals on or under the surface of land owned by another. Troublesome legal issues might arise in the future when activities deep underground intersect the vertical wedges of property owned by other persons. Until several decades ago, a landowner had control of the column of air between the surface and the heavens. The development of aviation led to the limitation of property rights upward. The development of subsurface space requires planning in order to prepare for legal problems which will arise concerning ownership.

1053. Tingerthal, Mary. Deciding to build an earth sheltered home. Archit. Minn., v. 6, no. 2, Apr. 1980: 36-8.

This article discusses obtaining financing to construct an earth-sheltered home. The factors to consider: a personal financial assessment; site assessment; design assessment; builder assessment. In addition, have a basic mortgage lending knowledge, make a checklist of items required by the lender to evaluate your application for a loan, i.e. plans, specifications, credit information, cost estimates, and information about the contractor, etc.

1054. TLH Associates, Inc. Earth-sheltered home financing, an introduction for lenders and appraisers. Prepared for the U.S. Dept. of Energy, Off. of Bldgs. Energ. Res. and Dev., Bldg. Syst. Div., St. Paul, MN, Sept. 1981.

1055. _____. Financing earth-sheltered housing: a report on a project to facilitate the loan process. Oak Ridge, TN: Oak Ridge Nat. Lab., Feb. 1982. 47 p. (Contract W-7405-ENG-26; NTIS, PC A03/MF A01).

Information is presented on the options available for short and long-term financing, shopping for a lending institution, lenders' obligations, the criteria lenders use in deciding eligibility for a loan, and presenting the borrower's case to the lending institution.

1056. Trek from Montana opens doors. Earth Shel. Dig. Energ. Rept., no. 8, Mar./Apr. 1980: 51-3.

A Montana earth-sheltered aficionado was denied an FHA-approved loan at home, so he took his case to the FHA in Washington, DC and eventually got the loan. A detailed record shows the sequence of events leading to approval of the loan.

1057. Underground Space Center. Earth sheltered housing: code, zoning and financing issues. By Ray Sterling, Roger Aiken, John Carmody. Washington, DC: Dept. of Hous. and Urb. Dev., Div. of Energ., Bldg. Tech. and Stand., 1980. Rev. ed. 1981. 141 p.

This work describes current financial, code, and zoning impediments to construction of earth-sheltered homes, and recommends changes in these areas that are needed to eliminate obstacles to this type of construction. Sections of this report deal with the concepts and development of earth-sheltered housing, advantages and disadvantages of such housing, building codes, zoning ordinances, and financing issues related to earth-sheltered homes.

1058. Vadnais, Kathleen. Building codes don't have to be a hassle. Earth Shel. Dig. Energ. Rept., no. 2, Mar./Apr. 1979: 12-3.

1059. _____. Energy costs threaten lenders' tradition. Earth Shel. Dig. Energ. Rept., no. 9, May/June 1980: 44-7.

The energy efficiency of a home is becoming a decisive factor in determining whether some lenders will finance home purchases.

1060. _____. FHA appraiser has practical approach. Earth Shel. Dig. Energ. Rept., no. 8, Mar./Apr. 1980: 18-21.

An FHA appraiser in the Minneapolis FHA office says his office has processed more earth sheltering loan guarantee applications than the five other offices in the region covering Indiana, Ohio, Michigan, Wisconsin, and Illinois. He uses the cost appraisal method. The solar credit program allows FHA to add up to 20 percent more to the insured value, and earth shelters might be more likely to qualify for the solar credit than would surface homes.

1061. _____. Insurance study favors earth sheltering. Earth Shel. Liv., no. 26, Mar./Apr. 1983: 26-8.
The underwriting manager of the Kemper Insurance Group coordinated a two-year study of the insurability of earth-sheltered housing. Their chief guideline is to avoid do-it-yourself efforts and insure only architect-designed and contractor-constructed earth shelters. The Earth Shelter Committee of the National Association of Mutual Insurance Companies issued an Energy Bulletin in Sept. 1981 to provide underwriting guidelines, highlight areas of concern, and provide a survey form for use in gathering information needed to underwrite an earth-sheltered home.

1062. _____. Subdivision owners require earth sheltering. Earth Shel. Liv., no. 26, Mar./Apr. 1983: 18-21.
Builders in Connecticut and Wisconsin have subdivisions with covenants restricting them to constructing only earth-sheltered houses.

1063. _____. Tour of earth shelters impresses money men. Earth Shel. Dig. Energ. Rept., no. 9, May/June 1980: 47.
A tour of earth-sheltered demonstration homes in Minnesota led to the inclusion of earth sheltering to the energy efficiency list of the Federal Home Loan Mortgage Corp.

1064. Warner, N. Thomas. Insurance considerations for earth-sheltered residences. Earth Shel. Bldgs. - Tech. Pap. TP-IIIK, 1983.

1065. White, Al. Banker favors earth sheltering. Earth Shel. Dig. Energ. Rept., no. 4, July/Aug. 1979: 41.
This banker gives steps to follow when trying to obtain financing on earth-sheltered housing.

1066. Ziebarth, A.M. Potential problems of legal liability in the design, construction, and ownership of an earth shelter. In Earth shelter 2: coll. pap., Earth Shel. Hous. Conf. and Exhib., Minneapolis, MN, Apr. 9-11, 1980. Minneapolis, MN: Univ. of Minn., Undergr. Sp. Ctr., 1980. p. 133-9.
Some potential legal problems regarding the design, construction, and ownership of an earth-sheltered home are discussed. The problems are in the areas of landscaping, struc-

tural engineering, waterproofing, insulation, the builder, and home tours.

1067. _____. Restrictive covenants: a barrier to earth sheltering. In Earth shelter 2: coll. pap., Earth Shel. Hous. Conf. and Exhib., Minneapolis, MN, Apr. 9-11, 1980. Minneapolis, MN: Univ. of Minn., Undergr. Sp. Ctr., 1980. p. 155-60.

The impact of restrictive covenants on earth sheltering are examined. Restrictive covenants affecting earth sheltering have not been tested in the courts. Advice is offered to prospective owners.

XXIII. PUBLIC POLICY

1068. As this issue went to press, the Solar Energy and Energy Conservation Bank was slated for elimination in the Reagan budget. Undergr. Sp., v. 6, no. 1, July/Aug. 1981: 5.

1069. Barker, Michael B. Earth-sheltered construction: thoughts on public policy issues. Undergr. Sp., v. 4, no. 5, Mar./Apr. 1980: 283-8.

Those with an interest in underground development must clarify policy issues and responses that will prove the value of underground construction and foster public interest. Issues of national policy that are discussed: defense, natural resources, energy, and transportation/urban form. Those of local importance: public utilities, building regulation, aesthetics, and public demand. Policy issues that demonstrate the value of subsurface construction and encourage public interest must be articulated by underground developers.

1070. Bedell, Berkley. Earth sheltered homes help to achieve energy independence. Earth Shel. Dig. Energ. Rept., no. 9, May/June 1980: 48-9.

Congressman Bedell of Iowa gave this message to an earth-sheltered housing seminar sponsored by the Iowa Chapter of the American Underground Space Association. He discusses his efforts to make Congress aware of earth sheltering and discusses the need for energy conservation.

1071. Bill introduced to promote use of underground. Underline, v. 5, no. 2, 1984: 5.

Public Policy

On Mar. 11, 1984, U.S. Rep. Pat Williams, Democrat of Montana, introduced a bill requiring the consideration of the use of underground structures for public buildings when possible.

1072. Bill would provide loans for earth sheltered homes. Underline, v. 1, no. 2, Jan. 1980: 3-4.

Minnesota's Fourth District Congressman Bruce Vento sponsored a Solar and Energy Conservation Bank bill to enable homeowners and developers to obtain long-term loans for installing efficient solar equipment in commercial and residential buildings.

1073. Congress studies earth shelter. Earth Shel. Dig. Energ. Rept., no. 1, Jan./Feb. 1979: 10.

The Vento Cave Amendment, sponsored by Congressman Bruce Vento, Democrat of Minnesota, directs the Secretary of HUD to conduct a feasibility study on residential construction underground.

1074. Energy-conscious design: entering architecture's mainstream. An interview with John Cable. Undergr. Sp., v. 6, no. 2, Sept./Oct. 1981: 84-7.

Cable is Director of the Buildings Division of the U.S. Dept. of Energy's Office of Buildings and Community Systems which promotes energy efficient building design through research, demonstration, and education.

1075. Federal subsidies for earth-sheltered structures available soon. News and comment. Undergr. Sp., v. 5, no. 4, Jan./Feb. 1981: 195.

The Solar Energy and Energy Conservation Bank Bill passed by Congress last July will make available subsidized loans for installing active or passive solar technologies, including earth-sheltering in residential or commercial buildings.

1076. Hamburger, Richard. Public policy considerations and earth covered settlements. In Proc., Alt. in Habitat: the Use of Earth Cov. Set., Conf., Fort Worth, TX, May 17-19, 1978. F.L. Moreland, ed. Washington, DC: U.S. Dept. of Energy, 1979. v. 2, Earth covered buildings and settlements, p. 1-6.

Public policies that promote energy conservation by encouraging the construction of earth-covered structures will work well if they reinforce each other. Policies should be developed which provide subsidies for conservation instead of for specific technologies, such as solar heating.

1077. _____. Strategies for legislative changes. In Proc., Alt. in Energ. Conserv.: the Use of Earth Cov. Bldgs., Conf., Fort Worth, TX, July 9-12, 1975. F.L. Moreland, ed. Washington, DC: U.S. G.P.O., 1976. p. 243-6.

A discussion of the implementation of public policy changes related to energy conservation to encourage more use of earth-covered buildings.

1078. Karpinski, David. Housing future is legislator's concern. Earth Shel. Liv., no. 19, Jan./Feb. 1982: 49-50.

The author works for the Minnesota State Senate and has done housing research for State Senator Frank Knoll. Their findings are discussed.

1079. Kneebone, T. The acceptance and role of earth-sheltered building systems within a public housing sector. In Proc., 1st Int. Conf. on Energ. Effic. Bldgs. with Earth Shel. Prot., Sydney, Aust., Aug. 1-6, 1983. L.L. Boyer, ed. Stillwater, OK: Okla. State Univ., Archit. Ext., 1983. p. 213-7.

This paper outlines the Victorian Ministry of Housing's changing attitudes to the use of non-traditional housing systems and materials for its public housing program. It traces the evolving interest in earth-sheltered construction with particular reference to the new self-build program promoting mud-brick buildings. It then discusses the problems, benefits, acceptance, and future role of earth-sheltered buildings in the public housing sector. --Auth. abstract.

1080. Knoll, Frank. A law maker's perspective. In Residential applications: transcripts of selected presentations, Going Under to Stay on Top, Minneapolis, MN, Oct. 1977. Minneapolis, MN: Univ. of Minn., Undergr. Sp. Ctr., 1979. p. 129-31.

Knoll is a state senator who introduced legislation regarding earth-sheltered housing to the Minnesota State Legislature.

1081. _____. A legislator lobbies. Earth Shel. Dig. Energ. Rept., no. 1, Jan./Feb. 1979: 12.

Minnesota State Senator Knoll supports legislation concerning underground construction of residential buildings in Minnesota.

1082. Labs, Kenneth B. Land-use regulation of underground housing. Chicago, IL: Am. Plan. Assn., May 1979. 8 p. (PAS memo).

1083. La Nier, Royce and Frank L. Moreland. Earth sheltered architecture and land use policy. Undergr. Sp., v. 1, no. 4, Aug. 1977: iii.

This editorial discusses the need to change our land-use habits and the laws governing them in order to significantly reduce energy consumption.

1084. Lee, Orville G. Is there a future for earth sheltered housing? In Residential applications: transcripts of selected presentations, Going Under to Stay on Top, Minneapolis, MN, Oct. 1977. Minneapolis, MN: Univ. of Minn., Undergr. Sp. Ctr., 1979. p. 161-2.

The author is the Director of the Building Technology and Standards Division of HUD. He discusses HUD's energy efficient residential program. Part of the research was a study of consumer acceptance of advanced technology in housing.

1085. Moe, Roger D. Technology and the legislator: the value of communication. Undergr. Sp., v. 4, no. 1, July 1979: 1-10.

Legislators and technical experts are considering many of the same problems and communication among them must be improved if underground space development is to become the boon it promises to be. The Underground Space Center is presented as an example of what experts and legislators can do when they combine forces.

1086. North Carolina Coalition aims at Legislature. Earth Shel. Dig. Energ. Rept., no. 5, Sept./Oct. 1979: 28-9.

On May 14, 1979, the Earth Shelter Committee of the North Carolina Coalition for Renewable Energy Resources lobbied the State Legislature by presenting the legislators with copies of Earth Shelter Digest and Energy Report.

1087. Riechers, Maggie. Federal activities in earth-sheltered and underground construction. Undergr. Sp., v. 5, no. 6, 1981: 275-8.

Nonresidential underground construction has received the majority of federal support, but the Dept. of Energy and the Dept. of Housing and Urban Development recently implemented several research and development projects to study energy consumption of earth-sheltered buildings, the technical aspects of their construction, and ways to gain market acceptance. Other recent support by the U.S. Government is discussed.

1088. Tax laws make pass at passive. Earth Shel. Dig. Energ. Rept., no. 14, Mar./Apr. 1981: 64.

Passive solar equipment, an important part of earth-sheltered designs, is still hard to define. They must not serve any significant structural function in order to be eligible for renewable energy credits under Federal law. However, some states are allowing either a property tax exemption, an income tax credit or a sales tax exemption for active and or passive solar equipment.

1089. USC info services adapt in response to Reagan budget cuts. <u>Underline</u>, v. 2, no. 6, Sept./Oct. 1981: 1, 8.
As a result of federal budget cuts, the Underground Space Center's technical inquiry response service began operating on a fee basis as of Oct. 1, 1981. The Center's Technical Response Group had been funded since May 1980 by the DOE to answer questions from consumers on the technical aspects of earth-sheltered design and construction.

XXIV. HAZARD MITIGATION

1090. Bambert, A.E. Fire protection in underground structures. <u>Fire J.</u>, Jan. 1975: 40-3+.

1091. Chester, C.V., H.B. Shapira, and G.A. Cristy. <u>Hazard mitigation potential of earth-sheltered residences</u>. Final rept., 1982-1983. Oak Ridge, TN: Oak Ridge Nat. Lab., Nov. 1983. 218 p. (NTIS, PC A10/MF A01).
This review of the literature on earth-sheltered housing provides an analysis of the protection potential against natural and technological hazards and a cost comparison with conventional construction. There is a discussion of institutional issues and policy options affecting the adoption of earth-sheltered structures.

1092. Christensen, Keith H. Send the wind up, around & away. <u>Earth Shel. Liv.</u>, no. 27, May/June 1983: 26-7.
Pt. 1 of a series on protection from wind discusses the value of wind-deflecting earth banks placed in a southwesterly direction from the exposed solar south glass wall, and the design of the connected but outreaching earth-retaining walls of a typical earth-sheltered house.

1093. _____. Use vertical fins and barn door shutters: design exposed wall components that protect you from severe wind storms. <u>Earth Shel. Liv.</u>, no. 28, July/Aug. 1983: 9-11.

Pt. 2 of a series on protection from wind recommends the use of vertical wall fins and heavy barn door shutters as parts of a coordinated severe storm protection system for earth-sheltered structures.

1094. Garland, Mark A. Earth covered buildings and fire. In Proc., 1st Int. Conf. on Energ. Effic. Bldgs. with Earth Shel. Prot., Sydney, Aust., Aug. 1-6, 1983. L.L. Boyer, ed. Stillwater, OK: Okla. State Univ., Archit. Ext., 1983. p. 151-8.

Some findings of a study into fire in earth-covered buildings are presented. The characteristics of earth-covered buildings under the effects of fire, smoke, and toxic gases are discussed. Recommendations are made for the appropriate use of certain fire prevention, detection, and control systems for this type of building. --Auth. abstract.

1095. _____. Earth covered buildings and fire. Geotecture, v. 2, no. 1, Jan. 1985: 18-33.

This paper deals with dangers occurring when fire originates within an earth-covered building. Prevention methods cover building materials, detection and extinguishing methods, ventilation, egress planning, and emergency lighting.

1096. _____. Fire dangers in earth covered buildings. Earth Shel. Liv., no. 36, Nov./Dec. 1984: 29-31.

This article lists steps to take to reduce the risk of fire, e.g. select non-combustible furnishings when possible, provide an adequate ventilation system to remove gases, equip the house with an extinguishing system, incorporate smoke detectors to initiate the extinguishing system, and design the structure to allow escape from all areas.

1097. Jensen, Rodney and Harry Roberts. A combined underground house and fallout shelter. In Proc., 1st Int. Conf. on Energ. Effic. Bldgs. with Earth Shel. Prot., Sydney, Aust., Aug. 1-6, 1983. L.L. Boyer, ed. Stillwater, OK: Okla. State Univ., Archit. Ext., 1983. p. 159-64.

Nuclear strike on Australia may expose many possible locations on the continent to high levels of fallout. An earth-protected house is an ideal basis for a shelter in both suburban and country areas. The cost of adding a shelter is justified if it can be used for some other purpose in peace time. The schematic design shows how a shelter could be built into a three-bedroom, earth-protected house for a normal flat site. The radiation protection given by the shelter is substantial; and if located in an area of high fallout, would certainly mean the difference between survival and slow painful death from radiation sickness. --Auth. abstract.

1098. Johnson, Terry A. How to survive natural & nuclear disasters, in an earth sheltered home. Portsmouth, OH: Underground Homes, 1981. 29 p.

This booklet concentrates more on the effects of a nuclear disaster and the protection an earth-sheltered house can afford than on natural disasters such as hurricanes, tornadoes, earthquakes, and fire. The author says that public fallout shelters are intolerably inadequate to support life for an extended period, and shows how an earth-sheltered home can be designed or modifed to act as a nuclear fallout shelter.

1099. Kiesling, Ernst W. Economical wind protection - underground. Undergr. Sp., v. 4, no. 5, Mar./Apr. 1980: 279-82.

Earth-sheltered houses offer degrees of occupant protection comparable to those presented by above-ground buildings with special features, and they offer higher degrees of protection against economic loss than is economically feasible in improved conventional houses. By reducing losses from wind storms, lower insurance rates can be obtained.

1100. _____ and Joseph E. Minor. Hazard mitigation through earth sheltering. In Proc., 1st Int. Conf. on Energ. Effic. Bldgs. with Earth Shel. Prot., Sydney, Aust., Aug. 1-6, 1983. L.L. Boyer, ed. Stillwater, OK: Okla. State Univ., Archit. Ext., 1983. p. 133-9.

Earth-sheltered buildings are inherently more resistant to some natural hazards than their above-ground counterparts. Greater protection from tornadoes is an important factor to some owners in choosing the earth-sheltered concept. The forces imposed by tornadic winds on a conventional building are presented, followed by discussion of some design features of conventional and earth-sheltered buildings which are important to their performance when subjected to these forces. Building response to earthquakes, hail, temperature extremes, and fire are discussed briefly. --Auth. abstract.

1101. Moreland, Frank. Earth-covered buildings: an exploratory analysis for hazard and energy performance. Final rept., Sept. 1979-Nov. 1981. 314 p. (NTIS, PC A14/MF A01).

The performance of earth-covered buildings is examined with regard to earthquakes, fire, nuclear detonation and radiation, storms, energy consumption, compatibility with solar energy systems, peak-load effects, soil and groundwater effects, air and climate effects, occupant evaluation, and resource management. Potential long-term benefits are assessed.

1102. Munson, Michael J.F. Fire safety characteristics of earth covered dwellings. In Proc., Alt. in Habitat: the Use of Earth Cov. Set., Conf., Fort Worth, TX, May 17-19, 1978. F.L. Moreland, ed. Washington, DC: U.S. Dept. of Energy, 1979. v. 1, Earth covered buildings: technical notes, p. 210-9.

This paper is divided into four sections: a brief description of the prototypical earth-covered dwelling; a general discussion of the characteristics of residential fires, based on recent empirical studies; a general discussion of the fire safety implications of earth-covered dwellings focusing on property losses and on human losses, the injuries and fatalities sometimes resulting from residential fires; and some general comments about the implications of earth-covered dwellings from the perspective of providers of fire protection services. It is concluded that the introduction of earth-covered dwellings will have a relatively minor impact on expected fire losses, although property losses to the structure may be reduced slightly.

1103. Schurer, Gerhard. Nuclear defence capability: yes or no! Geotecture, v. 1, no. 3, Apr. 1984: 5-6.

To promote earth-covered fallout shelters is to promote a false promise. Designers of geotectural structures have the responsibility to promote peace.

1104. Tornado jumps over earth shelter. Earth Shel. Dig. Energ. Rept., no. 17, Sept./Oct. 1981: 18-9.

An earth-sheltered house survived a St. Paul tornado, losing only the berm's ground cover.

XXV. NON-RESIDENTIAL APPLICATIONS

1105. Airplane lives high-underground. Earth Shel. Liv., no. 27, May/June 1983: 13-6.

An earth-sheltered hangar in northern Arizona at Montezuma Heights Air Park, Camp Verde, is described.

1106. All-weather wood makes its earth shelter debut. Earth Shel. Dig. Energ. Rept., no. 6, Nov./Dec. 1979: 48.

This all-wood earth shelter uses an engineering truss and beam combination for the roof. The Mouse House is a retail business structure in Redwood Falls, MN, built by Corkey U'Ren.

1107. Allen, Jonathan M. A 100 percent passive solar underground greenhouse. Alt. Energ., no. 45, Sept./Oct. 1980: p. 8.

The author built his house in one of the worst solar energy areas, Plattsburg, NY. By using a solar panel placed mostly inferior to an underground chamber, using the earth as heat storage mass, using gravity flow of air for circulating and distributing heat, the base temperature of the earth heat-store was maintained at 52 degrees and above during the coldest part of the year.

1108. Autumn Architecture Research Group. The human factors of underground work environments. J.A. Wise and Barbara K. Wise, eds. Seattle, WA: Univ. of Wash., 1984. 102 p.

This report was produced by the Autumn 1983 academic quarter undergraduate design research studio at the University of Washington, Dept. of Architecture. The students reviewed the state of the art of subsurface workplaces, each student writing a separate chapter. The chapters are entitled: Why underground environments? Psychosocial aspects; Health aspects; Emergency and safety aspects; Spatial aspects; Lighting; Interior furnishings and fabrics; and a Conclusion and underground building evaluation form. Available from J.A. Wise, JO-20 Architecture, University of Washington, Seattle, WA 98195.

1109. Bankers build securely into the environment. Earth Shel. Dig. Energ. Rept., no. 3, May/June 1979: 37.

1110. Barker, Michael B. Building underground for people: eleven selected projects in the United States. Washington, DC: Am. Inst. of Archit., 1978. 30 p.

This report to the Working Group on Subsurface Planning of the International Tunneling Association gives brief descriptions of 11 underground projects, including a library, bookstore, elementary school, cafeteria, and others. Data are given on design, construction techniques, cost, local geology, and date of completion for each of the projects, three of which are residential. A bibliography and list of architects are included.

1111. Barnes, Paul R. and Hanna Shapira. Passive solar heating and natural cooling of an earth-integrated design. In Proc., Earth Shel. Bldg. Des. Innov., Oklahoma City, OK, Apr. 18, 1980. L.L. Boyer, ed. Stillwater, OK: Okla. State Univ., 1980. p. VII. 29-36.

Innovative features of a new Oak Ridge National Laboratory building will reduce the energy needed for cooling, heating, and lighting. The energy efficiency of the design will be monitored over several years.

1112. Bennett, D.J. Earth sheltered buildings coupled with the sun: opportunities and constraints in design. In Potential of earth-sheltered and underground space: proc., Undergr. Sp. Conf. and Expos., Kansas City, MO, June 8-10, 1981. T.L. Holthusen, ed. Elmsford, NY: Pergamon Pr., 1981. p. 75-90.

The Civil and Mineral Engineering Building at the University of Minnesota in Minneapolis is programmed as an energy conservation demonstration, integrating underground construction with solar responsive components which include solar shading with plants, passive solar storage in water tubes, and a system of illuminating interior spaces with mirrors and optical lenses.

1113. _____ and T.P. Bligh. The energy factor -- a dimension of design. Undergr. Sp., v. 1, no. 4, Aug. 1977: 325-32.

The heat transfer and energy conserving characteristics of the underground Bookstore Building at the University of Minnesota are discussed.

1114. Brood barn to be bermed: earth sheltering to play large part in new horse farm. Earth Shel. Liv., no. 37, Jan./Feb. 1985: 15.

Brood barns will be earth bermed by their builder, Universal Design Group, Columbus, IN.

1115. Businesses cutting costs by covering up: small business is increasingly making use of earth sheltering. Earth Shel. Liv., no. 34, July/Aug. 1984:30-1.

Examples: a Washburn, WI, ice cream parlor, a radio station in Spring Grove, MN, a medical clinic in Lexington, NE, and a motel in Jackson, MN.

1116. Carter, Douglas N. Community and building official reaction to earth-covered buildings: a case study of Terraset Elementary School, Reston, Virginia. In Proc., Alt. in Habitat: the Use of Earth Cov. Set., Conf., Fort Worth, TX, May 17-19, 1978. F.L. Moreland, ed. Washington, DC: U.S. Dept. of Energy, 1979. v. 2, Earth covered buildings and settlements, p. 78-81.

This paper reviews the reactions from designers, cost consultants, public officials, and private citizens, and the building's users to the proposal to build an earth-covered elementary school. The author suggests that the review act as a guide to future designers who wish to avoid pitfalls. Because of the success of the school, a second commission was granted to build another earth-covered school which will have increased energy savings by simplifying the operation and maintenance of the mechanical system.

1117. _____. Don't look up, look down. Civ. Eng., v. 47, no. 7, July 1977: 57-60.

Designers arrived at an energy-conserving design for Terraset Elementary School in Reston, VA, by covering a series of circles with two to three feet of earth. They excavated the the top of a hill, poured concrete shells, then put the hill back on. The resulting high thermal mass allows the building to act as an energy reservoir, storing warmth or coldness, and delaying the impact of outside temperature changes.

1118. Center blends with natural setting. Earth Shel. Liv., no. 24, Nov./Dec. 1982: 18-9.

The Gordon Bubolz Nature Preserve Center in Appleton, WI, is earth sheltered. It was built by Natural Areas Preservation, Inc., Ben Seaborne, Douglas Marsh, Earth Shelter Corp. of America, and Gassner Realty and Construction, Inc.

1119. Company insures itself against future: Mutual of Omaha digs new office. Earth Shel. Dig. Energ. Rept., no. 5, Sept./Oct. 1979: 36-9.

A below-grade addition to the Mutual of Omaha Company's Home Office was completed in the Fall of 1979. The three-story 190,000 sq. ft. building is capped by a massive dome. A savings of 80 percent on energy costs is expected.

1120. Company protects computer with earth cover. Earth Shel. Dig. Energ. Rept., no. 9, May/June 1980: 14-7.

Protection from tornados and high winds was the primary reason Mass Merchandisers, Inc., Harrison, AR, housed their computer in a 10,000 sq. ft. earth-sheltered building.

1121. County building reclaims gravel pit, saves energy. Earth Shel. Dig. Energ. Rept., no. 8, Mar./Apr. 1980: 47.

The Operations and Maintenance Building for Multnomah County, OR, will be built in an unused gravel pit.

1122. Desert demo wins award. Earth Shel. Liv., no. 22, July/Aug. 1982: 55-6.

A 2,100 sq. ft. earth-sheltered building in the Mojave Desert is the visitor's center in Antelope Valley, California State Poppy Reserve, California.

185   Non-Residential Applications   **1123-1129**

1123. Dig this. Fam. W., Nov. 20, 1983.
Tom Erickson's Earth Inn in Jackson, MN, is the country's first earth-sheltered motel.

1124. Dorms sheltered on Kansas campus. Earth Shel. Liv., no. 22, July/Aug. 1982: 20-1.
Earth-bermed dorms at Barton County Community College in Great Bend, KS.

1125. Duke, Buford W., Jr. Incorporating earth shelter considerations into the design process for nonresidential buildings. In Proc., Earth Shel. Bldg. Des. Innov., Nat. Tech. Conf., Oklahoma City, OK, April 18, 1980. L.L. Boyer, ed. Stillwater, OK: Okla. State Univ., 1980. p. V. 25-30.
The nonresidential structures examined vary in size from 4,000 sq. ft. to 240,000 sq. ft., are primarily for office use, and are located in three climatic zones. They are the California State Office Building in Sacramento, the Los Alamos Laboratory Support Facility in New Mexico, and the small headquarters building for the National Art Education Association in Virginia.

1126. Earth sheltered businesses win energy awards. Earth Shel. Liv., no. 10, July/Aug. 1980: 64.
Two Minnesota earth-sheltered businesses were selected from 65 state entrants to be honored for their energy conservation programs in the fourth annual Energy Saver's Award of Excellence competition sponsored by the National Gas Council of Minnesota and the Minnesota Energy Agency. The businesses were Control Data Corporation's World Distribution Center in St. Paul (the state winner), and other was the Mouse House, a retail cheese store in Redwood Falls, MN; it was the runner-up.

1127. Earth sheltered motel keeps energy bills down. Underline, v. 6, no. 1, Oct./Dec. 1984: 1, 5.
The 6,900 sq. ft., 20-unit Earth Inn Motel in Jackson, MN, cost just $200 to heat in winter and $300 to air condition in the summer. The owners are considering building a chain.

1128. Earth sheltered Nature Center dedicated in Wisconsin. Underline, v. 3, no. 6, Sept./Oct. 1982: 1.
The 5,900 sq. ft. Gordon Bubolz Nature Preserve Center near Appleton, WI, incorporates earth sheltering, passive and active solar features, and a wind generator system. It was dedicated in May 1982.

1129. Farmer goes under whole hog: hog farmer beats the heat,

and cold, by going under: occupants have no complaints. Earth Shel. Liv., no. 34, July/Aug. 1984: 18-21.
A Plattsburgh, MO, hog farmer built a $150,000 earth sheltered farrowing house for temperature control. Davis Caves Construction, Inc. now builds earth-sheltered hog barns. Davis Caves is in Armington, IL.

1130. Fire HQ covered for 23 years. Earth Shel. Dig. Energ. Rept., no. 18, Nov./Dec. 1981: 4-5.
The St. Louis Fire Alarm Headquarters was built underground in 1958. It is built into a south-facing slope in Forest Park, a park in St. Louis, MO.

1131. Gagen, Joe. The underground church. Crosswinds, v. 1, no. 1, May 1968: 12-3.
A Malcolm Wells proposal.

1132. Garden offices bloom beneath desert. Earth Shel. Liv., no. 20, Mar./Apr. 1982: 53.
This 112,000 sq. ft. office building in Phoenix was designed by Ken O'Dell, of O'Dell and Wooldridge. The building contains a below-grade landscaped central garden.

1133. Geery, Daniel. Solar greenhouses: underground. Blue Ridge Summit, PA: TAB Books, 1982. 408 p.
Step-by-step construction techniques and details of underground greenhouse gardening are given. There is a discussion of how to plan and build a scale model to point at any flaws before building the full-scale structure. Three operational greenhouses are fully described. It is told how these structures optimize sunlight and radiation, thermal efficiency, radiation flows, heat transfer, humidity, etc.

1134. Georgetown University covers field house with field. Earth Shel. Dig. Energ. Rept., no. 8, Mar./Apr. 1980: 44-5.
Georgetown University is in Washington, D.C.

1135. Green, B.H., D.A. Summers, and N.B. Aughenbaugh. Design innovations for a new minerals engineering building. In Proc., Earth Shel. Bldg. Des. Innov., Nat. Tech. Conf., Oklahoma City, OK, Apr. 18, 1980. L.L. Boyer, ed. Stillwater, OK: Okla. State Univ., 1980. p. V. 17-22.
Conceptualization and planning of the new Civil and Mineral Engineering building, Univ. of Minnesota, are discussed. A unique feature of this project was the use of the existing subsurface rocks as walls in rooms in some areas of

the building. Other innovations include the use of high pressure water jets for excavation of the rock and the use of the excavated rock as building materials. The finished building includes large pretempering air intake plenums.

1136. Highway rest stop saves landscape. Earth Shel. Dig. Energ. Rept., no. 8, Mar./Apr. 1980: 23.
    This 1,786 sq. ft. rest stop is near Anchor Lake, MN. The method of construction is reinforced poured concrete.

1137. Hlavin, A.C. and A.A. Martin. Terraset: taking less from the earth. In Proc., Sol. World Mtg., Annu. Mtg., Int. Sol. Energ. Soc., Am. Sec., Orlando, FL, June 6, 1977.
Cape Canaveral, FL: Int. Sol. Energ. Soc., 1977. p. 38.19.
    An underground school is described. The mechanical system is an all electric solar-assisted heat pump/heat reclaim heating and cooling hydronic system. The solar collectors are evacuated tubular glass with reflector and an effective surface area of 448 sq. m. Solar cooling is provided by absorption chillers.

1138. Hoff, Eric, David Jenkins, and Jim Katomski. Noti solar greenhouses: performance and analysis. Eugene, OR: Univ. of Ore., 1977. 32 p.
    The performance of a passive solar-heated greenhouse is examined with respect to the intentions of its designers, its capacity for raising plants and vegetables and its viability for use in the Pacific Northwest. Recommendations are made that would improve greenhouse performance without any increase in operating cost. The greenhouse is below ground on the north side and the north slope of the roof has 12 inches of sod. Recycled and locally available materials are used where possible.

1139. Houghton, Dean. Going underground: hog building. Suc. Farm., v. 77, no. 11, Oct. 1979: 16-9.
    The earth-bermed building, i.e. earth contact on three sides, is most favored for this purpose. The main drawback is the need to heat incoming ventilating air.

1140. Interpretive center wins award. Earth Shel. Liv., no. 21, May/June 1982: 24-5.
    The earth-sheltered Oliver Hudson Kelly Interpretive Center in Elk River, MN, is the visitor center for a restored working farm of the 1850s.

1141. Johnson, Jay M. Sunspace Minnesota: passive solar design for winter resorts. Period covered, Aug. 1979-Oct. 1980. (DOE/R5/10130-2).

Minnesota winter resorts are discussed as to type, size, and use. Some new cabin designs and concepts are presented including earth-sheltered buildings. Some existing cabins are studied for energy conservation and solar retrofit possibilities.

1142. Kommendant, August E. Earth-covered structures. Undergr. Sp., v. 3, no. 6, May/June 1979: 279-84.
Some of the most suitable and economical systems for constructing underground facilities are discussed, facilities such as storage tanks, parking structures, factories, libraries, and community centers. The author asserts that underground buildings can be constructed easily and economically using existing technology.

1143. Largest earth shelter in San Francisco. Earth Shel. Dig. Energ. Rept., no. 9, May/June 1980: 37.
Called the largest earth-sheltered structure in the world, the Moscone Center covers 11 acres and contains 650,000 sq. ft. Also called the San Francisco Civic Center.

1144. Machowski, Barb. Earth shelters enrich American history. Earth Shel. Dig. Energ. Rept., no. 11, Sept./Oct. 1980: 48-51.
Two earth shelters have been recognized as state and national historic sites: Baldasare Forestiere's Underground Gardens in Fresno, CA, and an earth-sheltered museum and interpretive center showcasing an historic Civil War fort near Memphis, TN.

1145. _____. School designs deserve "A." Earth Shel. Dig. Energ. Rept., no. 14, Mar./Apr. 1981: 44-8.
Three new earth-sheltered school buildings are on the St. Paul Campus of the Univ. of Minnesota, in Riverheights, Canada, and in Poinciana, FL.

1146. Malott, R.W. Solar greenhouse as an integral part of an earth-sheltered home: the first two years. Sunpaper, v. 9, no. 1, Jan. 1984: 6-7.

1147. Mansfield, Jerry W. Dentist fills office with sunshine. Earth Shel. Liv., no. 21, May/June 1982: 50-1.
A passive solar earth-sheltered office building in Middletown, OH, is described. The floor plan is shown.

1148. Meixel, G.D., Jr. Energy use of non-residential earth-sheltered buildings in five different climates. In Potential of earth-sheltered and underground space: proc.,

Undergr. Sp. Conf. and Expos., Kansas City, MO, June 8, 1981. T.L. Holthusen, ed. Elmsford, NY: Pergamon Pr., 1981. p. 227-57.

The buildings are in Boston, MA; Washington, DC; Jacksonville, FL; San Diego, CA; and in Manila, the Philippines. These are earth-sheltered single-story office buildings and dry-storage warehouses. Computer analysis was used to associate energy loads with the wall, roof, windows and floor, to establish the energy load due to infiltration and ventilation and to estimate the internal load. The improvement in thermal performance due to earth sheltering is quantified.

1149. Minnesota tops underground space. Sol. Age, v. 4, no. 10, Oct. 1979: 40-1+.

Underground building activities at the Minneapolis campus of the Univ. of Minnesota are discussed. Several underground designs are illustrated, and the state and Federal government's involvement with the support of underground space research is reviewed. A state-financed earth-sheltered building demonstration program is described.

1150. Molding our man-made world. William Morgan. AIA J., v. 61, no. 2, Feb. 1974: 32-9.

Architectural shaping to blend with earth forms results in earth-bermed, subsurface, and earth-covered structures. Discussion of Riverfront Redevelopment, Memphis, TN; Florida State Museum, Gainesville, FL; an office building in Salisbury, MD; a cabin in Washington State; and the Dune Houses in Florida.

1151. Mom's subterranean root cellar/bungalow. Moth. Earth N., no. 74, Mar./Apr. 1982: 128.

This shelter was built in five days by two people using shovels, a mattock, and auger to dig the chimney, and a tile spade to smooth the interior. It has a solar chimney and an air vent at the threshold and maintains a closed-door temperature between 45 and 60 degrees F. year round. Good for storing vegetables, prechilling milk, and for smoking meat and or fish. The soil is heavily weathered and decomposed rock that is 30 to 35 percent clay. Total cost: about $60.

1152. Morton, David. The solar underground. Prog. Archit., v. 60, no. 4, Apr. 1979: 124-7.

The Plant Science Bldg. of the Cary Arboretum at Millbrook, NY, was designed by architect Malcolm Wells and engineer Fred Dubin.

1153. National Zoo "frees" great apes. Earth Shel. Liv., no. 23, Sept./Oct. 1982: 54-6.

The new multi-level Great Ape House at the National Zoological Park in Washington, DC, is warmed by the sun and protected by earth berms. It was designed by Joseph Wilkes of Wilkes, Faulkner, Jenkins, and Bass of Washington, DC.

1154. Nature center slips into prairie. Earth Shel. Dig. Energ. Rept., no. 17, Sept./Oct. 1981: 40-42.

The Pleasant Valley Outdoor Center near Chicago is earth sheltered; it was built by Hawkweed Group, Osseo, WI.

1155. Odello, R.J. Low-energy structures concepts. Final report Oct. 1977-Sept. 1980. Dec. 1980. 30 p. (AD-A--103107/9).

Different possibilities are discussed for energy conservation in Navy shore facilities. These include earth shelter, thermal mass concepts, passive solar designs, and also using conventional techniques. Both the advantages and disadvantages of the systems are discussed.

1156. Palmer, Brian. Earth integrated architecture for Tasmania's national parks and historic sites. In Proc., 1st Int. Conf. on Energ. Effic. Bldgs. with Earth Shel. Prot., Sydney, Aust., Aug. 1-6, 1983. L.L. Boyer, ed. Stillwater, OK: Okla. State Univ., Archit. Ext., 1983. p. F9-14.

Earth integration of buildings in areas under the control of the National Parks and Wildlife Service is proposed following consideration of the visual impact of buildings in aesthetically sensitive, historic sites and natural areas; and the economics of maintaining comfort conditions when incorporating passive solar design. The climate in many of Tasmania's National Park areas differs from much of the mainland. Selection of materials sometimes requires more than the usual consideration. One case study discussed related to an island historic site where transport and handling of materials imposes serious restrictions. Several projects are discussed and illustrated: including visitor reception and amenities buildings, a wildlife research center, aviaries, staff housing, and a generator house, with varying factors justifying, or modifying each design.

1157. Purdue adds underground to library. Earth Shel. Dig. Energ. Rept., no. 9, May/June 1980: 4.

The two-story, 100,000 sq. ft. library addition at Purdue University will be built underground to escape the noise of a heavily-traveled street and to preserve the master design of the campus.

1158. Quinn, Thomas. Energy analysis of Harvard's underground library. In Proc., Earth Shel. Perf. and Eval., 2nd Nat. Tech. Conf., Tulsa, OK, Oct. 16-17, 1981. Stillwater, OK: Okla. State Univ., Archit, Ext., 1981. p. 261-6.
 The energy performance of the Pusey Library is compared with that of adjacent above-ground buildings.

1159. Rest stops reflect prairie history. Earth Shel. Liv., no. 19, Jan./Feb. 1982: 10-1.
 There's a pair of earth-sheltered rest stops, one on each side of the highway in Wasta near Rapid City, SD, and a second pair in Salem near Sioux Falls in eastern South Dakota.

1160. Rest stops save energy, motorists. Earth Shel. Dig. Energ. Rept., no. 14, Mar./Apr. 1981: 24-6.
 Three earth-sheltered rest stops have been built in Minnesota: one on I-90 a mile east of Blue Earth, the Enfield rest area in northern Minnesota, and one at Anchor Lake.

1161. Restaurant successful underground. Earth Shel. Dig. Energ. Rept., no. 18, Nov./Dec. 1981: 38-9.
 Country Cook Inn in Greentown, IN, a 2,800 sq. ft. restaurant, was designed by LeRoy Troyer Architects, Mishawaka, IN.

1162. Rodale writes the book on earth efficient design. Earth Shel. Dig. Energ. Rept., no. 10, July/Aug. 1980: 24-5.
 Rodale Press contracted architect James Harter to design an energy efficient, environmentally sound, earth bermed 43,000 sq. ft. operations center in Emmaus, PA, for 300 workers at a cost of $2.1 million.

1163. Rolla Mines Building to go down. Earth Shel. Dig. Energ. Rept., no. 8, Mar./Apr. 1980: 39.
 The Mineral Engineering Building, School of Mines and Metallurgy at the University of Missouri, Rolla, is planned as an underground building to be built on the extreme west end of the Mall.

1164. School designed for Indiana. Earth Shel. Dig. Energ. Rept., no. 10, July/Aug. 1980: 56-7.
 The first earth-sheltered school for Indiana was meant to be tornado safe and energy efficient. Plans and sketches are shown.

1165. Schurke, Paul. University of Minnesota builds down again. Earth Shel. Dig. Energ. Rept., no. 6, Nov./Dec. 1979: 28-9.

The faculty and students of the Dept. of Civil and Mineral Engineering, Univ. of Minnesota, have established the Underground Space Center to be a national focal point for underground research and information exchange and are planning a new underground building to house the Dept. and the USC.

1166. Security building anchored into cliff. Earth Shel. Dig. Energ. Rept., no. 18, Nov./Dec. 1981: 48-9.
St. Paul's Ramsey County Detention Center is a seven-story pretrial holding facility that is built into rock cliffs above the Mississippi River.

1167. Solar-heated, earth-sheltered structures can be beautiful. Concr. Constr., v. 26, no. 2, Feb. 1981: 145.
On the Stark County District Library in Canton, OH.

1168. Swenson, Mark. Cost efficiency and earth sheltering. AIA J., v. 72, no. 1, Jan. 1983: 68-9.
A Midwestern industrial firm engaged two architectural/engineering firms to design a product research and testing laboratory, one design conventional, the other earth sheltered.

1169. Underground campus teaches savings. Earth Shel. Liv., no. 19, Jan./Feb. 1982: 14-6.
The Southfield, MI, campus of the Oakland Community College, is a 80,000 sq. ft. earth-sheltered one-building campus for 2,500 students.

1170. Underground museum expands Italian landmark. Earth Shel. Liv., no. 19, Jan./Feb. 1982: 28-9.
An underground addition was built to the museum honoring Giuseppe Garibaldi and Antonio Meucci in Staten Island, NY.

1171. Underground Space Center. Underground building design. By John Carmody and Raymond Sterling. New York, NY: Van Nostrand Reinhold, 1984.
This book, intended for a professional audience, focuses on underground designs for commercial and institutional buildings and discusses 20 case studies of existing structures. These include libraries, commercial buildings, educational facilities, visitor centers, and several special use facilities.

1172. Vadnais, Kathleen. Community wanted covered school. Earth Shel. Liv., no. 25, Jan./Feb. 1983: 38-40.
The Norwood-Young America Elementary School, Minnesota, is the first underground school in the upper Midwest. Total cost: $55.20 per sq. ft.

1173. A winner features earth, grass, landscaping ... and concrete. Concr. Constr., v. 25, no. 9, Sept. 1980: 678-9.

This is a description of Central Pre-Mix Concrete Company's earth-sheltered corporate office building in Spokane, WA.

1174. Wright, Rodney, Sydney Wright, Larry Dieckmann, and Robert Selby. An earth-integrated passive solar building. In Proc., 3rd Nat. Pass. Sol. Conf., San Jose, CA, Jan. 11-13, 1979. Newark, DE: Int. Sol. Energ. Soc., Am. Sec., 1979. p. 851-5.

This 2,000-sq. ft. building is designed to be integrated into the slope with only the south face open to the sun. It is planned as an environmental education center near Woodstock, IL. It has passive solar heating using direct gain (storage in the floor mass), natural convection air heaters and a Trombe wall. A self sustaining greenhouse is a teaching space.

XXVI. CONFERENCES

1175. Baggs, Sydney A. The first International Earth-Sheltered Building Conference. Undergr. Sp., v. 8, no. 3, 1984: 149.

This is the Australian Chairman's report on the Conference held Aug. 1-6, 1983 in Sydney, Australia.

1176. Boyer, Lester L. Earth shelter goes international. Undergr. Sp., v. 8, no. 3, 1984: 146-8.

This article discusses the past activities which led up to the 1983 International Conference on Energy Efficient Buildings with Earth Shelter Protection held in Sydney.

1177. Chinese to sponsor Symposium on Earth Architecture. Underline, v. 6, no. 1, Oct./Dec. 1984: 3.

The Architectural Society of China will sponsor a five-day International Symposium on Earth Architecture, Nov. 1985, in Beijing. English will be the official language of the Symposium.

1178. Conference focuses on large-scale applications of underground building. Undergr. Sp., v. 4, no. 5, Mar./Apr. 1980: 319.

The November 1979 conference, held in Minneapolis, sponsored by the Underground Space Center, featured presentations by engineers, researchers, legislators, regulatory agency officials, architects, construction company owners, and developers of underground space.

1179. Earth-sheltered housing conference and exhibition draws nearly 2,000. Undergr. Sp., v. 5, no. 2, Sept./Oct. 1980: 72.
Energy data for earth-sheltered homes and legal concerns were two of the topics discussed at the Minnesota Conference which included a trade exhibit.

1180. Financing earth-sheltered houses: conference recommendations. Undergr. Sp., v. 4, no. 3, Nov./Dec. 1979: 177-8.
A Conference on Financing Earth-Sheltered Housing was held in Feb. 1979 near Minneapolis made over 30 recommendations in the areas of means of persuading lending institutions to make loans available, methods of increasing the number of funding sources available and heightening awareness of earth-sheltered housing issues among regulatory agencies and methods of convincing lending institutions that there is a market for earth-sheltered housing.

1181. Group tours "Outback" shelters. Earth Shel. Liv., no. 30, Nov./Dec. 1983: 38-9.
This article describes the "Dugout" tour which followed the International Conference on Earth Sheltered Buildings, Sydney, Australia, Aug. 1983. There were visits to dugout homes in Coober Pedy, White Cliffs, Andamooka, and Burra.

1182. Innovative earth-sheltered designs discussed at Oklahoma City Conference. Undergr. Sp., v. 5, no. 2, Sept./Oct. 1980: 74.
The Conference featured presentations on consumer acceptance, energy performance, and new construction techniques.

1183. Iowa interest at peak. Earth Shel. Dig. Energ. Rept., no. 9, May/June 1980: 50.
A two-day seminar on earth sheltering sponsored by the Mid-Sioux Community Action Agency of Remsen, Iowa, was attended by 500 people.

1184. Schaefer, Steven E. Earth Sheltered Construction Conference held. Civ. Eng., v. 51, no. 1, Jan. 1981: 16.
World of Concrete Conferences and Concrete Construction Magazine sponsored the Conference in Chicago in October 1980. The Conference was oriented toward residential builders, poured-foundation wall contractors and those in-

terested in building earth-sheltered residences. Additional conferences on the subject were held in Atlanta, San Francisco, Boston, and Denver.

1185. 2nd International Conference to focus on earth sheltered design, analysis, construction. Underline, v. 6, no. 1, Oct./Dec. 1984: 1-2.
This is an announcement and call for papers on suggested topics: earth contact heat transfer, building design/use case studies, structures, waterproofing/drainage, building materials, landscape architecture, economics, physiological aspects, user acceptance/psychological aspects/interior design, urban/community applications, institutional issues.

1186. Seminar addresses underground space use in People's Republic. Underline, v. 4, no. 2, Nov./Dec. 1982: 1-2, 6.
A seminar on underground space engineering in China was sponsored by the Underground Space Center. Underground construction has been used by the Chinese for several thousand years and today approximately ten million Chinese live in earth-sheltered and underground dwellings.

1187. Stoiaken, Larry. Earth shelter 2: Conference report: Alt. Energ., no. 44, July/Aug. 1980: 28-30.
This is a report on the annual Earth Sheltered Housing Conference and Exhibition held April 9-11, 1980. The Conference proceedings are available from the Underground Space Center.

1188. Vadnais, Kathleen. Florida meets with enthusiasm. Earth Shel. Dig. Energ. Rept., no. 15, May/June 1981: 20-1.
The progress of earth sheltering in Florida includes the first earth-sheltered conference in Orlando, FL.

XXVII. ARCHITECTS/BUILDERS/ENGINEERS

1189. Andy Davis returns to Davis Caves, Inc. Earth Shel. Liv., no. 19, Jan./Feb. 1982: 51.
A. Davis, founder of Davis Caves, Inc., has reassumed control of the company which has 100 franchise dealers across the country.

1190. Architect, designer or ? Earth Shel. Liv., no. 39, May/June 1985: 12-3.
This article gives hints on how to choose someone to design your earth-sheltered house.

1191. Architect shows Missouri how. Earth Shel. Liv., no. 19, Jan./Feb. 1982: 52-3.
Larry Atkinson is an architect in Kansas City, active in passive solar energy, and now building his own earth-shelter home. He also builds for others. He stresses using salvaged materials and bartering with others for labor and supplies as ways of saving money.

1192. Australian team surveys U.S. earth shelters. Earth Shel. Dig. Energ. Rept., no. 6, Nov./Dec. 1979: 39.
Dr. Sydney Baggs and David Baggs toured the U.S. for five months in late 1979 to study earth-sheltering progress.

1193. Bailey, Brian. Selecting your contractor. Earth Shel. Liv., no. 36, Nov./Dec. 1984: 9.
Guidelines to use in choosing a competent contractor.

1194. Benedict, Frederic. Career camouflages buildings. Earth Shel. Dig. Energ. Rept., no. 13, Jan./Feb. 1981: 30-3.
The author is a former student of Frank Lloyd Wright who has been sinking buildings into the ground for more than 30 years. The featured house is his own in Aspen, CO.

1195. Blake, Peter. The fantastic world of Paolo Soleri. Archit. For., v. 114, no. 2, Feb. 1961: 105-10.
Soleri's earth houses in Paradise Valley near Phoenix, AZ.

1196. Busch, Akiko. Going underground: a New Mexico builder brings the wide open desert sky, light, and air into underground spaces. Res. Int., v. 5, no. 4, July/Aug. 1980: 74-5, 90.
Scott Pittman is a Santa Fe builder who specializes in adobe earth shelters.

1197. Business built on instinct. Earth Shel. Dig. Energ. Rept., no. 18, Nov./Dec. 1981: 50-1.
About Everstrong, Inc. which promotes earth-covered total wood buildings.

1198. Carpenter, E.E. Discussion of specific experiences and projects—panel. In Residential applications: transcripts of selected presentations, Going Under to Stay on Top, Minneapolis, MN, Oct. 1977. Minneapolis, MN: Univ. of Minn., Undergr. Sp. Ctr., 1979. p. 173-4.

The author is President of the Earth Sheltered Corp. of America. He discusses marketing and the advantages of living in an earth-sheltered house.

1199. Carter, Dave. A pioneer way of living is back—and doing well. Rur. Electr. Nebr., Dec. 1979.
Carter discusses his earth-sheltered home and philosophy.

1200. Cave company changes hands. Earth Shel. Dig. Energ. Rept., no. 10, July/Aug. 1980: 60-1.
Ownership of Davis Caves has changed hands, from Andy Davis to William Van Hagey, legal counsel for Davis Caves for several years. Relates the history of Davis Caves as a franchiser.

1201. Company bids for new market. Earth Shel. Dig. Energ. Rept., no. 15, May/June 1981: 56.
Anchor Block Co., St. Paul, MN, held a seminar on earth sheltering and displayed an earth-sheltered block home they'd built.

1202. Company complies: suspends operations. Earth Shel. Dig. Energ. Rept., no. 10, July/Aug. 1980: 7-8.
The Federal government caused Earth Shelter Corp. of America, Berlin, WI, to suspend all business between Oct. 21, 1979 and April 24, 1980, because a new Federal franchise law took effect, and the company discovered it was not in compliance. The business is now registered and official, but its activities as a franchiser continue to be monitored. The updating to keep the business legal will cost from $30,000 to $50,000 per year.

1203. Company is a means to an end. Earth Shel. Liv., no. 20, Mar./Apr. 1982: 50-1.
Tells how Gayle Scafe started the Terra Dome Corp.

1204. A down-to-earth architect. Moth. Earth N., no. 67, Jan./Feb. 1981: 174-5.
Angus Macdonald, an architect, designs earth-sheltered homes. Some of the homes he designed are described.

1205. Earth homes possible. Ariz. Repub., Aug. 14, 1977.
An interview with James Scalise, an Arizona State University professor.

1206. An earth integrated developer. <u>Earth Shel. Liv.</u>, no. 40, July/Aug. 1985: 28-30.
   Croasdale-Moore Construction Co., Inc. of Kansas City, MO, has built 60 single family earth-sheltered homes in the suburbs of Kansas City. Most are earth bermed with conventional roofs. The structural system, waterproofing, and insulation are described. Croasdale-Moore owns the earth-integrated subdivision Shelter Valley and is planning a 120-acre development called Shelter Haven. Energy costs in these homes average $200/heating season.

1207. Earth shelter group charts new directions. <u>Earth Shel. Liv.</u>, no. 33, May/June 1984: 35.
   Earth Shelter Corp. of America made major changes in its top management and marketing program. A new dealership program replaces franchises.

1208. The ESL interview: Dave Cavanaugh. <u>Earth Shel. Liv.</u>, no. 33, May/June 1984: 26-9.
   An owner of Minnesota Earth Shelter, Inc., discusses construction and marketing techniques.

1209. The ESL interview: Frank Moreland. <u>Earth Shel. Liv.</u>, no. 31, Jan./Feb. 1984: 30-1.
   Moreland is the 1983-85 past-President of the AUSA and President of Earth Covered Structures, Inc. in Fort Worth, TX. He's a critic of above-grade suburban housing.

1210. Feeck, Jeanne. Have a voice and dig in for underground housing in Iowa. <u>Earth Shel. Dig. Energ. Rept.</u>, no. 5, Sept./Oct. 1979: 23.
   The author is an official of the Iowa Chapter of the AUSA. She urges all interested parties to join.

1211. From Iowa to "down under." <u>Earth Shel. Liv.</u>, no. 40, July/Aug. 1985: 11.
   The formation of Terra-Domes of Australia is discussed. They've built two Terra-Dome homes so far, in Murota near Melbourne and in Brisbane.

1212. Home show models draw crowds. <u>Earth Shel. Liv.</u>, no. 22, July/Aug. 1982: 46.
   Home-show promoters are inviting earth-sheltered builders to erect models on show floors to attract people to this new market.

1213. An interview with Malcolm Wells. <u>Undergr. Sp.</u>, v. 3, no. 4, Jan./Feb. 1979: 214-6.

1214. Israel, Frank. Architecture: William Morgan. Archit. Dig., v. 36, no. 10, Dec. 1979: 86-93.
Florida architect William Morgan has gone to the architecture of prehistoric Americans, the mound-builders, for inspiration in building Forest House in northern Florida, a pair of earth mounds in the shape of truncated pyramids. One is a residence, the other the garage connected by a straight-covered walkway marking a north-south axis.

1215. Johnson, Jim. Cameron Park homes will have an earthy look. Sac. Bee, Sec. E, May 21, 1982: E1.
A Stockton firm, Earth Shelter Developers, announces plans for a 113-unit earth-sheltered housing project to be called Sun Earth Estates, scheduled to start in summer 1982. The units range in price from about $95,000 to about $150,000. The partners are Bruce Camper, Glen Camper, and Lon Simmons.

1216. Kellet, S. Mr. Davis builds himself a dream house -- not on a hillside but under it. People, v. 9, Jan. 9, 1978: 61-2.

1217. Lady converts to earth sheltering. Earth Shel. Dig. Energ. Rept., no. 16, July/Aug. 1981: 60-1.
An interview with Ann Kramer, a builder of earth-sheltered houses.

1218. Malcolm Wells speaks out. Earth Shel. Dig. Energ. Rept., no. 13, Jan./Feb. 1981: 60-2.
An interview with Wells.

1219. Manufacturer files Chapter 11. Earth Shel. Liv., no. 31, Jan./Feb. 1984: 25.
Effective Building Products, Inc. of Savage, MN, manufacturers of Bentonize waterproofing products have suspended production and sale of the products and have filed to reorganize under Chapter 11 of the Federal bankruptcy laws, because some Bentonize waterproofed homes had leaked, and claims for damages had obstructed their operations.

1220. McFadden, Pamm. Woman designer began as child. Earth Shel. Dig. Energ. Rept., no. 15, May/June 1981: 58.
The author built an earth-sheltered "fort" to play in as a child.

1221. Meter, Ken. Who is Tom Bligh, anyway? Alt. Energ., no. 26, June 1977: 29-31.
An interview with one of Minnesota's foremost designers of underground structures.

1222. Moreland speaks up. Earth Shel. Dig. Energ. Rept., no. 12, Nov./Dec. 1980: 60-1.
Frank Moreland's ideas and progress.

1223. Morgan, William. Environmental concern: shaping building to site preoccupies architect William Morgan. Interiors, v. 140, no. 3, Oct. 1980: 74-5+.

1224. Nebraska develops its underground. Earth Shel. Dig. Energ. Rept., no. 2, Mar./Apr. 1979: 35.
The Nebraska Underground Space Association is formed.

1225. New earth shelter association formed. Undergr. Sp., v. 8, no. 3, 1984: 142.
A new association for the advocacy of earth-sheltered structures has been formed by Dr. Sydney Baggs. It is named Geotecture International Association, headquartered in Sydney, Australia. It publishes the quarterly journal Geotecture.

1226. Patience, knowledge pay off. Earth Shel. Dig. Energ. Rept., no. 17, Sept./Oct. 1981: 52-3.
David Scott is an architect, educator, Asst. Dean of College of Engineering, Washington State University, Pullman, WA. He maintains a regional center for information on earth-sheltered design and construction activity in the Western states.

1227. Penfield, Louis A. Detroit rejected Wright's better idea: workers weren't interested in bermed home development plan. Earth Shel. Liv., no. 33, May/June 1984: 24-5.
In 1942, F.L. Wright designed an earth-bermed housing development for auto workers in Detroit. It was not built.

1228. Plowboy interview: David Wright. Moth. Earth N., no. 47, Sept./Oct. 1977: 16-22.
Wright discussed the passive conditioning of living space, i.e. the design and construction of space so the natural elements of the microclimate surrounding it are all that are necessary to make the space comfortable.

1229. Rosenberg, Barry. The underground man. Phila. Mag., v. 59, no. 3, Mar. 1968: 146-56.
Malcolm Wells.

1230. Rowlinson, K. Morel. Group to promote British earth sheltering. Earth Shel. Liv., no. 34, July/Aug. 1984: 28-9.
The British Earth Sheltering Association was formed in July 1983. This article discusses the need for earth-sheltered

architecture in Great Britain. Write: The British Earth Sheltering Association, c/o Vis Williams, Architects, 3 Merton Road, Bootle, Liverpool, Merseyside, LZO, 3BG England.

1231. Sale, Jonathan. How Arthur Quarmby is putting up roots. Times, Feb. 15, 1983: 12.

1232. Schurer, Gerhard. The Earth Covered Housing Association of South Australia. Geotecture, v. 2, no. 2, 1985: 5-7.
The ECHA conducts seminars and in general serves as a medium for the exchange of information and personal experiences as well as an entity which furthers the political interests of people who are interested in building earth-sheltered homes.

1233. Search for "quintessential house" satisfied. Earth Shel. Dig. Energ. Rept., no. 9, May/June 1980: 52-3.
An interview with Lon Simmons of Simmons and Sun in St. Louis, MO.

1234. Seitz, Don. Earth shelter association formed: N.E.S.B.A. will promote, be an information source for earth sheltering. Earth Shel. Liv., no. 37, Jan./Feb. 1985: 5.
The National Earth Shelter Builders Association has been formed to act as a national center for information on earth sheltering for builders and for the general public. It will also provide a vehicle for earth-shelter enthusiasts to meet, be a lobbying group in Washington to influence legislators on matters affecting earth sheltering, organize national and regional trade shows, and deal with problem areas affecting earth sheltering such as insurance, financing, and building codes. It hopes to educate and increase public awareness of earth sheltering. For additional information write: N.E.S.B.A., P.O. Box 268, Stillwater, MN 55082.

1235. _____. The ESL interview: Don and Julie Karsky. Earth Shel. Liv., no. 30, Nov./Dec. 1983: 28-33.
A discussion of the construction of and self-sufficient living in the interviewees' Wisconsin earth-sheltered home which employs a circular design.

1236. Steady pace pays off. Earth Shel. Dig. Energ. Rept., no. 14, Mar./Apr. 1981: 60-1.
About Eldon Morrison, a Minnesota architect who designs earth shelters.

1237. Undercover agent: he shot a bear on his roof. Earth Shel. Dig. Energ. Rept., no. 1, Jan./Feb. 1979:30-1.

About Mike Oehler, President of Hobbit Housing, Bonners Ferry, ID, who wrote The $50 & up underground house book.

1238. Vadnais, Kathleen. Franchising creates opportunities. Earth Shel. Dig. Energ. Rept., no. 10, July/Aug. 1980: 4-6.

Earth-shelter construction companies have started selling franchises, however, some of these companies have completed only one project. The franchiser (company) gets paid for selling its information to the franchisee (dealer) for a fee, and the franchisee makes money selling the product he or she has purchased rights to. Before purchasing a franchise, investigate the franchiser thoroughly, make sure the company is solvent, and will provide the promised information and sales assistance.
There is a Federal requirement that anyone entering a contract or agreement, even if oral, that involves marketing plans, trade names and fees, file a disclosure statement. Two publications on purchasing franchises are available from the International Franchise Association located in Washington, DC.

1239. _____. Owners complain, file suit against contractor. Earth Shel. Dig. Energ. Rept., no. 11, Sept./Oct. 1980: 6-7.

The first lawsuit has been brought against an earth-shelter contractor in Oklahoma who did not insulate at all and whose waterproofing job failed.

1240. _____. Underworld attracted to underground. Earth Shel. Dig.Energ. Rept., no. 13, Jan./Feb. 1981: 46-7.

Two scams involving earth shelters are exposed in Texas and Kansas. Readers are advised to be suspicious of high-pressure tactics.

1241. Wells, Malcolm. Mac Wells' summertime blues: what good is a low-impact house if you don't have low-impact people? New Shel., v. 2, no. 5, May/June 1981: 60-9.

Most of the visitors who flock to Wells' new earth-sheltered house in Cape Cod don't know how to conserve energy. Wells has produced a booklet of house rules which few of his guests follow. His house faces west and east, instead of north-south. It relies on other methods to achieve the status of low-energy shelter: internal gains, very good insulation, and thermal mass. There's an oil furnace on the north side of the building while a wood stove helps heat the south side. Berms and earth on the roof complete the earth-sheltered concept.

1242. _____. To build without destroying the earth. In Proc.,

Alt. in Energ. Conserv.: the Use of Earth Cov. Bldgs., Fort Worth, TX, July 9-12, 1975. F.L. Moreland, ed. Washington, DC: U.S. G.P.O., 1976. p. 211-32.
Wells tells how he turned into an earth-sheltered architect. Many of his designs are shown small-scale.

1243. Woods, Charles. Evolution of an "organic" architect. Earth Shel. Dig. Energ. Rept., no. 17, Sept./Oct. 1981: 56-61.
Charles Woods, a designer, has developed an "organic architecture" that is integrated with nature and uses natural local materials. Several of his designs are shown.

XXVIII. REGIONAL APPLICATIONS

Cold Climate

1244. Atkinson, L.J. Earth-sheltered housing/cold climate design. In The potential of earth-sheltered and underground space: proc., Undergr. Sp. Conf. and Expos., Kansas City, MO, June 8-10, 1981. T.L. Holthusen, ed. Elmsford, NY: Pergamon Pr. 1981. p. 187-90.
The earth-sheltered house that properly combines passive solar and the envelope design should be self-sufficient in terms of heating and cooling.

Developing Countries

1245. Sterling, Raymond L. and John C. Carmody. Potential use of earth-sheltered structures in developing countries. In Proc., 1st Int. Conf. on Energ. Effic. Bldgs. with Earth Shel. Prot., Sydney, Aust., Aug. 1-6, 1983. L.L. Boyer, ed. Stillwater, OK: Okla. State Univ., Archit. Ext., 1983. p. 15-8.
There are several features which make earth-sheltered construction desirable in developing countries: use of available materials, energy shortage, scarcity of flatlands, protection, severe climatic conditions, low maintenance. Construction and use issues, such as labor, materials, self-help possibilities, possibility of expanding living space, waterproofing, acceptability in underdeveloped societies, are discussed.

Hot/Arid Lands

1246. Berkowitz, Paul I. Site analysis for earth-sheltered buildings in hot arid climates. <u>Earth Shel. Bldgs. -- Tech. Pap.</u>, TP-IIA, 1983.

1247. Bircher, Tad L. Earth integration strategies in hot, arid regions. In <u>Proc., Annu. Mtg., Int. Sol. Energ. Soc., Am. Sec.</u>, Phoenix, AZ, June 2, 1980.
A finite difference model and analysis by the computer program SPICE have been used to study several of the variables related with earth integration of buildings in hot, arid regions. Results show that the design strategies for depth of soil, insulation, and glazing differ greatly from those used for structures in cold climates.

1248. _____. Ground-coupled cooling in hot, arid regions. In <u>Passive cooling: proc., Int. Pass. and Hybr. Cool. Conf.</u>, Miami Beach, FL, Nov. 6-16, 1982. Newark, DE: Int. Sol. Energ. Soc., Am. Sec., 1981. p. 136-40.
An evaluation is attempted of the impact of ground coupling on the cooling loads of desert structures based on the results from a computer simulation using the computer program SPICE.

1249. _____. Ground-coupling techniques for cooling in desert regions. In <u>Proc., Annu. Mtg., Int. Sol. Energ. Soc., Am. Sec.</u>, Philadelphia, PA, May 26, 1981.
A finite difference model and analysis by the computer program SPICE were used to study several of the variables that effect ground-coupling techniques for buildings in desert regions.

1250. _____. Thermal performance of earth covered buildings in hot, arid regions. In <u>Proc., 5th Nat. Pass. Sol. Conf.</u>, Amherst, MA, Oct. 19-26, 1980. Newark, DE: Int. Sol. Energ. Soc., Am. Sec., 1980. p. 332-6.
A finite difference model and analysis using the computer program SPICE were used to study the thermal impact of several variables related to earth integration of structures in hot, arid regions. The results show that burying a structure to a depth of two or more feet and insulating the roof will give the most benefits from ground coupling.

1251. Gelder, John. <u>Underground desert shelter.</u> B. Arch. thesis. Adelaide, Aust.: Univ. of Adelaide, 1977.

1252. Golany, Gideon, ed. Housing in arid lands: design and planning. London: Architectural Press; New York: J. Wiley, 1980. 257 p.

The book is organized under the headings: Vernacular responses, Subterranean innovations, Solar technology, House design and environment. Pt. 2 on Subterranean innovations contains chapters by G. Golany on Subterranean settlements for arid zones, K. Labs on Terratypes: underground housing for arid zones, W.J. Van Der Meer on the Possibilities for subterranean housing in arid zones, and N.B. Aughenbaugh on Underground housing.

1253. _____. Subterranean settlements for arid zones. In Proc., Alt. in Habitat: the Use of Earth Cov. Set., Conf., Fort Worth, TX, May 17-19, 1978. F.L. Moreland, ed. Washington, DC: U.S. Dept. of Energy, 1979. v. 1, Earth covered buildings: technical notes, p. 174-202. Also in Housing in arid lands. G. Golany, ed. London: Architectural Press, 1980. p. 109-22.

The author discusses incorporating the ancient systems of subterranean placement, passive ventilation, and cooling by evaporation in earth-covered settlements, particularly those in hot and dry areas of the equatorial regions. Settlement plans are discussed that show how these three cooling methods can be used in modern planning and development for flat or sloping terrain.

1254. Hayeem, E. An experimental study of earth temperature modification to provide cooling for earth contact buildings in the desert regions of Israel. M.S. thesis. San Antonio, TX: Trinity Univ., 1984.

1255. Kumar, Sudhir and J. Cheng-Chuan-Shih. Optimum subsurface and underground shell structures for better housing in hot-arid lands. Durham, NC: U.S. Army Res. Off., 1970. 164 p.

This report consists of two parts. Pt. 1 presents a case for subsurface and underground housing. A study was made of the climate, environmental conditions, and the subsurface thermal gradients of hot-arid regions. This, in combination with past developments in subsurface and underground housing, indicates that subsurface and underground living offers a definite possibility for using these as yet unexploited lands for the benefit of expanding populations. Various designs of modern housing are given including family dwellings, apartment houses, shopping centers, transportation tunnels, etc. Pt. 2 presents a study of optimization of subsurface and underground shells to reduce the quantity of materials needed for such underground structures.

1256. Sayigh, A.A.M. and T. Al-Jeda. Potential of earth coupled buildings in reducing the cooling load in Kuwait. In Proc., 1st Int. Conf. on Energ. Effic. Bldgs. with Earth Shel. Prot., Sydney, Aust., Aug. 1-6, 1983. L.L. Boyer, ed. Stillwater, OK: Okla. State Univ., Archit. Ext., 1983. p. 305-9.
  The paper outlines the importance of reducing cooling load during the summer period in Kuwait. It describes the weather patterns, water availability at various depths, evaporation rate, and the cooling load in Kuwait. It describes three different semi- and totally earth-coupled houses and outlines the amount of energy saving in such buildings. --Auth. abstract.

1257. Scalise, James W., ed. Earth-integrated architecture: an alternative method for creating livable environments with emphasis on arid regions. Tempe, AZ: Univ. of Ariz., Coll. of Archit., Archit. Found. Pubs., 1975. 284 p.
  This book deals with such topics as landscape concerns, moisture control, construction techniques, climatic and soil limitations and social constraints. The primary emphasis is on earth shelter for arid regions, but most data is applicable to the rest of the country as well.

1258. Shih, J.C. and S. Kumar. A case for subsurface and underground housing in hot-arid lands. Int. tech. rept., Durham, NC: U.S. Army Res. Off., Apr. 1976.

1259. U.S. Arm Res. Off. Subsurface and underground housing in hot-arid lands. A tech. rept. Durham, NC, 1964.

Humid Continental Regions

1260. Akridge, James M. and Charles C. Benton. Passive cooling for hot humid climates. In Passive cooling: proc., Int. Pass. and Hybr. Cool. Conf., Miami Beach, FL, Nov. 6-16, 1981. Newark, DE: Int. Sol. Energ. Soc., Am. Sec. 1981. p. 66-70.
  The authors discuss a possible cooling concept called "Detached Earth Tempering" (DET) which involves a coupling of some building elements to the earth as a heat sink. When properly used, the concept offers the advantages of below-ground earth-tempered construction without the structural, moisture, site, and cost disadvantages ordinarily linked with below-grade houses. A research program is presently investigating the idea. Data are presented on measured performance and predicted performance.

1261. Chester, C.F., H.B. Shapira, P.R. Barnes, and G.A. Cristy.

An earth covered residential concept for the humid continental region. In Proc., Alt. in Habitat: the Use of Earth Cov. Set., Conf., Fort Worth, TX, May 17-19, 1978. F.L. Moreland, ed. Washington, DC: U.S. Dept. of Energy, 1979. v. 1, Earth covered buildings: technical notes, p. 171-94.

The Oak Ridge National Laboratory is studying an earth-covered residential structure, incorporating passive solar heating and natural cooling features. The study addresses some of the problems associated with the humid continental region. The advantages of the concept and some of its problem areas as well, are discussed.

Australia

1262. Baggs, David W. Earth-integrated building: the importance of using Australian design data and detailing techniques. Sol. Prog., v. 4, no. 3, 1983: 12-3.

1263. _____. Earth integrated housing. Own. Build. (Melbourne), no. 8, June 1983: 30-4.

This article defines the terms: earth-integrated, earth-covered, earth-sheltered. It details the advantages of earth-integrated housing, and the necessity of using data for Australian conditions when building in Australia.

1264. _____. The lithotecture of Australia: with specific reference to thermal factors. In Proc., Earth Shel. Bldg. Des. Innov., Oklahoma City, OK, Apr. 18, 1980. L.L. Boyer, ed. Stillwater, OK: Okla. State Univ., 1980. p. II. 13-7. Also in Geotecture, v. 1, no. 4, July 1984: 21-5.

This paper discusses two case studies of occupied underground environments in the dugout community of Coober Pedy, Australia. Resulting cryptoclimatic and architectural survey data are presented. Some possible correlations are made between the ionized state of the interior air and health and anxiety factors. The thermal environment of two dugouts is studied, one a self-contained motel unit and the other a private residence.

1265. _____. Solar-underground housing in the Australian context. In Solar energy at work: proc., Int. Sol. Energ. Soc., Aust. and N.Z. Sec., Macquarie Univ., North Ryde, Aust., Nov. 25-27, 1981. p. 25-7.

1266. Baggs, Sydney, Joan Baggs, and David Baggs. Australian earth-covered building. Kensington, NSW, Aust.: New South Wales Univ. Pr., Mar. 1985. 146 p.

This practical manual covers site selection, financing, council applications, construction methods, building costs, maintenance, drainage, windows, landscaping, insulation, energy savings, soil types, insurance, swimming pools, and also mentions some of the disadvantages of this type of construction.

1267. _____. Australian underground housing for arid regions: user attitudes; remote prediction of periodic ground temperature; the role of certain landscape factors in soil temperature modification. Ph.D. thesis. Kensington, NSW, Aust.: Univ. of New South Wales, 1981. 2 v.

1268. _____. Building into the landscape. RIBA J., v. 89, no. 5, May 1982: 37.

About White Cliffs, NSW and Coober Pedy, SA.

1269. _____. Digging in. Archit. Aust., June/July 1978.

This letter to the editor discusses the differences between Australian dugout dwellings and modern earth-sheltered structures and the need for an Australian demonstration project.

1270. _____ and D.W. Baggs. An introduction to earth-covered housing: basic information for Australian conditions. Chatswood, NSW, Aust.: ECA Systems, 4 de Villiers Ave., 1983. 39 p.

1271. _____. The lithotecture of Australia: with specific reference to user health factors. In Proc., Earth Shel. Bldg. Des. Innov., Oklahoma City, OK, Apr. 18, 1980. L.L. Boyer, ed. Stillwater, OK: Okla. State Univ., 1980. p. II. 19-26.

First a brief historical review of the use of lithotecture in Australia is given. After presenting the results of recordings of ionized air in some underground residences, the author suggests a relationship between the ionized air conditions in the dwellings and some aspects of the health and state of anxiety of occupants of the underground and conventional above-ground dwellings. Discussion ensues of the effects of sensory deprivation, noise attenuation, and the extremes of light and heat intensity on the health of inhabitants of arid regions.

1272. _____. Remote prediction of ground temperature in Australian soils and mapping its distribution. Sol. Energ., v. 30, no. 4, 1983: 351-66.

Regional Applications

A method of determining ground temperature in Australia is used to assess site suitability for earth covered or underground housing.

1273. _____. Remote prediction of periodic ground temperature in Australia using isothermal contour maps. Undergr. Sp., v. 7, no. 2, Sept./Oct. 1982: 127-32.
In Australia, potential sites in the outback for the construction of earth-covered buildings are often geographically inaccessible. A method of remote prediction of ground temperature must be developed to evaluate site suitability. To meet this need, a mathematical model of the Southern Hemisphere was developed and tested, and isothermal contour maps of five Australian states were made based on ground temperature samples. Also discussed is a method of using thermal infrared sensing to detect soils with thermal characteristics required for earth-contact structures.

1274. _____. Underground architecture. Archit. Aust., Dec. 1977/Jan. 1978: 62-9.
This is an introductory type of article discussing the possible benefits and uses of earth-sheltered houses in Australia.

1275. Irwin, Colin B. Two prototype house designs for the hot, arid region of Australia. In Australasian proc., 1st Int. Conf. on Energ. Effic. Bldgs. with Earth Shel. Prot., Sydney, Aust., Aug. 1-6, 1983. S.A. Baggs, ed. Kensington, NSW, Aust.: Unisearch, Ltd., 1983. p. F15-21.
Designs of two prototype, earth-sheltered houses for a hypothetical mining town in the Pilbara, WA, are presented. These were intended to form part of a total town environment in which landscaping plays a role of major significance. --Auth. abstract.

1276. Keipert, J.D. and T.J. Williamson. The performance of an earth-bermed house in a hot, arid climate. In Proc., 1st Int. Conf. on Energ. Effic. Bldgs. with Earth Shel. Prot., Sydney, Aust., Aug. 1-6, 1983. L.L. Boyer, ed. Stillwater, OK: Okla. State Univ., Archit. Ext., 1983.
An experimental earth-bermed house has been constructed in the town of Port Augusta in the arid region of South Australia. A control house of similar floor plan was constructed on an adjacent site. Since completion in mid-1982, the performance of both houses has been continuously monitored. Construction techniques that were employed on the earth-bermed house are described, and the thermal performance of the earth bermed and standard houses are compared. --Auth. abstract.

1277. Machowski, Barb. Award smooths way for "down under" market. Earth Shel. Dig. Energ. Rept., no. 14, Mar./Apr. 1981: 4-5.

Earth sheltering has caught on in Australia in the last four years.

1278. Mann, Colin. Australians beat desert drought. Kan. City Star, Aug. 23, 1971.

The town of Coober Pedy in SA has most of its 3,000 population living underground in 70 degree homes while the surface reaches as high as 122 degrees. Sandstone is the matrix for this development, and the water is supplied from an additional depth of 300 ft. where natural reservoirs are tapped. Picture of solar still for water purification is shown.

1279. Schneider, Hans J. The Australian climate -- an overview. In Proc., 1st Int. Conf. on Energ. Effic. Bldgs. with Earth Shel. Prot., Sydney, Aust., Aug. 1-6, 1983. L.L. Boyer, ed. Stillwater, OK: Okla. State Univ., Archit. Ext., 1983. p. 11-4.

When comparing an overseas earth-covered building with one designed for Australian conditions, the (air) climate characteristics of both site locations should be taken into account (as the soil-climate is directly related to the ambient air climate); this means that comparisons between building designs and details on a thermal basis are only valid for Australian sites with homotypes in the climates of the Northern Hemisphere. Yet, such homotypes for climatic stations are extremely limited due to the position of the Australian continent in the subtropical and tropical latitudes of the Southern Hemisphere, the characteristics of the oceans to the west, south and east, and the shape and size of the continent itself. --Auth. abstract.

1280. Schurer, Gerhard A.K. A contemporary earth-sheltered project in the historical context of South Australia. In Proc., 1st Int. Conf. on Energ. Effic. Bldgs. with Earth Shel. Prot., Sydney, Aust., Aug. 1-6, 1983. L.L. Boyer, ed. Stillwater, OK: Okla. State Univ., Archit. Ext., 1983. p. 357-61.

In Burra, the earliest South Australian mining town, the underearth dwellings were born out of socio-economic limitations. Within this framework, several parameters coincided: the skill of the Cornish miner to use his pick for digging a home, the need for cheap temporary accommodation, and the favorable geological formation of the alluvial clay through which the creek had cut its bed. An underprivileged social status has been associated with the dugout occupants, emphasized by the refusal of the mining companies to give them employment. An attempt is made to put the usually isolated event of single earth-sheltered projects into a comprehensive planning framework. The paper examines the situation currently existing in South Australia and projects some rough cost benefit figures that could result from an earth-sheltered neighborhood.

1281. _____. Earth-integrated architecture in South Australia. Pt. One. Geotecture, v. 2, no. 2, 1985: 9-44. (Pt. Two of this series is listed under Earth Sheltered Houses--Case Studies, Australia).

This long article is divided into four sections. The first presents a brief history of earth shelters in South Australia. The second reports on a bushfire resistant home competition which was sponsored by the Boral Group of Companies in Adelaide. The author's submission was included for commendation and comment as one of the best in the competition. The third section presents excerpts from the author's report to the Competition: Design considerations for a bushfire resistant earth-integrated dwelling (6 p.). The fourth section gives detailed information about six earth-covered houses in South Australia.

1282. Siero, Gerhard C.W.H. Earth sheltered architecture in hot arid Australia. In Proc., Int. Conf. on Energ. Effic. Bldgs. with Earth Shel. Prot., Sydney, Aust., Aug. 1-6, 1983. L.L. Boyer, ed. Stillwater, OK: Okla. State Univ., Archit. Ext., 1983. p. 77-82.

Arid region housing in Australia is generally inadequately designed, southern, temperate-climate, suburban housing with little concession to the harsh climate. Bare desert soils are subject to high temperatures. Plants can be used to moderate and reduce earth temperature and modify microclimate. Using landforming and water-conservative irrigation methods, artificial oases of designed plant-communities can be established. Settlements could be built within these plant structures. Guidelines for earth-sheltered architecture in hot, arid climates are suggested. --Auth. abstract.

1283. _____ and C.B. Irwin. Earth sheltered architecture in hot arid regions of Australia. B. Arch. thesis. Sydney, Aust.: New South Wales Inst. of Technology, 1980. 5 v.

China

1284. Greenland, J.J. Alternative technology in the architecture and geotecture of China. In Australasian proc., 1st Int. Conf. on Energ. Effic. Bldgs. with Earth Shel. Prot.,

Sydney, Aust., Aug. 1-6, 1983. S.A. Baggs, ed. Kensington, NSW, Aust.: Unisearch, Ltd., 1983. p. C1-5.

How energy technologies are applied to traditional architecture by the LiuMing Ying Brigade and academics in Da Xing, China, is discussed. This is followed by descriptions of lithotecture (constructed using mining techniques) and recessed atrium type dwellings that combine lithotecture and terratecture (constructed by cut and cover techniques). Some 40 million Chinese choose to use geotecture (both lithotecture and terratecture) because of the thermal comfort it provides. Chinese academics are constructing and monitoring terratecture that represents an improvement to the conventional lithotecture of so-called "cave-dwellings," allowing the roofs to be developed for agriculture.

1285. Wright, Bruce N. China digs in. Archit. Minn., v. 7, no. 6, Dec./Jan. 1981-1982: 46-7.

This is a brief report on the People to People International exchange program on earth-sheltered structures which went to China in 1981.

Korea

1286. Kim, Heung Gon and Raymond L. Sterling. Integrating earth-sheltered design into the Korean terrain and tradition. Undergr. Sp., v. 7, no. 6, May/June 1983: 381-6.

This paper explores the design of earth-sheltered housing for hilly suburban areas unsuitable for above-grade construction. The designs suggested incorporate traditional Korean housing techniques with modern, passive energy and land-conserving construction techniques.

1287. _____ and _____. A study of home design combining earth sheltering and traditional Korean architecture. In Proc., 1st Int. Conf. on Energ. Effic. Bldgs. with Earth Shel. Prot., Sydney, Aust., Aug. 1-6, 1983. L.L. Boyer, ed. Stillwater, OK: Okla. State Univ., 1983. p. 231-6.
Also in Geotecture, v. 1, no. 5, Oct. 1984: 26-30.

This paper shows schematic house and community designs representing attempts at combining traditional Korean housing techniques with contemporary passive energy and land-conserving construction techniques. A proposal is briefly sketched for a hillside earth-sheltered community in the suburban area of Cheong Ju City in central Korea. The layout of the individual housing complexes is based on the garden colony housing layouts in Denmark.

Sweden

1288. Construction of as many as 10 demonstration earth-sheltered homes in Sweden may begin this year. Undergr. Sp., v. 6, no. 1, July/Aug. 1981: 4.

1289. Swedish firm plans earth sheltered housing demonstration project. Underline, v. 3, no. 4, May/June 1982: 1-2.
 An earth-sheltered housing demonstration project is planned for Sweden based on Minnesota's Earth Sheltered Housing Demonstration Project.

United States

1290. Grondzik, Walter T. and Lester L. Boyer. Earth shelter activity in the U.S. In Proc., 1st Int. Conf. on Energ. Effic. Bldgs. with Earth Shel. Prot., Sydney, Aust., Aug. 1-6, 1983. L.L. Boyer, ed. Stillwater, OK: Okla. State Univ., Archit. Ext., 1983. p. 237-41.
 Earth-sheltered buildings have found wide acceptance throughout much of the U.S. Interest is especially keen in a band of states running from Texas to Minnesota. Studies have shown this interest and activity to be directly related to energy conservation although other benefits are often quite important. Research and dissemination efforts in support of this activity have been crucial to the continued positive growth experienced by the earth-sheltered building phenomenon. --Auth. abstract.

1291. Labs, Kenneth and Don Watson. Regional suitability of earth tempering strategies. In Conf. proc., Earth Shel. Perf. and Eval., 2nd Nat. Tech. Conf., Tulsa, OK, Oct. 16-17, 1981. Stillwater, OK: Okla. State Univ., Archit. Ext., 1981. p. 39-51.
 A U.S. map is subdivided to indicate relative degrees of earth-shelter potential. Explanations and limitations on the use of earth sheltering are developed.

1292. Sterling, Raymond L. Earth sheltered buildings: construction activity and research in the U.S. Western SUN 1980 Solar Update Conf., Salt Lake City, UT, Sept. 24, 1980. p. 55-62.
 This paper discusses research, information, recent construction, and government programs.

Eastern U.S.

1293. Barnard, John. Earth sheltering in the eastern United States. In The potential of earth-sheltered and underground space: proc., Undergr. Sp. Conf. and Expos., Kansas City, MO, June 8-10, 1981. T.L. Holthusen, ed. Elmsford, NY: Pergamon Pr., 1981. p. 109-27.

Earth-sheltered structures, including residential, in the eastern U.S. are described.

1294. Gilbert, D.A. Earth-sheltered housing for Appalachia. Undergr. Sp., v. 6, no. 2, Sept./Oct. 1981: 89-92.

It is suggested that the strip mining areas of Kentucky provide possible sites for earth-sheltered housing developments.

Midwest U.S.

1295. Abercrombie, C.F. An earth-integrated direct gain passive solar home for the Great Plains. In Proc., 4th Nat. Pass. Sol. Conf., Kansas City, MO, Oct. 3-5, 1979. G. Franta, ed. Newark, DE: Int. Sol. Energ. Soc., Am. Sec., Univ. of Del., 1979. p. 760.

This design received the only Design Award in Kansas from HUD's 1978 Passive Solar Residential Design Competition and Demonstration. Passive design features include: thermal breaks, insulating glass with moveable insulation, external shade louvers, and a vestibule.

1296. Anderson, Brent D. Earth sheltering in the Mid-west. In The potential of earth-sheltered and underground space: proc., Undergr. Sp. Conf. and Expos., Kansas City, MO, June 8-10, 1981. T.L. Holthusen, ed. Elmsford, NY: Pergamon Pr., 1981. p. 129-33.

This paper discusses the building systems used in the upper Midwest when constructing earth-sheltered houses: steel culverts; shotcrete domes; fiberglass coating over wood; dry stacking block; treated wood; precast reinforced plank; precast, prestressed plank; post-tensioned concrete; reinforced block; and cast-in-place concrete.

1297. Boyer, Lester L. Earth shelter trends in the South Central Plains. Env. Com., July 1981: 4-9.

A survey project extended over nine states collected data on occupant and construction characteristics, habitability aspects and energy performance of earth-sheltered dwellings in the south central Plains. Profiles of the data are presented and recommendations for the future development of the earth-shelter idiom are provided.

1298. _____ and W.T. Grondzik. Habitability and energy performance of earth sheltered dwellings. In Proc., 3rd Int.

Conf. on Alt. Energ. Sources, Miami Beach, FL, Dec. 1980. Washington, DC: Hemisphere Pub. Corp., 1983. p. 39-64.

This paper addresses the earth-shelter phenomenon in mid-America: Iowa, Nebraska, Kansas, Missouri, Colorado, New Mexico, Oklahoma, and Texas. The need to achieve public, professional, and governmental acceptance is mentioned as well as the need for meticulous documentation of the energy conservation aspect of earth-covered dwellings, as well as other aspects. The need for energy performance data was approached by preparing a questionnaire which was sent to present earth-sheltered occupants. Other information requested: occupant profile, building decision process, cost and construction, financing and insurance, site characteristics, design formats, and building equipment.

1299. Grondzik, Walter T. and Lester L. Boyer. Earth sheltering trends: so goes the south central states, so goes the U.S.? Surveys reveal regional trends in earth sheltering. Earth Shel. Liv., no. 33, May/June 1984: 36-7.

Two surveys were made of earth-sheltered home owners in the eight south central states. Results and conclusions are similar to those obtained from ad hoc studies of the rest of the country.

1300. Kneeland, W.F. Underground dwellings built in Oklahoma. In Proc., Alt. in Habitat: the Use of Earth Cov. Set., Conf., Fort Worth, TX, May 17-19, 1978. F.L. Moreland, ed. Washington, DC: U.S. Dept. of Energy, 1979. v. 2, Earth covered buildings and settlements, p. 256-66.

Moderate soil temperatures provide an opportunity to greatly reduce the total heating and cooling energy requirements of an earth-sheltered residence. Many underground houses are now demonstrating to designers a number of possible efficient configurations and energy systems. A number of references are used to demonstrate the thermal benefits of underground houses in Oklahoma.

1301. McGuire, Steve. Design of low cost, passive solar/earth contact housing using an embankment wall concept. Final rept. Contract FG47-80R701150. May 1982. 26 p. (NTIS PC A03/MF A01; GPO Dep. Order No. DE 84007852).

This report discusses a grant proposal to research, design, and develop a system for building a low-cost passive solar/earth-contact house. The grant was considered a success. The energy savings potential of the dwelling was substantial. The amount of backup heat required made the house as efficient as any for the Midwest climate, making the concept more marketable with each utility cost increase.

1302. Riotte, Louise. Living underground—new shelter. Applewood J., no. 4, Nov. 1979: 42-7.
This article on earth sheltering in Oklahoma discusses soil analysis and responses to earthquakes.

1303. Wilkerson, Jerry. Earth shelter trend spreads in Midwest. Milw. J., Mar. 2, 1980.

Northwest U.S.

1304. Vadnais, Kathleen. Pacific Northwest: solar efforts continue. Earth Shel. Liv., no. 24, Nov./Dec. 1982: 20-2.
Earth sheltering in the Northwest is not as visible as in the Midwest but is used by solar heating advocates as a major design tool.

Southeast U.S.

1305. Langley, John B. Earth sheltered sun belt homes: 21 floor plans and perspectives. 2nd ed. Winter Park, FL: Sun Belt Earth Sheltered Research, P.O. Box 729, 1983. 104 p.
After a section on earth-sheltering concepts and their application in the southeastern U.S., the authors discuss in detail their preferred form of earth-sheltered construction, the barrel shell. Since buildings in the Southeast must be covered with three to six feet of earth to obtain maximum heating and cooling, the barrel shell built over a temporary plywood form with shotcrete and steel should be used to bear these great earth loads. Various design features for barrel shell structures are shown, and one section contains a detailed account of the construction of an earth-sheltered barrel shell home. Appendices contain 21-scaled floor plans and perspectives and a description of the installation of Bernold Plate in earth-sheltered structures.

1306. _____. Sun belt subsoil studied. Earth Shel. Dig. Energ. Rept., no. 12, Nov./Dec. 1980: 20-1.
Techniques and instruments for determining the subsoil temperature in Florida are discussed.

Southwest U.S.

1307. Behr, Richard, Ernst Kiesling, and Gary Boubel. Earth sheltered housing potentials for West Texas. Earth Shel.

Dig. Energ. Rept., no. 5, Sept./Oct. 1979: 24-5.
The authors briefly discuss the factors which make west Texas a good location for earth-sheltered construction and outline the earth-sheltered housing research and development being conducted in the Civil Engineering Dept. at Texas Tech University in Lubbock.

1308. Kiesling, E.W., R.A. Behr, and G.A. Boubel. Earth-sheltered housing for the Southwest. Lubbock, TX: Texas Tech. Univ., 1979. 31 p.

1309. Scalise, James W. Reduce existing data and compilation of additional data on earth sheltered housing in the Arizona-Sonoran Desert region. Minneapolis, MN: Control Data Corp., 1980.

1310. Selinfreund, Martin, Roger Farrer, and Peter Munding. Monitoring an earth-sheltered solar-assisted house. In Proc., 1st Int. Conf. on Energ. Effic. Bldgs. with Earth Shel. Prot., Sydney, Aust., Aug. 1-6, 1983. L.L. Boyer, ed. Stillwater, OK: Okla. State Univ., Archit. Ext., 1983. p. 345-9.
Construction of a sunspace/direct gain solar-assisted, earth-sheltered house has just been completed immediately east of Alamogordo, NM. The house is a classic example of an earth shelter, as opposed to the more frequently constructed berm homes, insofar as its north and east walls and its roof are integrated into the surrounding hillside. The house was designed and constructed by W.E. Givens (Sun Temple Associates) of Alamogordo, owner/builder, and Lundeen and Associates of Las Cruces, consulting architects. The New Mexico Solar Energy Institute is in the process of instrumenting the house and adjacent environs to ascertain temperature and other meteorological phenomena by placing thermocouples at varying depths within and under the floor slab, as well as at varying depths and distances in the earth surrounding the house. Additional instrumentation will provide meteorological data, including solar radiation and a record concerning the use of auxiliary heating and cooling. The data collected should provide information that will permit relating the internal performance of a passive solar earth-sheltered house to environmental conditions both above and below ground that are experienced during a one-year period. Although data are available on instrumented earth-sheltered homes from Oklahoma State University and the University of Minnesota, the data cannot be readily extrapolated to provide assistance to New Mexico homebuilders. --Auth. abstract.

1311. Smoot, Ralph C. Passive cooling of earth sheltered housing in Texas. In <u>Proc., 1st Int. Conf. on Energ. Effic. Bldgs. with Earth Shel. Prot.</u>, Sydney, Aust., Aug. 1-6, 1983. L.L. Boyer, ed. Stillwater, OK: Okla. State Univ., Archit. Ext., 1983. p. 75-6.

Discussion of variables and potential problem areas in the design of passive cooling in earth-sheltered homes in Texas. --Auth. abstract.

Western U.S.

1312. Scott, D.M. Earth-sheltered design and construction activity in the western states including Arizona, California, Nevada, Utah, Wyoming, Montana, Idaho, Oregon, and Washington. In <u>The potential of earth-sheltered and underground space: proc., Undergr. Sp. Conf. and Expos.</u>, Kansas City, MO, June 8-10, 1981. T.L. Holthusen, ed. Elmsford, NY: Pergamon Pr., 1981. p. 149-62.

A telephone survey was conducted to identify university faculty, architects, and builders who are leaders in earth-sheltered building. Designs of some specific buildings are described.

XXIX. CASE STUDIES

Australia

1313. Baggs, David W. Australia's first passive-solar, earth-covered dwelling: interim results of a limited monitoring program. <u>Sol. Prog.</u>, v. 4, no. 3, 1983: 1-2.

1314. _____. Australia's first passive-solar, earth-covered dwellings. In <u>Australasian proc., 1st Int. Conf. on Energ. Effic. Bldgs. with Earth Shel. Prot.</u>, Sydney, Aust., Aug. 1-6, 1983. S.A. Baggs, ed. Kensington, NSW, Aust.: Unisearch, Ltd., 1983. p. E2-8a.

The general advantages of the earth-covered concept are presented as an introductory discussion. Australia's first passive solar, earth-covered house was completed during May 1982 in the Hunter River Valley district of New South Wales, and the project is described in detail. This building was designed to achieve a specific interior comfort range using a ground temperature equation and computer simulation technique developed for Australian conditions. Post-occupational thermal monitoring records are compared with design predictions and the results evaluated. --Auth. abstract.

1315. _____. Earth-covered architecture: a case study. Bldg. Econ., Mar. 1983: 167-9.

1316. _____. Four earth-covered residences for New South Wales, Australia. Geotecture, v. 1, no. 5, Oct. 1984: 38-41.
Four earth-covered house projects show the variety of designs possible for sloping sites in hot temperature climates. The homes are planned for Bolwarra near Newcastle, Kurmond, Richmond, and Luddenham, the last two both on the Western Plains between the Blue Mts. and the coast.

1317. Baggs, Sydney A. The dugout dwellings of an outback opal-mining town in Australia. In Underground utilization. T. Stauffer, ed. Kansas City, MO: Univ. of Missouri - Kansas City, Dept. of Geosci., 1978. v. 4, p. 573-99.
A survey was conducted of the residents of dugouts in the opal-mining towns of White Cliffs, NSW and Coober Pedy, SA, to determine the attitudes of the residents to their underground homes. The natural history of these areas, the conditions inside the homes, and the attitudes of the residents are discussed.

1318. Contractor's home nears completion. Earth Shel. Dig. Energ. Rept., no. 14, Mar./Apr. 1981: 6.
Gerhard Schurer designed a 4,000 sq. ft. earth-covered home in Clarendon, SA, for the largest home builder in the state. Because of the complexity of the design, the project took three years to finish.

1319. Coober Pedy Community School. Coober Pedy dugouts. Written, researched, and photographed by students of the 11th and 12th year Humanities Class of the Coober Pedy Community School. Coober Pedy, SA, Aust.: Coober Pedy Community Printery, 1983. 24 p.
Everything you ever wanted to know about dugout living in Coober Pedy, Australia.

1320. Digging in to save the environment. Geotecture, v. 2, no. 3, 1985: 7.
This earth-sheltered home on the bank of the Naracoorte Creek was designed by Adelaide architect Peter Villis. About one-third of the house is built into the slope, and the entire roof is covered with 30 cm. of excavated soil and sown with

lawn seed. Planning officials insisted on larger than usual foundations because of the weight of the flat concrete roof and nearness to the creek.

1321. Dunlop, R. Town that went underground. <u>Pop. Mech.</u>, v. 155, Mar. 1981: 118-9+.
Coober Pedy, Australia's opal-mining center.

1322. Earth-sheltered projects in the Canberra district. <u>Geotecture</u>, v. 2, no. 1, Jan. 1985: 11.
Paul Hanley reports earth-sheltered projects underway. A copy of plans of his partly earth-covered house are shown.

1323. Forster, David J. Earth-sheltered accommodation for 55 people in a bush holiday camp. In <u>Australasian proc., 1st Int. Conf. on Energ. Effic. Bldgs. with Earth Shel. Prot.</u>, Sydney, Aust., Aug. 1-6, 1983. S.A. Baggs, ed. Kensington, NSW, Aust.: Unisearch, Ltd., 1983. p. E68-72.
The aim of Baanya Biami, a bush holiday camp, was to let people "get back to nature" with some "home comforts" provided in a manner appropriate to this environment. The use of earth-sheltered sleeping units fulfilled this ideally. Modified ferro-cement water tanks provided suitable buildings for up to 55 people. These units were readily available, prefabricated, and were easy to transport and install at less than half the cost of conventional buildings. A simple system of insulation and waterproofing that used readily available materials has helped these units provide adequate thermal stability. They remain well within comfort limits for the activities for which they were designed in Victoria's temperate but rapidly fluctuating climate. --Auth. abstract.

1324. Gillies, A.D.S., K.E. Mudd, and N.B. Aughenbaugh. Living conditions in underground houses in Coober Pedy, Australia. In <u>The potential of earth-sheltered and underground space: proc., Undergr. Sp. Conf. and Expos., Kansas City</u>, MO, June 8-10, 1981. T.L. Holthusen, ed. Elmsford, NY: Pergamon Pr., 1981. p. 163-77.
Hundreds of homes have been built underground in Coober Pedy, Australia, usually by excavating laterally into hillsides. Some underground spaces are mined using manual techniques, but most utilize mechanized hammers and mining machines used in opal mining. Some considerations in designing a "dugout" home in Coober Pedy are: the insulating properties of the rock cover, the interior temperature extremes, rock stability, and the design of interior space supported by pillars, etc., the use of auxiliary ventilation, provision for waste disposal, and others.

1325. Hadley, Philip. In-ground house survives Ash Wednesday bushfires. Own. Build., (Melbourne), no. 8, June 1983: 34, 36.

A two-story earth-sheltered home in the Adelaide Hills is constructed of fired brick and concrete. Window frames are aluminum, and the roof has a 600 mm. covering of earth. The owner stayed with the house during the fire.

1326. Hopkins, Nigel. Nothing spared in this subterranean palace. Advertiser (Adelaide), Jan. 6, 1984.

Gerhard Schurer, assisted by his partner Vera Trust, designed this palatial earth-sheltered home in Clarendon, SA, combining European style with the physical demands of Australian conditions. Long concrete spans support the earth-covered roof. Waterproofing consists of five protective barriers including a plastic membrane, building paper, and a type of hessian material, combined with other barriers and a system of agricultural drains to protect the walls. All rooms are five-sided, arranged in circular fashion.

1327. Mair, Robert W. Groundhouse: a fan-shaped, multi-level structure in North Queensland. In Australasian proc., 1st Int. Conf. on Energ. Effic. Bldgs. with Earth Shel. Prot., Sydney, Aust., Aug. 1-6, 1983. S.A. Baggs, ed. Kensington, NSW, Aust.: Unisearch, Ltd., 1983. p. E21-5. Also in Geotecture, v. 1, no. 5, Oct. 1984: 31-3.

The construction and design of an earth-covered dwelling is described. The building was built on a steeply sloping site in a rural area with a northerly aspect and minimizes disturbance to the environment and the effects of the prevailing winds and traffic noise. The resulting fan-shaped, earth-covered building effectively reduced road noise and environmental disturbance. Minimal temperature variations negated the need for air conditioning. —Auth. abstract.

1328. Mitchell, Paul B. On-going projects in South Australia. In Australasian proc., 1st Int. Conf. on Energ. Effic. Bldgs. with Earth Shel. Prot., Sydney, Aust., Aug. 1-6, 1983. S.A. Baggs, ed. Kensington, NSW, Aust.: Unisearch, Ltd., 1983. p. App. B1-5. Also in Geotecture, v. 2, no. 3, 1985: 28-37.

Brief descriptions are given of four earth-sheltered homes in Adelaide Hills, Murray Bridge, and Tailem Bend. One home survived the full force of the 1982 Adelaide Ash Wednesday bushfire.

1329. Moore, Kenny. Coober Pedy: opal capital of Australia's outback. Nat. Geog., v. 150, no. 4, Oct. 1976: 560-71.

1330. New lithotecture dwelling for Blue Mountains, NSW, Australia. Geotecture, v. 2, no. 1, Jan. 1985: 9.
Leigh Harris will build an underground house at Leura, NSW, that will have an enclosed pool and a squash court.

1331. Paton, David J. The "Terra Space" home. In Australasian proc., 1st Int. Conf. on Energ. Effic. Bldgs. with Earth Shel. Prot., Sydney, Aust., Aug. 1-6, 1983. S.A. Baggs, ed. Kensington, NSW, Aust.: Unisearch Ltd., 1983. p. E31-6. Also in Geotecture, v. 1, no. 5, Oct. 1984: 34-7.
The "Terra Space" project home situated in the foothills of the Gold Coast hinterland, Queensland, is described. This house features a unique light, ventilation, and seepage chamber around the earth-covered section of the house. The one m. wide chamber guarantees natural light from overhead sky domes and cross ventilation to habitable rooms. Monitoring to date indicates a measurable passive means of humidity control via the chamber. --Auth. abstract.

1332. Paul Mitchell's earth covered house in South Australia. Geotecture, v. 2, no. 1, Jan. 1985: 10.
The plan, a section, and a sketch of a view is shown.

1333. Residents of New South Wales, Australia, are being introduced to earth-sheltering through a display home built by Jewan Construction in Campbelltown. Undergr. Sp., v. 6, no. 4-5, Jan./Apr. 1982: 200.

1334. Schurer, Gerhard. Earth-integrated architecture in South Australia. Pt. Two. Geotecture, v. 2, no. 3, 1985: 9-19.
This article details five earth-sheltered houses in: Belair, Tailem Bend (on River Murray), and Adelaide Hills. They were designed by John Maitland of Maitland Architects, Paul Mitchell, Phil Hansen, and Villis Tossani Architects.

1335. _____. History of project. Earth Shel. Dig. Energ. Rept., no. 14, Mar./Apr. 1981: 6-7.
The author designed a very large earth-covered house, his main objective being environmental integration into the beautiful rural South Australian countryside. Started in 1979, at time of writing it was still not finished.

1336. Stanford, Greg. Down under dugouts - White Cliffs, Australia. Earth Shel. Dig. Energ. Rept., no. 7, Jan./Feb. 1980: 41-3.
This mining town is eastern Australia's largest underground community. The caves are dug out of moist, pliable claystone.

1337. Villis, Peter and Richard Tossani. Earth-sheltered houses, South Australia. In Australasian proc., 1st Int. Conf. on Energ. Effic. Bldgs. with Earth Shel. Prot., Sydney, Aust., Aug. 1-6, 1983. S.A. Baggs, ed. Kensington, NSW, Aust.: Unisearch, Ltd., 1983.
Villis Tossani Architects, N. Adelaide, have built four earth-sheltered houses. The design of an earth-sheltered child care center is also discussed.

1338. Wells, Malcolm. Down under, down under . . . or, how not to build underground. Prog. Archit., v. 49, no. 5, Mar. 1968: 164-5.
In the desert of central Australia, a group of opal miners has built an underground town to escape the hostile climate.

Bahamas

1339. Caribbean cove cave carved. Earth Shel. Dig. Energ. Rept., no. 14, Mar./Apr. 1981: 52-3.
Architect John Anderson has built his earth-sheltered house in the Bahamas. Illustrated.

Brazil

1340. Photo of earth sheltered house in Curitiba, Brazil: architects Eleanora Beltrao Barcik and Rodolfo Doubek. In The art of Brazil, by Carlos Lemos, Jose R. Teixeira Leite and Pedro Manuel Gismonti. New York, NY: Harper & Row, 1983. p. 274. (Icon Editions).

Canada

1341. Canadian architects opt for earth sheltering. Undergr. Sp., v. 5, no. 1, July/Aug. 1980: 6-7.
Several earth-covered house projects under construction in Canada are described.

1342. Czarnecki, M. Rabbits do it, but they never mow the roof. Macleans, v. 93, no. 8, Feb. 25, 1980: 44-5.
Earth-sheltered dwellings in Canada.

1343. Earth sheltered home "a dream": Toronto home show picks earth shelter as "dream home." Earth Shel. Liv., no. 31, Jan./Feb. 1984: 11.
Architect Robert Reimers of Toronto designed a 4,000 sq. ft. earth-sheltered home which was seen by 80,000 people at the 1983 National Home Show in Toronto. Cost estimate for the concrete home: $300,000.

1344. Meissner, John. Canadian farmer built in 1961. Earth Shel. Dig. Energ. Rept., No. 13, Jan./Feb. 1981: 34-7.

In 20 years, this earth-sheltered home in La Jord, Saskatchewan has been visited by over 20,000. The roof has not leaked since it was covered. A 15 kw windmill is on the roof.

1345. Nicholson, Nick. Autonomous house incorporates concepts. Earth Shel. Dig. Energ. Rept., no. 9, May/June 1980: 40-2.

The Canadian author is building an "Autonomous House" incorporating 52 percent earth sheltering, solar heating, zone controlled floor heating, parabolic roof construction, and other features.

1346. Pool easy victor: Canadian couple tops off earth shelter with pool. Earth Shel. Liv., no. 31, Jan./Feb. 1984: 38-9.

This 1,825 sq. ft. home in Castlegar, BC, has a swimming pool in front.

1347. Sawdust blocks insulate, too. Earth Shel. Dig. Energ. Rept., no. 14, Mar./Apr. 1981: 12-6.

With the objective of producing affordable housing, Du-Al Earth Sheltered Homes, Ltd., Vernon, BC, has built an earth-sheltered home out of sawdust blocks reinforced with steel and filled with concrete. The blocks are also a form of insulation, so only waterproofing is needed before backfilling. The 2,025 sq. ft. one-story is built into a hillside which was unsuitable for a conventional house.

1348. Shielke, Ty. Canadian father, son build. Earth Shel. Dig. Energ. Rept., no. 14, Mar./Apr. 1981: 16.

Author tells why he and his father built an earth-sheltered house in Vernon, BC, out of sawdust blocks.

China

1349. Raetzman, Ronald and Suzanne Wadsworth. Atrium and courtyard houses. Undergr. Sp., v. 7, no. 1, July/Aug. 1982: 12-3.

This is a photo essay about some underground homes built into the loess soil in north-central China.

England

1350. Exhibit draws international crowds. Earth Shel. Dig. Energ. Rept., no. 17, Sept./Oct. 1981: 63.

A model of a two-bedroom earth-sheltered home was exhibited at the Daily Mail Ideal Home Exhibition, "Energy in the Eighties," in London in the spring of 1981. The building plans were prepared by Ledward & McDonald Consulting Architects, London.

1351. If you can't beat 'em – bury 'em. Building, v. 237, no. 7107 (39), Sept. 28, 1979: 13.

This underground house design by Architect Frank Stovin-Bradford came about when the client's plan for a conventional house was rejected because the site bordered a greenbelt and the house would have obscured the view. In Amersham, Chiltern Urban District Council.

1352. Marsh, Jacqui. Under the hill. Archit. J., v. 165, no. 15, Apr. 13, 1977: 687.

"Underhill" residence, in Holme, Yorkshire, Eng., was designed by its owner, Arthur Quarmby, architect. It is between Manchester and Huddersfield.

1353. Spring, Martin. Architects' homes: the underground house in Holme, Yorkshire. Architect, Arthur Quarmby. Building, v. 236, no. 7092 (24), June 15, 1979: 49.

This is a brief report on Quarmby's house "Underhill."

1354. Trombley, Stephen. Arthur Quarmby's quandary. RIBA J., v. 89, no. 5, May 1982: 35.

Quarmby's house "Underhill" is built into a hill in West Riding. His main concern is integrating architecture into the landscape, not conserving energy.

1355. "Underhill," an underground house in Holme, Yorkshire. Concr. Q., no. 116, Jan./Mar. 1978: 2-7.

1356. Vadnais, Kathleen. English manor preserves village view. Earth Shel. Liv., no. 24, Nov./Dec. 1982: 6-9.

Architect Arthur Quarmby built this earth-sheltered home in the Pennine Mts. in western Yorkshire near the village of Holme. Quarmby puts architecture first and energy and ecology second.

France

1357. An instinctive house. Prog. Archit., v. 45, no. 5, May 1964: 186-93.

An earth-integrated house in Castellares-le-Neuf, Alpes-Maritime, France, was designed by Jacques Couelle. It has a cave-like form.

1358. Brown, Terry. The energy future in St. Pierre de Feric. Home Energ. Dig. Wood. Q., v. 5, no. 4, Spring 1981: 155-65.

This article describes the terraced, reinforced earth development designed and built by Architerra, a division of the Parisian firm La Terre Armée, in the hills outside of Nice, France. The architect and engineer responsible for the design is Henri Vidal. The reinforced earth technique may make mass developments of energy efficient, earth-sheltered homes possible. This method calls for putting metal strips between layers of compacted earth so that the ground itself acts as a wall.

1359. Daly, Les. In French caves, they live it up by living it down. Smithsonian, v. 14, no. 3, June 1983: 50-4+.

Some of the affluent French "haute bourgeoisie" have adopted cave dwelling. Several color photos show luxurious, tastefully decorated cave dwellings in and near the Loire Valley. The requirements for a "proper" cave home include: southern exposure, low humidity, and a history of the cave to try to determine its stability.

1360. Earth-covered protest symbol. Undergr. Sp., v. 8, no. 3, 1984: 143.

The Anti-Nuclear Association of the Region of Malville in France are building a self-sufficient solar house with earth cover a few miles from the Superphenix breeder reactor at Poleyrieu, France, to show that alternatives to nuclear power exist.

1361. Grigson, Geoffrey. Feeling at home in a cave house. Ctry. Life, v. 163, May 25, 1978: 1482, 1484.

The French cave houses in the Loire Valley are discussed. The author found these underground villages inhabited about 1960; but when he returned in 1977, many had been abandoned, and they had become tourist curiosities.

1362. Huet, Oliver. Ancient cliff dwellings are recycled. Earth Shel. Liv., no. 22, July/Aug. 1982: 47-9.

Cliff dwellings in France are being transformed into modern homes. The village of Villaines les Rochers was studied by the author.

1363. _____. Troglodyte habitations in France. Undergr. Sp., v. 6, no. 6, May/June 1982: 343-54.

Cliff dwellings and caverns in France have provided shelter and refuge since prehistoric times. Many of these troglodyte habitations have been modernized and are still inhabited.

1364. Large earth-sheltered housing complex nears completion. Undergr. Sp., v. 5, no. 2, Sept./Oct. 1980: 66.

Architerra, Inc. used a unique slope-stabilizing technique called Reinforced Earth to build a 47-unit housing complex into a steep hillside in Nice, France.

1365. Lord, David. Troglodyte communities in France. In Passive solar: subdivisions, windows, underground. Ed. by Herb Wade and others. Kansas City, MO: Am. Sol. Energ. Soc., Kansas City Chap., 1983. p. 200-18.

The troglodyte dwellings occur in highest density and largest numbers along the Loire River Valley. The geological formations of the Loire Valley are described. The underground dwellings occur either on the face of cliffs overlooking streams and rivers or on the surrounding backslope where there is perfectly flat terrain. About one-third are in absolutely flat country where access is vertical. The culture and daily life of the troglodytes in the Loire Valley and the different types of underground buildings there are described.

1366. Smay, V. Elaine. Under-hill village tames a plunging slope. Pop. Sci., v. 218, no. 2, Feb. 1981: 82-5.

Agora, an earth-integrated housing project at St. Pierre de Feric, near Nice, France, is built on a 50 percent slope using a special building method called Reinforced Earth^R. Built by Architerra, an architectural firm based in Paris, which has similar developments underway near Paris and Grenoble and near Madrid, Spain. The Reinforced Earth construction method is a patented process.

Mexico

1367. Legorreta, Ricardo. Desert housing in Baja California. In Desert housing: balancing experience and technology for dwelling in hot arid zones. Kenneth N. Clark and Patricia Paylore, eds. Tucson, AZ: University of Arizona Pr., 1980. p. 239-49.

The author designed two rows of beach condominium units burrowed into the dunes for a hotel in Cabo San Lucas.

1368. Smith, C. Ray. Resort condominium, Baja California: low density in the dunes. Prog. Archit., v. 57, Sept. 1976: 68-71.

These earth-sheltered condominiums designed by Mexican architect Ricardo Legorreta in Cabo San Lucas offer a low-profile, low-density form of beachfront resort housing.

New Zealand

1369. Earth sheltered house in New Zealand. Geotecture, v. 2, no. 1, Jan. 1985: 8.
 This 2,000 sq. m. concrete and steel house north of Auckland is built into a clay bank. It cost about 30-50 percent more per sq. m. to build than a conventional house.

1370. Robertson, Graeme. Low-energy passive solar earth sheltered house on Banks Peninsula, New Zealand. In Proc., 1st Int. Conf. on Energ. Effic. Bldgs. with Earth Shel. Prot., Sydney, Aust., Aug. 1-6, 1983. L.L. Boyer, ed. Stillwater, OK: Okla. State Univ., Archit. Ext., 1983. p. 103.
 The objectives of this paper are to study and define the design objectives for an earth-sheltered house on a rural north-facing slope on Banks Peninsula, South Island (43 degrees south), to study the available construction materials/systems using experience gained from other similar buildings, to study the overall economics of the final design in terms of capital cost and cost-in-use (energy and maintenance), and to study public acceptance of this form of housing. —Auth. abstract.

Norway

1371. Norwegian family readies home. Earth Shel. Liv., no. 23, Oct./Sept. 1982: 23.
 A couple built a 1,950 sq. ft., one-story earth-sheltered home on a farm in 1981. The difficulty of getting a home building loan in Norway is discussed.

Switzerland

1372. Seitz, Doug. Something different: a Swiss architect not content with the ordinary, uses new shapes for housing. Earth Shel. Liv., no. 36, Nov./Dec. 1984: 4-8.
 Architect Peter Vetsch has designed some of the most unconventional structures in Switzerland. Some of them are earth sheltered. One in Ascona is described. He's building four more in the Zurich area.

United States

Arizona

1373. Architect let fingers do walking. Earth Shel. Liv., no. 39, May/June 1985: 16-7.

The architect James Snider designed this earth-sheltered home in Arizona which has many passive solar features. It has 1,200 sq. ft., two bedrooms, and cost about $60,000 to build.

1374. Burgess, Hugh, Stanley Mumma, and John Yellott. Integrated architectural and mechanical design for the Arizona State University energy efficient house and laboratory. In Proc., Earth Shel. Bldg. Des. Innov., Oklahoma City, OK, Apr. 18, 1980. L.L. Boyer, ed. Stillwater, OK: Okla. State Univ., 1980. p. II. 4-10.

A building was designed to simulate a single family home to be later converted to a research laboratory. Recognizing that earth-integrated architecture further adds to a reduction in the cooling load, the first floor of the structure is designed to be partially below grade.

1375. Covered circles enhance Arizona yard. Earth Shel. Liv., no. 26, Mar./Apr. 1983: 6-8.

A small earth-covered studio on a 1960s subdivision lot with a conventional home in Glendale, AZ, is described. Designed by William P. Bruder, New River, AZ, it serves as a home workroom and a retreat. It was completed in Oct. 1982.

1376. Desert dictates design. Earth Shel. Dig. Energ. Rept., no. 16, July/Aug. 1981: 29-33.

This 2,000 sq. ft. custom-built earth-sheltered passive solar house is in Tempe, AZ.

1377. Desert model welcomes visitors. Earth Shel. Liv., no. 24, Nov./Dec. 1982: 13.

An Arizona home built by Concept 2000, Inc. utilizes steel culverts in earth-sheltered residential construction.

1378. Doney, Carl. Desert design. New Shel., v. 5, no. 6, Aug. 1984: 50-5.

This Tempe, AZ, home has sandy berms to shield it from heat on three sides.

1379. Machowski, Barb. Desert home harmonizes with sun, earth. Earth Shel. Liv., no. 20, Mar./Apr. 1982: 26-30.

This 1,820 sq. ft. earth and rock-covered home near Tucson has eight to twelve inches thick concrete block walls, reinforced and filled, and a sand-set brick floor. Cooled by an evaporative cooler, it is heated by an electric furnace.

1380. New home choices multiply. Earth Shel. Dig. Energ. Rept., no. 17, Sept./Oct. 1981: 43-5.

Two new spec homes are ready for purchase: a 1,800 sq. ft. house in Tucson, AZ, and a 2,148 sq. ft. home with luxury features in Dillsburg, PA.

1381. Saguaros and Dean Barber. Earth Shel. Liv., no. 40, July/Aug. 1985: 4-6.

This new 2,500 sq. ft. earth shelter in Cave Creek, AZ, utilized the Cal Hambro forming system in pouring the walls and roof.

1382. Scalise, James W. The Banen desert hillside house in Arizona. In Proc., 1st Int. Conf. on Energ. Effic. Bldgs. with Earth Shel. Prot., Sydney, Aust., Aug. 1-6, 1983. L.L. Boyer, ed. Stillwater, OK: Okla. State Univ., Archit. Ext., 1983. p. 197-202. Also in Geotecture, v. 1, no. 5, Oct. 1984: 21.

An approach to the design of an earth-sheltered residence in a hot, arid climate is in many ways exactly the opposite as in a cold, wet climate. These environmental conditions, capsulized in this report, were acknowledged in this desert hillside case study residence designed for Mr. & Mrs. Al Banen in Fountain Hills, AZ, a new planned community northeast of Phoenix. With significant aesthetic restrictions imposed by the community design review board, a desert site with a one in four slope and the owner's desire to integrate the building with the land and control summer heat gain, an earth-sheltered solution was quite natural. This report documents the special passive solar design detailing and construction considerations incorporated into this arid region hillside residence. --Auth. abstract.

1383. Unique home is traffic stopper. Earth Shel. Liv., no. 32, Mar./Apr. 1984: 5-8.

This Arizona home is a blend of curves, dips, and swirls. The exterior of this 3,400 sq. ft. earth-covered home in Paradise Valley, AZ, has few flat planes; it consists almost entirely of curved shapes.

1384. Wukasch, Eugene. Home wed technology and design: architect-engineer applauds rare combination of beauty and function. Earth Shel. Liv., no. 32, Mar./Apr. 1984: 8-9.

Arkansas

1385. Hayward, Roy. Owner "picks out" bluff dwelling. Earth Shel. Liv., no. 29, Sept./Oct. 1983: 24-7.

The author describes construction of his 2,600 sq. ft. home

built into a bluff in Arkansas. A spring runs into a pool in the house helping to cool it. This house is more expensive to heat than to cool.

1386. Pauley, Helen. Down on the farm. Earth Shel. Liv., no. 37-39, Jan./Feb. - May/June 1985.
A couple in their sixties are building an earth-sheltered home in Arkansas.

California

1387. Alexander House, Montecito, California. Architect: Roland Coate. Proc.: Archit., no. 21, Jan. 1981: 138-43.
The design of this 7,000 sq. ft. house is geared to the configuration of the site. Grading allowed the house to be incorporated into the hillside as a natural part of the landscape. It was finished in 1974.

1388. Baldasare Forestiere, Fresno, CA. Archit. Plus, v. 2, no. 4, July/Aug. 1974: 96-7.

1389. Barney, Alice Eichold. Zanettos' underground house. Winds of Change, v. 2, no. 8, Mar. 1981: 11.
Located in the Village Homes solar development in Davis, CA, this house of 1,025 sq. ft. is earth covered and bermed. Designed and built by Jim Zanetto, this wood structure has a concrete slab floor and is waterproofed with Hypalon, a synthetic rubber. It is adjacent to some houses with sod roofs.

1390. Buck, Claudia. A down-to-earth war on energy waste. Sac. Bee, Nov. 15, 1980: CL3.
Jim Zanetto, an architect, has built an earth bermed, passive solar house in Village Homes, Davis, CA. Thirty-five sensors are installed on the roof, walls, slab floor, and imbedded in the berms to monitor temperatures. The house is grouped with three other less extensively earth-blanketed homes. The structure is made of specially treated wood. The entire framework is draped top to toe in a synthetic rubber material called Hypalon. Cost of house: approx. $30,000.

1391. Dean, Andrea O. Underground movement widens. AIA J., v. 67, no. 13, Nov. 1978: 34-49.
Four subsurface buildings are studied: Alexander House, Montecito, CA, by Roland Coate; Malcolm Wells' Solaria House, Indian Mills, NJ; Philip Johnson's Geier House in suburban Cincinnati; and the Clark-Nelson House in River Falls, WI, designed by Michael McGuire.

1392. Earth shelter crowns California hilltop. <u>Earth Shel. Dig. Energ. Rept.</u>, no. 7, Jan./Feb. 1980: 24-7.

This 2,400 sq. ft. California earth-sheltered home perches on a hill in the Santa Cruz Mountains.

1393. Feuille, House, the Sea Ranch, California. Architect: David Wright of SEAgroup. <u>Proc.: Archit.</u>, no. 21, Jan. 1981: 150-1.

This 1,854 sq. ft. house on the California north coast has a sod roof and earth berms. It was completed in March 1979.

1394. Goldberger, Paul. The house in the hill. <u>N.Y. Times Mag.</u>, Aug. 7, 1977: 42-4.

Alexander House, near Santa Barbara, CA, was designed and built by Roland Coate, Jr. for photographer and film maker Jesse Alexander.

1395. Goodykoontz, James R. Subterranean house with solar screen. <u>Sunworld</u>, no. 4, May 1977: 26-7.

TMC Co., P. O. Box 237, Woodland Hills, CA, have designed a two-bedroom subterranean house built around a central patio open to the sky. It is heated by a conventional forced-air furnace. The garage and front entrance foyer are above ground. The patio can be covered by a "solar screen" consisting of stationary metal louvers which are tilted toward the south so that noontime midsummer sun is blocked and the patio is in total shade.

1396. Hines, Thomas S. Coate. <u>Prog. Archit.</u>, v. 57, no. 8, Aug. 1976: 58-61.

Alexander House, Montecito, CA, designed by Los Angeles architect Roland Coate is a controversial earth-covered house of board-formed concrete which takes a provocative approach to the use of raw materials for domestic design. The site plan and floor plans of the three-level house are given, as well as photographs of the interior and grounds.

1397. Johnson, Jim. Homes that blend into the terrain. <u>Sac. Bee</u>, Sept. 25, 1981: F1.

This earth-sheltered house is located in the Sierra foothills near Auburn, CA, on red clay soil. It was designed by Pierre Prodis, architect of San Francisco, and built by Steve Johnson, the current occupant. Red clay berms the east side. There are 18 inches of soil on the roof, seeded with grass. They used materials generally found in heavy commercial construction: precast concrete panels up to eight inches thick supported by steel beams. The owner describes it as a passive solar home partially earth sheltered. Natural insulation from earth supplements the R-30 in the ceiling and R-19 in the west wall. The house has three bedrooms, two and half baths, 2,950 sq. ft. of living area, and an oversized detached two-car garage.

1398. Machowski, Barb. Luxury development is efficient, too. Earth Shel. Dig. Energ. Rept., no. 17, Sept./Oct. 1981: 8-9.
Honey Springs is a 2,200-acre luxury development with 389 home sites east of San Diego. It's the largest earth-sheltered passive solar project yet developed. A unique feature will be a system of underground earth pipes modeled on those found in the Middle East to allow earth-cooled air to enter the homes.

1399. Olmsted, Lorena Ann. Human mole: Baldasare Forestiere's "underground gardens" were a labor of love. Am. Mer., v. 90, no. 434, Mar. 1960: 137-40.
Forestiere built 65 rooms, gardens and grottos underground using pick and shovel over a period of 38 years.

1400. Rental property features quality. Earth Shel. Liv., no. 24, Nov./Dec. 1982: 3-5.
Whittet Construction, Walnut Creek, CA, chose the All-Weather-Wood Foundation system for walls and a fiberglass-insulated, treated wood roof structure for this two bedroom, two bath, 1,520 sq. ft. house plus garage.

1401. Retirement home ready. Earth Shel. Liv., no. 19, Jan./Feb. 1982: 38-40.
This 1,385 sq. ft. home overlooks the Pacific Ocean at Sea Ranch in northern California. The direct gain system utilizes a front face of windows, sloped roof for added height, a loft room, clerestory windows, and a wind-tower.

1402. Sanoff, Henry. Seven acres of underground shelter. AIA J., v. 47, no. 2, Feb. 1967: 66-8.
Starting in 1908 and working for 38 years, Baldasare Forestiere created a subterranean labyrinth including living quarters and gardens.

1403. Specs designed for climate. Earth Shel. Dig. Energ. Rept., no. 18, Nov./Dec. 1981: 43-6.
The homes are in the Riverside area of California, in the Sun Valley resort area in Idaho, and in Haslett, MI, 5 miles east of Lansing.

1404. Stoumen, Jonathan. A passively heated and cooled earth

integrated home and a passively cooled residence in a hot humid climate. In Proc., 4th Nat. Pass. Sol. Conf., Kansas City, MO, Oct. 3-5, 1979. G. Franta, ed. Newark, DE: Int. Sol. Energ. Soc., Am. Sec., 1979. p. 760.
    This paper discusses two solar homes located in northern California and in Hawaii. The California home is set into a hillside meadow. The Kauai residence is a traditional home.

1405. Tomorrow's house. Sunset, Apr. 1977: 132-4.
    Architect David Wright designed an underground, passive structure in Sea Ranch, CA. The south wall slopes 75 degrees with the structure only 20 feet deep. The back wall is composed of one foot of concrete and acts as a heat storage medium. The rooms are side by side with all but the bathroom receiving direct sunlight. The outside of the concrete wall is waterproofed and covered with two inches thick polystyrene insulation panels. Fiberglass insulation was placed between the roof joists with a half inch of plywood and a waterproof barrier. Six inches of sod covers the roof.

1406. Underground in California. Architects Steve Badanes and Jim Adamson of Jersey Devil. Domus, no. 610, Oct. 1980: 3.
    Hill House is near La Honda on top of a hill overlooking San Francisco. It is built inside the mountain, the house structure following the line of the hillside enclosing the garden area and protecting it from the wind. Load-bearing external walls are of reinforced concrete, and all interior walls are of wood, either exposed or plaster surfaced. The roof is a series of wooden and tubular steel beams covered with plywood and then gravel separated by insulating material.

1407. Underground in Fresno. Sunset, v. 119, no. 2, Aug. 1957: 21.
    Baldasare Forestiere's underground caverns are located on Shaw Avenue five and a half miles north of Fresno's traffic circle and two blocks west of U.S. Highway 99.

1408. Vadnais, Kathleen. Oceanside house perches on cliff. Earth Shel. Liv., no. 25, Jan./Feb. 1983: 21-5.
    The California Coastal Commission required this couple to preserve the ocean view by sinking their retirement home into the ground.

1409. Woodbridge, Sally. Against nature. Prog. Archit., v. 62, no. 6, June 1981: 78-85.
    The 3,300 sq. ft. Kirlin House (p. 82) in the Napa Valley,

CA, is bermed on three sides providing a warm winter living court on the south. It was designed by Batey and Mack, architects.

1410. Zanetto, J. and D. Harding. Earthshelter: performance evaluation of a northern California residence. In Proc., Annu. Mtg., Int. Sol. Energ. Soc., Am. Sec., Philadelphia, PA, May 26, 1981. 4.2, p. 1116-9.

A passive solar, earth-sheltered house in Davis, CA, is constructed of pressure-treated wood. East, west, and north sides of the house are bermed. There is a sod roof. By comparing indoor and outdoor temperatures during two data collection periods, this house was shown to be well adapted to the local climate.

Colorado

1411. Colosol's earth-sheltered energy saver. Moth. Earth N., no. 62, Mar./Apr. 1980: 136-7.

Built by Colosol Construction near Dillon, CO, the floor of the underground portion of the house is four feet below the surface. The removed earth was used to berm the walls which protrude above ground level creating a combination underground/earth-bermed structure. The energy efficiency of the home depends upon three major features: the heat-saving capabilities of earth sheltering, the collection of solar warmth through an atrium and skylights, and the retention of heat in concrete, rock, and tile flooring.

1412. Crowther House, Denver, Colorado. Architect: Richard L. Crowther. Proc.: Archit., no. 21, Jan. 1981: 80-3.

The north side of the 6,400 sq. ft. house is earth bermed to the roofline. Construction is pre-cast prestressed concrete that, with the earth covering, acts as a thermal mass. The house was completed in Nov. 1979.

1413. Earth shelter profiles. Earth Shel. Liv., no. 31, Jan./Feb. 1984: 16-7.

Floor plans are shown for earth-sheltered homes in Breckenridge, CO; Northfield, MN; Clyde, Ohio; Kenosha, WI; and Valparaiso, IN.

1414. Earth shelter profiles. Earth Shel. Liv., no. 35, Sept./Oct. 1984: 20-1.

Photos and floor plans of earth-sheltered homes in Boulder, CO; Bend, OR; Hanover, IL; Elk River, MN; and Tucson, AZ, are shown.

1415. Earth sheltered Colorado house is 100% solar heated. Undergr. Sp., v. 4, no. 6, May/June 1980: 403-4.

The 1,800 sq. ft. Sun Earth House designed and built by Colorado Sunworks, Boulder, CO, is discussed. Its energy performance was monitored by IBM computerized tracking equipment.

1416. Earth-sheltered housing project is being built on Colorado slope. Undergr. Sp., v. 6, no. 6, May/June 1982: 317.

Architerra, Inc. has begun a 12-unit luxury housing complex in Vail, CO, using the slope stabilization method (Reinforced Earth) they have developed.

1417. Elk roam on home. Earth Shel. Dig. Energ. Rept., no. 10, July/Aug. 1980: 52-5.

This 1,750 sq. ft. earth-sheltered home is at 8,500 ft. alt. and 25 miles west of Vail, CO. The walls are eight inches thick. The roof areas are 80 percent covered with a maximum of 18 inches of earth. The living room area is waterproofed with Butyl rubber sheets. Insulation is three inches thick (R-13-5). This solar hybrid was designed as a passive direct gain structure, but it also includes a bank of hydronic solar hot water collectors. The total cost came to $51/sq. ft.

1418. F. Lloyd Wright student builds into land. Earth Shel. Dig. Energ. Rept., no. 13, Jan./Feb. 1981: 28-9.

In 1962, Frederic Benedict built an earth-sheltered rambler in the Colorado Mts. His present north-facing earth-sheltered home in Aspen, CO, is 6,000 sq. ft. on two stories. He favors clusterings instead of separate houses to increase energy efficiency and preserve low profiles.

1419. Factory-built modules. Earth Shel. Liv., no. 36, Nov./Dec. 1984: 10-2.

The sections for a 2,400 sq. ft. earth-covered house near Denver, CO, were built in a factory and assembled at the site.

1420. Mitchell, Stephen. Large mountain home shelters family. Earth Shel. Liv., no. 22, July/Aug. 1982: 30-3.

The Switzer's 4,000 sq. ft., two-story, earth-sheltered house is in Estes Park, CO, in the Rockies.

1421. A sandstone cave. N.Y. Times, Feb. 21, 1980, Sec. C: 8.

A two bedroom, three story, 1,940 sq. ft. house was built in a sandstone cave in Loma, CO. The owner, Charles Nystrom, chose the site as much for its beauty as for its ability to keep energy bills down. The average heating bill is $91.25/yr.

1422. Shippee, Paul. Minimal energy use-performance of the Sunearth House. In <u>Proc., 4th Nat. Pass. Sol. Conf.</u>, Kansas City, MO, Oct. 3-5, 1979. G. Franta, ed. Newark, DE: Int. Sol. Energ. Soc., Am. Sec., 1979. p. 760.

Colorado Sunworks designed and constructed the Sunearth House during 1977 and 1978. It is an earth-covered passive solar-heated and naturally-cooled residence.

1423. _____. Performance of the Sunearth House. In <u>Proc., 2nd Annu. Sol. Heat. and Cool. Syst. Oper. Res. Conf.</u>, Colorado Springs, CO, Nov. 27, 1979.

The operation of the Sunearth House demonstrates minimal energy usage. This earth covered passive solar-heated and naturally-cooled home is located in Longmont, CO. Its performance is monitored by IBM computerized tracking of 90 energy sensors that were built in during construction. Results of the monitoring are published by the DOE under the National Solar Data Program.

1424. _____. The Sunearth Home. In <u>Proc., 2nd Nat. Pass. Sol. Conf.</u>, Philadelphia, PA, Mar. 16-18, 1978. Newark, DE: Int. Sol. Energ. Soc., Am. Sec., 1978. v. 1, p. 91-3. Also in <u>Solar Diversification: proc., Annu. Mtg., Int. Sol. Energ. Soc., Am. Sec.</u>, Denver, CO, Aug. 28, 1978. Newark, DE: Int. Sol. Energ. Soc., Am. Sec., 1978. p. 235-7.

A description is given of an earth-covered passive solar heated and cooled home built in Longmont, CO. It features massive water-filled drum walls, Beadwall, concrete structure, one-foot thick earth cover with full berms, a passive tank water heater, 45 degree skylight wells, and full five-year performance documentation by the National Bureau of Standards.

1425. The Sunearth House. <u>Sol. Age</u>, v. 5, no. 2, Feb. 1980: 10-7.

This earth covered passive solar heated and naturally cooled house is located near Longmont, CO. It was designed, built, and marketed by Paul Shippee's Colorado Sunworks in 1977-78. Low energy use was achieved by mxing load reduction techniques, passive solar heating, and thermal/architectural design. Data are given on insulation and heating load, passive solar system, back up heating, summer cooling performance, weather conditions, and energy savings.

1426. A 20th century cliff house. <u>Moth. Earth N.</u>, no. 64, July/Aug. 1980: 124-6.

This house is based on Hopi design ideas. Native Americans enjoyed the warmth and security of natural cave shelters over a thousand years ago. Located just west of Grand Junction, CO, it was blasted out of sandstone. It has 1,920 sq. ft., three stories, and cost about $40-45 per sq. ft. The heating and cooling expense is about 34 cents a day. Appropriate cliff-bearing rock formations span the country from Mexico to Canada in a 500 mile wide swath. It took less than a year to complete the dwelling.

1427. Two-story soaks up sun. Earth Shel. Dig. Energ. Rept., no. 18, Nov./Dec. 1981: 33-7.
This 2,400 sq. ft. house in Golden, CO, has a passive solar plan and no heating bills. Architect: Ron Abo.

Connecticut

1428. Landis and Pamela Gore's semi-subterranean "house for all seasons." Moth. Earth N., no. 49, Jan./Feb. 1978: 64-5.
This 4,000 sq. ft. house in New Canaan, CT, is approximately 2/3 below ground. Most heat comes from the earth by means of a unique buried-loop/heat-pump system.

1429. Philip Johnson goes underground. Art Amer., July 1966.
The roof of the Johnson Gallery (the private gallery on the estate of architect Philip Johnson) is covered with sand contained within parapets projecting just through the surface. It is in New Canaan, CT.

Florida

1430. Dean, Andrea Oppenheimer. Sculpting with the earth. AIA J., v. 72, no. 1, Jan. 1983: 61.
A house in Florida designed by William Morgan consists of two truncated pyramids wrapped in berms, topped and outlined with strips of stuccoed reinforced masonry. The north unit contains a garage and storage space; the south unit is the residence.

1431. _____. Underground architecture. AIA J., v. 67, no. 4, Apr. 1978: 34-51.
Five underground structures are studied and described: W. Morgan's Dune House in Atlantic Beach, FL; his Hilltop House in central Florida; the church of St. Benedict's Abbey in Benet Lake, WI; and Terraset School, Reston, VA.

1432. An earth-bermed house for Florida. Alt. Energ., no. 33, Aug. 1978: 14-5.
This typical Florida concrete block house is earth bermed to reduce heating and cooling costs. Estimated savings: about 40 percent of costs before it was earth-bermed.

1433. Earthform house by William Morgan echoes Florida's pre-colonial past. Archit. Rec., v. 159, no. 6, mid-May 1976: 106-7.

Morgan's earth-mound house in central Florida is constructed of reinforced concrete beams with tie beams and a concrete slab. All exterior walls are earth covered except where glazing occurs. Thomas A. McCrary was project architect; Howard Woodward was the contractor.

1434. Forest House. Central Florida, 1979. Architect: William Morgan. Archit. Urb., no. 7 (118), July 1980: 52-4.
Article in English and Japanese.

1435. Forest House. Central Florida. Architects: William Morgan Architects. Proc.: Archit., no. 21, Jan. 1981: 130-7.

Two truncated pyramids of earth are interconnected by an entry canopy in a 60-acre oak forest. It was completed in Jan. 1979.

1436. Haponski, Don. Steel is tops. Earth Shel. Liv., no. 38, Mar./Apr. 1985: 12-4.

After living in an earth-bermed house since the early 1970s, the author and his wife decided to build one in Florida. They installed a steel deck to support the earth cover. The completed shell for the house cost around $4,000.

1437. Hilltop House, Central Florida. Architects: William Morgan Architects. Proc.: Archit., no. 21, Jan. 1981: 126-9.

This 3,300 sq. ft. pyramidal earth-bermed structure was completed in 1975.

1438. Matthews, Mindy A. Collaborative learns building skills. Earth Shel. Liv., no. 23, Sept./Oct. 1982: 4-5.

A construction collaborative of six people helped to build a 1,075 sq. ft. earth-sheltered home near Orlando, FL, using the Bernold structural system.

1439. Morgan, William. Building as landscape: five current projects by William Morgan. Archit. Rec., v. 152, no. 3, Sept. 1972: 129-136.

Five of Morgan's projects are shown which used earth form as a principal design element: Police and Courts Facility in Jacksonville, FL; Morgan's residence in Atlantic Beach, FL; Hilltop House, Central Florida; Whaley Condominium, Ocean City, MD; and the Dune Houses in Amelia Island, FL.

1440. A naturally cooled Florida house. Moth. Earth N., no. 70, July/Aug. 1981: 158-9.
Through well-planned design, heat is controlled in this earth-bermed house in subtropical north Florida.

1441. On the Florida coast, a double beach house nestles under the sand in concrete eggshells. Archit. Rec., v. 162, no. 3, mid-Aug. 1977: 74-5.
Dune House in Atlantic Beach, FL, by owner-architect William Morgan, is two apartments in a pair of thin (four inches) concrete domes (grass covered) acting in compression to resist earth load.

1442. Private residence, Gainesville, Florida. Archit. Rec., v. 167, mid-May 1980: 114-6.
This earth-sheltered house by Wm. Morgan consists of two separate truncated pyramids recalling Indian earth mounds. Engineers: H.W. Keister Associates (structural) and Roy Turknett (mechanical/electrical); contractor: T.J. Kimbrell; landscape architect: Diversified Environmental Planning.

Georgia

1443. Contractor at home underground. Earth Shel. Dig. Energ. Rept., no. 12, Nov./Dec. 1980: 34-7.
This 2,676 sq. ft. earth-sheltered home in rural Atlanta, GA, was designed by Richard Sibley and built with the owner acting as general contractor.

1444. Dixon, John Morris. Farm housing near Pembroke, GA. Working the land. Prog. Archit., v. 60, no. 4, Apr. 1979: 142-3.
Earth is cut and mounded into forms in a plan by Emilio Ambasz for an energy self-sufficient multifamily farm. The plan calls for living units to be dug into the south-facing slopes, insulated by the earth on all but the exposed sunny side.

1445. Sibley, Richard M. A remote, mass storage, passive/hybrid solar solution architecturally integrated for heating and cooling in the Southeast. In Proc., 4th Nat. Pass. Sol. Conf., Kansas City, MO, Oct. 3-5, 1979. G. Franta, ed. Newark, DE: Int. Sol. Energ. Soc., Am. Sec., 1979. p. 761.
This paper describes the advantages of a hybrid Trombe wall heated home utilizing earth berms and earth-cooling tubes. The two homes under discussion are in Georgia.

Idaho

1446. Mountain shelters home. Earth Shel. Dig. Energ. Rept., no. 18, Nov./Dec. 1981: 22-5.

This 1,735 sq. ft. earth-sheltered home in Idaho overlooks Mica Bay on Lake Coeur d'Alene. The problems encountered when building the house are discussed.

1447. Oehler, Mike. A $2,000 house can be built. Earth Shel. Liv., no. 23, Sept./Oct. 1982: 6-9.

A couple built a 1,100 sq. ft. earth-sheltered home in northern Idaho for $2,000 using the author's PSP (Post/Shoring/Polyethylene) method.

1448. Rawlings, Roger. Dig it yourself. New Shel., v. 3, no. 1, Jan. 1982: 23-6.

This owner-built earth shelter in the Bitterroot Mountains of Idaho has 18 inches of soil and gravel on the roof and walls of reinforced concrete. The roof consists of 28-foot-long concrete planks. Insulation is sprayed-on urethane foam.

1449. Scott, Margaret. Moving underground. Earth Shel. Dig. Energ. Rept., no. 18, Nov./Dec. 1981: 26-7.

The builder of an earth-sheltered house in Coeur d'Alene, ID, tells problems of getting financing and what it's like to live in their new house.

1450. Scott, Robert B. Going underground: an owner/builder's experience. In The potential of earth-sheltered and underground space: proc., Undergr. Sp. Conf. and Expos., Kansas City, MO, June 8-10, 1981. T.L. Holthusen, ed. Elmsford, NY: Pergamon Pr., 1981. p. 351-62.

This paper details the building process and materials used in an earth-sheltered home in northern Idaho. Potential owner/builders are advised on potential pitfalls. The home's energy performance is evaluated using temperature charting data for the four-month period December 1980 through March 1981.

Illinois

1451. Davis, Andy. My cave. Undergr. Sp., v. 2, no. 3, Apr. 1978: 151-2.

This is a description of the author's earth-sheltered house in Armington, IL.

1452. Earth shelter profiles. Earth Shel. Liv., no. 37, Jan./Feb. 1985: 18.

Photos and floor plans are shown for earth-sheltered homes in Greenfield, IL; Fayetteville, AR; and Lake Havasu City, AZ.

1453. Gettings, T.L. Digging in: how a family lives underground. Org. Gard., June 1978: 98-100.

Andy Davis' house in Armington, IL, is described as three bedrooms, kitchen, dining room, living room, one and a half baths with a country view.

1454. Jackewicz, Shirley A. New cave dwellers save on energy bills, keep comfortable. Wall St. Jr., May 24, 1979: 1.

Douglas Stevens, a builder and developer, built a three-bedroom earth-sheltered home in Curran Township, IL, a suburb of Springfield.

1455. Largest residence in Illinois. Earth Shel. Dig. Energ. Rept., no. 12, Nov./Dec. 1980: 50-1.

This 7,060 sq. ft. home is in Bloomington, IL: 12 rooms, swimming pool, garage.

1456. Murphy, Jim. Cooperate with nature. Moth. Earth N., no. 66, Nov./Dec. 1980: 115-6.

This solar and wood-heated earth-bermed home in southern Illinois combines a variety of existing technologies and materials to provide both efficiency and comfort. It is rectangular in shape with a shed-style roof and contains 1,360 sq. ft. of floor space. The main floor is slate. Insulation: side walls made of concrete blocks filled with vermiculite backed with two inches of polyurethane on the outside and two inches of fiberglass on the inside--R-value 24.

1457. New models are team effort. Earth Shel. Dig. Energ. Rept., no. 16, July/Aug. 1981: 38-41.

These new earth-sheltered homes are located in Barrington Hills, IL; St. Joseph, MO; and Bellevue, OH.

1458. The plowboy interview: Andy Davis. Moth. Earth N., no. 46, July/Aug. 1977: 18-28.

Andy Davis of Armington, IL, together with his wife and children, designed and built a 1,200 sq. ft., three-bedroom house for $15,000 which costs virtually nothing to heat and cool. The house is octagonal in shape, walls are poured concrete imbedded with rocks.

1459. Portland Cement Association. Earth-sheltered concrete homes. 1981. 4 p. (Spec. Rept., no. 31).

Three earth-sheltered homes are shown: Illinois, Iowa, Washington State.

1460. Swimming pool makes splash. <u>Earth Shel. Dig. Energ. Rept.</u>, no. 6, Nov./Dec. 1979: 14-5.
This 4,200 sq. ft. earth shelter in Granite City, IL, contains a swimming pool.

1461. Team accepts design challenge. <u>Earth Shel. Dig. Energ. Rept.</u>, no. 18, Nov./Dec. 1981: 28-32.
A case study of a 1,800 sq. ft. earth-sheltered house in Casey, IL, designed by Thomas Miller.

1462. Vadnais, Kathleen. Barren land sculpted and reclaimed. <u>Earth Shel. Liv.</u>, no. 26, Mar./Apr. 1983: 22-4.
An Illinois couple decided to build their earth-sheltered home on reclaimed coal mine strippings.

1463. _____. Multi-systems house has concrete, wood, steel culverts. <u>Earth Shel. Liv.</u>, no. 26, Mar./Apr. 1983: 30-4.
This two-story house in Pittsfield, IL, combines conventional frame construction, steel-reinforced poured concrete, and ribbed, steel culverts.

Indiana

1464. Alcorn, Jane. First underground dwelling in New Albany. <u>Tribune, New Albany, Indiana</u>, Apr. 27, 1978.

1465. Energy savings with passive solar and earth sheltering. <u>Concr. Constr.</u>, v. 27, no. 4, Apr. 1982: 364.
This earth-sheltered residence at Muir Woods, IN, was built with cast-in-place concrete walls and a concrete-topped steel-bar joist roof system. Earth covers the roof and both east and west sides, and the north side is sheltered by an attached garage.

1466. Fire destroys house, ignites dream: house combines elements of the old and new. <u>Earth Shel. Liv.</u>, no. 32, Mar./Apr. 1984: 40-1.
This earth shelter in Indiana was designed by Daniel Gobin of Columbus, IN.

1467. Levy, M.T. Designer's first experience with troglodyte subculture. In <u>Earth shelter 2: coll. pap., 1st Earth Shel. Hous. Conf. and Exhib.</u>, Minneapolis, MN, Apr. 9-11, 1980. Minneapolis, MN: Univ. of Minn., Undergr. Sp. Ctr., 1980.
The paper describes a 1,900 sq. ft. residence built into a southeast facing slope in northeast Indiana. It features an en-

closed atrium courtyard open to the sky. Construction information is given. The designer's other earth-sheltered projects in progress are briefly reviewed.

1468. Open house nets charity dollars. Earth Shel. Dig. Energ. Rept., no. 12, Nov./Dec. 1980: 48.
On August 16-18, 1980, an earth-sheltered home in Royal Center, IN, was open for inspection for an admission fee donated to the Lions Club leader dog and hearing conservation programs.

1469. Promotion carefully planned. Earth Shel. Dig. Energ. Rept., no. 15, May/June 1981: 35-6.
Bay Development Corp. in Indianapolis, IN, built the state's first earth-sheltered solar condominium in Muir Woods.

1470. Sklare, Bruce. A down to earth solution. In Proc., 5th Nat. Pass. Sol. Conf., Amherst, MA, Oct. 19-26, 1980. Newark, DE: Int. Sol. Energ. Soc., Am. Sec., 1980. p. 1270-3.
A passive solar-heated house was developed for an area receiving only a small amount of winter sun. It was designed by Bay Development Corp. of Indianapolis, IN, in Sept. 1979 and constructed in the Company's residential development Muir Woods. The one-story, 1,950 sq. ft. house was constructed with poured concrete exterior walls and a steel bar joist structural roof system. Thermal convection in the home is illustrated.

1471. Wood homes marketed. Earth Shel. Liv., no. 22, July/Aug. 1982: 43-5.
Designer Michael Cavanaugh worked through a local bank, the FHA, and the VA to obtain financing for the first earth shelter in Indianapolis. Larry Weber, Under-the-Earth dealer in Bayfield, WI, built a 1,738 sq. ft. home in Cable, WI.

1472. Zook, Wayne. Indiana two-story pleases owners. Earth Shel. Liv., no. 24, Nov./Dec. 1982: 30-1.
The house is near Delphi, IN, overlooking the Wabash River Valley.

Iowa

1473. Bermed, covered homes for sale. Earth Shel. Liv., no. 21, May/June 1982: 43-6.
Four earth-sheltered homes on the market in Canton, GA; Mars, PA; Arlington, TX; and Boone, IA. Floor plans are shown.

1474. Block, David A. and Laurent Hodges. Earth-integrated direct gain residence using concrete cored slab. In Proc., 3rd Nat. Pass. Sol. Conf., San Jose, CA, Jan. 11-13, 1979. Newark, DE: Int. Sol. Energ. Soc., Am. Sec., 1979. p. 771-8.

An earth integrated direct gain home in Ames, IA, is sunk into the ground, bermed on the north, east, and west sides and has 500 sq. ft. of glazing on the south side. The floor, consisting of an eight-inch thick concrete cored slab, provides thermal storage. It has long cylindrical holes running the length which serve as supply-return ducts for a forced air system. The home is estimated to be approximately 85 percent solar and needs six million BTU auxiliary in a typical 6800-degree day heating season.

1475. Dahlin, Dennis. Loess is more: tunneling in Iowa. Earth Shel. Dig. Energ. Rept., no. 13, Jan./Feb. 1981: 55-7.

The owners took advantage of special loess soil conditions to tunnel their earth shelter into a steep bluff near Onawa, IA. Although some interior work remained, at time of interview total cost had been $3,500.

1476. Earth shelter profiles. Earth Shel. Liv., no. 33, May/June 1984: 14-5.

Photos and floor plans are given for homes in Shenandoah, IA; Oliver, BC; Briarcliff Manor, NY; Cross Plains, WI; and Trinity, TX.

1477. Earth shelter profiles. Earth Shel. Liv., no. 34, July/Aug. 1984: 12-3.

Photos and floor plans are given for earth-sheltered homes in Letts, IA; Sidney, MT: Boulder, CO; Red Cloud, NE; and McNeal, AZ.

1478. Earth shelter profiles. Earth Shel. Liv., no. 39, May/June 1985: 22-5.

A bermed 1,600 sq. ft. home in Tipton, IA, and a 2,000 sq. ft. covered home in Tulsa, OK, are described.

1479. Educators study earth shelters. Earth Shel. Dig. Energ. Rept., no. 10, July/Aug. 1980: 48-9.

In Algona, IA, two teachers built a fiberglass home custom ordered from American Solartron.

1480. Hodges, L. Hodges residence: performance of a direct gain passive solar home in Iowa. In Proc., 5th Nat. Pass. Sol. Conf., Amherst, MA, Oct. 19-26, 1980. Newark, DE: Int. Sol. Energ. Soc., Am. Sec., 1980.

The Hodges residence is a 2,200 sq. ft. earth covered direct gain passive solar home in Ames, IA. Its energy performance was studied during the 1979-80 heating season, and results are given.

1481. Spec list grows. Earth Shel. Dig. Energ. Rept., no. 12, Nov./Dec. 1980: 42-6.

These new earth-sheltered homes are in Boone, IA (Southridge Estates, an earth-sheltered development); Everett, WA; Minneapolis (the Sticks and Stones House); and Altamonte, FL.

Kansas

1482. Double domes circles built - rectangle next. Earth Shel. Dig. Energ. Rept., no. 5, Sept./Oct. 1979: 34-5, 42-3.

These two earth-sheltered domes in Hiawatha, KS, built side by side, have approximately 1,200 sq. ft. each. Heat is supplied by an electric furnace in one, heat pump in the other. A third house is rectangular and has an arched dome.

1483. Early owner assesses project. Earth Shel. Dig. Energ. Rept., no. 17, Sept./Oct. 1981: 50-1.

A 1,400 sq. ft. home in Wichita, KS, was built below grade, then topped with a 460 sq. ft. conventional second story that houses an entry and the equipment for the active solar system.

1484. An earth shelter for independence. Moth. Earth N., no. 65, Sept./Oct. 1980: 132-4.

This article describes a Kansas family's well-planned stone and earth-bermed house. Details are given on post and beam construction, waterproofing, passive solar features, energy efficiency (the cost of lights and appliances was $30 per month). The total cost of the 3,400 sq. ft. house was $80,000.

1485. Ernst, F. Gene. Compact home conserves owners' energy. Earth Shel. Dig. Energ. Rept., no. 3, May/June 1979: 24-6.

A case study of a house in Manhattan, KS.

1486. Family joins in serene compound. Earth Shel. Dig. Energ. Rept., no. 12, Nov./Dec. 1980: 12-7.

A retired home builder in eastern Kansas built a compound of four earth-sheltered homes for his sons and daughters and their families. They call it "Hobbit Hollow."

1487. For sale: two-story spec. <u>Earth Shel. Liv.</u>, no. 19, Jan./Feb. 1982: 41-2.
   This house in Derby, KS, has a 300 sq. ft. top story which looks like a conventional house, but 2,000 sq. ft. of the living space is hidden under the front lawn.

1488. House remains uncovered: house was built to be earth covered but owner changed his mind. <u>Earth Shel. Liv.</u>, no. 37, Jan./Feb. 1985: 22-3.
   Worried about leaks, this owner-builder in Mayetta, KS, decided to just berm.

1489. Kansas couple to sell. <u>Earth Shel. Dig. Energ. Rept.</u>, no. 12, Nov./Dec. 1980: 49.
   This couple built their windowless home in Topeka in 1966 to protect them from radioactive fallout.

1490. Knapp, Gifford. We did our best. <u>Earth Shel. Dig. Energ. Rept.</u>, no. 7, Jan./Feb. 1980: 21-3.
   The author describes the construction of his home near Desoto, KS.

1491. Plains family creates passive design. <u>Earth Shel. Dig. Energ. Rept.</u>, no. 7, Jan./Feb. 1980: 20.
   This 2,450 sq. ft. earth-sheltered passive-solar two-story home is located outside Desoto, KS.

1492. Radiation-proof home survives, since 1966. <u>Earth Shel. Dig. Energ. Rept.</u>, no. 3, May/June 1979: 27-9.
   In 1966, the Lawsons built an almost totally underground structure; only the garage and patio are above ground.

1493. Rickman, Gary A. and Leonard E. Bennett. <u>Go underground and save</u>. Wellsville, KS: Rickman and Bennett, 1979. 81 p.
   A step-by-step description is given of the construction of Rickman's home near Wellsville, KS, from site planning to interior finishing. Cost: less than $15 per sq. ft.

1494. Shindelar, Carol Ann. A suburban earth sheltered home at a sensible price. <u>Bet. Homes Gard.</u>, v. 59, no. 3, Mar. 1981: 87-91.
   This earth-sheltered home in a tract development in Salina, KS, is windowless on three sides, south side is open to the sun. Quarry tile covers the floor, and there's five and a half inches of concrete under that. There are thermal shutters on the windows.

1495. Two-story is independent of utilities. <u>Earth Shel. Dig. Energ. Rept.</u>, no. 11, Sept./Oct. 1980: 34-7.
　This two-level solar 2,000 sq. ft. earth-sheltered home is in Concordia, KS. Through solar energy, the earth and wind power, it is energy self-sufficient.

1496. Widmar, Barbara. Owner radiant over passive solar, earth-banked home. <u>Kan. City Star</u>, Feb. 1980.

Kentucky

1497. Couple builds first in area. <u>Earth Shel. Dig. Energ. Rept.</u>, no. 15, May/June 1981: 51-3.
　This three-bedroom 2,340 sq. ft. house is the first earth shelter in southeastern Kentucky. It's in Williamsburg. Waterproofing: hot asphalt covered with heavy gauge plastic. Heating: woodburning stove in fieldstone fireplace with backup electric radiant heat ceiling panels.

1498. House went up while rains came down: worst weather in half-century, construction began at same time. <u>Earth Shel. Liv.</u>, no. 31, Jan./Feb. 1984: 36-7.
　This 2,700 sq. ft. earth-covered home is near Lexington, KY.

1499. Marcum, D.S. Affordable, earth sheltered, passive solar house. In <u>Earth shelter 2: coll. pap., 1st Earth Shel. Hous. Conf. and Exhib.</u>, Minneapolis, MN, Apr. 9-11, 1980. Minneapolis, MN: Univ. of Minnesota, Undergr. Sp. Ctr., 1980. p. 185-6.
　A 2,700 sq. ft. earth-sheltered house in Kentucky is described. It was constructed at 60 to 75 percent of the current cost of above-ground housing. The house has a conventional roof and incorporates passive solar heating techniques.

Louisiana

1500. Louisiana comfort covered by berms. <u>Earth Shel. Liv.</u>, no. 25, Jan./Feb. 1983: 26-9.
　A 3,500 sq. ft. earth-bermed home in Baton Rouge is described. It has a shingled roof and poured concrete walls eight inches thick. Steel reinforces the monolithically-poured shell, the monolithic-grade beam, and the four inches thick slab. The contractor hit water at four feet so eight ft. pilings were put under the footings of the house and on the garage corners. Drainage consists of four-inch plastic pipes at the base of the walls and eight-inch wide gutters behind the wood fascia lead-

ing to downspouts around the structure. Soil is bermed around 60 percent of the house and 75 percent of the garage to within one foot of the roof. Architect: Roy J. Hotard, Jr., Port Allen, LA.

Maryland

1501. Block home faces north. <u>Earth Shel. Dig. Energ. Rept.</u>, no. 13, Jan./Feb. 1981: 48-52.
    This 3,600 sq. ft. home is built into a hill north of Baltimore, MD. It has 12-inch thick reinforced block walls filled with concrete. The house is completely earth covered except for two entries, a garage door, and a roof skylight. The owner-engineer Ray Scott wrote <u>How to build your own underground home</u>.

1502. Branson, Gary. An earth-sheltered solar home. <u>Fam. Hand.</u>, v. 32, no. 9, Nov. 1982: 120.
    "Terra Vista" is on three and a half acres near Frederick, MD. The cost was 15-20 percent higher than a conventional home would have been because of reinforced concrete construction, superior insulation, and Bentonite waterproofing. Plans are available from Milliner Construction Co., Inc., 302-A East Patrick St., Frederick, MD, 21701.

1503. Manion, Thomas. Earth sheltered design in Maryland. <u>Des. Act.</u>, Jan./Feb. 1983: 6-7.
    Sunshine Farm in Columbia, MD, was designed by the author. It is a three-story earth-bermed house. The Brian House in Columbia was designed by Ferd Johns of Annapolis. Riddermark in Frederick, an extended linear earth-sheltered prototype, was designed by the author. Terra Vista by Mike Milliner, a HUD-sponsored project, is in Frederick. The Harris House by Ward Bucher of Washington, DC, is in Rock Creek Park.

1504. Milliner, Michael S. Terra Vista. <u>Env. Com.</u>, July 1981: 10-5.
    The Dept. of Housing and Urban Development conducted a passive solar design competition in 1979. The earth-sheltered house, Terra Vista, designed by M.S. Milliner Construction, Inc. in Frederick, MD, was one of 91 selected to receive partial funding for construction. The design, construction, heating and cooling systems, and their operation are discussed.

1505. _____. Terra Vista: HUD award winning passive solar earth sheltered house. In <u>The potential of earth-shel-</u>

tered and underground space: proc., Undergr. Sp. Conf. and Expos., Kansas City, MO, June 8-10, 1981. T.L. Holthusen, ed. Elmsford, NY: Pergamon Pr., 1981. p. 363-72.

Terra Vista is an earth-sheltered home which uses direct and indirect solar gain as well as passive cooling. It was constructed under the Cycle 5 Residential Solar Demonstration Program administered by HUD. Construction of the home was started in late 1980 and completed in spring 1981 near Frederick, MD. This paper discusses site, configuration, floor plan, solar features, the structure, thermal and moisture protection, and glazing.

Massachusetts

1506. Barnard, John. Ecology House. Pamphlet distributed by the author.

1507. East Coast's earliest is most copied. Earth Shel. Dig. Energ. Rept., no. 7, Jan./Feb. 1980: 37-9.
This home in Stowe, MA, was designed by John Barnard, Jr. It is similar to Ecology House but has an exposed front.

1508. Ecology House II: architect of Ecology House applied lessons learned to Ecology House II. Earth Shel. Liv., no. 37, Jan./Feb. 1985: 24-6.
Ecology House II is a few hundred feet away from Ecology House I and incorporates the ideas developed during Barnard's (the architect) more than ten years of earth-sheltered construction experience. He says it cost about 15 percent less per sq. ft. than a custom built wood frame house.

1509. Experimental atrium house built completely underground. NAHB J., v. 2, Dec. 3, 1973: 33.
Floor plan is shown for J. Barnard's Ecology House in Marstons Mills, MA.

1510. Futuristic home is self-sufficient. Earth Shel. Dig. Energ. Rept., no. 14, Mar./Apr. 1981: 42-3.
This hybrid home designed by Steven Strong of Solar Design Associates, Lincoln, MA, receives 100 percent of its heat and hot water requirements from the sun. It will generate its own electricity with an array of silicon photovoltaic solar cells on the roof.

1511. Li, Lindsay. The Lewis House, Medfield, Mass. Archit. Rec., v. 170, mid-May 1982: 96-9.

This atrium-style earth-sheltered house by architect Don Metz is sheltered by earth temperatures which range from 45 to 50 degrees year round. Solar heating is provided by sunlight through a south window wall enhanced by the thermal storage capacity of the structural materials, tile floors, and interior masonry walls.

1512. Saving by going underground. AIA J., v. 61, no. 2, Feb. 1974: 48-9.

Ecology House in Marstons Mills, MA, was built in the winter of 1973-74. It is an atrium-style earth shelter with walls of poured concrete reinforced with steel rods. The waterproofing is three-ply pitch and asbestos-felt membrane. Cost - about $24,000.

1513. Smay, V. Elaine. Underground living in this Ecology House saves energy, cuts building costs, preserves the environment. Pop. Sci., v. 204, no. 6, June 1974: 88-9.

Ecology House, Marstons Mills, Cape Cod, MA, built by John Barnard.

1514. Wells, Malcolm. Earth shelter on Cape Cod. Fine Homebldg., no. 7, Feb./Mar. 1982: 34-9.

A long triangular skylight fills with light a house without a southern exposure.

Michigan

1515. Beadles, Joyce. The earth has won our hearts. Moth. Earth N., no. 52, July/Aug. 1978: 96-9.

An owner-builder in Michigan tells about his experience in building his 2,304 sq. ft. house, and how he reached the decision to go underground.

1516. Bumke, David. The underground arch. New Shel., v. 5, no. 1, Jan. 1984: 46-9, 76.

The Loveless family live in a two-story earth-covered arch in Grand Haven, MI, designed by John Loveless and Jeremy Berg. The wooden arch is formed of glued-together "Arch-Tech Panels," an invention of the designers.

1517. 4-H operates earth shelter. Earth Shel. Dig. Energ. Rept., no. 10, July/Aug. 1980: 58.

The resident manager for the 4-H Leader Training Camp in Tustin, MI, has a new energy efficient earth-sheltered house. Some details of construction are given.

1518. Go underground in Michigan. Moth. Earth N., no. 54, Nov./Dec. 1978: 112-3.

This earth-sheltered house built by Daniel Rinker uses all-weather, pressure-treated wood construction rather than concrete or cement blocks, plus a layer of six-mil black polyethylene waterproofing (between the wood and the earth) on all of the building's earth-facing surfaces. Twenty-two percent of the outer surface is exposed.

1519. Lees, Al W. Enemies of the underground. Pop. Sci., v. 224, no. 3, Mar. 1984: 144-5.

An earth-bermed home built in a Michigan township met with strenuous objections from a neighbor who filed suit, claiming that the main level was a walk-in basement which violated the township's requirement that homes have at least 1,600 sq. ft. of above-grade living area.

1520. Machowski, Barb. Lake home has commanding view. Earth Shel. Liv., no. 22, July/Aug. 1982: 34-7.

A 2,050 sq. ft. home on Grand Traverse Bay near Traverse City, MI, was designed by architect John Dyksterhouse of Traverse City.

1521. Michigan plans show models. Earth Shel. Dig. Energ. Rept., no. 11, Sept./Oct. 1980: 65.

Two earth-sheltered models were designed by architect E.T. Vermulen: one for the Western Michigan Energy Show in Grand Rapids, Oct. 23-26, 1980, the other for the Detroit Show, Nov. 13-16, 1980.

1522. Mother Earth News, Inc. Mother's homebuilding & shelter guide. Hendersonville, NC, 1983. 200 p.

Section 1 features seven earth-sheltered homes. They are in Michigan, North Carolina, Minnesota, Texas (Rod Rylander's Vertical Crawl Space House), Illinois, Kansas, and Rob Roy's Log-End Cave in New York.

1523. New House has old flavor. Earth Shel. Liv., no. 20, Mar./Apr. 1982: 34-7.

Because of their interest in antiques, the owners' earth-covered house near Riverdale, MI, was built of recycled old barn wood and stone foundations, in addition to poured concrete walls. They copied many features of a very old house built in 1704.

1524. "Plan," suggests teacher: earth shelter owner-teacher tells his students to plan, plan, plan. Earth Shel. Liv., no. 31, Jan./Feb. 1984: 28-9.

The owner-builder of this earth-sheltered home in Portage, MI, relates his experiences with building his house in adult education classes.

1525. Two more models open. Earth Shel. Liv., no. 23, Sept./Oct. 1982: 48-50.
Model homes for sale in Grand Rapids, MI, and in Buffalo, WY.

1526. Two years underground! Moth. Earth N., no. 61, Jan./Feb. 1980: 38.
Architect Daniel Rinker built an earth-sheltered house in Michigan for his daughter two years ago. The R-value of the earth-covered roof is estimated to be more than 100. Figures on year-round temperature and humidity are given.

1527. Vadnais, Kathleen. Arched house is at end of search. Earth Shel. Liv., no. 28, July/Aug. 1983: 17-21.
This house near Rockford, MI, is built with steel plates that form a curved structure. Bentonite waterproofing system failed on the southwest front corner of the house.

Minnesota

1528. Air from earth moderates temperature in above ground home. Undergr. Sp., v. 5, no. 1, July/Aug. 1980: 9-10.
Homes in Dalton, MN, and Dayton, OH, have two systems which permit above-grade homes to utilize the temperature-moderating properties of the earth--one uses air and the other uses water.

1529. Baby earth sheltered since birth. Earth Shel. Dig. Energ. Rept., no. 15, May/June 1981: 34.
Baby's 1,800 sq. ft. earth-sheltered home in Preston, MN, is for sale.

1530. Bloedoorn, Seph. "Breakthrough" is affordable for family living. Earth Shel. Dig. Energ. Rept., no. 4, July/Aug. 1979: 35-40.
John Coleman Construction built an affordable two-bedroom earth-sheltered home in Elk River, MN. It cost less than $80,000.

1531. Brief: the first six months of energy use data for an earth sheltered home in suburban Minneapolis. Undergr. Sp., v. 5, no. 3, Nov./Dec. 1980: 140.
Reports that the home is operating extremely well with regard to energy use.

1532. Couple sells: to build again. Earth Shel. Dig. Energ. Rept., no. 13, Jan./Feb. 1981: 15.

Shakopee, MN, earth shelter sold, and the owner-builder will build another.

1533. Earth, garage shelter two-story. Earth Shel. Dig. Energ. Rept., no. 14, Mar./Apr. 1981: 51.

This large, two-story earth-bermed house in Hugo, MN (bermed on three sides to 13 feet) has wood construction, fiberglass insulation on the inside, and polystyrene insulation on the outside below the frostline.

1534. Earth-bermed housing project built in Minneapolis suburb. Underline, v. 3, no. 5, July/Aug. 1982: 1, 3.

Grasslands is an earth-bermed multiple-residential development in Coon Rapids, MN, designed to accommodate physically disabled people.

1535. Earth shelter profile. Earth Shel. Liv., no. 38, Mar./Apr. 1985: 26.

Photos and floor plans are shown for earth-sheltered houses in Belle Plaine, MN; Vinemont, AL; and Shelby County, OH.

1536. Earth shelter profiles. Earth Shel. Liv., no. 36, Nov./Dec. 1984: 20-1.

Photos and floor plans are shown for homes in Renville, MN; Maple Grove, MN; Knoxville, TN; Mayetta, KS; and Bel Air, MD.

1537. Earth sheltered home profile. Underline, v. 6, no. 1, Oct./Dec. 1984: 4.

This 1,600+ sq. ft. earth-sheltered home in Inver Grove Heights, MN, features an elevational design with southern exposure. It is 100 percent earth covered on roof and walls.

1538. Earth sheltered home sale. Underline, v. 2, no. 2, Jan./Feb. 1981: 3.

An earth-bermed house in Burnsville, MN, is described.

1539. Earth sheltered home sales. Underline, v. 2, no. 6, Sept./Oct. 1981: 2.

Two homes are described, one in Minneapolis and one in Redwood Falls, MN.

1540. Earth sheltered home sales. Underline, v. 3, no. 4, May/June 1982: 3.

New earth-covered homes are available in Coon Rapids and Plymouth, MN.

1541. Earth sheltered home sales. Underline, v. 4, no. 1, Nov./Dec. 1982: 5.

Two earth-sheltered houses for sale in Edina and Mendota, MN, share the same features.

1542. Earth sheltered home sales. Underline, v. 4, no. 2, Jan./Mar. 1983: 4.

Two houses are for sale, one in New Brighton, MN, a suburb of St. Paul, and a Seward townhouse near downtown Minneapolis.

1543. Earth sheltered house draws 150,000 fairgoers. Underline, v. 4, no. 1, Nov./Dec. 1982: 1.

A 1,175 sq. ft. earth-sheltered house was built on the Minnesota State Fairgrounds. It was designed by Earth Integrated Technics and built by Division 7 Corp., Minneapolis. It's fully bermed on the east and north sides, half-bermed on the west side, and exposed on the south. The roof is covered with 18 inches of soil. The house will not be occupied but will be shown occasionally during the year.

1544. Egerstrom, Lee. Minnesota "earth shelters" may catch on in the capital. St. Paul Pion. Pr., Oct. 20, 1977.

1545. Ellison, Tom and John Carmody. Earth sheltered houses: two case studies. Archit. Minn., v. 6, no. 2, Apr. 1980: 42-4.

House no. 1 is built into a steeply sloping, heavily wooded site with earth on roof and walls and openings on both north and south side. It's a two-level plan with 2,000 sq. ft. House no. 2 is on a steeply-sloping heavily-wooded site with vehicular access on the south side. The house is detached from and up the hill from the garage. The house has one level and 1,900 sq. ft. The advantages and disadvantages of the two designs are discussed.

1546. First demo open: for sale sign goes up. Earth Shel. Dig. Energ. Rept., no. 3, May/June 1979: 16-7.

The first earth-sheltered house completed under the sponsorship of the Minnesota Housing Finance Agency Solar/Earth Sheltered Demonstration Housing Program, opened by State Senator Frank Knoll, April 1979, Burnsville, MN.

1547. First resale listed. Earth Shel. Dig. Energ. Rept., no. 9, May/June 1980: 21.

This 1,800 sq. ft. concrete earth shelter is in Preston, MN.

1548. Fourth Minnesota demo for sale. Earth Shel. Dig. Energ. Rept., no. 8, Mar./Apr. 1980: 36-7.
This 1,884 sq. ft. earth shelter in Waseca, MN, was built using a $17,000 grant from the Minnesota Housing Finance Agency.

1549. Fourth Minnesota demo sold. Earth Shel. Dig. Energ. Rept., no. 15, May/June 1981: 39.
The fourth MHFA demonstration home sold for $65,000.

1550. Germer, Jerry. Earth-sheltered apartments. Sol. Age, v. 9, no. 12, Dec. 1984: 20-2.
St. John's University, Collegeville, MN, has built some earth-sheltered apartments for students. Five earth-sheltered dormitories each contain four apartments. The wedge-shaped buildings open to the south. Energy bills for 1983 suggest that the units are well within the range of energy-efficient buildings but fall short of expectations. Consumption of electricity exceeded predictions by 49 percent.

1551. Haynes, George. George Haynes' earth-sheltered passive-solar abode. Alt. Energ., no. 39, Sept./Oct. 1979: 11-2.
This article is about the author's home on the Net River near Holyoke Township, MN.

1552. House built for site. Earth Shel. Dig. Energ. Rept., no. 16, July/Aug. 1981: 12-5.
This 2,240 sq. ft. house in Eyota, MN, is of masonry construction. The roof is eight inches of prestressed concrete covered with three inches of poured concrete. The five-acre lot has a hill into which the house is nestled.

1553. House "revealed" itself on slope. Earth Shel. Dig. Energ. Rept., no. 11, Sept./Oct. 1980: 11-4.
This 2,500 sq. ft. home in Stillwater, MN, has solar water heating, double-pane windows, and an entry airlock.

1554. Hutson, Ken. Swedes tour Minnesota home. Earth Shel. Dig. Energ. Rept., no. 13, Jan./Feb. 1981: 64.
A group of 20 Swedes associated with a Swedish cement production firm toured a 2,700 sq. ft. two-story earth shelter under construction near Morris, MN.

1555. Lane, Barbara. Lakeville, Minnesota. Earth Shel. Liv., no. 35, Sept./Oct. 1984: 28-9.

This earth-sheltered home in Lakeville, MN, was modified for wheelchair use.

1556. Lane, C.A. A supplemental paper to the design of an earth sheltered energy-efficient home in North Oaks, Minnesota. Plan B. project. Minneapolis, MN: Univ. of Minn., Fall 1978. 160 p.

1557. Low cost wood, concrete homes open. Earth Shel. Dig. Energ. Rept., no. 14, Mar./Apr. 1981: 38-41.
Two all-weather wood projects in Minnesota (near Malmo and in New Ulm) and a poured concrete earth-sheltered house in North Lauderdale, FL, are described.

1558. Machowski, Barb. Minnesota park rangers get new homes. Earth Shel. Dig. Energ. Rept., no. 12, Nov./Dec. 1980: 4-7.
The reinforced concrete block earth-sheltered homes for park rangers are in Camden State Park, St. Croix Wild River Park, and Whitewater State Park. A table gives construction data for each home.

1559. McDill, Dana. Gopher state underground owner built home: photo story. Alt. Energ., no. 33, Aug. 1978: 6-8.
Home of Ben and Ann Preusser of Zimmerman, MN, begun in July 22, 1977, finished the end of November.

1560. The Midwest digs new ideas. Archit. Minn., v. 7, no. 6, Dec./Jan. 1981-82: 48-9.
The earth-sheltered projects described are in Minnesota, Colorado, Iowa, and Wisconsin.

1561. Murphy, Jim. House in the hill. Prog. Archit., v. 61, no. 10, Oct. 1980: 72-5.
This design by Daryl Hansen of Minneapolis won the first award in the Innovations in Housing competition. The built version, constructed by R.B. Fitch, Jr., has several energy-conserving features. An energy analysis of the house is included. The house includes a greenhouse, berming, rock bed heat storage, shading, venting and optional active solar collectors. The greenhouse was built partially below grade on the living room/den side, and the house is bermed on the two other sides.

1562. North woods surround two-story. Earth Shel. Dig. Energ. Rept., no. 7, Jan./Feb. 1980: 7-9.
The home of Floyd and Millie Borchert is a 2,150 sq. ft. structure in Walker, MN, surrounded by trees and earth.

1563. Olson, Myron and Dorothy. An energy-conserving subterranean home. Elk River, MN: The Olsons, 14461 NE 95th St., 1977. 8 p.

This is a description of the construction of a home in Wright County, MN (Elk River area), employing an earth temperature stabilized, underground structure to demonstrate a practical, socially and ecologically acceptable, single-family dwelling.

1564. _____. Low cost underground headaches. Alt. Energ., no. 39, Sept./Oct. 1979.

In Elk River, MN, the growth rate of earth-sheltered homes exceeds that of solar homes. Three trouble areas: structural integrity, waterproofing, and ventilation. Pilasters or internal reinforcing are a must. Water in the soil on the roof can stay for days. A good masonry surface is needed, and non-water-soluble waterproofing materials. Air must be brought in either through adjustable vents and windows or through a power-vent system.

1565. One state's approach: Minnesota, an underground hotbed. Earth Shel. Dig. Energ. Rept., no. 1, Jan./Feb. 1979: 8, 10.

Most of the serious activity in earth-sheltered design is in Minnesota, although there are centers of interest in other parts of the country.

1566. Pauls, Susan Maas. Passive solar underground home. Alt. Energ., no. 33, Aug. 1978: 10-3.

A 2,700 sq. ft. passive solar underground house in St. Cloud, MN, is described. It is earth bermed, built on grade, and was completed in Nov. 1977. Dirt from a nearby swamp was used to berm the structure. Two to three feet of dirt are piled on the roof. Glazing on the south side provides passive solar heat as well as daylighting. The open design is described and illustrated.

1567. Rain plagues builder. Earth Shel. Dig. Energ. Rept., no. 2, Mar./Apr. 1979: 25-7.

A case study of an earth-sheltered house in Maple Plain, MN.

1568. Resales marketed in city, country. Earth Shel. Liv., no. 19, Jan./Feb. 1982: 43-4.

These earth shelters are for resale in Spring Lake, MN, and in rural Ladysmith, WI.

1569. Ritter, Alexander. Demonstration homes. Archit. Minn., v. 5, no. 2, Mar./Apr. 1979: 46-7.

259 Case Studies   1570-1577

1570. Rollin, Carol Kubasche built an earth-sheltered home. Rur. Minn. N., Apr. 1981.

1571. Second demo house for sale. Earth Shel. Dig. Energ. Rept., no. 4, July/Aug. 1979: 18-9.
 This 1,848 sq. ft. Minnesota house was built by the Carpentry II students at the Willmar Area Vocational-Technical Institute.

1572. Seward West Redesign. Move down to earth sheltered townhouses. Minneapolis, MN.

1573. Shank, Ben. Earth-sheltered Housing Demonstration Project, Minnesota Housing Finance Agency. Undergr. Sp., v. 3, no. 5, Mar. 1979: 259-68.
 This paper describes the project from the initial legislation and design of the project goals through the design selection process and the construction phase. The project consisted of six rangers' homes built on state park lands.

1574. Specific examples of earth-sheltered structures. Eye of the Falcon, Sept. (?) 1980.

1575. Sterling, Ray and Mary Tingerthal. Building costs and construction problems in the Minnesota Earth Sheltered Housing Demonstration Program. Undergr. Sp., v. 6, no. 1, July/Aug. 1981: 13-20.
 This article analyzes the cost and construction problems encountered in the MHFA Demonstration Program houses and highlights some of the more significant points discovered during the course of the program. This experience revealed problems, all of which are avoidable, in the design, marketing, construction, and cost of earth-sheltered houses.

1576. Third demo open: townhouses for sale. Earth Shel. Dig. Energ. Rept., no. 5, Sept./Oct. 1979: 12.
 The prices of the Seward West earth-sheltered townhouses in Minneapolis ranged from $66,419 for two bedrooms to $76,419 for three bedrooms.

1577. Tingerthal, Mary. MHFA Solar/Earth Sheltered Demonstration Housing Program: seven case studies. Archit. Minn., v. 6, no. 2, Apr. 1980: 45-8.
 In 1978, the Minnesota Housing Finance Agency developed this program in response to a mandate from the Minnesota Legislature that the Agency demonstrate various energy-conserving techniques in housing.

1578. Toedter, Wendell. Fair report: small unit built in short time. Earth Shel. Liv., no. 24, Nov./Dec. 1982: 25-7.
Ark Energy Systems, Staples, MN, built a model earth-sheltered house for the 1982 Wadena County Fair.

1579. Townhouse for sale. Earth Shel. Dig. Energ. Rept., no. 5, Sept./Oct. 1979: 12.
The 12-unit Seward West earth-sheltered townhouses go on sale.

1580. Townhouses for sale. Earth Shel. Liv., no. 26, Mar./Apr. 1983: 10-1.
Two of the Seward townhouses in Minneapolis were for sale. Details of purchase conditions are given: financing, prices, interest rates, etc.

1581. Two communities of energy-efficient homes are being developed by Eldon Morrison Architects, White Bear Lake, Minnesota. Undergr. Sp., v. 6, no. 1, July/Aug. 1981: 4.

1582. Two-story hideaway faces woods. Earth Shel. Dig. Energ. Rept., no. 8, Mar./Apr. 1980: 28-31.
This two-story earth shelter in Preston, MN, was cut into an outcropping of rock.

1583. Unique project halted: illness stops earth shelter project: available to someone wanting to complete it. Earth Shel. Liv., no. 34, July/Aug. 1984: 33.
The site of this project is eight miles from New Ulm, MN.

1584. Vadnais, Kathleen. House full of unusual characteristics. Earth Shel. Liv., no. 22, July/Aug. 1982: 26-9.
Wayne and Sandra Kimber's earth-sheltered house in Redwood Falls, MN.

1585. _____. Minnesota house uses heat against cold. Earth Shel. Liv., no. 25, Jan./Feb. 1983: 18-20.
This two-story, 3,000 sq. ft. home is designed to fit into a corner site of three city lots, 138 x 165 ft. It has underfloor rock bed heat storage.

1586. _____. Two-story puts sun to work. Earth Shel. Liv., no. 23, Sept./Oct. 1982: 26-9.
This 3,000 sq. ft. solar heated earth shelter in Northfield, MN, is 70 percent earth covered.

Case Studies

1587. Uncommon adversities plague owners. Earth Shel. Dig. Energ. Rept., no. 15, May/June 1981: 16-9.

A Minnesota couple lost $5,000 because a general contractor did not finish the job of building their house, and they had to hire another. An earth-sheltered home builder in Billings, MT, received a permit to build an earth-sheltered home, but his neighbors called it a "basement" in violation of the subdivision's restrictive covenants, and he was taken to court. A house in Provo, UT, was vandalized and destroyed, and eventually the lot and its ruins were sold by the builder. A builder in Illinois built an earth-sheltered home without a building permit.

1588. Where you can see earth-sheltered structures. Mpls. Trib., May 16, 1981.

Earth-sheltered structures in the Twin Cities (St. Paul/Minneapolis).

1589. Williams, Monty. Earth shelters sell themselves. Earth Shel. Dig. Energ. Rept., no. 9, May/June 1980: 51.

Missouri

1590. An earth-sheltered duplex is under construction in Springfield, Missouri. Undergr. Sp., v. 6, no. 3, Nov./Dec. 1981: 131.

1591. An earth-sheltered triplex has been built in Independence, Missouri by locally-based Terra Dome Corp. Undergr. Sp., v. 6, no. 3, Nov./Dec. 1981: 132.

1592. Fagan, Pat. The Fagan residence. In Proc., 4th Nat. Pass. Sol. Conf., Kansas City, MO, Oct. 3-5, 1979. G. Franta, ed. Newark, DE: Int. Sol. Energ. Soc., Am. Sec., 1979. p. 759.

This 1,800 sq. ft. earth-bermed hybrid solar home in Columbia, MO, includes shuttering, external foundation insulation, an R-45 ceiling, and R-30 walls. The energy features include 220 sq. ft. of direct gain surface, an attached greenhouse, 450 sq. ft. of air collector, and a 32-ton rock storage bin. During the very cold winter of 1979, it required one cord of wood for heating.

1593. Golubski, Steven E. Passive solar projects in the Midwest by Steven Golubski/Earthworks. In Proc., 4th Nat. Pass. Sol. Conf., Kansas City, MO, Oct. 3-5, 1979. G. Franta, ed. Newark, DE: Int. Sol. Energ. Soc., Am. Sec. 1979. p. 763.

The projects of Earthworks include hybrid heating and cooling, earth integration, and natural cooling.

1594. Haupert, David. Energy-smart earth-sheltered housing. Bet. Homes. Gard., v. 59, no. 9, Sept. 1981: 44-9.

Lon Simmons' 2,235 sq. ft. home in Missouri is built of post-tensioned poured concrete. The heating system consists of a solar greenhouse, a pair of Trombe walls, and a wood-burning stove. Three ft. of earth cover the roof.

1595. Lakeside home is a solid retreat. Earth Shel. Liv., no. 19, Jan./Feb. 1982: 34-7.

This 6,000 sq. ft. castle-like home on the Lake of the Ozarks (Central Missouri) has rounded turrets protruding through the earth covering, arched windows, and a curving stairway. The home is heated by an electric floor system.

1596. Machowski, Barb. Berms shelter Ozark development. Earth Shel. Dig. Energ. Rept., no. 18, Nov./Dec. 1981: 54-7.

Stoneshire development in Highlandville, MO, in an Ozark Mountain ridge has 200 to 250 sites intended for low cost, energy efficient custom homes, many of which are earth sheltered. They are encouraging new site buyers to build earth-sheltered homes.

1597. Missouri berm keeps costs low. Earth Shel. Liv., no. 25, Jan./Feb. 1983: 6-8.

Earth bermed 2,400 sq. ft. home in Rolla, MO, was built by Dale and Kathy Elifrits.

1598. Modular model opens in Missouri. Earth Shel. Dig. Energ. Rept., no. 7, Jan./Feb. 1980: 32.

Terra Dome Corp. in Independence, MO, structures the 24 sq. ft. modules with one pour of concrete over steel for the exterior and interior walls and ceilings.

1599. Modules answer aesthetic needs. Earth Shel. Dig. Energ. Rept., no. 13, Jan./Feb. 1981: 52-4.

Gayle Scafe, a Terra Dome dealer, built his first Terra Dome for his own family. The 3,600 sq. ft. home is in Independence, MO. It consists of a basic domed module of poured concrete.

1600. Moore, Gordon L. A groundswell is sweeping the Midwest. Earth Shel. Dig. Energ. Rept., no. 3, May/June 1979: 9-10.

263 Case Studies

At time of writing, 75-85 new earth-contact homes were planned or already built in Missouri.

1601. _____ . A groundswell that is sweeping the Midwest -- facts and fancies. Columbia, MO: Univ. of Missouri, Columbia Ext. Div. 4 p. (Eng. Sci. and Tech. Guide 5520). Also in Underground utilization. T.S. Stauffer, ed. Kansas City, MO: Univ. of Missouri, Dept. of Geosci., 1978. p. 750-3.
The variety of earth-contact homes in Missouri is great.

1602. Retired couple builds down. Earth Shel. Dig. Energ. Rept., no. 16, July/Aug. 1981: 34-7.
This owner-built 1,800 sq. ft. earth shelter in Poplar Bluff, MO, has east and west bedroom wings attached to a hexagonal central living area.

1603. Simmons, John D., Jerry O. Newman, and R.E. Harrison. Case history: earth sheltered house in Versailles, Missouri. In Potential of earth sheltered and underground space: proc., Undergr. Sp. Conf. and Expos., Kansas City, MO, June 8-10, 1981. T.L. Holthusen, ed. Elmsford, NY: Pergamon Pr., 1981. p. 379-91.
Two design features are suggested for reducing energy consumption in a residence: solar energy and earth embankment. The interaction of three supplemental heating systems with solar energy as a primary heat source is discussed. The heating systems are: heat pump, electric resistance, and wood stove.

1604. Spec developments come through. Earth Shel. Dig. Energ. Rept., no. 10, July/Aug. 1980: 34-9.
Earth-sheltered developments are being planned or built: Kiva Ridge in Oak Grove, MO; near Traverse City in northern Michigan; Muir Woods, a condominium development in Indianapolis; townhouses in St. Paul; campus student housing at State University Agricultural and Technical College in Morrisville, NY.

1605. Subdivision underway. Earth Shel. Dig. Energ. Rept., no. 16, July/Aug. 1981: 37.
Twin Springs Estates near Poplar Bluff, MO, is a 100-acre subdivision restricted to earth-sheltered homes.

1606. Vadnais, Kathleen. Double envelope concept applied to earth sheltering. Earth Shel. Dig. Energ. Rept., no. 13, Jan./Feb. 1981: 4-7.
Architect Larry Atkinson of Kansas City, MO, has a 3,800

sq. ft. double envelope earth shelter that is open on two sides, southeastern and southwestern.

Montana

1607. "Big sky country" home built. Earth Shel. Dig. Energ. Rept., no. 12, Nov./Dec. 1980: 30-3.
This 1,930 sq. ft. home is in Deer Lodge, MT.

1608. Geodome opens in Montana. Earth Shel. Dig. Energ. Rept., no. 15, May/June 1981: 47-9.
An earth-sheltered geodesic structure in Missoula, MT, has traditional tilt-slab construction.

1609. Machowski, Barb. Lady rancher ignores "good" advice. Earth Shel. Liv., no. 20, Mar./Apr. 1982: 38-40.
This earth-integrated house on a Sheridan, MT, cattle ranch is not built into a hill; earth had to be brought in (for almost $5,000) to cover this 1,512 sq. ft. home. It has concrete walls and slab and a wood roof; bentonite waterproofing. It was designed by John Frechette; the contractor was John Benedict.

1610. Smith, Barb. FmHA commits to earth sheltering. Earth Shel. Liv., no. 22, July/Aug. 1982: 18.
Montana's first Farmers' Home Administration-financed earth shelter was built in Belgrade by Harry Annear of Earthhome Corp.

Nebraska

1611. Mound belies living space below. Earth Shel. Dig. Energ. Rept., no. 8, Mar./Apr. 1980: 24-5.
The front of this 2,000 sq. ft. earth shelter in Martell, NE, is a garden room enclosed by 420 sq. ft. of glazing.

1612. Omaha model opens. Earth Shel. Dig. Energ. Rept., no. 8, Mar./Apr. 1980: 38.
Down-to-Earth Homes in Omaha, NE, uses a two-story earth-shelter model home as their office.

Nevada

1613. Temperature study proves point: earth shelter savings measured in degrees. Earth Shel. Liv., no. 41, Sept./Oct. 1985: 12-6.
Fred O. Swanson, the owner/builder of this 2,000 sq. ft.

earth shelter in Silver City, NV, intended it to be used as a model for earth sheltering and built monitoring devices into the home to record its performance. The home was designed and engineered by Brent Anderson & Associates.

New Hampshire

1614. Architect details with wood. Earth Shel. Dig. Energ. Rept., no. 5, Sept./Oct. 1979: 17-9.
A case study of Don Metz's Baldtop Dugout in Lyme, NH.

1615. Back to the earth. House Gard., v. 152, no. 4, Apr. 1980: 158-61.
This is the fifth in a series on energy-efficient houses. This earth-covered house by architect Don Metz has a window in every room and passive solar features.

1616. Dropouts drop into new home. Earth Shel. Dig. Energ. Rept., no. 15, May/June 1981: 30-2.
This 2,500 sq. ft. two-story passive solar earth shelter in Thornton, NH, has buried roof and three walls. It has no conventional heating system.

1617. Earthtech 5, Lyme, New Hampshire. Architect: Don Metz. Proc.: Archit., no. 21, Jan. 1981: 156-8.
The design of this 2,000 sq. ft. house uses the walls, the slab, and the earth-covered roof as a thermal mass to absorb solar gain and slowly disperse it back into the house long after the sun has set. The house was completed in the summer of 1979.

1618. Hut is smallest home yet. Earth Shel. Dig. Energ. Rept., no. 14, Mar./Apr. 1981: 37.
A 480 sq. ft. earth-sheltered summer home in Franconia, NH, is described.

1619. Metz, Don. Designing today for the future. In Residential applications: transcripts of selected presentations, Going Under to Stay on Top, Minneapolis, MN, Oct. 1977. Minneapolis, MN: Univ. of Minn., Undergr. Sp. Ctr., 1979. p. 101-11.
This architect built his first earth-sheltered house (Winston House in Lyme, NH) in 1971 as an example of non-architecture, not as an energy efficient building. He describes the house, giving many useful construction details.

1620. Metz House, Lyme, New Hampshire. Architect: Don Metz. Proc.: Archit., no. 21, Jan. 1981: 152-5.

The east and west walls are bermed and the north walls totally buried. This house has 2,000 sq. ft. and was completed in June 1977.

1621. Smay, V. Elaine. Solar goes underground in new house designs. Pop. Sci., v. 216, no. 5, May 1980: 83-8.
These new passive solar earth-sheltered houses are: Baldtop Dugout in Lyme, NH, designed by Don Metz, Underhill in Grand Rapids, MI, the home and office of Malcolm Wells on Cape Cod, Suncave in Santa Fe, NM, and several others.

1622. Underground house designed by architect Don Metz in Lyme, NH. N.Y. Times, Mar. 22, 1979, III: 1.

1623. Winston House, Lyme, New Hampshire. Archit. Rec., v. 155, mid-May 1974: 52-63.

New Jersey

1624. Article on underground buildings in New Jersey and illustrations of the underground office of Michael J. Lenny that was designed by Malcolm B. Wells. N.Y. Times, Jan. 6, 1980, XI: 16.

1625. Bliss, Steve and Jerry Germer. An underground archetype. Sol. Age, v. 9, no. 4, Apr. 1984: 28-9.
Solaria, designed by Malcolm Wells.

1626. Contractor picks block, wood. Earth Shel. Dig. Energ. Rept., no. 17, Sept./Oct. 1981: 30-4.
This 2,200 sq. ft. home is the only earth shelter in southern New Jersey. It is built on flat land and is waterproofed with Karnak, an elastomeric membrane.

1627. Edmund Scientific Co. Solaria: on the threshold of environmental renaissance. By Bob and Nancy Homan, Harry Thomason, and Malcolm Wells. Barrington, NJ, 1975. 57 p.
Describes the construction of the earth-covered home of Robert and Nancy Homan designed by Malcolm Wells. It contains the Solaris System, a solar heating system developed by Harry Thomason in southern New Jersey.

1628. Family blends into Solaria comfort. Earth Shel. Dig. Energ. Rept., no. 1, Jan./Feb. 1979: 18-9.
Solaria, designed by Malcolm Wells, is being occupied by the couple who acted as general contractors for the project.

The 2,800 sq. ft. home in Indian Mills, NJ, is not completely earth covered, but it has 24 inches of earth on the timber and wood deck roof. The north and south sides are exposed.

1629. House is family project. Earth Shel. Liv., no. 30, Nov./ Dec. 1983, 4-7.
   A ski lodge in Hidden Valley, NJ, incorporating superinsulation, passive solar and earth sheltering, supports the designer's theory that the temperature of the house is moderated by seasonally stored heat in the ground, rather than by daily storage of the sun's heat.

1630. Olcott, Morrow. "Earth sun" home nestles snugly into a hillside. Chr. Sci. Mon., Aug. 26, 1981: 15.
   Terrasol Farms in Newton, NJ, has seven-eights of its circumference underground. Its designer, Frank Fracasso, says construction costs were 25 percent below that for a comparable conventional home.

1631. Smay, V. Elaine. Super-tech house: a double shell earth sheltered solar house in Vernon, NJ, designed by M. Arace. Pop. Sci., v. 223, no. 5, Nov. 1983: 90-3.
   The lower level of this house and the atrium are earth sheltered. The hollow walls deliver earth-tempered air to the windows above. A ground-loop heat pump stores heat under the house in summer and uses the warm earth as a heat source during the winter.

1632. Szigethy, Les. "Underground gutters" drain flat site. Earth Shel. Dig. Energ. Rept., no. 17, Sept./Oct. 1981: 30-1.
   The author's flat land earth-sheltered house in Estell Manor, NJ, has an underground gutter drainage system using polyethylene sheeting extended from the roof and wrapped around a perforated drainage pipe lined with gravel and covered with salt hay to prevent dirt from clogging the pipe. The perforated pipe is joined with a vertical "downspout" at the edge of the walls.

1633. Wells, Malcolm. Architect's hideaway. Bldg. Prog., Aug. 1969: 12-3. Malcolm Wells' Cherry Hill, NJ, office.

New Mexico

1634. Fitzgerald House, Santa Fe, New Mexico. Architect: David Wright of SEAgroup. Proc.: Archit., no. 21, Jan. 1981: 148-9.
   In northern New Mexico, this 1,385 sq. ft. earth-covered

house integrates traditional pueblo design with current lifestyle requirements. The structural materials are adobe, concrete, and brick. It was completed in March 1977.

1635. Foehr, Stephen. A funny little house in the desert. Home Energ. Dig. Wood Q., v. 5, no. 4, Spring 1981: 140-52.

Architect Michael Reynolds built, from recyclable materials, a set of desert houses that are partially buried in rocky ground near Taos, NM.

1636. A house heated solely by the sun. House Gard., v. 151, no. 10, Oct. 1979: 176-9.

The Fitzgerald house in Santa Fe, NM, was designed by David Wright and built by Karen Terry. It has heat-retaining adobe walls and on the north and northeast sides the walls are underground, as is two-thirds of the roof. It has 1,550 sq. ft. and four rooms.

1637. McKinney, Robin. Paradox House. N.M. Mag., v. 55, no. 2, Feb. 1977: 30-5.

Modeled after Indian pit houses and pioneer sod huts. Earth covered and bermed, it's a traditional Southwestern house.

1638. Pittman, Scott, Wayne Pittman, and Gail Haggard. Adobe mixed with earth houses. Earth Shel. Dig. Energ. Rept., no. 13, Jan./Feb. 1981: 11-4.

These three adobe, earth-sheltered houses in Cerrillos, NM, were built on lots deed-restricted to earth sheltering and berming. All must be invisible to their neighbors.

1639. Semi-subterranean house designed to employ passive solar energy, built in 1980 in unbaked earth by architects Georgina and John MacGowan near Santa Fe, NM. In Down to earth: adobe architecture, an old idea, a new future. New York, NY: Facts on File, 1983. p. 184.

1640. Wright, David. Karen Terry's other house. Sol. Age, v. 2, no. 10, Oct. 1977: 16-9.

The design of a passive solar heated 1,500 sq. ft. house in Santa Fe, NM, is described by the architect. All walls, except the south facing wall are underground. Considerations that led to the design including microclimate and aesthetic blending with the landscapes are discussed. Back-up heating is provided solely by two sculptured fireplaces. Experiences in financing the construction are related.

1641. _____. Two natural solar houses. In Desert housing:

balancing experience and technology for dwelling in hot arid zones. Kenneth N. Clark and Patricia Paylore, eds. Tucson, AZ: Univ. of Arizona Pr., 1980. p. 301-11.

The Terry Residence, built in 1975, in the Sangre de Cristo Mountains near Santa Fe, NM, is an adobe with exterior cement stucco. The north side is earth integrated. The Suncave (Fitzgerald Residence), also near Santa Fe, is of adobe, is dug into the side of a southwest-facing hill and is partly covered by a sod roof. It was built in 1977 and has 1,385 sq. ft. The roof is of timber beam, supporting two inches of roughsawn wood decking, and has 12 inches of earth.

New York

1642. Exhibit features earth-shelter models. Underline, v. 3, no. 5, July/Aug. 1982: 3.

The exhibition "Shelter: models of native ingenuity" was held at the Katonah Gallery, Katonah, NY, Mar. 12 - May 23, 1982. It included seven models of partially or completely earth-sheltered dwellings and photographs of four such dwellings.

1643. Ford, Barbara. Safe city: apartment living inside a mountain. Sci. Dig., v. 66, no. 2, Aug. 1969: 16-7.

"Safe City" is an extensive apartment complex now being built 150 ft. deep in the rock of a New York mountain. It is being built to protect vital records of firms and those firms' key personnel, safe from fallout in case of nuclear attack. It is being built by New York Underground Facilities near Rosendale, NY.

1644. Home offers "birds eye" view: show home offers "crow's nest" to view Rochester skyline. Earth Shel. Liv., v. 31, Jan./Feb. 1984: 14-5.

This completely earth covered 3,200 sq. ft. home designed by Carlton DeWolff is in Rochester, NY.

1645. Jacobson, Sebby Wilson. Crow's nest peeps out from "castle retreat": underground house uses earth to cut down on energy needs. Roch. Times-Union, Aug. 14, 1983.

This earth-sheltered house designed by architect Carlton DeWolff has a window tower which provides a view of the Rochester skyline. The house is 60 percent beneath the ground and has two feet of earth on the roof.

1646. _____. You can share the dreams of 8 designers: Architecture 83. Roch. Times-Union, Sept. 28, 1983.

Eight new houses by eight different architects are shown, including Carlton DeWolff's 60 percent earth-covered house, built by Mendon Country Homes.

1647. Low-tech house is comfortable. Earth Shel. Dig. Energ. Rept., no. 11, Sept./Oct. 1980: 52-5.
The Log End Cave of Rob and Jaki Roy in West Chazy, NY, has 910 sq. ft., is heated with wood, and has a 12 volt wind system.

1648. Machowski, Barb. Circular house "contains" climate. Earth Shel. Liv., no. 19, Jan./Feb. 1982: 20-3.
This 5,000 sq. ft. hillside north-facing earth shelter uses neither passive solar gain nor active solar systems. The New York State home is heavily covered and has few openings. It was designed by Carlton DeWolff of Fairport, NY.

1649. Multi-units attract students. Earth Shel. Dig. Energ. Rept., no. 17, Sept./Oct. 1981: 24-9.
Terra Domus of Oneida, NY, has built off-campus housing for students of nearby State University Agricultural and Technical College, Morrisville, NY. It consists of three earth-sheltered buildings with 18 apartments each.

1650. New York design grew from clients' ideas. Earth Shel. Dig. Energ. Rept., no. 8, Mar./Apr. 1980: 48-9.
Sketches of a 3,000 sq. ft. home under construction are shown.

1651. Room at the bottom. Newsweek, May 3, 1965: 87.
A model underground home was displayed at the New York World's Fair by G.B. (Jerry) Henderson, President of the Underground World Home Corporation.

1652. Roy, Robert L. Building a round earth shelter. Earth Shel. Liv., no. 21, May/June 1982: 12-6.
The stages in the building of Earthwood, a round two-story cordwood, masonry earth shelter is shown in 20 photos. The roof has 12 inches of earth cover, and the walls are 40 percent bermed on the north side.

1653. _____. Earthwood -- an integrative design. Alt. Energ., no. 56, July/Aug. 1982: 17-9.
Author and his wife built Log End and then built Earthwood nearby, a cylindrical two-story earth shelter of predominantly cordwood masonry construction, built around a 25-ton Russian masonry stove. Attending to all facets of living in the house during the design stage is stressed.

1654. _____. Earthwood: owner sends an update. <u>Earth Shel. Liv.</u>, no. 27, May/June 1983: 18.
The cordwood earth shelter, Earthwood.

1655. _____. A log-end cave. <u>Moth. Earth N.</u>, no. 67, Jan./Feb. 1981: 110-1.
The author and his wife built an earth-sheltered log-end panel-walled house, the log-ends being of cordwood. The house has 924 sq. ft. Construction began in 1977, and they moved in in Feb. 1978.

1656. _____. Open homestead - inquire below. <u>Earth Shel. Liv.</u>, no. 19, Jan./Feb. 1982: 45-6.
The author describes his Log End Homestead which he offers for sale at $63,500.

1657. Vadnais, Kathleen. New Yorker spreads the word. <u>Earth Shel. Liv.</u>, no. 27, May/June 1983: 5-7.
William Dyer, Middleburgh, NY, designed and built a 1,360 sq. ft. home for less than $35,000. Financing was difficult, but achieved.

North Carolina

1658. Construction experience will be remembered. <u>Earth Shel. Dig. Energ. Rept.</u>, no. 2, Mar./Apr. 1979: 20-2.
A case study of a home in Burnsville, NC.

1659. A critical look at my mother's house. <u>Moth. Earth N.</u>, no. 80, Mar./Apr. 1983: 140-2.
Mistakes are laid bare. Areas where costs could have been cut are revealed.

1660. Feleki, Henry. Secluded home satisfies retirees. <u>Earth Shel. Liv.</u>, no. 28, July/Aug. 1983: 22-5.
Retired couple builds earth-sheltered home in Rockingham, NC.

1661. Hibernate in a hobbitat! <u>Moth. Earth N.</u>, no. 68, Mar./Apr. 1981: 128-9.
Lloyd Remington, a professor of chemistry at the Univ. of North Carolina's Asheville campus, began building the home in October 1977 and moved in the following May. The cost of the 1,927 sq. ft. house came to over $80,000. Solar heat is supplemented by a wood and coal stove.

1662. Kennedy, Richard. An earth-integrated design — the Rem-

ington Residence: the construction experience. In <u>Proc.,
3rd Nat. Pass. Sol. Conf.</u>, San Jose, CA, Jan. 11-13, 1979.
Newark, DE: Int. Sol. Energ. Soc., Am. Sec., 1979. p.
626-9.

Sunspace Designer/Builder, Burnsville, NC, constructed the
Remington Residence in the fall of 1977. The structural features
of the 1,700 sq. ft. home included stepped ceilings, a 500 sq. ft.
skylight, over 6,000 masonry units including fluted block, exterior insulation, a prestressed concrete plank roof, a new three-fourths-inch thick nylon open weave mesh drainage system, a
special rubber-based waterproofing, and a four mode heating
and cooling system.

1663. Macdonald, Angus W. Building the Sun Cottage. Pts. 1-6.
<u>Moth. Earth N.</u>, nos. 81-86, May/June 1983-Mar./Apr.
1984.

Pt. 1: Site selection: gives the criteria for selecting a site
for a passive solar, earth-sheltered home. Pt. 2. Cost control:
making and maintaining a budget. Pt. 3. Pouring the footings,
foundation, and floor slab for this earth sheltered, passive solar
home. Pt. 4. Walls and beams are discussed. Pt. 5. The structural
frame: erecting the roof-supporting frame. Pt. 6. Waterproofing,
insulating, and finishing the Sun Cottage.

1664. Mother's $10-per-square-foot (or less!) earth-sheltered
house. Pts. 1-3. <u>Moth. Earth N.</u>, nos. 84-86, Nov./Dec.
1983-Mar./Apr. 1984.

Pt. 1. Mother's Eco-Village is building a homestead whose
1,000 sq. ft. house is earth sheltered. Its block walls are convexly curved to better withstand the weight of the earth and
hydrostatic pressure so the house is circular. Pt. 2. Framing,
rafters, and roofing the house. Pt. 3. Experimental waterproofing techniques are used.

1665. My mother's house. Pts. 1-7. <u>Moth. Earth N.</u>, nos. 70-77,
July/Aug. 1981-Sept./Oct. 1982.

Pt. 1 describes the initial phases of the building of an
earth sheltered, passive solar house at Mother's Eco-Village
in western North Carolina. Pt. 2 describes the wooden post
and beam construction which supports the sod-covered roof.
Pt. 3. Two earth-sheltered waterproofing materials are tested.
P. 4. Cooling tubes and backfilling provide natural air conditioning. Pt. 5. The hybrid solar heating/storage system is
described. Pt. 6. A passive solar batch water heater and a
pair of solar chimneys are installed. Pt. 7. The construction
of the Russian masonry fireplace is related.

1666. Thomas, Wendell. The self-heating, self-cooling house. Moth. Earth N., no. 10, July 1971: 76-9
   The author designed and built two underground houses in the mountains of western North Carolina in 1948 and 1957. This article describes their design and provisions for heating and cooling.

North Dakota

1667. Circles connect design with ideals. Earth Shel. Liv., no. 29, Sept./Oct. 1983: 16-9.
   This 2,300 sq. ft. two-story house in Bismarck, ND, has a curved shell that increases wall stability, maximizes interior space, cuts down on exterior wall space, reducing material cost and heat loss.

1668. Hawley, J. Earth-covered home made of wood. N.D. REC Mag., v. 29, no. 8, Feb. 1983: 40-1.
   This underground house was constructed of wood at a cost of less than $20 per sq. ft. The roof is supported by 13-inch thick laminated 2 x 6s, covered with three layers of rolled roofing, three layers of sheet plastic, four inches of foam board insulation, and 12 inches of dirt. The exposed south wall features six feet high thermal pane glass, and there is a 30-inch roof overhang to keep the summer sun off the glass. In 1982, 2,290 kw hours of electricity was used for heat, cooking, lights, and all appliances.

1669. Navrat home "in tune" with nature. N.D. REC Mag., v. 29, no. 8, Feb. 1983: 38-9.
   The design of a 4,400 sq. ft. home in North Dakota utilizes earth berming to the roof on the north and west walls. Built to utilize solar energy, a bank of 38 windows on the south side admits solar gain which is stored in brick columns.

1670. Vadnais, Kathleen. Indians get funds to study modern version of past housing. Earth Shel. Dig. Energ. Rept., no. 5, Sept./Oct. 1979: 31-3.
   The Fort Berthold Reservation, ND, was given $350,000 by the U.S. Dept. of Housing and Urban Development to build ten demonstration earth shelters.

Ohio

1671. Dawson, Sue. Underground home provides modern living at low cost. Ohio Farm., Feb. 5, 1977: 60.
   The Ackermans in Allen County, OH, constructed a ten-

room house with eight-inch thick concrete slabs on walls and six-inch concrete slabs on the roof. The walls and ceiling are insulated with one inch of styrofoam. Some errors are discussed.

1672. Geier House, Cincinnati, OH. Archit. For., v. 138, no. 1, Feb. 1973: 67. Architect Philip Johnson designed this house built in 1965.

1673. Humphrey, John B. House features no waterproofing. Earth Shel. Liv., no. 35, Sept./Oct. 1984: 4-8.
This owner-built earth-sheltered house is under construction in Ashtabula, OH.

1674. Johnson underground. Prog. Archit., v. 48, no. 4, Apr. 1967: 146.
The Geier House in Cincinnati, OH, by architect Philip Johnson, is underground but overlooks a lake.

1675. Kawecki, Joseph J. Ohio's first all solar home development -- Genesis: direct earth contact passive residence: energy consumption and performance of several passive homes in central Ohio. In Proc., 4th Nat. Pass. Sol. Conf., Kansas City, MO, Oct. 3-5, 1979. G. Franta, ed. Newark, DE: Int. Sol. Energ. Soc., Am. Sec., 1979. p. 762.
Nearly 60 percent of the Genesis community is complete. Twelve homes will be built on the 32-acre site, featuring innovative thermal systems, contemporary styling, minimal maintenance, and maximum energy usage rates. Marketing points are presented, and four passive homes are compared: a direct gain earth berm, a sun tempered, a hybrid, and an isolated gain.

1676. Kremers, Jack Alan. An earth-berm, wood foundation passive solar home in Kent, Ohio. In Proc., 3rd Nat. Pass. Sol. Conf., San Jose, CA, Jan. 11-13, 1979. Newark, DE: Int. Sol Energ. Soc., Am. Sec., 1979. p. 630-3.
Huth-Westwood Builders of Kent, OH, constructed an earth-bermed residence which was designed to conserve heat energy. Features of the home include: a center, glass-covered atrium, a conventional electric cooling and gas-fired heating system, and an underground fresh air intake system. Construction was completed in August 1978.

1677. Laukes, Jim. Northern climate underground home. Alt. Energ., no. 33, Aug. 1978: 9.
This 2,200 sq. ft. earth shelter was designed and built by

Sun/Earth Builders in Columbus, OH. The shell is covered with foam insulation, a water barrier, then two feet of earth. It cost $32 per sq. ft.

1678. Passively heated underground houses can be beautiful, too! Moth. Earth N., no. 51, May/June 1978: 101-3.
The house is located in northwest Columbus, OH, built for Buck Vaile by Solar-Earth Energy.

1679. Stetzel, Warren. A building for all time. Earth Shel. Liv., no. 34, July/Aug. 1984: 6-9.
Progress on Locust Hill, at Raven Rocks, OH, designed by Malcolm Wells, is described. The energy conservation features of the structure are stressed.

1680. _____. "Raven Rocks" leads to "Locust Hill." Earth Shel. Liv., no. 33, May/June 1984: 38-40.
A 19-person corporation bought 1,000 acres in Ohio to save it from strip mining. Solely a preservation effort at first, an underground home is being built there to house all the members. It was designed by Malcolm Wells and called Locust Hill.

1681. Vaile, Janitye. Woman discovers secure environment. Earth Shel. Dig. Energ. Rept., no. 3, May/June 1979: 18-9.
The author is the wife of Buck Vaile, a builder in Westerville, OH.

1682. Van der Meer, Wybe J. Down to earth housing. Sol. Age., Sept. 1976.
About Raven Rocks, OH, an earth-sheltered community.

Oklahoma

1683. Architect designs own home. Earth Shel. Dig. Energ. Rept., no. 3, May/June 1979: 20-3.
Elbert Wheeler is the architect/owner of this Enid, OK, home.

1684. Boyer, Lester L. The Oklahoma experience. Earth Shel. Dig. Energ. Rept., no. 2, Mar./Apr. 1979: 32-5.
Briefly describes recent improved site developments in Oklahoma.

1685. Carter, Joe. A year-round energy winner. New Shel., v. 5, no. 7, Sept. 1984: 74-7.
Architect Joe Hylton designed this 2,548 sq. ft. house in Norman, OK, with extensive berming to fend off winter winds.

1686. Custom home saves energy. Earth Shel. Dig. Energ. Rept., no. 15, May/June 1981: 12-5.
This 3,100 sq. ft. concrete home is in Shawnee, OK. Waterproofing by acrylic latex coating. Heating by electric heat pump and woodburning stove.

1687. Earth shelter profiles. Earth Shel. Liv., no. 32, Mar./Apr. 1984: 32-3.
Photos and floor plans of earth-sheltered homes in Newcastle, OK; Northfield, MN; Brasstown, NC; St. Peter, MN; and Chippewa Falls, WI.

1688. Encore! Earth Shel. Liv., no. 38, Mar./Apr. 1985: 6-7.
This two-story earth shelter in Edmond, OK, was designed by architect Joe Hylton.

1689. Faubion, Roy. Patented design includes garden. Earth Shel. Dig. Energ. Rept., no. 6, Nov./Dec. 1979: 16-8.
This 2,232 sq. ft. earth shelter in Tulsa, OK, is by Geobuilding Systems of Hereford, TX. This article is excerpted from their publication Underground Gardens and Homes.

1690. Home safe in family compound. Earth Shel. Dig. Energ. Rept., no. 10, July/Aug. 1980: 29-32.
A 2,380 sq. ft. fire, burglar, and tornado-proof house was built in Newcastle, OK. Only skylights and vent pipes are visible from the road. The entrance to the home is from a tunnel-like entrance beside the garage. Windows are narrow. The home was designed by Joe Hylton of Norman, OK, with eight-inch thick concrete walls and roof, footings 12 by 24 inches, waterproofing with five coats of Hydroside, and a tar base sealer. There's an innovative ventilation system.

1691. Johnston, T.L., ed. A tour of selected Oklahoma earth shelters II. Stillwater, OK: Okla. State Univ., Archit. Ext., 1981. 32 p.
Tour held in conjunction with the Conference on Earth Shelter Peformance and Evaluation, sponsored by the Oklahoma State University Architectural Extension with assistance from the American Underground Space Association and the Earth Shelter Digest and Energy Report.

1692. Resales set market values. Earth Shel. Dig. Energ. Rept., no. 15, May/June 1981: 37-8.
Two earth-sheltered homes for resale: one near Norman, OK and the other in Chaska, MN.

1693. Speer, Bonnie. Going underground: house of tomorrow. Orbit Mag., Sunday Oklahoman, Apr. 10, 1977.
This is a review of several underground homes in Oklahoma with reactions from their owners.

1694. Wheeler, Elbert M. Design/development process for Underhill, a residence. In Proc., Earth Shel. Bldg. Des. Innov., Nat. Tech. Conf., Oklahoma City, OK, Apr. 18, 1980. L.L. Boyer, ed. Stillwater, OK: Okla. State Univ., 1980. p. V. 5-13.
A discussion of the design and development of an earth sheltered house on a gently sloping site in Enid, OK. This house utilizes passive solar energy for heating, many windows for natural light and ventilation, and a lower level below grade to serve as protection from storms and excessive heat and cold. A north-entry atrium and a south-facing garden room are featured.

Oregon

1695. Bolton, Steve. An interview with Norm Clark. Energ. Alt., v. 2, no. 4, Winter 1979: 8-10, 36-7.
Clark's residence is an underground, active/passive solar-heated single family residence in suburban Portland, OR.

1696. Ecological village begun in Oregon. Earth Shel. Dig. Energ. Rept., no. 5, Sept./Oct. 1979: 29.
Cerro Gordo, OR, is being planned as an environmentally-sound community which may contain a family cluster of underground homes.

1697. House blends with neighborhood. Earth Shel. Dig. Energ. Rept., no. 9, May/June 1980: 24-9.
This 2,200 sq. ft. earth shelter with atrium is in Portland, OR.

1698. Lambert, Brian. Planning for energy needs: a look at three new communities. Undergr. Sp., v. 5, no. 6, May/June 1981: 362-9.
Passive solar and earth-sheltering techniques are used in the energy planning for developing and redeveloping communities in Cerro Gordo, OR; Rock Ridge Community, WI; and Soldiers Grove, WI.

1699. Two greenhouses heat, cool home. Earth Shel. Dig. Energ. Rept., no. 16, July/Aug. 1981: 50-1.
This 1,830 sq. ft. bilevel demonstration home is in Aloha,

OR, on a 7,800 sq. ft. sloping lot. The entry is above grade at street level, and the lower level living area is built into the hill and covered with two feet of earth.

1700. Vadnais, Kathleen. Hillside house fits site. Earth Shel. Liv., no. 21, May/June 1982: 26-9.
Tedd Chilless designed and built a 2,462 sq. ft. white stucco house on a slope in Portland, OR. It has 18 inches of earth cover and berms on the north and east sides.

Pennsylvania

1701. Bregman, Lillian. Keeping down with the Joneses. Phila. Mag., v. 72, Sept. 1981: 227-9, 232-3.
Briefly describes an earth-sheltered home in the Delaware Valley, especially its construction.

1702. Meanor, Linda L. Underground living: fears and obstacles overcome. Earth Shel. Liv., no. 41, Sept./Oct. 1985: 10.
The author acceded to her husband's desire to build an earth-sheltered house in York County, PA. It was built within four months, and heating bills are less than $100 a year.

1703. Nearhoof, Steve, Bob Kobet, Harry Gordon, and David Lage. The same solar salad with different kinds of dressing. In Proc., 4th Nat. Pass. Sol Conf., Kansas City, MO, Oct. 3-5, 1979. G. Franta, ed. Newark, DE: Int. Sol. Energ. Soc., Am. Sec., 1979. p. 761.
Burt Hill Kosar Rittleman Associates of Butler, PA, have designed three structures to prove that solar heating does work in western Pennsylvania. One house in Valencia, PA, is partially underground. Another is an underground structure which utilizes a double glazed south wall.

1704. Solar atrium opens house. Earth Shel. Dig. Energ. Rept., no. 4, July/Aug. 1979: 15-7.
This Murrysville, PA, earth shelter is owned by Nancy DiGioia of Solar-Earth Energy, Inc.

Rhode Island

1705. Reeves, Melissa-Jo. "Home sweet home": a subterranean solar sanctuary. Chr. Sci. Mon., Sept. 9, 1982: 18.
This earth-shelter house is in Middletown, RI. Some construction details are given, especially waterproofing.

South Carolina

1706. An experimental, earth-insulated house is being monitored in rural South Carolina. Undergr. Sp., v. 3, no. 3, Nov./Dec. 1978: 148-9.

South Dakota

1707. Earth shelter profiles. Earth Shel. Liv., no. 30, Nov./Dec. 1983: 8-9.
    Profiles earth-sheltered houses in Bonesteel, SD; Duluth, MN; Fort Worth, TX; Osage, IA; and Catalina, AZ.

1708. Electrical engineer gets results. Earth Shel. Dig. Energ. Rept., no. 9, May/June 1980: 30-3.
    The owner-builder of this 1,356 sq. ft. reinforced concrete earth shelter in Rapid City, SD, is an electrical engineer who is monitoring the home's performance for the S.D. Housing Development Authority and for the National Solar Passive Heating Conference.

1709. Feisel, Lyle D. Economic design considerations for an underground house. In Passive solar: subdivisions, windows, underground. Ed. by H. Wade and others. Kansas City, MO: Am. Sol. Energ. Soc., Kan. City Chap., 1983. p. 231-44.
    The author's underground house near Rapid City, SD, has been designed to conserve energy. Considered are: the advantages and disadvantages of some of the unique features and the details of construction of the home. Temperature is being monitored using thermistors inside the structure and in the soil outside the concrete walls and in the earth on the roof.

1710. _____. Underground house in South Dakota. In Proc., Alt. in Habitat: the Use of Earth Cov. Set., Conf., Fort Worth, TX, May 17-19, 1978. F.L. Moreland, ed. Washington, DC: U.S. Dept. of Energy, 1979. v. 2, Earth covered buildings and settlements, p. 267-72.
    The site planning, construction details, and a two-year performance record are reported for an owner-designed underground house in South Dakota. Site preparation in a small ravine required plans for de-watering a natural drainage area. The house features electric heating and a maximum use of natural light and ventilation.

Tennessee

1711. Flannery, Herschel K. Temperature nears constant. Earth Shel. Dig. Energ. Rept., no. 14, Mar./Apr. 1981: 33.

The author's mid-Tennessee earth shelter demonstrates that thermal mass can be used to achieve nearly constant temperatures in the house throughout the year.

1712. Massive home performs well. Earth Shel. Dig. Energ. Rept., no. 14, Mar./Apr. 1981: 30-2.
This 2,640 sq. ft. earth shelter is in mid-Tennessee.

1713. Woods, Melvin. A $10,000 earth shelter. Moth. Earth N., no. 78, Nov./Dec. 1982: 10.
Pressure-treated lumber was used to construct the frame of this 960 sq. ft. home in eastern Tennessee.

Texas

1714. Basic concepts home. Earth Shel. Liv., no. 27, May/June 1983: 41.
Eugene Wukasch, Austin, TX, plans to use the fibrous sprayed concrete dome for residential buildings. Using this design, he has developed "The Basic Concepts Home," a self-sufficient habitat containing a hydroponic greenhouse to provide domestic heating, as well as vegetables, fruit, and flowers. Tanks can grow warm-water fish and seafood. His ideas are borrowed from work done at the Integral Urban House, Berkeley, CA, and by the New Alchemists, Woods Hole, MA.

1715. Breezes air condition house. Earth Shel. Liv., no. 19, Jan./Feb. 1982: 24-7.
This 1,782 sq. ft. earth shelter in Parker County, TX, was designed by architect Ray Boothe. The house won a passive design award from HUD and DOE in 1978.

1716. Bumke, David. Designed for deep Texas. New Shel., v. 3, no. 1, Jan. 1982: 27-30.
Frank Moreland helped in the design of this house. It is north facing, all-electric, has 2,176 sq. feet, and cost about $120,000 to build. The owners are satisfied with it because it is an effective answer to finding comfort during the very hot Texas summers.

1717. Earth sheltered home sales. Underline, v. 2, no. 4, May/June 1981: 2.
Two houses are described: Terra Grande house in Lubbock, TX and an earth-bermed house in Little Canada, a suburb of St. Paul, MN.

1718. Free-form buildings: shape of housing in Texas communities limited only by the imagination. Earth Shel. Liv., no. 36, Nov./Dec. 1984: 32-4.

These very unusual homes are heavily rebarred ferroconcrete structures built in shapes to suit the owners. They are in Rainbow Valley and in White Hawk, near Denton, TX.

1719. Is this the house of the future? Empire Mag., Denver Post, Feb. 27, 1966: 12-9.

Jay Swayze's underground house in Plainview, TX, is discussed.

1720. Kiesling, E.W. and Gary A. Boubel. Ashford earth-covered residence, Muleshoe, TX. In Proc., Alt. in Habitat: the Use of Earth Cov. Set., Conf., Fort Worth, TX, May 17-19, 1978. F.L. Moreland, ed. Washington, DC: U.S. Dept. of Energy, 1979. v. 2, Earth covered buildings and settlements, p. 273-7.

A low-cost house using the most appropriate construction techniques for the area was the goal of the owner and the planners. Some design concepts, such as the use of earth forms for the concrete shell, and modifications of standard construction methods are discussed. The initial costs of construction were higher than for an above-grade house of the same size.

1721. _____, _____, and Richard Behr. Earth forms Texas house. Earth Shel. Dig. Energ. Rept., no. 4, July/Aug. 1979: 8-11.

The authors consulted on the design and monitoring of this earth-covered residence in Muleshoe, TX, as part of an ongoing research program at Texas Tech University.

1722. Kilroy, Karen. Earth sheltered security. Earth Shel. Liv., no. 30, Nov./Dec. 1983: 42.

Home in rural north central Texas provides security from depredations of nature and man.

1723. McKown, Cora, ed. Texas: earth sheltered. Lubbock, TX: Texas Tech. Univ., Coll. of Home Econ., Dept. of Fam. Mgmt. Hous. and Cons. Sci., 1982. 109 p.

This work uses examples of earth-sheltered homes in Texas to illustrate chapters on siting, design and construction, interior design, economic considerations, law/codes and consumer concerns related to earth sheltering. This report is an account of work sponsored by the Texas Energy and Natural Resources Advisory Council.

1724. Southern house features pillars, atrium. <u>Earth Shel. Dig. Energ. Rept.</u>, no. 7, Jan./Feb. 1980: 10-3.
 This 2,100 sq. ft. north-facing home is a combination six-foot pit and earth berm, with a colonial facade complete with pillars. It is in Austin, TX.

1725. Texan builds a dreamhouse underground: living it up way down. <u>Life</u>, v. 56, no. 17, Apr. 24, 1964: 53, 56.
 Jay Swayze's ten-room house in Plainview, TX, is a sunken concrete shell. It cost $80,000 to build.

1726. Texas family happy with their large underground house. <u>Mpls. Trib.</u>, July 17, 1977: 16F.

1727. Texas home pleases family. <u>Earth Shel. Liv.</u>, no. 20, Mar./Apr. 1982: 31-3.
 This 2,176 sq. ft. earth-covered home near Decatur, TX, was designed by Frank Moreland. The house is all-electric, including an electric heat pump. It has 12-inch poured concrete walls and prestressed planks on the roof.

1728. Tubes cool off Texans: earth tubes keep house cool, even in the Texas heat. <u>Earth Shel. Liv.</u>, no. 31, Jan./Feb. 1984: 12-3.
 A 2,256 sq. ft. earth-bermed home in Harker Heights, TX, is cooled by earth tubes buried 14 feet underground.

1729. Underground home of the future debuts at the Fair. <u>Elect. World</u>, v. 161, no. 15, Apr. 20, 1964: 165.
 Jay Swayze constructed a model underground home for the New York World's Fair similar to one he built for his family in Plainview, TX. The home is all electric and electricity costs are about half what they would be above ground. The article predicts unlimited possibilities for underground construction.

1730. World's Fair visitors view life underground. <u>Today's Hlth.</u>, v. 42, no. 9, Sept. 1964: 12.
 An underground house similar to one built by Jay Swayze in Plainview, TX, was exhibited at the New York World's Fair. The house is an oblong shell of waterproof concrete 130 x 90 ft. whose top is three feet below the earth's surface. Some details of design, including the lighting system, are given.

Utah

1731. Chamberlain, David. Underground condo (Survive Tomorrow's project in La Verkin, Utah). Roll. Stone, June 11, 1981: 14.

Terrene Ark I is a condominium complex located in La Verkin in southwestern Utah. Plans call for 250 units ($39,000 for a 360 sq. ft. one-bedroom, $78,000 for a 720 sq. ft. two-bedroom) buried under eight inches of reinforced concrete and at least three and a half feet of dirt.

1732. The Paul Isaacson family lives in the house of the future. Moth. Earth N., no. 50, Mar./Apr. 1978: 101-3.

The underground house is topped with two clear plastic geodesic domes, one inside the other. The dome above creates a solar energy trap and greenhouse, the smaller one is the ceiling of a sunken courtyard. Financing problems are discussed.

1733. Sunbird 2000: a Utah mountain-top home doubles as a laboratory. Earth Shel. Liv., no. 41, Sept./Oct. 1985: 5-9.

This ultramodern earth-sheltered home, ten minutes from Salt Lake City in the Wasatch Mountains, resembles a flying saucer. The home is earth covered to the base of the dome-roof which consists in part of opaque acrylic panels and white fiberglass. The roof can be opened. The house is for sale: approx. $450,000.

1734. Vadnais, Kathleen. Multi-unit survival community marketed. Earth Shel. Dig. Energ. Rept., no. 16, July/Aug. 1981: 4-7.

Terrene Ark 1, a Survivalist community southwestern Utah, offers 240 underground residences each with a nuclear fallout shelter and four years' supply of food for one person.

1735. Vicker, Ray. Underground condominium offers haven for pessimists. Undergr. Sp., v. 5, no. 6, May 1981: 356-7.

This article was originally printed in the Wall Street Journal. There are 266 windowless residences buried under eight inches of reinforced concrete and three and a half feet of earth in La Verkin, UT. This community was developed for survivalists by Survive Tomorrow, Inc., Ronald B. Boutwell, President.

Vermont

1736. Article on underground home designed by architect Mark Simon in Vermont. N.Y. Times, Mar. 22, 1979, sec. III: 1.

1737. Crowell House, Vermont. Architect: Mark Simon of Moore Grover Harper. Proc.: Archit., no. 21, Jan. 1981: 144-7.

A small house (900 sq. ft.) is set into the side of a large hill; a deep sod roof is covered with 18 inches of earth. It has a southern exposure. It was completed in Oct. 1975.

1738. Filler, Martin. Little house off the prairie. Prog. Archit., v. 60, Dec. 1979: 72-5.

Mark Simon of Moore Grover Harper, designed Crowell House, Washington, VT, a small vacation house, earth-bermed, inspired by the sod house of the prairie in the nineteenth century.

1739. Holland, Elizabeth. Underground retreat. Fine Homebldg., no. 16, Aug./Sept. 1983: 50-3.

Don Metz designed this 900 sq. ft. house in Vermont and Bob Schultz built it.

Virginia

1740. The $15,000 solar arcade. Moth. Earth N., no. 74, Mar./Apr. 1982: 134-5.

This one bedroom, 800 sq. ft. earth shelter cost under $15,000 to build. It has a solar water heater and a wood burning stove. The designer/builder has developed a precut, heavy timber roof framing kit which can be secured to the home's masonry shell with a drill. The prototype is near Orange, VA.

1741. Huggins, Geoffrey G. One owner-builder's approach: a Virginia couple pass along some helpful hints. Earth Shel. Liv., no. 41, Sept./Oct. 1985: 24-8.

1742. Macdonald, Angus W. The solar carriage house. Moth. Earth N., no. 94, July/Aug. 1985: 140-1.

Two homes in Virginia have been built using this plan which incorporates earth tempering, superinsulation, and solar direct gain.

Washington (State)

1743. County builds park retreat. Earth Shel. Dig. Energ. Rept., no. 17, Sept./Oct. 1981: 12-4.

The Park Ranger and his family in Wawawai Park, WA, live in a 2,600 sq. ft. earth-sheltered home overlooking a wide 2,000 ft. deep canyon of the Snake River. The house was designed by architect David Scott.

1744. Croston, Dennis I. Home ideal for Northwest: couple designs and builds home they believe best for Northwest. Earth Shel. Liv., no. 31, Jan./Feb. 1984: 4-5.

Electricity costs for this all-electric, 1,900 sq. ft. home are approximately $26 per month. No electric heating is necessary in the Maple Valley, WA, earth shelter.

1745. Earth-sheltered home profile. Underline, v. 5, no. 2, 1984: 5.

Resident/architect Harry G. Merrick built this 2,996 sq. ft. home in Spokane, WA.

1746. Earth sheltered/solar community being planned. Underline, v. 2, no. 2, Jan./Feb. 1981: 4.

A self-reliant cooperative community in south central Washington state called Ponderosa Village features earth-sheltered solar houses.

1747. Farmer builds retirement home. Earth Shel. Dig. Energ. Rept., no. 6, Nov./Dec. 1979: 2-4.

This 1,000 sq. ft. owner-built house is in Spokane, WA. No insulation was used.

1748. Home combines world of experience. Earth Shel. Dig. Energ. Rept., no. 17, Sept./Oct. 1981: 35-9.

A case study of an earth-covered retirement home in the San Juan Islands, WA, on a hillside. It was occupied in 1978.

1749. Lewis, Linda. Go underground young man, says John Strickler. Seattle Post-Intel. N.W., Mar. 6, 1977.

Strickler's earth shelter is located on Camano Island, WA.

1750. Parsons, Mark. Remote underground home completed. Earth Shel. Liv., no. 21, May/June 1982: 36-40.

This owner-built home is in Washougal, WA, in the Washington State Cascades.

1751. Rambo, Forrest. The "EVAC" house that Jack built. Moth. Earth N., no. 58, July/Aug. 1979: 106-7.

This 1,536 sq. ft. EVAC (Energy at Very Acceptable Cost) house was built in 1976 in Camano Island, WA.

West Virginia

1752. All mine and paid for! Earth Shel. Liv., no. 40, July/Aug. 1985: 17.

The roof of an all-wood, 1,250 sq. ft. earth-covered home

in West Virginia can support about 600-700 lbs. per sq. ft. It has a cellar, and will cost less than $20 per sq. ft. finished.

1753. Ashelman, Randall B. and Gary C. Hagen (illustrator). Construction details of an earth-sheltered, passive solar, thermosiphon air house. Proc., 5th Nat. Pass. Sol. Conf., Amherst, MA, Oct. 19-26, 1980. Newark, DE: Int. Sol. Energ. Soc., Am. Sec., 1980. p. 1146-50.
   Construction details of "Sunrise" a passive solar, earth-sheltered house in eastern West Virginia are offered. Particular attention is given to structural, waterproofing and insulation details, and to the thermosiphon air system.

1754. Vadnais, Kathleen. Hog Lick Holler becomes Terra Lake. Earth Shel. Liv., no. 28, July/Aug. 1983: 26-9.
   Ron Cutlip, a student in landscape architecture from Olney, MD, chose as his senior project the reclamation for residential use of an unclaimed surface mine area in West Virginia, using a combination of earth sheltering and bermed structures.

Wisconsin

1755. Couple built earlier than planned. Earth Shel. Liv., no. 19, Jan./Feb. 1982: 30-3.
   This 3,200 sq. ft. owner-built home in Wisconsin was designed by Rolf Anderson.

1756. Disasters point way to earth shelters. Earth Shel. Dig. Energ. Rept., no. 8, Mar./Apr. 1980: 11-4.
   The owners of this 2,100 sq. ft. home in Wautoma, WI, wanted to be safe from tornadoes and fire.

1757/58. Earth sheltering no obstacle for handicapped: special earth shelters were designed for wheelchair use. This one in Milwaukee, WI. Earth Shel. Liv., no. 35, Sept./Oct. 1984: 26-30.

1759. Home began new family corporation. Earth Shel. Dig. Energ. Rept., no. 7, Jan./Feb. 1980: 44-5.
   This earth-sheltered house in Berlin, WI, is also the headquarters of the Earth Shelter Corp. of America.

1760. Homes ready for city markets. Earth Shel. Liv., no. 20, Mar./Apr. 1982: 43-4.
   These homes were built in Wisconsin and British Columbia, Canada.

1761. House has "cardinal" virtues. Earth Shel. Dig. Energ. Rept., no. 4, July/Aug. 1979: 12-4.
This earth-sheltered home belongs to Buzz and Jan Carpenter of Berlin, WI.

1762. Jones, Mary. Beneath the surface. House Beaut., v. 121, no. 11, Nov. 1979: 102, 104.
A 1,500 sq. ft. home on the St. Croix River in Wisconsin is discussed. It cost about the same to build as a conventional house, but fuel costs are lower. It has a wood burning stove and a back-up electric downdraft furnace. A third heat source is a passive solar heating system, but it's not needed. Insulation is polystyrene foam insulation.

1763. Machowski, Barb. Specs, model open in 7 states. Earth Shel. Dig. Energ. Rept., no. 15, May/June 1981: 40-6.
Two earth-sheltered models in Oregon, WI and New Hampton, IA and six spec homes in Frederick, MD; Plymouth, MN; Burnsville, MN; Omaha, NE; Norman, OK; and Charlottesville, VA are described.

1764. _____. Subdivisions top new home list. Earth Shel. Dig. Energ. Rept., no. 13, Jan./Feb. 1981: 38-43.
Two Terra Dome subdivision models are described, one in Oregon, WI and the other near Grand Junction, CO. Other new homes are in Post Falls, ID, one in Johnston, IA, an Earth Systems concrete dome in Phoenix, AZ, and a moderately-priced "starter" earth shelter in Bend, OR.

1765. _____. Sunspaces built to fit owners' needs. Earth Shel. Liv., no. 22, July/Aug. 1982: 4-7.
The Greisbachs of Hortonville, WI, put a site-built, six by 50 feet sunspace across the south face of their 1,800 sq. ft. earth-sheltered home as a thermal break and growing area. Harry Annear's 2,400 sq. ft. earth shelter in Bozeman, MT, has been retrofitted with a sunspace which acts as an airlock entry and provides heat to the home.

1766. _____. Tourist attraction opens in Dells. Earth Shel. Liv., no. 22, July/Aug. 1982: 16-7.
A 3,600 sq. ft. Terra Dome in Wisconsin Dells, WI, was built for owners who want to promote earth sheltering.

1767. Plans are complete for an earth-sheltered townhouse complex in Fond du Lac, Wisconsin. Undergr. Sp., v. 6, no. 3, Nov./Dec. 1981: 132.

1768. Quality features built in. Earth Shel. Dig. Energ. Rept., no. 2, Mar./Apr. 1979: 23-4.

1769. Redmann, DuWayne K. Getting into it. Earth Shel. Liv., no. 25, Jan./Feb. 1983: 12-3.
Central County Builders, Inc., Weyauwega, WI, constructed a house to provide time and cost figures for a planned FmHA earth-sheltered apartment project. Afterwards ten appraisers arrived at ten different values.

1770. Their home is like others. Earth Shel. Dig. Energ. Rept., no. 2, Mar./Apr. 1979: 36-7.
Home of Corrine and Derrick Jones on the east bank of the St. Croix River, WI.

1771. Tornado takes trees--leaves earth shelters. Earth Shel. Liv., no. 29, Sept./Oct. 1983: 42-3.
Three earth-sheltered homes in Cable, WI, survived a tornado with little or no damage.

1772. Two more specs listed. Earth Shel. Dig. Energ. Rept., no. 10, July/Aug. 1980: 16-8.
Two more earth shelters have been placed on the market; a three bedroom, 1,932 sq. ft. earth shelter with a 696 sq. ft. garage on a 5.34 lot in Waukesha County, WI, will be the model for an eight-parcel site. The first earth shelter in Waterloo, IA, is a 1,482 sq. ft., three-bedroom, one and one-half bath spec house built by Youngblut Corp., Washburn, IA. Plans are shown.

1773. Unique tube home fits into earth. Earth Shel. Dig. Energ. Rept., no. 1, Jan./Feb. 1979: 20-2.
This 2,700 sq. ft. home built in 1972 near River Falls, WI, consists of two culverts connected by a hallway.

1774. Vadnais, Kathleen. Earth mounds form underground prototype. Earth Shel. Liv., no. 22, July/Aug. 1982: 22-5.
A 5,000 sq. ft. underground home being built by Gerald Keller in Hubertus, WI, is described.

1775. _____. Mobile house pleases crowds. Earth Shel. Dig. Energ. Rept., no. 16, July/Aug. 1981: 48-9.
The Wisconsin Ready Mixed Concrete Assn. has purchased a model of a three-bedroom, earth-sheltered home which is featured at home shows, architectural exhibits, fairs, conventions, etc.

1776. _____. Parallels separated by two states. Earth Shel. Liv., no. 29, Sept./Oct. 1983: 30-1.

Two houses with very similar features were built in Gilman, WI and Marion, ND.

1777. _____. Small house has serene impact. Earth Shel. Liv., no. 29, Sept./Oct. 1983: 20-3.
This 950 sq. ft. home in Wisconsin outside Stillwater, MN, is set into the earth, has built-in furniture and redwood siding. It cost about $55,000 with well and septic tank.

1778. _____. Steel house goes on market. Earth Shel. Liv., no. 23, Sept./Oct. 1982: 34-7.
An early underground home in Wisconsin is for sale. It was built in 1972. Michael McGuire built this home of steel arches sprayed with urethane foam.

1779. Wisconsin resale market tested. Earth Shel. Dig. Energ. Rept., no. 16, July/Aug. 1981: 42.
This 2,100 sq. ft. home is in Waupaca, WI.

1780. Wright, David. A fiberglass domed earth integrated farmhouse. In Conf. proc., Earth Shel. Perf. and Eval., 2nd Nat. Tech. Conf., Tulsa, OK, Oct. 16-17, 1981. Stillwater, OK: Okla. State Univ., Archit. Ext., 1981. p. 53-63.
The energy design of an innovative two-story domed earth shelter in Wisconsin is described, including a greenhouse, rockbed, and sod roof. Computer energy performance simulations are also given.

Wyoming

1781. Experimental underground survival home. Undergr. Sp., v. 9, no. 2-3, 1985: 78-9.
An underground nuclear war shelter will be built in the mountains of Wyoming. It will be the site of a family survival experiment. Participants and supporters are solicited.

1782. Lee, Vincent. Berms fit mountain sites. Earth Shel. Liv., no. 23, Sept./Oct. 1982: 30-2.
The author has built many earth-bermed homes in Wyoming.

Location Not Specified

1783. Barnard, John E., Jr. Covered vs. conventional. Earth Shel. Dig. Energ. Rept., no. 12, Nov./Dec. 1980: 27-9.
This article compares the costs of construction, upkeep, and the thermal performance of a south-facing, linear design earth shelter with a traditional above-grade Cape Code house. The earth shelter wins.

1784. Bartos, Michael. Underground buildings: energy savers. Civ. Eng., v. 49, no. 5, May 1979: 80-5.
Case histories illustrate various aspects of underground construction, energy conservation, and preservation of open space.

1785. The Beale solar-heated subterranean guest house. Moth. Earth N., no. 45, May/June 1977: 80.
A 16 x 30 ft. one-room plus bath cottage passively heated by direct solar radiation plus insulation of six inches of fiberglass in walls and ceilings, double-pane glass, set into the side of a south-facing hill.

1786. Bogart, J. Earth sheltered home has two floors and dozens of innovations. Workbench, v. 37, Jan./Feb. 1981: 80-4+.

1787. Brown, Denise. Family rebuilds after fire. Earth Shel. Dig. Energ. Rept., no. 12, Nov./Dec. 1980: 56.
An earth-bermed house was destroyed by lightning-caused fire. Roof windows with pull-down ladders in the owners' new house are described.

1788. Brown, Terry. Ancient simplicity meets modern art. Home Energ. Dig. Wood. Q., v. 5, no. 4, Spring 1981: 32-4.
The Arcadian Berm House design of architect Emilio Ambasz is described. The house is covered and surrounded by a gently sloping earth berm and is designed to use only 30 percent of the heating and cooling energy of a conventional house of the same size. Heat comes mainly from two large solar collectors.

1789. Campbell, Stu. Buried alive: the first year. Alt. Energ., no. 53, Jan./Feb. 1982: 8-11.
The author rented the house the first winter to a tenant who experienced moisture condensation problems because he didn't understand the ventilation needs and because he was only there on weekends. The source of the condensation problem was still-wet concrete.

1790. Carter, Dave. Why I dug in. Earth Shel. Dig. Energ. Rept., no. 8, Mar./Apr. 1980: 26-7.
This article is excerpted from the author's Digging in. He reveals that he did it because of high fuel costs.

1791. Dean, T. Earth-sheltered house versus super-insulated conventional home. Workbench, v. 39, Jan./Feb. 1983: 38+.

1792. A down-to-earth idea: the roof of this underground house provides great insulation and a spot for picnics. House Beaut., v. 124, Jan. 1982: 50+.

1793. Earth sheltered home saves fuel. Cottonwood Curr., Sept. 18, 1980.

1794. Edwards, Steve. Ideal home goes underground. Bldg. Des., no. 536, Mar. 13, 1981: 24.

1795. Family digs life together. Earth Shel. Dig. Energ. Rept., no. 5, Sept./Oct. 1979: 46-7.
This owner-builder is constructing a compound of earth-sheltered homes for his family members.

1796. Fowler, Beth and Tom Miller. Some earth shelter buying tips. Earth Shel. Liv., no. 41, Sept./Oct. 1985: 18.
The authors bought a 2,400 sq. ft. earth-sheltered home that was unfinished and had been on the market for two years.

1797. Fox, Greg. Low cost earth sheltered housing. Alt. Energ., no. 48, Mar./Apr. 1981.
This house cost less than $30/sq. ft. to build, qualified for FmHA financing and needed a half cord of wood to be heated last winter.

1798. Hultgren, Dale. Owners berm fourth home. Earth Shel. Liv., no. 28, July/Aug. 1983: 14-6.
This conventional house has berming and bentonite waterproofing.

1799. Johnson, Mark. Former bridge bridges style gap: builder believes model home makes best use of earth sheltering and superinsulation. Earth Shel. Liv., no. 36, Nov./Dec. 1984: 36-8.
This house is called Bridge House because its heavy timbers were taken from a demolished railroad bridge and because the house bridges the gap between superinsulated and earth-sheltered houses.

1800. Kramer, Ann. Shingling our home with a bulldozer. Earth Shel. Dig. Energ. Rept., no. 7, Jan./Feb. 1980: 35-6.
This is a humorous account of building the author's earth-sheltered home.

1801. La Tona, T. and V. La Tona. Earth sheltered home sited on city lot. Workbench, v. 39, Jan./Feb. 1983: 4-6+.

1802. La Tona, Vincent C. Sunburrows, an earth contact/passive solar development. In Proc., 4th Nat. Pass. Sol. Conf., Kansas City, MO, Oct. 3-5, 1979. G. Franta, ed. Newark, DE: Int. Sol. Energ. Soc., Am. Section, 1979. p. 644-7.

The paper discusses site and size considerations, financing for the homes and for the development, marketing strategy, and getting builders to construct speculative earth-contact homes.

1803. Laur, Jeff. Composite energy system designed. Earth Shel. Dig. Energ. Rept., no. 14, Mar./Apr. 1981: 17-20.

The author's earth-bermed envelope house has a composite energy system including active solar collectors, a water heater, heat pump, and a geothermal well.

1804. Lees, A. Earth sheltered, sod-roofed home. Pop. Sci., v. 217, Sept. 1980: 96-7.

1805. Little house moves on the prairie. Earth Shel. Liv., no. 26, Mar./Apr. 1983: 12-3.

The experience of moving an earth-sheltered house. It was a 779 sq. ft. fair display model which, because of being built of lumber, was heavier than expected.

1806. Machowski, Barb. High-end home is investment. Earth Shel. Liv., no. 23, Oct./Sept. 1982: 21-5.

This high-priced ($400,000) earth shelter was built to be 100 percent efficient in anticipation of rising energy costs.

1807. Model merits double exposure. Earth Shel. Dig. Energ. Rept., no. 17, Sept./Oct. 1981: 62.

A 1,296 sq. ft. earth-sheltered model designed by Richard Ohanian was shown at the Ohio State Fair in Aug. 1981 and at the Texas State Fair in Oct. 1981.

1808. Modular duo cuts costs. Earth Shel. Liv., no. 19, Jan./Feb. 1982: 47-8.

Two earth-sheltered homes built side by side were built by Central Pre-Mix of Spokane, WA and Bowen Construction of Post Falls, ID.

1809. Montgomery, T.E., C.D. Elifrits, and T.L. Holthusen. Earth-bermed passive-solar house: case study of an actual project. In The potential of earth-sheltered and underground space: proc., Undergr. Sp. Conf. and Expos., Kansas City, MO, June 8-10, 1981. T.L. Holthusen, ed. Elmsford, NY: Pergamon Pr., 1981. p. 191-208.

This paper discusses the decision and the plan to construct an earth-bermed passive solar house. Included are details of site considerations, architectural considerations, and a synopsis of the plans and specifications for the house.

1810. Morgan, William. Earth architecture: up to earth. Prog. Archit., v. 60, no. 4, Apr. 1979: 84-7.

Numerous examples of earth-related architecture in the U.S. built in the past 40 years are reviewed. The examples shown were designed before the energy crisis developed.

1811. Newman, Jerry O. and Luther C. Godbey. Multi-therm solar-earth house with retreat area - design considerations. In Proc., 1st Int. Conf. on Energ. Effic. Bldgs. with Earth Shel. Prot., Sydney, Aust., Aug. 1-6, 1983. L.L. Boyer, ed. Stillwater, OK: Okla. State Univ., Archit. Ext., 1983. p. 109-13.

An innovative house is a combination of features that have been pulled together into an integrated functional system. Therefore, the success or failure of innovative housing systems is measured as the resultant of its combined attributes which includes successful, partially successful, and unsuccessful features. To objectively evaluate such a system or house, one must dissect it and identify those components that should be perpetuated into future designs. The multi-therm, solar-earth house is a coalition of selected features or components that have been extracted from the Rural Housing Research Unit's (RHRU) solar-attic, solar-earth, greenhouse-residence, and other energy and cost-efficient designs. Features of the multi-therm will now be evaluated for use in future housing systems. The multi-therm house is a relatively small 1,000 sq. ft. three-bedroom residence; however, its effective size has been increased by adding an 800 sq. ft. live-in solar sunspace onto its south wall which provides an abundance of space for multiple household activities. --Auth. abstract.

1812. Radice, Phil. 20th century cliff dwellers. Empire Mag., Denver Post, Feb. 5, 1978: 16-8.

1813. Ruehl, Peter. Going underground in Hartford. Balt. Sun., Feb. 5, 1978.

1814. Schonberg, David. The floor-storage thermal-loop home. Moth. Earth N., no. 77, Sept. 1982: 144-6.

A 1,800 sq. ft., four-bedroom home with three walls built into the earth has walls of eight-inches thick reinforced poured concrete insulated on the outside with two-inch thick polystyrene. The plumbing is accessed by providing removable floor panels.

1815. Secrist, Don. Earth-sheltered homes in self-reliant villages. In Proc., 4th Nat. Pass. Sol. Conf., Kansas City, MO, Oct. 3-5, 1979. G. Franta, ed. Newark, DE: Int. Sol. Energ. Soc., Am. Sec., 1979. p. 762.
Self-reliant decentralized villages are planned by Solar-Earth Energy. They expect to achieve self reliance in five areas: the earth-sheltered passive solar home, the home's energy, transportation energy, food and water, plus products and knowledge to sell for additional profits.

1816. Slesin, Suzanne. Down to earth: two houses. N.Y. Times, Mar. 22, 1979: C1.

1817. Smay, V. Elaine. Year-round energy miser. Pop. Sci., v. 219, no. 2, Aug. 1981: 64-5.
This earth-sheltered house is built into a south-facing hillside and blanketed with 18 inches of earth. The alternative backup heat source is a heat pump.

1818. Solberg, Jean. Passive solar underground: a hybrid takes root. Alt. Energ., no. 39, Sept./Oct. 1979: 10-1.
The north and east sides of the author's passive/active solar wind-assisted home are earth covered.

1819. Steiger, R.W. and M.K. Hurd. Building underground. Concr. Constr., v. 23, no. 2, Feb. 1978: 90-5.
This introductory type of article discusses some of the best-known underground structures.

1820. Tracking the sale of an earth sheltered home. Earth Shel. Dig. Energ. Rept., no. 2, Mar./Apr. 1979: 9-10.
Earth-sheltered homes are hard to sell.

1821. Traylor, Everett. What to do in the meantime. Earth Shel. Liv., no. 40, July/Aug. 1985: 12-3.
The author has built models of earth-sheltered homes. He will build one when he retires and tells how he maintains his interest level and plans.

1822. Wells, Malcolm. An earth sheltered home. Blair Ketchums Ctry J., Sept. 1982: 48-51.

1823. Wistinghausen, N. Groundhouse: a low cost solar home. In Renewable alternatives: proc., 4th Sol. Energ. Soc. of

Can. Conf., London, Can., Aug. 20, 1978. Winnipeg, Can.: Sol. Energ. Soc. of Can., 1978.

This earth sheltered U-shaped concrete and steel structure features a private courtyard for light, a hydroponic integral greenhouse, and solar panels on the greenhouse for heat. Long range heat storage below the living room floor offers warmth even when the power has failed. The home is designed for economy, weather resistance, insulation quality, and the interior partitions are movable to suit growing families.

1824. Wolfe, Betty L. No place like an earth shelter. Earth Shel. Liv., no. 32, Mar./Apr. 1984: 31.

Her earth-sheltered home is everything she expected.

1825. Woods, Charles S. A designer looks at his house: a noted earth shelter designer tells what went right, and wrong, when building his home. Earth Shel. Liv., no. 34, July/Aug. 1984: 14-7.

The author designed and built a 1,100 sq. ft. earth-sheltered house consisting of two studios for him and his wife. He recommends a roof with no or very little earth on it. A super-insulated roof with ivy on it does well.

CONFERENCES CITED

1975

Symposium on the Development and Utilization of Underground Space, Kansas City, MO, Mar. 5-7, 1975. Proceedings. Washington, DC: National Science Foundation, 1975.
Alternatives in Energy Conservation: the Use of Earth Covered Buildings, Conference, Fort Worth, TX, July 9-12, 1975. Proceedings. Frank L. Moreland, ed. Washington, DC: U.S. G.P.O., 1976.

1976

IAHS International Symposium on Housing Problems, Atlanta, GA, 1976. Proceedings. Parvis F. Rad, ed. Coral Gables, FL: International Association for Housing Science, 1976. 2 vols.
Alternative Energy Sources Conference: Technology and Applications for Minnesota, Minneapolis, MN, April 1976.

1977

Aspen Energy Forum, 4th, May 27-29, 1977. Workshop on Solar Energy Applications. Solar architecture: proceedings. Ann Arbor, MI: Ann Arbor Science Publishers, Inc., 1978.
International Solar Energy Society, American Section, Annual Meeting, Orlando, FL, June 6, 1977. Proceedings. Cape Canaveral, FL: International Solar Energy Society, 1977.
Solar Energy Society of Canada, Conference, 3rd, Edmonton, Alberta, Can., Aug. 22, 1977. Solar energy update '77. Edmonton, Alberta, Can.: University of Alberta, 1977.
Going Under to Stay on Top, Minneapolis, MN, Oct. 1977. Residential applications: transcripts of selected presentations. Minneapolis, MN: University of Minnesota, Underground Space Center, 1979. 174 p.

1978

National Passive Solar Conference, 2nd, Philadelphia, PA, Mar.

16-18, 1978. Proceedings. Newark, DE: International Solar
Energy Society, American Section, 1978.

Alternatives in Habitat: the Use of Earth Covered Settlements,
Conference, Fort Worth, TX, May 17-19, 1978. Proceedings.
Frank L. Moreland, ed. Washington, DC: U.S. Dept. of Energy, 1979. 2 vols. Vol. 1: Earth covered buildings: technical
notes. Vol. 2: Earth covered buildings and settlements.

Earth Sheltered Housing Workshop, Helena, MT, July 13, 1978.
Proceedings. Helena, MT: Montana Dept. of Natural Resources and Conservation, Energy Division, 1978. 105 p.

Solar Northwest Conference, Portland, OR, July 14, 1978.
Proceedings.

Solar Energy Society of Canada, Conference, 4th, London, Can.,
Aug. 20, 1978. Renewable alternatives. Winnipeg, Can.:
Solar Energy Society of Canada, 1978.

International Solar Energy Society, American Section, Annual
Meeting, Denver, CO, Aug. 28, 1978. Solar diversification.
Newark, DE: International Solar Energy Society, American
Section, 1978. 2 vols.

American Underground Association, Annual Meeting, Toronto,
Can., Oct. 1978.

Midwest Energy Conference, Chicago, IL, Nov. 1978.

American Society of Agricultural Engineers, Winter Meeting,
Chicago, IL, Dec. 18-20, 1978. Papers. St. Joseph, MO:
ASAE, 1978.

1979

National Passive Solar Conference, 3rd, San Jose, CA, Jan.
11-13, 1979. Proceedings. Newark, DE: International Solar
Energy Society, American Section, 1979.

National Conference and Exhibition on Technology for Energy
Conservation, 3rd, Tucson, AZ, Jan. 22, 1979. Silver Spring,
MD: Information Transfer, 1979.

American Society for Engineering Education, College Industry
Education Conference, Tampa, FL, Jan. 29-Feb. 2, 1979.
Proceedings.

American Underground Association, Annual Meeting and Underground Housing Conference, Kansas City, MO, Mar. 1979.

U'Bahn International Earth Sheltered Conference, Granite City,
IL, Mar. 1979.

American Underground Association, Conference, Atlanta, GA,
June 1979.

International Conference on Environmental Psychology, University of Surrey, Guildford, Eng., July 16-20, 1979.

National Passive Solar Conference, 4th, Kansas City, MO, Oct.
3-5, 1979. Proceedings. G. Franta, ed. Newark, DE: International Solar Energy Society, American Section, 1979.

299 Conferences Cited

International Conference on Energy Use Management, Los Angeles, CA, Oct. 22, 1979. Changing energy use futures. New York, NY: Pergamon Press, 1979.

Annual Solar Heating and Cooling Systems Operational Results Conference, Colorado Springs, CO, Nov. 27, 1979.

DOE/ASHRAE Conference, Orlando, FL, Dec. 1979. Thermal performance of the exterior envelopes of buildings..

American Society of Agricultural Engineers, Winter Meeting, New Orleans, LA, Dec. 11-14, 1979. Papers, St. Joseph, MO: ASAE, 1979.

1980

UMR-DNR Conference on Energy, 7th, University of Missouri - Rolla, 1980. Rolla, MO: Univ. of Missouri, 1980.

Solar Passive and Hybrid Cooling, DOE Conference, Washington, DC, Feb. 1980.

American Underground Space Association, Annual Meeting, Minneapolis, MN, Apr. 1980.

Earth Sheltered Housing Conference and Exhibition, 1st, Minneapolis, MN, Apr. 9-11, 1980. Earth shelter 2: collected papers. Minneapolis, MN: University of Minnesota, Underground Space Center, 1980. 236 p.

Earth Sheltered Building Design Innovations, Oklahoma City, OK, Apr. 18, 1980. Proceedings. Lester L. Boyer, ed. Stillwater, OK: Oklahoma State University, 1980.

International Solar Energy Society, American Section, Annual Meeting, Phoenix, AZ, June 2, 1980. Proceedings.

Western SUN 1980 Solar Update Conference, Salt Lake City, UT, Sept. 24, 1980.

National Passive Solar Conference, 5th, Amherst, MA, Oct. 19-26, 1980. Proceedings. Newark, DE: International Solar Energy Society, American Section, 1980.

International Conference on Alternative Energy Sources, 3rd, Miami Beach, FL, Dec. 1980. Washington, DC: Hemisphere Pub. Corp., 1983.

1981

Earth Integration for Cooling Seminar, Oklahoma State University, 1981. Proceedings.

DOE Solar Passive and Hybrid Cooling Update Conference, Oakland, CA, Jan. 1981.

Passive Solar and Earth-Sheltered Housing Conference, Birmingham, AL, Feb. 19, 1981.

Earth-Sheltered Farm Building Conference, West Lafayette, IN, Mar. 5, 1981.

Passive Solar Earth-Sheltered Construction Training Seminar, St. Louis, MO, May 1-2, 1981.
International Solar Energy Society, American Section, Annual Meeting, Philadelphia, PA, May 26, 1981. Proceedings.
Underground Space Conference and Exposition, Kansas City, MO, June 8-10, 1981. The potential of earth-sheltered and underground space: proceedings. T.L. Holthusen, ed. Elmsford, NY: Pergamon Press, 1981. 503 p.
American Society of Engineering Education, 89th Annual Meeting, Los Angeles, CA, June 21, 1981. Education and industry, a joint endeavor: proceedings. Washington, DC: ASEE, 1981.
American Society of Agricultural Engineers, Annual Meeting, Orlando, FL, June 21-24, 1981.
National Passive Solar Conference, 6th, Portland, OR, Sept. 8-12, 1981. Progress in passive solar energy.
Earth Shelter Performance and Evaluation, National Technical Conference, 2nd, Tulsa, OK, Oct. 16-17, 1981. Conference proceedings. Stillwater, OK: Oklahoma State University, Architectural Extension, 1981.
International Passive and Hybrid Cooling Conference, Miami Beach, FL, Nov. 6-16, 1981. Passive cooling: proceedings. Newark, DE: International Solar Energy Society, American Section, 1981.
International Solar Energy Society, Australian and New Zealand Section, Macquarie University, North Ryde, Australia, Nov. 25-27, 1981. Solar energy at work: proceedings.
DOE-ORN/ASTM Conference, Clearwater Beach, FL, Dec. 8-11, 1981.
Conference on Thermal Insulation Materials and Systems for Energy Conservation in the '80s, Florida, Dec. 1981. Proceedings.

1982

American Society of Civil Engineers, Conference, 1982.
International Solar Energy Society, American Section, Annual Meeting, 1982. Proceedings.
American Society of Mechanical Engineers, Solar Energy Conference, Albuquerque, NM, Apr. 26, 1982. Solar engineering. New York, NY: ASME, 1982.
Symposium on Design Strategies for Earth Covered Buildings, May 8-9, 1982. Proceedings. S.A. Baggs, ed. Kensington, NSW, Australia: University of New South Wales, Graduate School of the Built Environment, 1982.
American Council for an Energy Efficient Economy, Conference, Santa Cruz, CA, Aug. 1982. Proceedings.
Energex '82: a Forum on Energy Self-Reliance: Conservation,

Production and Consumption, Regina, Saskatchewan, Can., Aug. 23-29, 1982. Conference proceedings. Fred A. Curtis, ed. Winnipeg, Can.: Solar Energy Society of Canada, 1982.
Passive and Hybrid Energy Conference, DOE, Washington, DC, Sept. 1982.
International PLEA Conference, 1st, Bermuda, Sept. 13-15, 1981. Passive and low energy alternatives I. New York, NY: Pergamon Press, 1982.
Forming Economical Concrete Buildings, International Conference, Lincolnshire, IL, Nov. 8-10, 1982. Proceedings.

1983

ASHRAE (American Society of Heating, Refrigeration and Air Conditioning) Conference, Atlantic City, NJ, Jan. 1983.
National Bureau of Standards, Center for Building Technology Conference: Thermal Properties of Soil and Earth Contact Heat Transfer, Mar. 1983.
American Solar Energy Society, Annual Meeting, Minneapolis, MN, June 1983. Proceedings.
International Conference on Passive and Low Energy Alternatives, 2nd, Crete, Greece, June 28-July 1, 1983. Proceedings. Oxford, Eng.: Pergamon Press, 1983.
International Conference on Energy Efficient Buildings with Earth Shelter Protection, 1st, Sydney, Australia, Aug. 1-6, 1983. Proceedings. L.L. Boyer, ed. Stillwater, OK: Oklahoma State University, Architectural Extension, 1983. And Australasian proceedings. S.A. Baggs, ed. Kensington, NSW, Australia: Unisearch, Ltd., 1983.

SERIALS CITED

Adobe Today

The Advertiser (Adelaide)

African Arts   Afr. Arts

Age (Melbourne)

Alternative Sources of Energy   Alt. Energ.

American Institute of Architects   AIA J.
  Journal

American Mercury   Am. Mer.

American Society of Agricultural   ASAE Trans.
  Engineers, Transactions

American Society of Civil   ASCE Proc.
  Engineers, Proceedings

American Way   Am. Way

Annual Review of Energy   Annu. R. Energ.

Applewood Journal   Applewood J.

Architects' Journal   Archit. J.

Architectural and Engineering News   Archit. Eng. N.

Architectural Digest   Archit. Dig.

Architectural Forum   Archit. For.

Architectural Record   Archit. Rec.

Architectural Science Review   Archit. Sci. R.

Serials Cited

Architecture and Urbanism: Kenchiku to toshi (Tokyo)	Archit. Urb.
Architecture Australia	Archit. Aust.
Architecture Minnesota	Archit. Minn.
Architecture Plus	Archit. Plus
The Arizona Republic	Ariz. Repub.
Art in America	Art Amer.
Arts and Architecture	Arts Archit.
American Society of Heating, Refrigerating and Air Conditioning Engineering, Transactions.	ASHRAE Trans.
Australian House and Garden	Aust. House Gard.
Baltimore Sun	Balt. Sun
Belle (Sydney)	
Better Homes and Gardens	Bet. Homes Gard.
Blair Ketchum's Country Journal	Ctry. J.
Boston Magazine	Bost. Mag.
Building	
Building Design (London)	Bldg. Des.
Building Economist (Sydney)	Bldg. Econ.
Building Ideas (Sydney)	Bldg. Ideas
Building Progress	Bldg. Prog.
Building Research: the Journal of the Building Research Institute	Bldg. Res.
Building Systems Design	Bldg. Syst. Des.

Buildings

California Real Estate   Calif. R. Est.

Charette (Pennsylvania Society
   of Architects)

Chartered Quantity Surveyor   Chart. Quant. Surv.

Christian Science Monitor   Chr. Sci. Mon.

Civil Engineering   Civ. Eng.

Coeur d'Alene Press

CoEvolution Quarterly   CoEv. Q.

Concrete Construction   Concr. Constr.

Concrete Quarterly   Concr. Q.

Congressional Record   Cong. Rec.

Construction Specifier   Constr. Spec.

Consumer's Research   Consum. Res.

Cottonwood Current (Lyon County,   Cottonwood Curr.
   KS).

Country Life   Ctry. Life

Crosswinds (Albany)

Current Health (Highwood, IL)   Curr. Hlth.

Daily Pacific Builder (San   Daily Pac. Build.
   Francisco, CA)

Dallas Morning News   Dallas Morn. N.

Denver Post

Design Action   Des. Act.

Domus (Milan)

305 Serials Cited

Dynamic Years	Dyn. Yrs.
Earth Journal (Minneapolis, MN)	Earth J.
Earth Sheltered Buildings - Technical Papers (Tempe, AZ: Arizona State University, College of Architecture, 1983-)	Earth Shel. Bldgs. - Tech. Pap.
Earth Shelter Digest & Energy Report	Earth Shel. Dig. Energ. Rept.
Earth Shelter Living	Earth Shel. Liv.
Economist	
Electrical World	Elect. World
Energy (Oxford)	
Energy & Alternatives	Energ. Alt.
Engineering Journal (Montreal)	Eng. J.
Environmental Comment (Washington, DC: Urban Land Institute)	Env. Com.
Eye of the Falcon (Ottertail County, MN)	
Family Handyman	Fam. Hand.
Family Weekly	Fam.W.
Farmstead	
Fine Homebuilding	Fine Homebldg.
Fire Journal	Fire J.
Florida Architect	Fla. Archit.
Ford Times	
The Futurist	

Geotecture: Journal of the
Geotecture International Association (Chatswood, NSW, Australia)

Heating and Ventilating Engineer and Journal of Air Conditioning (London)

Home Energy Digest and Wood Burning Quarterly (Minneapolis, MN)

Home Plan Ideas, Better Homes and Gardens (Des Moines, IA)

Horizon

House and Garden

House Beautiful

Housing

Housing and Society

Interiors

International Journal of Housing Science and Its Application (Elmsford, NY)

Journal of Social, Political and Economic Studies

Journal of Solar Energy Engineering

Journal of the Soil Mechanics and Foundations Division, American Society of Civil Engineers

Kansas City Star

Ladies' Home Journal

Landscape

Landscape Architecture

Learning How (Howe Furniture Corp.)

Geotecture

Heat. Vent. Engr. J. Air Cond.

Home Energ. Dig. Wood. Q.

Home Plan Ideas

House Gard.

House Beaut.

Hous. Soc.

Int. J. Hous. Sci. Appl.

J. Soc. Pol. Econ. Stud.

J. Sol. Energ. Eng.

J. Soil Mech. Found. Div., ASCE

Kan. City Star

Ladies' Home J.

Land. Archit.

Serials Cited

Life	
Lighting Research and Technology (London)	Light Res. Tech.
Living Alternatives	Liv. Alt.
Log Home Builder and Alternative Housing	Log Home Build. Alt. Hous.
Los Angeles Times	L.A. Times
Maclean's	
Mainlines (United Airlines)	
Mechanical Engineering	Mech. Eng.
Mechanix Illustrated	Mech. Illus.
Medical Economics	Med. Econ.
Military Engineer	Mil. Engr.
Milwaukee Journal	Milw. J.
Minneapolis Tribune	Mpls. Trib.
Moneysworth	
Mother Earth News	Moth. Earth N.
Multi-Housing News	Multi-Hous. N.
National Association of Home Builders, Builder	NAHB Build.
National Association of Home Builders, Journal-Scope	NAHB J.-Scope
The National Experience	Nat. Exper.
National Geographic	Nat. Geog.
National Geographic World	Nat. Geog. World
Navy Civil Engineer	Nav. Civ. Engr.

New Mexico Architecture					N.M. Archit,

New Mexico Magazine					N.M. Mag.

New Roots

Rodale's New Shelter					New Shel.

New York Times						N.Y. Times

News World

Newsweek

North Dakota REC (Rural Electric Cooperatives) Magazine					N.D. REC Mag.

Ohio Farmer						Ohio Farm.

Omni

Orbit Magazine: the Sunday Oklahoman					Orb. Mag.

Organic Gardening					Org. Gard.

The Owner Builder (Berkeley, CA)			Own. Build.

Owner Builder (Melbourne)				Own. Build. (Melbourne)

People

Philadelphia Magazine					Phila. Mag.

Planning, S.A. (South Australia)

Plant Energy Management				Plant Energ. Mgmt.

Popular Mechanics					Pop. Mech.

Popular Science						Pop. Sci.

Process: Architecture (Tokyo)				Proc.: Archit.

Progressive Architecture				Prog. Archit.

Serials Cited

Real Estate Today	R. Est. Today
Realites	
Residential Interiors	Res. Int.
Royal Institute of British Architects, Journal	RIBA J.
Rochester Times-Union	Roch. Times-Union
Rolling Stone	Roll. Stone
Rural Electric Nebraskan	Rur. Electr. Neb.
Rural Minnesota News (Alexandria, MN)	Rur. Minn. N.
Sacramento Bee	Sac. Bee
St. Paul Pioneer Press	St. Paul Pion. Pr.
Science Digest	Sci. Dig.
The Sciences	
Seattle Post-Intelligencer Northwest	Seattle Post-Intel. N.W.
Seller/Servicer	Sell./Serv.
Smithsonian	
Solar Age	Sol. Age
Solar Energy	Sol. Energ.
Solar Progress	Sol. Prog.
Southern Living	South. Liv.
Sports Afield	
Subterranea Britannica	Sub. Brit.
Successful Farming	Suc. Farm.

Sunpaper

Sunset

Sunworld

Times (London)

Today's Health   Today's Hlth.

Toronto Sun   Tor. Sun.

The Tribune (New Albany, IN)

Underground Space: the Journal of   Undergr. Sp.
  the American Underground Space
  Association

Underline

Uniken (Kensington, NSW, Australia:
  University of New South Wales)

The UNSW Quarterly (Kensington, NSW,   UNSW Q.
  Australia: University of New South
  Wales)

Venture

Vogue Living (Sydney)

Wall Street Journal   W. St. J.

Washington Post   Wash. Post

Washington Star   Wash. Star

Wentworth Institute Bulletin   Went. Inst. Bull.

Winds of Change (Winters, CA)

Wisconsin State Journal   Wisc. State J.

Workbench

AUTHOR INDEX

Abercrombie, C.F. 1295
Adams, Larry 1008
Advanced Waterproofing, Inc. 576
Ahmed, Syed Faruq 618
Ahrens, Donna 380
Aiken, Roger G. 986, 1057
Akridge, James M. 203, 735-736, 1260
Alabama Energy Extension Service 2
Alcorn, Jane 1464
Al-Jeda, T. 1256
Allan, Jerry 800
Allen, Gerald E. 419
Allen, Jonathan M. 1107
Allen, Peter C. 801
American Underground Space Association 1009-1010
American Underground Space Association. Iowa Chapter. 3.
Anderson, Brent 394-395, 557, 577-580, 802-804, 1296.
Anderson, Carol 4
Anderson, Philip B. 291
Anderson, Richard 627
Andre, John 396
Andreadaki-Chronaki, Eleni 272
Angel, Craig 581
Appleton, Bonnie L. 846
Apthorp, D. 743
Ashelman, Randall B. 1753
Atchison, Tom 1012
Atkinson, Larry J. 1244
Aughenbaugh, Nolan B. 216

757, 814, 988, 1002, 1135, 1324
Autumn Architecture Research Group 1108

Baggs, David W. 8, 18, 218, 293, 400, 558, 582, 644, 808, 847, 1262-1266, 1313-1316
Baggs, Joan C. 218, 582, 645, 808, 1266
Baggs, Kate L. 922
Baggs, Sydney A. 9, 10-18, 170, 217-220, 254, 582, 805-808, 848-849, 923-924, 954, 969, 1175, 1266-1274, 1317
Bailey, Brian 401, 1193
Baker, D. 273
Balcomb, J. Douglas 620
Balsara, J.P. 438
Bambert, A.E. 1090
Bannon-Harwood, Barbara 19, 583
Bargabus, Dave 402
Barker, Joel 925
Barker, Michael B. 1069, 1110
Barnard, John E., Jr. 20, 294, 1293, 1506, 1783
Barnes, Paul R. 1111, 1261
Barnes, Steven R. 618
Barney, Alice Eichold 1389
Bartos, Michael 1784
Baum, Gregory T. 21
Beadles, Joyce 1515

Bechtel, Robert B. 926
Becklian, Barbara 621
Bedell, Berkley 1070
Behr, Richard A. 403-405, 868-869, 1307, 1721
Bell, J.L. 927
Belsheim, Rod W. 694
Benedict, Frederic A. 646, 1194
Bennett, David J. 221, 899, 1112-1113
Bennett, Leonard E. 1493
Bennett, Randy 406
Benton, Charles C. 203, 1260
Berkowitz, Paul I. 1246
Berman, Jean 989
Bethany, Marilyn 22
Bibliographic Research Library, San Jose, CA 204
Bice, Thomas Neal 647-648, 661
Bircher, Tad L. 737, 1247-1250
Blake, Peter 1195
Blick, E.R. 738
Bligh, Thomas P. 23-26, 295-297, 559-562, 569, 649-659, 739-748, 782, 870, 1113
Bliss, Steve 1625
Block, David A. 1474
Bloedoorn, Seph 1530
Boeing Co., Seattle, WA 622
Boer, Andrew J. 21
Bogart, J. 1786
Bohn, C. 408
Bolton, Steve 1695
Booker, Frank 27
Boubel, Gary A. 405, 871, 1307, 1720-1721
Bourdier, Jean-Paul 274
Bowen, A. 275
Boyer, Lester L. 28-31, 298-299, 358-359, 648, 660, 684, 686-687, 759, 761, 900-904, 970-973, 987, 1176, 1290, 1297-1299, 1684

Brann, Donald R. 409
Branson, Gary 1502
Bregg, Gary 872
Bregman, Lillian 1701
Brent Anderson Associates, Inc. 300
Bressler, Gary 873
Brite, Steve E. 713, 893
Brown, Denise 1787
Brown, G.Z. 810
Brown, James J. 410, 563, 585, 874
Brown, Terry 32, 1358, 1788
Brown, F.R. 1013
Brubaker, S.E. 116
Buck, Claudia 1390
Bumke, David 1516, 1716
Burgess, Debora 34
Burgess, Hugh 1374
Burnett, Ronald A. 36
Burns, Donna M. 586
Burnside, Brad 421
Busch, Akiko 1196

Cabonne, Pierre 37
Calvert, Terri 413
Cambell, Stu 38, 1789
Capoccia, Stephen 39
Cargo, Douglas B. 223, 966
Carleton, Joseph G. 965
Carmody, John C. 180-181, 276, 748, 895, 990, 1005, 1057, 1171, 1245, 1545
Carpenter, E.E. 1198
Carter, David 40-41, 414, 1199, 1790
Carter, Douglas N. 1116-1117
Carter, Joe 1685
Carter, M.W. 954
Chalmers, Larry S. 302
Chamberlain, David 1731
Cheng-Chuan-Shih, J. see Shih, Jason C.
Chester, C.V. 1091, 1261

Childress, R.S. 403
Christensen, Keith H. 1092-1093
Clark, Rod 905
Clearinghouse for Earth Covered Settlements see Texas University at Arlington. Clearinghouse for Earth Covered Settlements
Cole, Robert S. 255, 277, 284
Collins, Belinda Lowenhaupt 928-929
Collins, J.B. 906
Colliver, D.G. 749
Combs, E. Raedene 1024
Coober Pedy Community School 1319
Cook, G. Robert 419
Cook, Jeffrey 187
Cook, Marcia J. 931
Cooper, B.L. 44
Costello, Michael J. 811-812
Cottrell, Richard 420
Cristy, George A. 750, 893, 1091, 1261
Croley, Victor A. 256
Crosbie, Michael J. 278
Croston, Dennis I. 1744
Cunningham, Gregory W. 623
Cunningham, Kim 45
Curry, Marianne 932
Czarnecki, M. 1342

Dahlin, Dennis 1475
Dalton, Ann P. 907
Daly, Les 1359
Daniel, James I. 421
Darvas, Robert M. 422
Davidoff, Linda 991
Davies, Gary R. 666
Davis, Andy 1451
Davis, Evelyn 912

Davis, Martin A. 355, 915-916
Davis William B. 751
Davy, James 423
Dawson, Sue 1671
Dean, Andrea O. 49, 1391, 1430-1431
Dean, Tom 50, 1791
DeBord, David Douglas 813
DeCourcy Hinds, Michael 876
Dempewolff, Richard F. 51-52
Deppen, Dave 53-54, 224
Derr, Douglas 276
DeSaventhem, E.M. 1017
Diamond, Stuart 55
Dick, Chester J., Jr. 424
Dieckmann, Larry 1174
Dike, G.A. 667
Dimitriadou, E. 280
Dirr, T. 752
Dixon, John Morris 1444
Doney, Carl 1378
Donovan, Hamester and Rattien, Inc. 1018
Drucker, E.E. 669
Duffy, Brian J. 908
Duke, Buford W., Jr. 1125
Dunbar, Thomas R. 813
Duncan, James M. 426-427, 505
Dunlop, R. 1321
Dupont, William C. 753
Dynamic Integrations, Fairlee, VT 316

Earth Habitats 428
Earth Integrated Technics, Inc. 317
Earth Shelters, Inc. 205
Earth Systems, Inc. 430
Eckert, E.R.G. 744, 755
Edelhart, Mike 63, 322
Edmund Scientific Co. 1627

Edwards, Steve 1794
Effective Building Products, Inc. 588
Egerstrom, Lee 1544
Eggert, Jim 64
Eijadi, David A. 899
Eikens, Ron 890
Elias, Michel R. 829
Elifrits, C. Dale 756-757, 814, 1809
Eller, Kenneth R. 589
Ellison, Tom 380, 1545
Ellison Design and Construction 323
Elmer, Donald B. 768
Elnicky, Gail 1005
Emery, A.F. 671-672, 878
Engelken, Ruth 279
Erb, Ellsworth R., III 433
Ernst, F. Gene 1485
Evans, N. 688
Evans, R.S. 673-674

Fagan, Pat 1592
Fagerson, M. 690
Fairhurst, Charles 226, 675-676
Fanchiotti, A. 280
Farnan, William 181
Faubion, Roy 1689
Feduniw, Leon O. 436
Feeck, Jeanne 1210
Fehr, Robert L. 749
Feisel, Lyle L. 674, 677, 879, 1709-1710
Feleki, Henry 1660
Filler, Martin 1738
Filmart Productions, Inc. 78
Findley, Stephen M. 887
Firbank, James J. 437
Fischer, Hank 1020
Fitzgerald, Daniel K. 760, 971
Fitz-Hugh, Sarah 590
Flannery, Herschel K. 1711

Flathau, W.J. 438
Flecknoe-Brown, A.E. 591
Flint, Benny 281
Flouquet, Francoise 710
Foehr, Stephen 1635
Ford, Barbara 1643
Forster, David J. 1323
Forwood, Bruce 626
Fossum, J.E. 403
Foster, Eugene L. 227
Foute, Steven J. 966
Fowler, Beth 1796
Fox, Greg 1797
Frank, Robert 66
Franks, James 67
Frenette, Edward R. 325-326
Friedberg, M. Paul 850
Friedman, Jonathan Block 327
Furst, Terry 68, 328

Gagen, Joe 1131
Gangnes, David 69
Garcia-Chavez, Jose R. 851
Garland, Mark A. 1094-1096
Garland, Steven R. 852
Geery, Daniel 1133
Gelder, John 1251
Germer, Jerry 1550, 1625
Gettings, T.L. 1453
Gilbert, D.A. 1294
Gillies, A.D.S. 756-757, 1324
Givoni, Baruch 72, 758
Glenn-Wells, Sam 387
Godbey, Luther C. 355, 787, 916, 1811
Golany, Gideon S. 75, 1252-1253
Goldberg, Louis F. 678-683
Goldberger, Paul 1394
Goldfinger, Myron 282
Golubski, Steven E. 1593
Goodykoontz, James R. 1395
Gordon, Ann 853-854
Gordon, Harry 1703

Gorman, James 76-77
Grald, E.W. 650
Gray, Donald H. 855
Green, Bruce Hamilton 79-80, 440-441, 627, 1135
Green, Larry 81
Green, Melvyn 1021
Green, Terence M. 82
Greenland, J.J. 1284
Grendell, Eric A. 933
Griffith, Kenneth J. 466
Grigson, Geoffrey 1361
Grondzik, Walter T. 83, 299, 648, 660-662, 684-687, 759-761, 900-901, 934, 971-974, 979, 987, 1290, 1298-1299
Gruber, K.A. 593
Guy, Homer L. 880

Hadley, Philip 1325
Hagen, Gary C. 1753
Haggard, Gail 132, 1638
Hagstrom, Jim V. 856
Haines, J.T. 669
Hait, John 762-765
Hall, Charles L. 258
Hamburger, Richard 651, 1076-1077
Hammes, Jeffrey L. 594, 815
Hanna, A.M. 688, 766
Hanna, S.A. 766
Hannula, John Karl 228, 816
Hanzal-Kashi, Amy 1023-1024
Haponski, Don 1436
Haran, Siva Kumar 760
Harding, D. 1410
Harrington, K. 772, 776
Harris, Ron 84
Harrison, Lloyd, Jr. 881, 992
Harrison, Robert E. 485, 1603
Hassall, David N.H. 442
Haupert, David 329, 443, 1594
Hauser, Leroy 993

Hausmann, Manfred R. 540-541
Haves, P. 719
Hawkins, Donald 330
Hawley, J. 1668
Hayeem, E. 1254
Haynes, George 1551
Hayward, Roy 1385
Heerwagen, D.R. 671-672, 878
Helm, Bob 979-980
Herman, L. Vance 86
Heyder, Katherine 259
Higgs, Forrest S. 1025
Hines, Thomas S. 1396
Hlavin, A.C. 1137
Hodges, Laurent 1474, 1480
Hodgkinson, Allan 817
Hoff, Eric 1138
Holland, Elizabeth 332, 1739
Hollon, Steven D. 935, 939
Holmes, William Whittaker 767
Holthusen, T. Lance 508, 1809
Hopkins, Nigel 1326
Horsbrugh, Patrick 229-232
Houghton, Dean 1139
Hourmanesh, Mo 768
Hourmanesh, Ray 768
Huet, Olivier 1362-1363
Huggins, Geoffrey G. 1741
Hughey, Joseph B. 936
Hull, M. 445
Hultgren, Dale 1798
Humphrey, John B. 1673
Hurd, M.K. 1819
Hurst, Homer T. 446
Hutchinson, M. 690
Hutson, Ken 1554
Hylton, Joe 91, 333-334, 628, 691, 818

Impson, Loren C. 447-448
Ingersoll, John 937
Irwin, Colin B. 1275, 1283

Isaacson, Paul 335
Isakson, H.R. 1026
Israel, Frank 1214

Jackewicz, Shirley A. 1454
Jacobs, Sol 994
Jacobson, Sebby Wilson 1645-1646
Jaffe, Martin 161
Jansson, B. 94
Jenkins, David 1138
Jensen, Harley R. 453
Jensen, Rodney 1097
Johnson, B.R. 878
Johnson, Jay M. 1141
Johnson, Jim 1215, 1397
Johnson, Mark 1799
Johnson, Richard F. 938, 975
Johnson, Terry A. 206, 410, 454, 563, 585, 629, 874, 1098
Johnston, Timothy L. 686, 759, 761, 900, 903, 1691
Jones, C.D. 692
Jones, D. Earl 819
Jones, Edward 95
Jones, Jeremy A. 302
Jones, LaVerne Koelsch 207-208
Jones, Lloyd S. 96-97
Jones, Mary 1762

Kahn, Terry 1027
Karpinski, David 1078
Katomski, Jim 1138
Katz, Martin A. 769
Kawecki, Joseph J. 1675
Kearney, Robert P. 909
Keating, Bern 98
Keehn, Pauline A. 209
Keipert, J.D. 1276
Kellet, S. 1216
Kendall, Philip C. 935, 939

Kennedy, Richard J. 255, 283-284, 1662
Kern, Barbara 99
Kern, Ken 99
Kiesling, Ernst W. 403-405. 868, 1099-1100, 1307-1308, 1720-1721
Kilroy, Karen 1722
Kim, Heung Gon 1286-1287
Kimber, Wayne, Jr. 456, 693-694
Kimura, K. 770
Kinney, L.F. 667
Kippenhan, C.J. 671-672, 878
Kis, Babette 857
Kistler, Eugene C. 457
Klepper, M.R. 820
Kliewer, Tim 336
Klodt, Gerald 142, 458
Klump, E.H. 459
Knapp, Gifford 1490
Kneebone, T. 1079
Kneeland, William F. 630, 1300
Kness, Roger 733
Knoll, Frank 1080-1081
Knoth, B.H. 659, 741, 743, 782
Kobet, Bob 1703
Kommendant, August E. 1142
Konarske, Jim 695
Korell, Mark L. 1028
Kramer, Ann 858, 940-941, 1800
Kramer, Charlene Kahlor 100
Kremers, Jack Alan 1676
Kubota, H. 696
Kuehn, Thomas H. 771, 796, 798
Kumar, Sudhir 1255, 1258
Kusuda, Tamami 821

Labs, Kenneth B. 101, 187, 210, 233-234, 260-262, 631,

772-777, 822-827, 995,
    1029, 1082, 1291
Lage, David 1703
Lambert, Brian 1698
Landa, Edward R. 955-956
Lane, Barbara 1555
Lane, Charles A. 102-106,
    595-596, 632, 682, 778,
    828, 883, 1556
Langa, Frederic S. 568
Langewiesche, Wolfgang 107
Langfeldt, Steffen 910
Langley, John B. 460-462,
    779, 829, 884, 1305-1306
La Nier, Royce, 235, 967, 1083
Lash, David Michael 463
La Tona, T. 1801
La Tona, Vincent C. 1801-1802
Laubach, Darrell 402
Laufer, A. 464
Laukes, Jim 1677
Laur, Jeff 1803
LaVigne, A.B. 697
Lawler, Barry 236
Leach, V.A. 954
Lee, Orville G. 1084
Lee, Vincent 1782
Lees, Al W. 108-109, 337-345, 633, 1519, 1804
Lefebvre, Guy 427
Legorreta, Ricardo 1367
Lesiuk, Stephen 830, 859
Levy, M.T. 1467
Lewis, Linda 1749
Li, Lindsay 1511
Linton, Marilyn 110
Liu, Tony C. 473
Loker, Rex 465
Lord, David 957, 1365
Lorenz, Ray 112-113
Lowing, Arnold E. 346, 466-469, 597
Lu, John C.M. 860
Luhrsen, Wolfgang 710
Lunde, Martin R. 470-471, 698, 780, 885

Lunstrum, Kurt 472
Lytton, Robert 831

MacArthur, J.W. 781
McClarin, Jim 115
McCray, J.W. 116
McCreath, D.R. 701
McCrone, Susan J. 117
McDill, Dana 1559
Macdonald, Angus W. 1663, 1742
McDonald, James E. 473
McFadden, Charles B. 263
McFadden, Pamm 1220
McGough, Kenis 1031
McGrath, D.J. 474
McGroarty, Bryan W. 347, 598-601
McGuire, Steve 1301
Machowski, Barb 118, 285,
    699-700, 886, 911, 1144-1145, 1277, 1379, 1398,
    1520, 1558, 1596, 1609,
    1648, 1763-1766, 1806
Macintosh, James C., Jr. 21
McKinney, Robin 1637
McKown, Cora 912, 943-944
    949, 976-977, 983-984,
    1723
McNeil, R.D. 674, 677
McWilliams, Donald B. 887
Mair, Robert W. 1146, 1327
Malott, R.W. 1146
Manion, Thomas 1503
Mann, Colin 1278
Mansfield, Jerry W. 211, 1147
Manson, Dean A. 1032
Marcum, D.S. 1499
Marier, Don 119-121
Marsh, Jacqui 1352
Martin, A.A. 1137
Martindale, David 120
Mason, Roy 237, 996
Mason, Susan 1033

Matthews, Mindy A. 1438
May, H. 958
Meanor, Linda L. 1702
Meier, R.L. 238
Meissner, John 1344
Meixel, George D., Jr. 560-561, 569, 653, 657, 717, 740, 742, 748, 782, 793, 1148
Mendenhall, Norman 239
Meter, Ken 1221
Metz, Don 240, 348-350, 475, 602, 1619
Meyer, William T. 888
Miley, N. 696
Miller, J.R. 997
Miller, Thomas R. 351
Miller, Tom 1796
Milliner, Michael S. 1504-1505
Minh-Ha, Trinh T. 274
Mink, John Woodward 913
Minke, Gernot 479
Minnesota Masonry Institute 122, 353, 480
Minor, Joseph E. 1100
Mirtsios, J. 280
Misra, Prem K. 481
Missouri Dept. of National Resources 123
Mitchell, D.E. 701
Mitchell, Paul B. 1328
Mitchell, Stephen 1420
Moe, C.E. 212
Moe, Roger D. 1085
Montgomery, T.E. 1809
Moore, Gordon L. 603, 703, 783, 1600-1601
Moore, Kenny 1329
Moreland, Frank L. 124-125, 998-1000, 1083, 1101
Morgan, William 264-265, 1223, 1439, 1810
Morton, David 1152
Mosena, David R. 1036
Mother Earth News, Inc. 1522
Mott, Larry 483

Moulds, Matthew 784
Moumtzidou, F. 280
Mudd, K.E. 1324
Mullan, Jane 99
Mullan, Otis 99
Muller, C.A. 1037-1038
Mulligan, Helen C. 286-288
Mumma, Stanley 1374
Munding, Peter 1310
Munson, Michael J. 1102
Murphy, Jim 1456, 1561

National Association of Mutual Insurance Companies 1039
Natural Spaces, North Branch, MN 354
Neal, Wallace 126
Nearhoof, Steve 1703
Nelson, C. 690
Nelson, George 1001
Nelson, James 484
Nelson, Susan R. 161
Nero, Anthony V. 959
Newberry, James R. 785
Newman, Jerry O. 355-356, 485, 635, 786-787, 916, 949, 1603, 1811
Nicholson, Nick 1345
Niskern, Diana 213
Norsted, Steven 935, 939
Norton, Willard S. 486-489
Novitski, Barbara-Jo 810
Noziska, Howard 491

Oddo, Sandra 127
Odello, R.J. 1155
Oehler, Mike 128, 492, 1447
Ohanian, Richard 357, 493, 604
Oklahoma State University. Architectural Extension 358-359
Oklahoma State University. Center for Natural Energy Design 182

Oklahoma State University.
  School of Architecture 704
Olcott, Morrow 1630
Oliver, Gordon 494
Olmsted, Lorena Ann 1399
Olson, Dorothy 1563
Olson, Myron 635, 1563-1564
O'Neil, Bill 129
Orlowski, Henry 637
Orr, A. 299
Osten, Robert J., Jr. 640
Oswald, Richard A. 960
Otto, Lorrie 861

Palmer, Brian 1156
Parker, B.F. 749
Parsons, Mark 1750
Paton, David J. 1331
Patterson, Ann 131
Pauley, Helen 1386
Pauls, Susan Maas 1566
Paulus, Paul B. 945
Paylore, Patricia 999
Pearcey, Dale 495
Pearcey, Gene 495
Peck, Carolyn 983
Pendergast, Robert E. 496
Penfield, Louis A. 1227
Perkins, Jerry 1040
Peterman, Jeffrey D. 946
Peterson, Roger A. 705
Pfender, E. 744
Pfister, Peter 638
Pholeros, Paul 830
Pick, E. 788
Pittman, Scott 132, 1638
Pittman, Wayne 132, 1638
Plant, C.G.H. 906
Pleimann, L.G. 396
Portland Cement Association
  133-134, 498-499, 1459
Poulos, J.F.J. 706
Powell, Evelyn J. 362
Pringle, Murray T. 135
Puri, V.M. 707

Quarmby, Arthur 365
Quigley, Donald W. 505
Quinn, Thomas 1158

Raab, Richard 1041
Radice, Phil 1812
Raetzman, Ronald 914, 1349
Raff, S.J. 789
Raman, K. 708
Raman, R.J. 766
Rambo, Forrest 1751
Ramsey, J.W. 714
Rand, George 961-962
Randall, Frank A., Jr. 606
Randall, William J. 137
Ranganathan, P. 707
Rawlings, Roger 138, 1448
Redmann, DuWayne K. 1769
Reeves, Melissa-Jo 1705
Reindl, Wilhelm 790
Replogle, K.K. 658
Reynoldson, George 366
Ribot, Jesse C. 710
Rickman, Gary A. 1493
Riechers, Maggie 1087
Riewerts, John L. 507
Riotte, Louise 1302
Ritter, Alexander 1569
Rivard, Mike 1042
Rivers, W. Joel 979-980
Roberts, Harry 1097
Robertson, Graeme 1370
Rockaway, John D. 988,
  1002
Rocky Mountain Research
  Center 764
Rogers, Patsy 139
Rollwagen, Mary 242, 508
Rose, Michael A.H. 367
Rosenberg, Barry 1229
Rosenfeld, Arthur H. 710
Routh, Barbara 947
Rowlinson, K. Morel 1230
Roy, Robert L. 140, 509-511,
  791, 889, 1652-1656

Rudofsky, Bernard 266
Rue, Roger L. 842, 1004
Ruehl, Peter 1813
Ruppel, Dennis L. 711
Rush, Richard 512
Rylander, Rod 368-370

Sale, Jonathan 1231
Salomone, Lawrence A. 833
Samuel, Barbara 712
Sanoff, Henry 1402
Sayigh, A.A.M. 1256
Scafe, Gayle R. 141, 514-515
Scafe, John C. 514
Scalise, James W. 371, 981, 1257, 1309, 1382
Schaefer, Steven E. 1184
Schlosser, François 516
Schmidt, Mark 1043
Schmitt, Greg 890
Schmitz, R.J. 677
Schneider, Dick 1044
Schneider, Hans J. 1279
Schonberg, David 1814
Schramm, Donald R. 142
Schuldt, M.A. 697
Schurer, Gerhard A.K. 289, 1103, 1232, 1280-1281, 1334-1335
Schurke, Paul 1165
Scott, David M. 1045, 1312
Scott, Margaret 1449
Scott, Norman L. 517
Scott, Ray G. 143-145
Scott, Robert B. 1450
Secrist, Don 891, 1815
Seitz, Doug 146, 607, 1234-1235, 1372
Selby, Robert 1174
Selde, Vernon 608
Selinfreund, Martin 1310
Selkowitz, Steve 187
Severson, J.L. 570
Seward West Redesign 1572
Seybert, Jeffrey A. 948

Shank, Ben 1573
Shapira, Hanna B. 713, 893, 1091, 1111, 1261
Shen, L.S. 714
Shick, Wayne L. 834
Shielke, Ty 1348
Shih, Jason C. 148, 519-521, 1255, 1258
Shindelar, Carol Ann 1494
Shipp, Paul H. 560-561, 569, 653, 715
Shippee, Paul 1422-1424
Shukuya, M. 770
Shurcliff, William A. 149-150
Sibley, Richard M. 1445
Siero, Gerhard C.W.H. 1282-1283
Simmons, John D. 915, 1603
Simmons, Lon B. 151, 372, 523-525, 716
Sklare, Bruce 1470
Skorusa, Mike 571, 609
Slater, Donald E. 526, 836-838
Slesin, Suzanne 1816
Smay, V. Elaine 152, 373, 527, 1366, 1513, 1621, 1631, 1817
Smith, Barb 1610
Smith, C. Ray 1368
Smith, E.A. 743, 782
Smoot, Ralph C. 1311
Solberg, Jean 1818
Solomon, Nancy 894
Solomonson, Gary 1047
Spears, R.E. 498
Speer, Bonnie 1693
Speltz, Jerome J. 717-719, 792
Spring, Martin 1353
Stafford, Lannon 529
Stall, James P. 530
Stanford, Greg 720-721, 982, 1336
Stauffer, Truman, Sr. 154, 214, 1003

Steiger, R.W. 1819
Steiner, Robert M. 610
Stephens, D. 155
Sterling, Raymond L. 149, 156-161, 179-181, 375, 380, 532-533, 722, 793, 839, 895, 990, 1005, 1048, 1057, 1171, 1245, 1286-1287, 1292, 1575
Stetzel, Warren 1679-1680
Stewart, Donald R. 723
Stewart, Kay K. 943, 949, 976, 983-984
Stoiaken, Larry 1187
Stoumen, Jonathan 1404
Strayer, Richard D. 794
Strong, Steven J. 640
Sudjic, Deyan 162
Sullivan, M. 534
Summers, D.A. 441, 1135
Swayze, Jay see Julian H. Swayze
Swayze, Julian H. 163, 376
Sweaney, Anne L. 985
Swenson, Gregory S. 1049
Swenson, Mark 1168
Szigethy, Les 612, 1632
Szydlowski, Richard F. 795-798

Tait, David B. 537
Tanabe, S. 770
Tarlock, A. Dan 1050-1051
Tatz, Vicki 164
Taylor, R.A. 1037
Taylor, Susan 508
Terman, Max R. 243, 725-726, 968
Terra-Dome Corp. 377
Texas University at Arlington. Clearinghouse for Earth Covered Settlements 538
Thomas, Craig R. 917
Thomas, Marshall 851

Thomas, Wendell 1666
Thomas, William A. 1052
Thompson, Irene 167
Thompson, L.K. 168
Thorsen, Gerald W. 842, 1004
Tingerthal, Mary 378, 532, 1053, 1575, 1577
TLH Associates, Inc. 1054-1055
Toedter, Wendell 1578
Tollin, Gale 169
Tossani, Richard 383, 1337
Towson, Peter G. 540-541
Traylor, Everett V. 542, 1821
Tremblay, Kenneth R., Jr. 985
Triantafillou, Menelaos 914
Trombley, Stephen 170, 1354
True, D.G. 543
Trull, J. R. 171
Tye, Robert L. 936

Undercurrent Design Research 843
Underground Homes 174, 379
Underground Space Center 179-182, 380, 986, 1005, 1057, 1171
U.S. Army Research Office, Durham, NC 1259
Uttley, James P. 1006

Vadnais, Kathleen 183, 267, 381-382, 545-552, 573-575, 613-614, 641, 699, 897, 918, 1007, 1058-1063, 1172, 1188, 1238-1240, 1304, 1356, 1408, 1462-1463, 1527, 1584-1587, 1606, 1657, 1670, 1681, 1700, 1734, 1754, 1774-1778

Vaile, Buck 553
Vaile, Janitye 553
Van der Meer, Wybe J. 729, 1682
Varde, K.S. 730
Varey, G.B 672
Veen, James C. 919
Viceps, Karlis 615
Vicker, Ray 1735
Villagran, Nora E. 189, 554
Villis, Peter 383, 1337
Volkman, Nancy 950
Von Fraunhoffer, Hermann, J. 184, 384, 616
Von Ranson, Jonathan 185
Vosbeck, R. Randall 385

Wade, Herb 186-187, 642
Wadsworth, Suzanne 1349
Wampler, Louis 188
Wampler, M.S. 268
Warde, William D. 979-980
Warner, N. Thomas 1064
Warnock, J. Gavin 245
Waterbury, Norman L. 189
Watson, David 935, 939
Watson, Don 1291
Weaver, Rose S. 215
Weber, Margaret J. 972-973, 987
Weiss, Peter Michael 190
Weiss, Piera Millicent Antonia 864
Wells, Malcolm 191-195, 246-252, 269-270, 386-387, 920, 1241-1242, 1338, 1514, 1633, 1822
Wendt, Robert L. 731-732
Wheeler, Elbert M. 1694
White, Al 1065
White, Bret Milford 196, 844
White, George 617
Whitford, Graham 197
Widmar, Barbara 1496
Wigington, Fred J. 733

Wilcox, Joe Stephen 921
Wilcox, R. Peter 271
Wilkerson, Jerry 1303
Willard, T. 746
Williams, Monty 643, 1589
Williamson, T.J. 1276
Wimble, E. Douglas 865
Winter, Ruth D. 952
Wirtanen, Linda K. 198
Wirth, Thomas E. 866
Wise, Barbara K. 1108
Wise, J.A. 1108
Wistinghausen, N. 199, 1823
Wolf, R. 200
Wolfe, Betty L. 1824
Wollan, Otis 201
Wood, A.M. Muir 253
Woodbridge, Sally 1409
Woodrum, Dave 898
Woods, Charles G. 388-390, 1243, 1825
Woods, Melvin 1713
Wright, Bruce N. 1285
Wright, David 1640-1641, 1780
Wright, Rodney 391, 1174
Wright, Sydney 391, 1174
Wuelpern, Thomas D. 845
Wukasch, Eugene 392, 556, 1384
Wunderlich, Elizabeth 953
Wylie, Jim 867

Yellott, John 1374
Yost, Michael B. 713, 893

Zanetto, James 1410
Zang, J.W. 684
Ziebarth, Allan M. 202, 1066-1067
Zook, Wayne 1472

GEOGRAPHIC INDEX

Adelaide, SA, Aust. 1320, 1337
Adelaide Hills, SA, Aust. 1325, 1328, 1334
Alabama 1046, 1535
Alamogordo, NM 1310
Albuquerque, NM 752
Aledo, IL 381
Algona, IA 1479
Allen County, OH 1671
Aloha, OR 1699
Altamonte, FL 1481
Amarillo, TX 878
Amersham, Eng. 1351
Ames, IA 1474, 1480
Anchor Lake, MN 1136, 1160
Andalusia, Spain 254
Andamooka, SA, Aust. 1181
Appalachia 1294
Appleton, WI 1118, 1128
Arizona 495, 529, 752, 828, 981, 1105, 1132, 1195, 1373-1384, 1414, 1452, 1477, 1707, 1764
Arkansas 268, 1120, 1385-1386, 1452
Arlington, TX 1473
Armington, IL 381, 1451, 1453, 1458
Ascona, Switzerland 1372
Asheville, NC 305
Ashtabula, OH 1673
Aspen, CO 1194, 1418
Atlanta, GA 310, 502, 828, 1443
Atlantic Beach, FL 1431
Auburn, CA 1397
Auckland, New Zealand 1369

Austin, TX 1714, 1724
Australia 8, 289, 558, 645, 720-721, 848, 924, 954, 969, 982, 1079, 1097, 1156, 1175-1176, 1181, 1211, 1225, 1262-1283, 1313-1338

Bahamas 1339
Baja California, Mexico 1367
Baltimore, MD 1501
Banks Peninsula, New Zealand 1370
Barrington Hills, IL 1457
Baton Rouge, LA 1500
Bel Air, MD 1536
Belgrade, MT 1610
Belle Plaine, MN 1535
Bellevue, OH 1457
Bend, OR 1414, 1764
Benet Lake, WI 1431
Berlin, WI 1202, 1759, 1761
Beulah, CO 381
Billings, MT 1587
Bismarck, ND 1667
Bitterroot Mts., ID 1448
Bladensburg, MD 407
Bloomington, IL 1455
Blue Earth, MN 1160
Bolwarra, Aust. 1316
Bonesteel, SD 1707
Bonners Ferry, ID 1237
Boone, IA 1473, 1481
Boston, MA 893, 1148
Boulder, CO 724, 1414, 1415, 1477
Bozeman, MT 1765

Brasstown, NC 1687
Brazil 1340
Breckenridge, CO 1413
Briarcliff Manor, NY 1476
Brisbane, Queensland, Aust. 1211
Buffalo, WY 1525
Bulla Regia, Tunisia 255, 279, 283
Burnsville, MN 1538, 1546, 1763
Burnsville, NC 1658, 1662
Burra, SA, Aust. 289, 1181, 1280
Butler, PA 1703

Cable, WI 1471, 1771
Cabo San Lucas, Baja, California, Mex. 1367-1368
Cadillac, MI 494
California 194, 752, 1122, 1125, 1143-1144, 1148, 1215, 1388-1403, 1405-1407, 1409-1410
Camano Island, WA 1749, 1751
Cambridge, MN 397
Camp Verde, AZ 1105
Campbelltown, NSW, Aust. 1333
Canada 308, 1341-1348
Canberra, Aust. 1322
Canton, GA 1473
Canton, OH 1167
Cape Cod, MA 1241, 1541, 1621
Cappadocia, Turkey 254
Carrboro, NC 315
Casey, IL 1461
Castellares-le-Neuf, Alpes-Maritime, France 1357
Castlegar, BC, Can. 1346
Catalina, AZ 1707
Cave Creek, AZ 1381

Cerrillos, NM 1638
Cerro Gordo, OR 1696, 1698
Charlottesville, VA 1763
Chaska, MN 1692
Cheong Ju City, Korea 1287
Cherry Hill, NJ 248, 1633
Chicago, IL 729, 1184
China 254, 276, 1186, 1284-1285, 1349
Chippewa Falls, WI 1687
Cincinnati, OH 234, 1391, 1672, 1674
Clarendon, SA, Aust. 1318, 1326
Clyde, OH 1413
Coeur d'Alene, ID 1449
Collegeville, MN 1550
Colorado 381, 490, 724, 956, 1194, 1411-1427, 1477, 1560, 1764
Columbia, MD 1503
Columbia, MO 1592
Columbus, IN 1114, 1466
Columbus, OH 891, 1677-1678
Concordia, KS 1495
Connecticut 1046, 1062
Coober Pedy, SA, Aust. 954, 969, 1181, 1268, 1278, 1317, 1319, 1321, 1324, 1329, 1338
Coon Rapids, MN 1534, 1540
Cross Plains, WI 1476
Curitiba, Brazil 1340
Curran Township, IL 1454

Da Xing, China 1284
Dalton, MN 621, 1528
Davis, CA 1389-1390, 1410
Dayton, OH 1528
Decatur, TX 1727
Deer Lodge, MT 1607
Delaware Valley, PA 1701
Delphi, IN 1472
Denton, TX 1718

Geographic Index

Denver, CO 1412, 1419
Derby, KS 1487
Desoto, KS 1491
Detroit, MI 1227
Dillon, CO 1411
Dillsburg, PA 1380
Duluth, MN 1707
Durango, CO 490

Easley, NC 787
Eastern U.S. 1293-1294
Edina, MN 1541
Edmond, OK 1688
Elk River, MN 1140, 1414, 1530, 1564
Emmaus, PA 1162
Enid, OK 1683, 1694
England 254, 367, 1230, 1350-1356
Estell Manor, NJ 1632
Estes Park, CO 1420
Europe 380, 710
Everett, WA 1481
Eyota, MN 1551

Fairport, NY 1648
Fayetteville, AR 1452
Fenton, MO 381
Florida 264, 461, 752, 1145, 1148, 1150, 1188, 1214, 1306, 1430-1442, 1481, 1557
Fond du Lac, WI 1767
Fort Berthold Reservation, ND 1670
Fort Smith, AR 268
Fort Worth, TX 1000, 1007, 1209, 1707
Fountain Hills, AZ 1382
France 290, 1357-1366
Franconia, NH 1618
Frederick MD 1502-1505, 1763

Fresno, CA 752, 1144, 1388, 1399, 1402, 1407

Gainesville, FL 1150, 1442
Georgia 310, 502, 828, 1046, 1443-1445, 1473
Germany 479
Gilman, WI 1776
Glendale, AZ 1375
Goreme Valley, Anatolia, Turkey 281
Golden, CO 1427
Grand Haven, MI 547, 1516
Grand Junction, CO 1426, 1764
Grand Rapids, MI 1525, 1621
Grand Traverse Bay, MI 1520
Granite City, IL 1460
Great Bend, KS 1124
Greece 280
Greenfield, IL 1452
Greentown, IN 1161
Grenoble, France 1366

Harker Heights, TX 1728
Harrison, AR 1120
Haslett, MI 1403
Hawaii 1404
Hendersonville, NC 1663-1665
Hereford, TX 1689
Hiawatha, KS 1482
Hidden Valley, NJ 1629
Highlandville, MO 1596
Holme, Yorkshire, Eng. 1352-1356
Holyoke Township, MN 1551
Hortonville, WI 1765
Houston, TX 893
Hubertus, WI 1774
Hudsonville, MI 416
Hugo, MN 1533

Earth-Sheltered Residences 326

Hunter River Valley, NSW, Aust. 1314

Idaho 1237, 1403, 1446-1450, 1764
Illinois 194, 381, 729, 1046, 1174, 1184, 1414, 1451-1463, 1587
Independence, MO 482, 1591, 1598-1599
Indian Mills, NJ 1391, 1628
Indiana 828, 1046, 1114, 1161, 1164, 1413, 1464-1472, 1604
Indianapolis, IN 828, 1469-1470, 1604
Inver Grove Heights, MN 1537
Iowa 381, 754, 1070, 1183, 1210, 1459, 1473-1481, 1560, 1707, 1763-1764, 1772
Israel 1254

Jackson, MN 1115, 1123, 1127
Jacksonville, FL 1148-1439
Japan 451-452
Jesup, IA 381
Johnston, IA 1764

Kansas 545, 723, 752, 936, 1003, 1029, 1124, 1191, 1206, 1240, 1482-1496, 1536, 1606
Kansas City, KS 545, 752, 936, 1003, 1191, 1206, 1606
Katonah, NY 1642
Kauai, HI 1404
Kenosha, WI 1413

Kent, Oh 1676
Kentucky 1497-1499
Knoxville, TN 893, 1536
Korea 1286-1287
Kurmond, Aust. 1316
Kuwait 1256

La Honda, CA 1406
La Jord, Sask., Can., 1344
La Verkin, UT 1731, 1735
Ladysmith, WI 1568
Lake Coeur d'Alene, ID 1446
Lake Havasu City, AZ 1452
Lake of the Ozarks, MO 1595
Lake Oswego, OR 307
Lakeville, MN 812, 1555
Las Vegas, NV 319
Latin America 479
Laura, IL 381
Letts, IA 1477
Leura, NSW, Aust. 1330
Lexington, KY 1498
Lexington, NE 1115
Lincoln, MA 1510
Little Canada, MN 1717
Liverpool, Eng. 1230
Loire Valley, France 1359, 1361, 1365
Loma, CO 1421
Longmont, CO 1423-1425
Los Alamos, NM 997, 1125
Louisiana 1500
Lubbock, TX 1717
Luddenham, Aust. 1316
Lyme, NH 234, 1614, 1617, 1619-1623

McNeal, AZ 1477
Madrid, Spain 1366
Maine 1046
Malmo, MN 1557

327 Geographic Index

Manhattan, KS 1485
Manilla, The Philippines 1148
Maple Grove, MN 1536
Maple Plain, MN 1567
Maple Valley, WA 1744
Marion, ND 1776
Mars, PA 1473
Marstons Mills, MA 1509, 1512-1513
Martell, NE 1611
Maryland 407, 1150, 1501-1505, 1536, 1763
Massachusetts 639, 658, 893, 1046, 1148, 1241, 1506-1514, 1541, 1621
Matmata, Tunisia 277, 279, 283
Mayetta, KS 1488, 1536
Medfield, MA 1511
Mediterranean area 284
Memphis, TN 1144, 1150
Mendota, MN 1541
Metamora, IL 381
Mexico 1367-1368
Miami, FL 752
Mica Bay, ID 1446
Michigan 416, 494, 547, 1169, 1227, 1403, 1515-1527, 1604, 1621
Middleburgh, NY 1657
Middletown, RI 1705
Middletown, OH 1147
Midwest U.S. 285, 707, 729, 1295-1303
Millbrook, NY 1152
Milwaukee, WI 1757-1758
Minneapolis, MN 58, 221, 241, 649, 670, 752, 878, 893, 951, 1060, 1112-1113, 1149, 1178, 1180, 1491, 1531, 1539, 1542, 1561, 1572, 1576, 1579-1580, 1588
Minnesota 58, 60, 221, 241, 290, 303-304, 306, 352, 397, 504, 551, 621, 649, 670, 682-683, 690, 693, 700, 705, 752, 812, 878, 892-893, 938, 951, 964, 975, 1007, 1029, 1049, 1060, 1063, 1072-1073, 1078, 1080-1081, 1104, 1106, 1112-1113, 1115, 1123, 1126-1127, 1136, 1140, 1141, 1149, 1160, 1166, 1172, 1178, 1180, 1201, 1219, 1413-1414, 1481, 1528-1589, 1604, 1687, 1692, 1707, 1717, 1763, 1777
Mishawaka, IN 1161
Missoula, MT 568, 1608
Missouri 381, 482, 1046, 1129-1130, 1163, 1233, 1457, 1590-1606
Mojave Desert, CA 1122
Montana 568, 1056, 1071, 1477, 1587, 1607-1610, 1765
Montecito, CA 1387, 1391, 1396
Montgomery City, MO 381
Morris, MN 1554
Morrisville, NY 1604, 1649
Mounds, IL 381
Muir Woods, IN 1465, 1469-1470
Muleshoe, TX 405, 1720-1721
Multnomah County, OR 1121
Murota, Victoria, Aust. 1211
Murrysville, PA 1704

Napa Valley, CA 1409
Nebraska 1115, 1119, 1224, 1477, 1611-1612, 1763
Nevada 319, 1613
New Albany, IN 1464
New Brighton, MN 1542
New Canaan, CT 234, 1046, 1062, 1428-1429

Earth-Sheltered Residences 328

New Hampshire 234, 332,
    1046, 1614-1623
New Hampton, IA 1763
New Hanover, IL 1414
New Jersey 248, 1391,
    1624-1633
New Mexico 752, 997, 1125,
    1196, 1310, 1621, 1634-
    1641
New River, AZ 1375
New South Wales, Aust. 8
New Ulm, MN 1557, 1583
New York 194, 314, 364,
    1041, 1046, 1107, 1152,
    1369-1370, 1476, 1604,
    1642-1657
New Zealand 1369-1370
Newcastle, OK 1687, 1690
Newton, NJ 1630
Nice, France 1364, 1366
Nora Springs, IA 754
Norman, OK 309, 1685,
    1692, 1763
North America 254, 265,
    710
North Carolina 305, 315,
    787, 1086, 1658-1666,
    1687
North Dakota 700, 1667-
    1670, 1776
North Lauderdale, FL 1557
North Oaks, MN 1556
Northfield, MN 1413, 1586,
    1687
Norway 1371
Norwood, MN 1172
Nottingham, Eng. 254

Oak Grove, MO 1604
Ohio 234, 891, 1147, 1167,
    1391, 1413, 1457, 1528,
    1535, 1671-1682
Oklahoma 309, 393, 648,
    660-661, 687, 760, 972-974,
    978-979, 987, 1239, 1302,
    1478, 1683-1694, 1763
Oliver, BC, Can. 1476
Omaha, NE 1119, 1612,
    1763
Onawa, IA 1475
Oneida, NY 1649
Orange, VA 1740
Oregon 307, 1121, 1414,
    1695-1700, 1764
Oregon, WI 1763-1764
Orlando, FL 1188, 1438-
    1439, 1441
Osage, IA 1707
Osseo, WI 1154
Owasso, OK 393

Pacific Northwest 697,
    1138, 1304, 1744
Paradise Valley, AZ
    1383
Parker County, TX 1715
Pawtucket, RI 313
Pembroke, GA 1444
Pennsylvania 194, 1029,
    1046, 1162, 1380, 1473,
    1701-1704
The Philippines 1148
Phoenix, AZ 495, 529,
    752, 828, 1132, 1195,
    1764
Pilbara, WA, Aust. 1275
Pittsfield, IL 1463
Plainview, TX 1719, 1725,
    1729-1730
Plattsburg, NY 1107
Plattsburgh, MO 1129
Plymouth, MN 304, 1540,
    1763
Poinciana, FL 1145
Poleyrieu, France 1360
Poplar Bluff, MO 1602, 1605
Port Augusta, SA, Aust. 1276
Portage, MI 1524
Portland, OK 1695, 1697,
    1700

Geographic Index

Post Falls, ID 1764
Preston, MN 1529, 1547, 1582
Provo, UT 1587, 1732
Pullman, WA 1226

Queensland, Aust. 1327, 1331

Rapid City, SD 702, 1159, 1708-1709
Raven Rocks, OH 1675, 1679-1680, 1682
Red Cloud, NE 1477
Redwood Falls, MN 504, 551, 693, 1106, 1126, 1539, 1584
Remsen, IA 1183
Renville, MN 1536
Reston, VA 1117, 1431
Rhode Island 313, 1046, 1705
Richmond, Aust. 1316
River Falls, WI 1391, 1773
Riverdale, MI 1523
Riverheights, Canada 1145
Riverside, CA 1403
Rochester, NY 314, 1644-1646
Rock Ridge, WI 1698
Rockford, MI 1527
Rockingham, NC 1660
Rocky Mts. 1420
Rolla, MO 1163, 1597
Rosendale, NY 1643
Royal Center, IN 1468

Sacramento, CA 1125
St. Cloud, MN 1566
St. Croix River, WI 1762, 1768, 1770
St. Joseph, MO 1457
St. Louis, MO 1130, 1233
St. Paul, MN 58, 649, 828, 893, 989, 1007, 1104, 1126, 1166, 1201, 1542, 1588, 1604
St. Peter, MN 1687
St. Pierre de Feric, France 1358, 1366
Salem, SD 1159
Salina, KS 1494
Salisbury, MD 1150
Salt Lake City, UT 551, 893
San Diego, CA 1148, 1398
San Francisco, CA 1143
San Juan Islands, WA 1748
Sangre de Cristo Mts., NM 1641
Santa Barbara, CA 1394
Santa Cruz Mts., CA 1392
Santa Fe, NM 752, 997, 1125, 1196, 1310, 1621, 1634, 1636, 1639-1641
Santorini, Greece 280
Savage, MN 1219
Scandinavia 1003
Sea Ranch, CA 1393, 1401, 1405
Seattle, WA 828, 878
Shakopee, MN 1532
Shawnee, OK 1686
Shelby County, OH 1535
Shenandoah, IA 1476
Sheridan, MT 1609
Sidney, MT 1477
Silver City, NV 1613
Sioux Falls, SD 1159
Snake River, WA 1743
Soldiers Grove, WI 1698
Sonoran Desert 581, 981
South Australia 1232, 1281, 1332, 1334-1335, 1337
South Carolina 1046, 1706
South-Central U.S. 684, 979, 1297

Earth-Sheltered Residences 330

South Dakota 700, 702, 1159, 1707-1710
Southhampton, Long Island, NY 364
Southeast U.S. 1305-1306
Southfield, MI 1169
Southwest U.S. 581, 1307-1311
Spain 254, 290, 324, 1366
Spokane, WA 1173, 1747
Spring Grove, MN 1115
Spring Lake, MN 1568
Springfield, MO 1590
Stanwood, IA 381
Staples, MN 1578
Stillwater, MN 303, 1553, 1777
Stockton, CA 1215
Stowe, MA 1507
Suffolk, VA 381
Sun Valley, ID 1403
Sussex Downs, England 367
Sweden 799, 1288-1289
Switzerland 1372
Sydney, Aust. 1175-1176, 1181, 1225

Taos, NM 1635
Tasmania, Aust. 1156
Tempe, AZ 1376, 1378
Tennessee 893, 1144, 1150, 1536, 1711-1713
Texas 194, 369, 405, 878, 893, 977, 1000, 1007, 1209, 1240, 1307, 1311, 1473, 1476, 1689, 1707, 1714-1730
Thornton, NH 1616
Tipton, IA 1478
Tokyo, Japan 451-452
Topeka, KS 1489
Traverse City, MI 1520, 1604
Trinity, TX 1476
Tucson, AZ 1380, 1414

Tulsa, OK 1478, 1689
Tunisia 255, 277, 279, 283-284, 290
Turkey 254, 281, 290
Tustin, MI 1517

United States 67, 78, 230, 242, 285, 380, 420, 436, 581, 660, 684, 707, 774, 822, 825, 845, 894, 979, 1290-1303, 1305-1306, 1307-1312
Upper Volta 274
Utah 551, 893, 1587, 1731-1735

Vail, CO 1416-1417
Valencia, PA 1703
Valparaiso, IN 1413
Vermont 1736-1739
Vernon, BC, Can. 1347-1348
Vernon, NJ 1631
Versailles, MO 1603
Victoria, Aust. 1079
Villaines les Rochers, France 1362
Vinemont, AL 1535
Virginia 381, 1046, 1117, 1431, 1740-1742, 1763

Wabash River, IN 1472
Walker, MN 1562
Walnut Creek, CA 1400
Wasatch Mts., UT 1733
Waseca, MN 1548
Washburn, IA 1772
Washburn, WI 1115
Washington, DC 1134, 1148, 1153
Washington, VT 1736-1738
Washington State 828,

Geographic Index

878, 1173, 1226, 1459, 1743-1751
Washougal, WA 1750
Wasta, SD 1159
Waterloo, IA 1772
Waukesha County, WI 1772
Waupaca, WI 1779
Wautoma, WI 1756
Wawawai Park, WA 1743
Wellsville, KS 1493
West Chazy, NY 1647
West Virginia 1752-1754
Western U.S. 1312
Westerville, OH 1681
Weyauwega, WI 1769
White Bear Lake, MN 1581
White Cliffs, NSW, Aust. 720-721, 954, 982, 1181, 1268, 1317, 1336
Wichita, KS 723, 1483
Williamsburg, KY 1497
Willmar, MN 306
Wisconsin 700, 938, 1062, 1115, 1118, 1128, 1154, 1202, 1235, 1413, 1431, 1471, 1476, 1560, 1568, 1687, 1698, 1755-1780
Wisconsin Dells, WI 1766
Woodland Hills, CA 1395
Woodstock, IL 1174
Wright County, MN 1563
Wyoming 1525, 1781-1782

York County, PA 1702
Young America, MN 1172

Zimmerman, MN 1559
Zurich, Switzerland 1372

SUBJECT INDEX

Abo, Ron, architect 1427
acceptance 154, 925, 928, 934, 936-937, 940, 942-943, 946, 953, 1182, 1370
accident risks 149, 1021
acoustical aspects 970
active solar collectors see solar collectors
active solar houses see solar houses: active
Adamson, Jim, architect 1406
adobe houses 1196, 1634, 1638, 1641
advantages 1, 3, 8, 149, 151-154, 201, 238-239, 246, 248, 252, 320, 322, 350, 936, 1198, 1263, 1709
aesthetics 351, 1069
Aglite for backfilling 550 (see also backfilling)
Agora housing development, St. Pierre de Feric, France 1358, 1366
air collectors see air intake systems
air conditioning 104, 440, 619, 669, 751
air infiltration 908
air intake systems 1592, 1676
air quality see indoor air quality; ionized interior air
air raids 301
air-to-air heat exchangers 634, 641, 753
airlock entries 1553, 1765

air-tight houses 632, 957, 960
Alexander, Jesse, owner 1394
Alexander House, Montecito, CA 1391, 1394, 1396
All-Weather Wood Foundation System 343, 446, 1400
Ambasz, Emilio, architect 324, 1444, 1788
American Solartron Corporation 413, 435, 518, 1479
American Underground Space Association 325, 675, 825, 1070, 1210, 1691
Ames Laboratory 797
Anasazi Pueblo architecture 258 (see also pueblo design)
Anchor Block Company, St. Paul, MN 1201
Anderson, Brent & Associates 1613
Anderson, John, architect 1339
Anderson, Philip B., architect 306
Anderson, Rolf, architect 1755
animal confinement buildings 536
Annear, Harry, owner/builder 1610, 1765
antennas 846
apartments 1002, 1256, 1550, 1643, 1649, 1769

Subject Index

appraisal 890, 1011, 1060, 1769
appropriate technology 368
Arace, M., architect 1631
Arcadian berm house design 1788
arches 397, 405, 444, 481-482, 527, 545, 548, 868, 1516; Roman 444; steel 548, 1527, 1778
Arch-Tech curved panels 547, 1516
architects and designers 206, 209, 225, 322, 508, 1110, 1190-1192, 1194-1195, 1204-1205, 1209, 1213-1214, 1218, 1220-1223, 1226-1229, 1231, 1236, 1241-1243, 1406
Architerra, Inc. 4, 429, 432, 1358, 1364, 1366, 1416
arid regions 623, 737, 851, 924, 1246-1259, 1267, 1276, 1282-1283, 1382
Arizona State University 1205, 1374
Ark Energy Systems, Staples, MN 1578
Art Bunker of Philip Johnson, New Canaan, CT 234
art galleries 234, 257
artificial lighting see lighting, artificial
Ash Wednesday bushfires, South Australia 1325, 1328
Ashford residence, Muleshoe, TX 1720-1721
Atkinson, Larry, architect 1191, 1606
Atomic Age 376
atrium house designs 276, 302, 320, 322, 329, 419, 566, 1284, 1349, 1411, 1467, 1506-1509, 1511-1512, 1631, 1676, 1697, 1724

attitudes 922-924, 927, 930, 932, 938, 947, 949, 969, 976, 978, 989, 993-994, 1317 (see also acceptance; psychological aspects)
aviaries 1156

Baanya Biami Holiday Camp, Victoria, Australia 1323
backfilling 487, 526, 550, 577, 590, 606, 809, 963, 1665; Aglite 550
Badanes, Steve, architect 1406
Baggs, David, architect 318, 1192
Baggs, Sydney, architect 1192, 1225
Baldtop Dugout, Lyme, NH 1614, 1621
Banen Residence, Fountain Hills, AZ 1382
banks 1109
Barcik, Eleanora Beltrao, architect 1340
Barnard, John, architect 1506-1509, 1513
barns, brood see brood barns
barrel shell construction see construction: barrel shell
Barton County Community College, Great Bend, KS 1124
basements 107, 120, 401, 409, 561, 584, 653, 1519, 1587
Batey and Mack, architects 1409
bathhouses 618
Bay Development Corporation, Indianapolis, IN 1469-1470
Beale House 1785
beams 1663; reinforced concrete 1433

bedrock 816
Bell Labs, NJ 918
Benedict, Frederick, architect 1418
Benedict, John, builder 1609
Bennett House, Minneapolis, MN 241
Berbers, Tunisia 277, 279
Berg, Jeremy, architect 1516
Berg and Associates, Inc., Plymouth, MN 304
bermed houses see earth bermed houses
Bernold metal sheets see Bernold plate systems
Bernold plate systems 460, 548, 550, 1305, 1438
Blackbeard, Geoff, architect 308
Bligh, Tom, architect 1221
blocks: concrete 349, 491, 862; dry stacking 1296; Loffelstein concrete 862; polystyrene 439; reinforced concrete 1558
bonding, surface see surface bonding
book sellers 209
bookstores 1110, 1113
Boothe, Ray, architect 1715
Boral Group of Companies, Adelaide, Australia 1281
Borchert, Floyd 1562
Borchert, Millie 1562
Boutwell, Ronald B., Pres., Survive Tomorrow, Inc. 1735
Bowen Construction, Post Falls, ID 1808
box-type prefabricated modules 464 (see also prefabricated module building systems)
Brian House, Columbia, MD 1503
bricks 1634
Bridge House 1799

British Earth Sheltering Association 1230
British market 67
British Thermal Units 1474
brood barns 1114
Bruder, William P., architect 1375
Bubolz, Gordon, Nature Preserve Center, Appleton, WI 1118, 1128
Bucher, Ward, architect 1503
builders 206, 209, 508, 1312
building codes 6, 38, 43, 54, 179-181, 193, 320, 875, 905, 986, 994, 1014-1015, 1021, 1025, 1040-1041, 1043, 1045, 1048, 1057-1058, 1234, 1723
building orientation 834, 839
building standards 412
Bullock, Ralph 413
burglar protection 1690
burglary 149
Burt Hill Kosar Rittleman Associates, Butler, PA, architects 1703
bus transportation 1000
bush holiday camp 1323
bushfire-resistant homes 1281, 1325 (see also fire: resistance)
buying 875, 1796

cabins 344, 389, 1141, 1150
Cable, John, director, Buildings Division, U.S. Dept. of Energy 1074
cafeterias 1110
Cal Hambro forming system 1381
California Coastal Commission 1408
California State Office Building, Sacramento, CA 1125

Subject Index

Camper, Bruce, builder 1215
Camper, Glen, builder 1215
canyons 997
Cape Cod houses 294, 1783
capillary draw 577
Carpenter, Buzz, owner/ builder 1761
Carpenter, Jan, owner/ builder 1761
Cary Arboretum, Millbrook, NY 1152
cast-in-place concrete see concrete: cast-in-place
catastrophe theory 238
cattle ranches 1609
Cavanaugh, Dave, builder 1208
Cavanaugh, Michael, architect 1471
cave homes 266, 281-282, 1284, 1359, 1361-1362, 1365, 1421, 1426
CCA see Chromated Copper Arsenate
ceilings: concrete 19; stepped 1662
cellars 1752 (see also root cellars)
Central County Builders, Inc., Weyauwega, WI 1769
Central Pre-Mix Concrete Co., Spokane, WA 1173, 1808
chalk formations 367
chamber houses 329
Chapter 11 (federal bankruptcy law) 1219
Chilless, Tedd, owner/ builder 1700
Chimacoff/Peterson, architects 374
chimney rock bins 627 (see also energy: storage; heat: storage; rock bed heat storage)
chimneys 846 (see also solar chimneys)
Chromated Copper Arsenate 456, 547 (see also wood: treated)
churches 1131
circular designs 1235
Clark, Norm 1695
Clark-Nelson House, River Falls, WI 1391
classes 146, 1524 (see also courses)
clay 182, 1369, 1397
claystone rock deposits 721, 1336
clerestory windows 1401 (see also windows)
cliff houses 258-259, 283, 1362-1363, 1385, 1426
climate 53, 810, 823, 828, 1005, 1244, 1279 (see also climatically stressed areas); cold 1244; control 255, 631, 822-823, 825, 843, 910; ground 826, 845; hot 1246-1248, 1250, 1253, 1255, 1258-1260, 1404; humid 1260-1261, 1404; temperate 243
climatically stressed areas 75
clinics see medical clinics
coal mine reclamation 1294, 1462, 1754 (see also mine reclamation)
Coate, Roland, architect 1387, 1391, 1394, 1396
codes see building codes
cold climate design 1244
Coleman, John, Construction, Elk River, MN 1530
Colorado Sunworks, Boulder, CO 622, 724, 1415, 1422-1425
Colosol Construction, Dillon, CO 1411
comfort assessments 880, 900-901
commercial buildings 215,

Earth-Sheltered Residences 336

322, 386, 393, 420, 866, 1072, 1075, 1171
Committee of Inquiry into Technological Change in Australia 18
community centers 1142
community development 989-991, 993-994, 1000, 1005
commuting 646 (see also transportation)
competitions, design see design competitions
Comprehensive Underground Space Insurance Policy (CUSIP) 1038
computer models 717, 737, 750, 878, 896
computer simulation to analyze thermal performance see energy: performance, computer simulation of
computerized tracking equipment 1415, 1423
computers, electronic analog 669
Concept 2000, Inc., builder 184, 1377
concrete 417, 425, 473, 486-489, 1634 (see also shotcrete); blocks 349, 491, 862; cast-in place 515, 1296, 1465; ceilings 19; construction 488-489, 498-499, 703, 1459, 1502; cracks 424; curing 486; floors 19, 487; masonry 480, 555, 620; post-tensioned 443, 523, 1296, 1594; precast 406, 429, 500-501, 503, 549, 1397; precast prestressed 1296, 1412, 1727; precast reinforced 1296; reinforced 340, 349, 464, 483, 512, 1136; reinforcing calculations 790; slabs 301, 399, 455, 484, 486-487, 1389-1390, 1474; walls 19, 470-471, 493, 1296, 1379, 1406, 1448, 1465, 1500-1501, 1727, 1814
condensation 349, 773, 843, 917, 1789
condominiums 321, 358, 362, 1367-1368, 1469-1470, 1604, 1731, 1735
conduction 823
conductivity, thermal 758, 833
conduit construction 529
Conference on Financing Earth-Sheltered Housing, Minneapolis, MN, 1979 1180
conservation of resources 148 (see also land conservation)
construction 116, 148, 186, 243, 393-556, 1110, 1182, 1257, 1266, 1701, 1705, 1709-1710, 1723, 1784 (see also structural considerations); All-Weather Wood Foundation System 343, 446, 1400; barrel shell 460-462, 868, 1305; Bernold plate system 460, 548, 550, 1305, 1438; Cal Hambro forming system 1381; concrete 488-489, 498-499, 703, 1459, 1502; concrete block 1432; conduit 529; cordwood masonry 1652-1655; C/Shells 502; culvert 419, 527, 531, 1296, 1377, 1463, 1773; CW-100 hardwall structural system 399; Enviromass System 483; Ho-Vert shoring system 522; inflatable forms 393, 445, 554; post

and beam 443, 1484, 1665; poured-in place post-tensioned concrete 443; PSP (post-shoring-polyethylene) 128, 1477; rammed earth 479, 537; rebarred ferroconcrete 1718; reinforced concrete 1558, 1708; Reinforced Earth^R 432, 516, 1358, 1364, 1366, 1416; sawdust blocks 1347-1348; steel plate 1527; Terra Dome system 514-515, 1764, 1766; tilt-up 484, 1608; wood 338, 411, 693, 1296, 1533, 1557, 1752; Wood-Tech^{TM} panelized wood system 434; zero lot line 453

consumer concerns 124, 1723

<u>Consumer's guide to earth sheltered housing</u>, by M. Rollwagen, S. Taylor, T. Holthusen 875

contractors 40, 938, 975, 1193, 1239, 1443, 1587

Control Data Corporation, St. Paul, MN 1126

Control Data/Terra Tech Division, Criteria, Inc. 419

convection 823; thermal 1470

convection air heaters <u>see</u> heaters: convection air

cooling 34, 182, 186, 623, 630, 736, 740, 754, 759, 772-773, 775, 878, 903, 1111, 1244, 1248-1249, 1253-1254, 1256, 1260-1261, 1379, 1385; Detached Earth Tempering (DET) 1260; evaporative 774, 1253; ground coupled 1248-1249, 1256, 1260; loads 752, 896, 1248, 1256; passive 304, 642, 851, 1260, 1311, 1422-1424; tubes <u>see</u> earth tubes

cordwood masonry construction 1652-1655

Cornish miners 1280

costs (<u>see</u> <u>also</u> low-cost housing): construction 104, 112, 393, 428, 464, 709, 719, 868-869, 878, 883, 885, 893, 896, 1048, 1720, 1740; energy 163, 885, 896; estimates 874; lifecycle 8, 869, 871, 887, 894, 1026, 1048; operating 138, 878, 893; overruns 872

Couelle, Jacques, architect 1357

Country Cook Inn, Greentown, IN 1161

courses 146 (<u>see</u> <u>also</u> classes)

courtyard house designs <u>see</u> atrium house designs

courtyards 374, 1349, 1395, 1732, 1823

crawl space <u>see</u> vertical crawl space

Creative Financing, Inc. 1019

Croasdale-Moore Construction Co., Inc., Kansas City, MO 1206

Crowell House, Washington, VT 1737-1738

Crowther, Richard L., architect 1412

Crowther House, Denver, CO 1412

C/Shells (precast modular shells) 502

culvert construction <u>see</u> construction: culvert

CUSIP <u>see</u> Comprehensive Underground Space In-

surance Policy
cut and fill 292, 327
Cutlip, Ron 1754
CW-100 hardwall structural system 399
Cycle 5 Residential Solar Demonstration Program 304, 1505

Daily Mail Ideal Home Exhibition 1350
dampproofing 598, 601 (see also waterproofing)
Daniel, Maurice, inventor 911
Davis, Andy, builder 1189, 1216
Davis Caves Construction, Inc., Armington, IL 381, 1129, 1189, 1200
daylighting 182, 193, 255, 367, 396, 704, 902, 904, 913, 921, 970-971, 1566 (see also lighting)
Deco Homes, Bladensburg, MD 407
defense 1069
dentist's office 1147
desert areas see arid regions; desert buildings
desert buildings 284, 322, 737, 981, 1248, 1251, 1367, 1378-1379, 1382, 1635
design 6, 34, 38, 40, 53-54, 75, 112, 148, 160, 179-181, 184, 186, 193, 210, 217, 243, 246, 323-324, 328, 330-335, 341, 343, 347 349, 351-363, 366-368, 371, 373, 375, 377-392, 394, 413-414, 421, 485, 527, 802, 805, 817, 826, 828, 837, 844, 914, 984, 1110, 1117, 1244, 1247, 1262, 1723; for elderly 362; for handicapped 362, 1534, 1555, 1757/58; hillside 4, 322, 379, 432, 1382; interior see interior design; linear 1783; passive solar see passive solar design
design competitions 293, 298, 304, 318, 321, 325-326, 352, 358-359, 361, 825, 1295, 1561
designers see architects and designers
developing countries 1245
De Vido, Alfredo, architect 633
De Wolff, Carlton, architect 1645-1646, 1648
Digging in, by Dave Carter 1790
Digioia, Nancy, owner/builder 1704
disadvantages 8, 121, 149-151, 201, 320, 322, 350, 936, 1266, 1709
disaster protection 182 (see also fire: protection; hazard protection)
Diversified Environmental Planning, landscape architects 1442
Division 7 Corp., Minneapolis, MN 1543
domes 403-405, 425, 430-431, 445, 448-449, 472, 482, 495, 527, 545, 554, 556, 868, 1119, 1296, 1482, 1732; concrete 396, 495, 1441, 1599, 1714, 1764; elliptical 528; fiberglass 1780; geodesic 144, 335, 396, 1608, 1732; precast 472; shotcrete 1296
doors 563, 839
dormitories 1550 (see also student housing)

339 Subject Index

Doubek, Rodolfo, architect 1340
double-envelope houses 350, 1606 (see also envelope houses)
Down-to-Earth Homes, Omaha, NE 1612
drainage 149, 418, 486, 577, 581, 587, 590-592, 594, 607, 614, 814, 963, 1266, 1500, 1632; mesh system 1662; tiling 963
dry stacking blocks 1296
Du-Al Earth Sheltered Homes, Ltd., Vernon, BC, Can. 1347
Dubin, Fred, engineer 1152
dugout dwellings, Australian 720-721, 969, 982, 1181, 1264, 1268-1269, 1278, 1280, 1317, 1319, 1321, 1324, 1336, 1338 (see also frontier dugouts)
Duguay, Michael 918
Dune House, Amelia Island, FL 1150, 1439
Dune House, Atlantic Beach, FL 1150, 1431, 1441
duplexes 1590 (see also triplexes)
Dyer, William, designer 1657
Dyksterhouse, John, architect 1520

earth-air heat exchangers 210, 768
earth-bermed houses 21, 338-339, 342, 379, 401, 468, 597, 622, 635, 698-699, 707, 719, 749, 780, 885, 896, 1114, 1206, 1276, 1393, 1397, 1410, 1432, 1440, 1445, 1456, 1476, 1484, 1488, 1500, 1503, 1519, 1533-1534, 1538, 1543, 1561, 1592, 1597, 1620, 1637, 1669, 1717, 1782, 1787-1788, 1809
earth contact heat transfer 717, 735-799, 833, 901
Earth-covered buildings: an exploratory analysis for hazard and energy performance, by Moreland Associates 65
Earth Covered Housing Association of South Australia 1232
earth covered roofs see roofs: earth covered
Earth Covered Structures, Inc., Fort Worth, TX 1209
Earth Inn Motel, Jackson, MN 1123, 1127
Earth-integrated building construction, Portland Cement Association 606
Earth Integrated Technics 1543
earth movements 835 (see also fault movements)
earth pipes see earth tubes
Earth Shelter Corporation of America, Berlin, WI 1118, 1198, 1202, 1207, 1759
Earth Shelter Data Bank 46-48
Earth Shelter Developers, Stockton, CA 1215
Earth Shelter Developments of Canada 308
Earth Sheltered Construction Conferences of 1980: Atlanta, Boston, Chicago, Denver, San Francisco 1184
Earth Sheltered Demonstration Program 378

Earth sheltered housing: an evaluation of energy-conservation potential, by R. L. Wendt 709
Earth Sheltered Housing Conference and Exhibition, 1980 1187
Earth sheltered housing design, by R. Sterling and others 119, 157, 159, 839
Earth Sheltered Housing Design Competition 361
Earth Shel-Tours, St. Paul, MN 58
Earth Systems, Phoenix, AZ 495
Earth Systems kit houses 431, 490, 495, 1764 (see also kit houses)
earth tubes 621, 753-754, 756-757, 764, 776, 827, 1398, 1445, 1665, 1728
Earthhome Corp., builder 1610
earthquake resistant engineering 469 (see also earthquakes)
earthquakes 346, 466-469, 597, 1098, 1100-1101, 1302
Earthwood, NY 1652-1654
Earthworks, MO 1593
Ecology Houses, Marstons Mills, MA 96, 1506-1509, 1512-1513
economics 868, 876, 879-881, 891, 1723 (see also costs)
Eco-Village, Hendersonville, NC 1664-1665
Effective Building Products, Inc., Savage, MN 1219
elastomeric membrane see waterproofing: elastomeric membrane
elderly, design features for 362
electric radiant panels see heating: radiant heat panels
electrical systems 186
electronic analog computers see computers, electronic analog
elevational house designs 243, 329, 1537
elevators see hydraulic elevators
Elifrits, Dale, builder 1597
Elifrits, Kathy, builder 1597
Eljen Drainage System 592
Ellison Design and Construction 319
emergency escape 1014, 1021 (see also fire: egress
energy: conservation 33, 97, 112, 238, 646, 651, 654-655, 662-663, 675, 677, 685, 695, 701, 704, 731-732, 859, 916, 987, 995, 1016, 1068, 1072, 1075-1077, 1113, 1117, 1266, 1577, 1679, 1709, 1784; consumption 43, 104, 179-181, 649, 653, 664-665, 671, 710, 723, 730, 734, 972, 974, 978, 1087, 1101, 1148, 1550, 1603, 1675; costs see costs: energy; performance 126, 210, 280, 287, 645, 667, 689, 691, 709, 712, 718, 737, 752, 797, 869, 883, 887, 893, 896, 995, 1182, 1450, 1480, 1675, 1780; performance, computer simulation of 671-672, 674, 717, 878, 896, 1314, 1780; performance monitoring 647-648, 652, 657-661, 666, 670-672, 678-683,

341 Subject Index

686-687, 690, 692, 696-697, 702, 704, 706, 708-710, 712, 714, 720-726, 728, 735, 894, 970-971, 1148, 1250, 1276, 1310, 1390, 1410, 1415, 1422-1423, 1450, 1480, 1484, 1531, 1613, 1709-1710, 1721, 1780; policy 925; storage 79, 627 (see also heat: storage; chimney rock bins; rock bed heat storage)
Engan, Richard, architect 311
envelope houses 336, 1606, 1244, 1803 (see also double-envelope houses)
Enviromass System 483
environmental aspects 97, 800, 965-968, 995
environmental education center 1174
evaporation 823 (see also cooling: evaporative)
evapotranspiration 848
exercising equipment 910

face brick 346
factories 1142, 1171
Fagan Residence, Columbia, MD 1592
fallout shelters 1097-1098, 1103, 1489, 1492, 1643, 1734 (see also nuclear war shelters; survival shelters)
Farmer's Home Administration 1610, 1769
Farnan, William T., designer 345
farrowing houses 1129 (see also hog buildings)
fault movements 426-427 (see also earth movements)

Federal Emergency Management Agency, U.S. 65
Federal Home Loan Mortgage Corporation, U.S. 1063
Federal Housing Administration, U.S. 1056, 1060
ferrocement 447-448; structures 1718
Feuille House, Sea Ranch, CA 1393
FHA see Federal Housing Administration, U.S.
FHLMC see Federal Home Loan Mortgage Corporation, U.S.
fiber optic wires (for interior lighting) 911
fiberglass: homes 518, 1479, 1780; panels 435, 1733; reinforced plywood panels 413, 1296
field houses 1134
films 60, 78, 173
financing 38, 40, 43, 112, 116, 320, 430, 873, 1008-1010, 1012-1013, 1015-1016, 1018-1020, 1023-1024, 1026, 1028, 1030-1034, 1042, 1044-1045, 1053-1057, 1065, 1180, 1234, 1266, 1449, 1471, 1580, 1640, 1657, 1732, 1802
finite element analyses 426, 746
fire: egress 1045; lightning-caused 1787; protection 491, 1045, 1048, 1090, 1094-1096, 1100-1101; resistance 1281, 1325, 1690; safety 1101-1102, 1756
fireplaces 563, 1640, 1655
Fitch, R.B., Jr., builder 1561
Fitzgerald House, Santa Fe,

Earth-Sheltered Residences 342

NM 1621, 1634, 1636, 1641
flashing failures 602
flat sites 869
Fleckenstein Associates Architects, Rochester, NY 314
floor plans 163, 186, 300, 305-315, 325, 372, 377, 379-380, 413, 428, 495, 1413-1414, 1452, 1473, 1476-1477, 1505, 1535-1536, 1687
floors 436, 484, 1663; concrete 19, 487; heating 910, 1345, 1595; slab-on-grade 210, 714; subgrade 210
Florida State Museum, Gainesville, FL 1150
FmHA see Farmer's Home Administration
food storage 212
footings 476-477, 497, 542, 1663, 1690
forced-air systems see furnaces: forced-air
Forest House, Central Florida 1214, 1434-1435
Forestiere, Baldasare 1144, 1388, 1399, 1402, 1407
The $40 and up underground house book, by Mike Oehler 1237
foundations 64, 817, 836, 1663; wood 465, 1676
Four-H Leader Training Camp, Tustin, MI 1577
Fourier-series boundary method (to analyze thermal performance) 714
Fracasso, Frank, architect 1630
frames 1663
franchise law 1202 (see also franchises)
franchises 1207, 1238 (see also franchise law)
Frechette, John, architect 1609
frontier dugouts 256, 285 (see also dugout dwellings, Australian)
frost heave 809
fuel savings 1762, 1793
furnaces (see also heating): direct-vent 624; electric 1379, 1482, 1762; forced-air 1395, 1474
furnishings 1096, 1108
future development 221-222, 225-226, 237, 241, 244, 248, 267, 895, 996,

gardens see roof gardens
Garibaldi, Giuseppe 1170
Gassner Realty and Construction, Inc. 1118
Geier House, Cincinnati, OH 234, 1391, 1672, 1674
Genesis Community, Central Ohio 1675, 1680, 1682
Geobuilding Systems, Hereford, TX 1689
geologic considerations 814, 820, 988, 1002, 1110
Georgetown University, Washington, DC 1134
Geosphere, Inc. 528
Geotecture International Association 1225
geotextiles 540-541
Gephart, Ken, designer 341, 343
Givens, W.E., designer/builder 1310
glass: double-pane 1785; thermal-pane 1688 (see also glazing)

343 Subject Index

glazing 1247, 1474, 1505, 1611 (see also glass)
Gober, John L. 522
Gobin, Daniel, architect 1466
Golubski, Steven, builder 1593
Gore, Landis, owner 1428
Gore, Pamela, owner 1428
grading 53
Grass on the roof (film) 60, 78, 173
Grasslands, Coon Rapids, MN 1534
gravel pits 1121
greenbelts 223
greenhouses 366, 396, 733, 927, 1107, 1133, 1138, 1146, 1561, 1592, 1594, 1699, 1714, 1723, 1780, 1811, 1823
Greisbach House, Hortonville, WI 1765
ground climate 826, 845
ground cover 821, 858
ground temperature see soil: temperature
ground tubes see earth tubes
ground water 577, 817, 838-839, 1101, 1500 (see also water table)
guardrails 1045
Gurunsi people, Upper Volta 274
gutter systems 1500, 1632

habitability 148, 1297-1298
Hagans, G. Walker, architect 315
Hagconsult AB, Sweden 799
hail 1100
Hait, John 568
hallways 428
handicapped, design features for 362, 1534, 1555, 1757/58
hangars 1105
Hanley, Paul 1322
Hanover Insurance Co., Worcester, MA 1022, 1046
Hansen, Daryl, architect 1561
Harris, Leigh 1330
Harris House, Washington, DC 1503
Harter, James, architect 1162
Harvard University, Pusey Library 1158 (see also libraries)
Hawkweed Group, Osseo, WI, builders 1154
hazard protection 894, 1090-1104 (see also disaster protection; fire: protection)
health factors 233, 954, 958, 1271 (see also physiological aspects)
heat (see also heating): exchange methods 643, 754, 768; exchangers see air-to-air heat exchangers and earth-air heat exchangers; flow 126, 779, 792-793, 1113, 1133; loss 6, 53-54, 649, 1667; storage 620, 627, 708, 762-765, 799, 901, 1107, 1474, 1511, 1665, 1669, 1824 (see also rock bed heat storage; chimney rock bins; energy: storage); transfer see earth contact heat transfer
heat pumps 757, 1428, 1482, 1603, 1631, 1686, 1727, 1803, 1817
heaters: convection air 1174

heating 34, 104, 186, 315, 343, 627, 757, 875, 891, 1603, 1616, 1662, 1665-1666 (see also heat pumps; heaters; furnaces); electric 891, 1379, 1603, 1710, 1727, 1744; passive solar 182, 304, 366, 622, 642, 774, 1111-1112, 1174, 1261, 1422-1424, 1499, 1566, 1694; radiant heat panels 636, 1497; solar 144, 366, 396, 635, 654, 1345, 1665, 1703 (see also solar hot water systems; photovoltaic arrays); systems 315, 343, 754, 875, 1474, 1616, 1627, 1662, 1665
heliostats 899
Henderson, G.B. (Jerry) 1651
Heritage International, Salt Lake City, UT 551
highway rest stops 1136, 1159-1160
Hill House, La Honda, CA 1406
hillside designs 4, 322, 379, 432, 1382 (see also hilly terrain)
Hilltop House, Central Florida 1431, 1437, 1439
hilly terrain 128, 1286-1287, 1382 (see also hillside designs)
history 120, 148, 154, 217, 223, 254-271, 287
Hobbit Housing, Bonners Ferry, ID 1237
Hodges Residence, Ames, IA 1480
hog buildings 1129, 1139 (see also farrowing houses)
Homan, Nancy, owner 1627
Homan, Robert, owner 1627
Home Building Plan Service, Portland, OR 341, 343
Hopi Indians 1426
hot water systems see solar hot water systems; heating: solar
Hotard, Roy J., Jr., architect 1500
hotels 279 (see also motels; resorts)
House Beautiful's Climate Control Project 107
Housing and Urban Development, U.S. Dept. of 133, 304, 986, 1043, 1073, 1084, 1087, 1504-1505, 1670
housing developments 24, 1416, 1604-1605 (see also subdivisions); multiple-unit 870, 895, 1416, 1469-1470, 1534, 1576, 1604, 1649, 1731, 1734, 1767
Housing Warranty Corporation, Indianapolis, IN 551
Ho-Vert shoring system 522
How to build your own underground home, by Ray Scott 1501
humidity 6, 54, 126, 186, 272, 1133, 1331 (see also water vapor)
Hunter Valley Residence, NSW, Australia 8, 1314
hurricanes 1098
Huth-Westwood Builders, Kent, OH 1676
HVAC systems design 704
hybrid solar heating/storage system 1665
hydraulic elevators 301
hydrology 820
hydronic systems see solar hot water systems: hydronic
Hylton, Joe, architect 309, 1685, 1688, 1690

345 Subject Index

ice cream parlors 1115
Ihrke, Gene 1019
Illuminating Engineering Society 298
indigenous materials see materials: indigenous
indoor air quality 182, 632, 908, 957, 961-962, 964 (see also ionized interior air)
industrial buildings 215
inflatable forms 393, 445, 554
infrared sensing 1273
Innovations in Housing Competition 1561
Innovative Structures Program, U.S. Dept. of Energy 172, 709, 731, 840
insulation 19, 43, 79, 101, 104, 175, 179-182, 186, 193, 304, 322, 349, 386, 402, 418, 448, 492, 557-575, 609, 653, 719, 729, 735, 741, 749-750, 769-771, 774, 796, 798, 880, 901, 978, 1066, 1206, 1239, 1247, 1266, 1295, 1323, 1347-1348, 1425, 1448, 1533, 1592, 1662-1663, 1668, 1747-1748, 1753, 1762; extruded polystyrene 557, 564; fiberglass 605, 1400, 1405, 1456, 1533, 1785; Foil-Ray^{TM} 572; foam 539, 1448, 1677; glazing 304, 566, 1295; manufacturers 563; placement 769; polystyrene 1814; polystyrene bead board 564; polystyrene foam 557, 1533, 1762; polystyrene panels 1405, 1814; polyurethane 564, 1456; polyurethane foam 396; sawdust blocks 1347-1348; styrofoam 1671; Thermocurve 550; urethane foam 1448, 1778; Warm-N-Dri fiberglass foundation insulation 605
insurance 875, 891, 1017, 1022, 1037-1039, 1046, 1048, 1061, 1064, 1099, 1234, 1266; rates 138, 163, 1099
Integral Urban House, Berkeley, CA 1714
Integrated Building Systems, Grand Haven, MI 434, 547
interior decoration 907, 909
interior design 704, 901, 904, 907, 910, 912, 914 1723, 1730; thermal 704, 821, 1425
International Conference on Energy Efficient Buildings with Earth Shelter Protection, 1st, Sydney, Australia, 1983 231, 956, 1175-1176, 1181
International Franchise Association 1238
International Inventory of Geospacial Facilities and Conditions 231
International Tunneling Association, Working Group on Subsurface Planning 1110
ionized interior air 958, 1264, 1271 (see also indoor air quality)
irrigation systems see trickle irrigation systems
Isaacson, Paul 1732
isolation 149

Jefferson, Thomas 271
Jewan Construction, Aus-

Earth-Sheltered Residences 346

tralia 1333
Johns, Ferd, architect 1503
Johnson, Philip, architect 1391, 1429, 1672, 1674
Johnson, Steve, builder 1397
Johnson Gallery, New Canaan, CT 1429
Jones, Corrine, owner 1770
Jones, Derrick, owner 1770

Kaplan, Richard D., architect 364
Karsky, Don 1235
Karsky, Julie 1235
Kassel University see University of Kassel
Katonah Gallery, Katonah, NY 1642
Keister, H.W., Associates, structural engineers 1442
Keller, Gerald, builder 1774
Kelley, Oliver Hudson, Interpretive Center, Elk River, MN 1140
Kemper Insurance Group 1061
Kimber, Sandra 1584
Kimber, Wayne 1584
Kimbrell, T.J., builder 1442
Kirlin House, Napa Valley, CA 1409
kit houses 431, 490, 495, 1740, 1764
Kneeland, William, engineer 412
Knoll, Frank, State Senator, Minnesota 1078, 1081, 1546
Kramer, Ann, builder 1217

L-shaped houses 337, 341
labor personnel 40
ladders, pull-down 1787

land conservation 97, 944, 1286-1287 (see also land use)
land use 54, 75, 149, 1027, 1082-1083 (see also land conservation)
landscape design 228, 813
landscaping 6, 54, 325, 386, 577, 846-867, 1066, 1266
Lane Metal Products 531
Lash, David 500
Lawsuits 1239, 1519
leakage 440, 584, 612, 615, 875, 1219, 1488 (see also seepage)
Ledward & McDonald Consulting Architects, London, Eng. 1350
legal aspects 233, 1040-1041, 1050-1052, 1066, 1219, 1723
legislation 1071-1073, 1075, 1080-1081
Legorreta, Ricardo, architect 1368
Lenny, Michael J. 1624
Lewis House, Medfield, MA 1511
libraries 257, 1110, 1142, 1152, 1157-1158, 1171
Library of Congress, U.S. 213
life-cycle costs see costs: life-cycle
light shafts 344 (see also roofs: penetration)
lighting 186, 976, 978, 984, 1108, 1111; artificial 1730; natural 38, 255, 358, 374, 450, 899, 910, 915-916, 970, 1045, 1331, 1824; natural lighting simulation 910; sunlight 911, 918
lightning-caused fires see fire: lightning-caused
linear design houses 1783

347 Subject Index

liquid-applied waterproofing see waterproofing: liquid-applied
Liu Ming Ying Brigade, Da Xing, China 1284
loads see structural considerations: loads; cooling: loads
loans, mortgage 1023-1024
Locust Hill, Raven Rocks, OH 1679-1680
loess soil see soil: loess
Loffelstein concrete blocks 862
Log End Cave, West Chazy, NY 1522, 1647, 1655-1656
Lord's Power Company, Nora Springs, IA 754
Los Alamos Scientific Laboratory 1125
lotteries 352
louvers, external shade 442, 1295, 1395 (see also shading)
Loveless, John, architect 1516
low-cost housing 99, 128, 511, 870, 877, 889, 897-898, 1002, 1447, 1557, 1720, 1797
lumber see construction: wood; wood
Lundeen and Associates, Las Cruces, NM 1310

McCrary, Thomas A., architect 1433
Macdonald, Angus, architect 398, 1204
MacGowan, Georgina 1639
MacGowan, John 1639
McGuire, Michael, architect 303, 1391, 1778
maintenance 1266

Maitland, John, architect 1334
Majid, Johnathan, architect 312
marketing 892, 912, 922, 1005, 1026, 1033, 1047, 1198, 1802
Marsh, Douglas, builder 1118
Martin Organization, Atlanta, GA 310
masonry, concrete 480, 555, 620
Mass Merchandisers, Inc., Harrison, AR 1120
mass production 141, 515, 895
materials 6, 40, 54, 430, 485, 802; indigenous 414
medical clinics 1115
Mendon Country Homes, builder 1646
Merrick, Harry G., owner/architect 1745
mesh drainage system see drainage: mesh system
Metz, Don 1511, 1614-1615, 1617, 1619-1623, 1739
MHFA see Minnesota Housing Finance Agency
Mid-Sioux Community Action Agency, Remsen, IA 1183
Midwest Savings and Loan, Minneapolis/St. Paul, MN 1020
military uses 97
Miller, Thomas, architect 1461
Milliner, Mike, builder 1503
Milliner Construction Co., Frederick, MD 1502, 1504
mine reclamation 811-812, 1294, 1462, 1754

mined space 214
miners, Cornish 1280
mines, sand and gravel 811-812
Minnesota Earth Shelter, Inc. 1208
Minnesota Energy Agency 1126
Minnesota Housing Finance Agency 378, 682, 1548-1549; Solar/Earth Sheltered Demonstration Program 352, 378, 532, 678-679, 728, 1034, 1289, 1546, 1573, 1575
Minnesota Renaissance Festival 528
Minnesota State Fair 1543
Minnesota State Legislature 1080
misconceptions 106
missions 1171
Mitchell, Paul 1332, 1334
moisture (see also humidity; leakage; seepage; water vapor): control 598, 606, 1257; sources of 577
Montezuma Heights Air Park, Camp Verde, AZ 1105
Moore, Grover, Harper, Architects 1738
Moreland, Frank, architect 1209, 1222, 1716, 1727
Moreland Associates, Ft. Worth, TX 65
Morgan, William, architect 1214, 1223, 1430-1431, 1433-1435, 1439, 1441-1442
Morgan, William, Architects 1435, 1437
Morris, Robert Stirling, architect 313
Morrison, Eldon, Architects 1236, 1581
mortgages see loans, mortgage
Moscone Center see San Francisco Civic Center
motels 1115, 1123, 1127, 1264 (see also hotels; resorts)
mottling, soil see soil: mottling
mound-builders 1214
mound-houses 1433, 1442
mounds 292
Mouse House, Redwood Falls, MN 1106, 1126
movable partitions 1824
multiple-unit developments see housing developments, multiple-unit
museums 1170
Mutual of Omaha 1119

NAMIC see National Association of Mutual Insurance Companies
National Art Education Association 1125
National Association of Home Builders 319
National Association of Mutual Insurance Companies 875; Earth Shelter Committee 1061
National Building Code see building codes
National Bureau of Standards, U.S. 724, 821, 1424; Geotechnical Engineering Group 833
National Concrete Masonry Association 555
National Earth Shelter Builders Association 1234
National Parks and Wildlife Service, Tasmania, Australia 1156

349 Subject Index

National Solar Data Program 1423
National Zoological Park, Washington, DC 1153
Natural Areas Preservation, Inc. 1118
natural gas 963
Natural Gas Council of Minnesota 1126
natural lighting see lighting: natural
natural lighting simulation see lighting: natural lighting simulation
Navy, U.S. 896, 1155
Nebraska Underground Space Association 1224
New Mexico Solar Energy Institute 1310
New York Underground Facilities 1643
New York World's Fair 1651, 1729-1730
noise protection 138, 894, 944-945, 1271, 1327
North Carolina Coalition for Renewable Energy Resources, Earth Shelter Committee 1086
Northern States Power Company 700
Northwestern Bank of Minneapolis 361
Norton, Willard 546
Norwood-Young America Elementary School, Minnesota 1172
NSW Building Society Design Competition, Australia 293, 318
nuclear war 1101 (see also nuclear war shelters)
nuclear war shelters 1097-1098, 1643, 1781 (see also fallout shelters; survival shelters)
Nystrom, Charles, owner 1421

Oak Ridge National Laboratory 713, 883, 894, 1111, 1261
Oakland Community College, Southfield, MI 1169
O'Dell and Wooldridge, Phoenix, AZ, architects 1132
office buildings 248, 693, 1125, 1132, 1147-1148, 1150, 1171, 1173, 1612
office-residence complex 419
Ohanian, Richard, architect 1807
Ohio State Fair 1807
Oklahoma State University 358-359, 903, 971, 1310; School of Architecture Extension 177, 1691
opinion surveys see surveys
orientation see building orientation
outback, Australian 1181, 1317
overhangs, roof 346, 1668
Owens-Corning fiberglass 605
ownership of subterranean space 1050-1052

PAHS see passive annual heat storage
panels: acrylic 1733; fiberglass 435; plywood 413; Waffle-Crete precast 503; wall 398
Paradox House, NM 1637
parapets 346, 418, 1429
park ranger residences 1558, 1573, 1743
parking 149
parking buildings 1142
partitions, movable see movable partitions

Earth-Sheltered Residences 350

passive annual heat storage 568, 763-765
passive cooling see cooling: passive
passive earth coupling 210 (see also cooling: ground-coupled)
passive solar design 186, 294, 704, 971, 973, 989, 1141, 1155, 1174, 1362, 1427
passive solar equipment, tax laws concerning 1088
passive solar houses see solar houses, passive
patents 301
patio covers 346
patio homes 302, 1000, 1395
pavilion homes 302
Pei, I.M., and Partners 593
penetrational designs 329
People to People International 1285
periscopes 920
phase lag interval 805
photovoltaic arrays 639-640, 1510
physiological aspects 954-964, 1108, 1264, 1271 (see also health factors)
pilasters 1564
pillar extraction methods 1002, 1324
pillars 1724
pit houses, Indian 1637
pitch coating see waterproofing: pitch coating
Pittman, Scott, builder 1196
planning 40, 64, 161, 175, 229, 231-232, 508, 590, 950
plants see vegetation
plasticizers 507
PLATO (Control Data education system) 43
plumbing 186
plywood 349

pollution, indoor see indoor air quality
polystyrene 1814; blocks 439; bead board 564; foam 557, 1533, 1762; panels 1405, 1814
polyurethane 564, 1456; foam 396
pools see swimming pools
portals, precast 481
post-tensioning 486-487, 523-525
prefabricated module building systems 406, 413, 435, 464, 504, 551, 1419; box-type 464
prehistoric earth architecture 264-265
pressure-treated wood see wood: pressure-treated
pressures, earth 426, 505, 809; lateral 477, 496
Preusser, Ann, owner 1559
Preusser, Ben, owner 1559
Preusser Home, Minneapolis, MN 241, 1559
prisons 1166, 1171
privacy 149, 971, 984
Prodis, Pierre, architect 1397
property rights see ownership of subterranean space
property values 1033
psychological aspects 38, 75, 356, 909, 922-953, 1108, 1264, 1271
public housing 1069
public policy issues 1068-1089
public works 386
pueblo design 1634 (see also Anasazi Pueblo architecture)
Purdue University, Library 1157 (see also libraries)
pyramidal forms 292, 1214, 1430, 1435, 1437, 1442

351 Subject Index

Quarmby, Arthur, architect 1231
questions 5, 12, 83, 103-105, 123, 125, 136, 142, 145, 251

R-values 573-574, 1526
radiant heat panels see heating: radiant heat panels
radiation 823; monitoring 954-955; solar 821
radio stations 1115
radon concentrations 954-956, 958-960, 963
radon daughters, carcinogenic effects of 954
rammed earth construction 479, 537
Ramsey County Detention Center, St. Paul, MN 1166
real estate market 1013, 1026 (see also resale)
reclamation, coal mine see coal mine reclamation
Reduce existing data and compilation of additional data on earth sheltered housing in the Arizona-Sonoran Desert, by James W. Scalise 981, 1205
Regional analysis of ground and above-ground climate, by Kenneth Labs 840-841
regulations 154, 1069 (see also building codes)
Reimers, Robert, architect 1343
reinforced concrete beams 1433
Reinforced Earth^R see construction: Reinforced Earth^R
Remington, Lloyd, owner/builder 1661
Remington Residence, Burnsville, NC 1662
remote view optics 918, 920
resale 1547, 1692, 1779, 1796 (see also real estate market; selling)
research 148, 156-157, 230-232, 325, 1028, 1721
Residential Solar Heating and Cooling Demonstration Program 304, 1505
resorts 1141, 1367-1368
resource conservation see conservation of resources
rest stops, highway 1136, 1159-1160
restaurants 1161
restrictive covenants 1062, 1067, 1587
retirement homes 542, 1401, 1408, 1660, 1748, 1821
Reynolds, Michael, architect 1635
RHRU see Rural Housing Research Unit
Riddermark, Frederick, MD 1503
Rinker, Daniel, builder 1518, 1526
risks see accident risks
Riverfront Redevelopment, Memphis, TN 1150
rock bed heat storage 627, 694, 750, 1561, 1585, 1592, 1780 (see also heat: storage; energy: storage; chimney rock bins)
Rodale Press Operations Center, Emmaus, PA 1162
Roman arches 444
roof gardens 849-850, 854
roofs 38, 64, 398, 402, 404-405, 410, 418, 423, 475, 479, 482, 1106, 1400, 1406, 1641, 1668, 1671; diagonal 302; earth cov-

Earth-Sheltered Residences 352

ered 79, 210, 738, 761, 791; framing kits 1740; insulation 741; joist roof system 1465, 1470; log 398; parabolic 1345; penetration see skylights and light shafts; precast 493-494; prestressed concrete 1552, 1662; shingled 1500; sloped 492, 601, 1456; sod 21, 1393, 1410, 1405, 1641; 1780, 1804; superinsulated 1825; thermal 727, 780, 885; truss 398, 402; truss and beam 1106; vaulted 272; waffle slab 593
root cellars 510, 1151
Rowles, W., designer 301
Roy, Jaki, owner/builder 1647
Roy, Rob, builder 1647
runoff 577, 995
Rural Housing Research Unit 635, 1811
Rylander, Rod, architect 1522

Safe City, Rosendale, NY 1643
safety considerations 65, 148, 233, 1021, 1108 (see also fire: safety)
St. Benedict's Abbey, Benet Lake, WI 1431
St. John's University, Collegeville, MN 1550
St. Louis Fire Alarm Headquarters 1130
sand and gravel mines see mines, sand and gravel
sandstone 282, 1278, 1421, 1426
San Francisco Civic Center 1143
saunas 910

sawdust blocks see insulation: sawdust blocks and construction: sawdust blocks
Scafe, Gayle, builder 482, 1203, 1599
scams 1240
schools 1110, 1116-1117, 1137, 1145, 1164, 1172, 1431
Schultz, Bob, builder 1739
Schurer, Gerhard, architect/builder 1318, 1326
Science Museum of Minnesota 290
Scott, David, architect 1226, 1743
Seaborne, Ben, builder 1118
Seedorf, Richard 502
seepage 814 (see also leakage; moisture)
selling 892, 1692, 1820 (see also resale)
seminars 44, 177, 299, 1183, 1186, 1201, 1232
sensory deprivation 1271
septic tanks 1777
Seward West Townhouses 1542, 1572, 1576, 1579-1580
shading 762, 834, 848, 1561 (see also louvers, external shade)
shed-style roofs see roofs: sloped
shell structures 404-405, 407, 432, 493, 520, 534, 868, 1117, 1255, 1305, 1441, 1667, 1720, 1725; precast modular 502
Shelterra Earth Homes 493
shelters see fallout shelters; nuclear war shelters; survival shelters
Shippee, Paul 1425
shopping centers 1255

353 Subject Index

shoring 522
shotcrete 415, 483, 539
Shurcliff, William 108-109
Sibley, Richard, architect 310, 502, 1443
Simmons, Lon, builder 1215, 1233, 1594
Simon, Mark, architect 1736-1738
siting considerations 6, 34, 38, 43, 53, 64, 104, 149, 179-182, 186, 577, 590, 800-845, 970-971, 995, 1005, 1053, 1246, 1266, 1493, 1505, 1663, 1710, 1723, 1802, 1809 (see also flat sites)
sky-mining 246
skylights 340, 374, 396, 450, 905, 919, 1331, 1411, 1424, 1501, 1514, 1662, 1690; skyflex 450
slab-on-grade floors see floors: slab-on-grade
slabs, concrete see concrete: slabs
slopes 812, 842, 855, 858, 1004, 1316, 1327, 1694; stabilization 855, 1416
snail plans 302
Snider, James, architect 1373
sod houses 120, 256, 285, 1637
soil 496, 606, 611, 831, 837, 839, 955, 963, 1005, 1101; analysis 803-805, 809, 837, 844, 865, 1302; bearing capacity 817; classification 809, 1266; climate 822, 827, 840-841, 843, 848; composition 809; cover 126, 438; depth 846; evaluation 186; expansion 819, 836; loess 276, 1349, 1475; moisture 846; mottling 815; pressure see pressures, earth; settlement 809; stability 835; stratification 830; swelling 809; temperature 735, 741, 743, 745, 751, 768, 772-773, 776-777, 787, 789, 805-807, 821-822, 829, 833, 840, 843, 1267, 1272-1273, 1300, 1306; tests 832-833, 844, 865; thermal conductivity 210, 833; thermal resistivity 833;
solar chimneys 618, 1151, 1665
solar collectors 1137, 1561, 1788, 1803
solar credit program 1060 (see also taxation)
solar design, passive see passive solar design
Solar Design Associates, Inc., Lincoln, MA 639, 1510
Solar-Earth Energy Conservation Bank Bill 1068, 1072, 1075
solar hot water systems 304, 627, 891, 1417, 1553, 1561, 1665, 1740, 1788, 1803; hydronic 1137, 1417
solar houses 91, 271, 334, 366, 374, 1046, 1360, 1586, 1641, 1818, 1823; active 723, 891; passive 132, 331, 343, 372, 697, 750, 891, 1174, 1261, 1295, 1301, 1313-1314, 1370, 1376, 1390, 1397, 1404, 1422, 1427, 1445, 1470, 1480, 1491, 1496, 1499, 1505, 1566, 1616, 1753, 1809
solar optics 899, 918
solar stills 1278
Solar Thermal Energy Conversion Documentation

Project 210
Solaria House, Indian Mills, NJ 1391, 1625, 1627-1628
Solaris System (solar heating system) 1627
Soleri, Paolo, architect 1195
Solomonson, Gary, and Associates, Minneapolis, MN 951
sound/slide presentation 133
South Dakota Housing Development Authority 879, 1708
Southern Regional Housing Research Project 985
Southridge Estates, Boone, IA 1481
space perception 223
SPICE computer program 1247-1250
standards, building 412
Stark County District Library, Canton, OH 1167
State University Agriculture and Technical College, Morrisville, NY 1604, 1649
Stearns, David 416
stepped ceilings 1662
Stevens, Douglas, builder 1454
Sticks and Stones House, Minneapolis, MN 1480
stills, solar 1278
Stoneshire Development, Highlandville, MO 1596
storage, food 212
storage facilities 1171; tanks 1142
storm protection 1093, 1101 (see also tornado protection)
stoves, wood-burning 1497, 1594, 1603, 1686, 1740, 1762
Stovin-Bradford, Frank, architect 1351
Strickler, John, owner 1749
strip mining areas 1294, 1462, 1680, 1754
Strong, Steven, architect 1510
structural considerations 175, 970, 1021 (see also construction); design 43, 179-181, 488, 804, 1045, 1753; engineering 112, 410; grids 855 (see also slopes: stabilization); loads 410, 478, 521, 544, 1441; systems 104, 148, 514-515, 533, 1206, 1764, 1766
stucco 1430, 1641, 1700
student housing 1604, 1649 (see also dormitories)
subcalc (heat loss algorithm) 767
subcontractors 40
subdivisions 545, 1000, 1062, 1206, 1215, 1398, 1481, 1604-1605, 1763 (see also housing developments)
Sullivan, Louis 389
Sun belt earth sheltered architecture, by Langley and Gay 779
Sun Cottage, Hendersonville, NC 1663
Sun Earth Estates, CA 1215
Sun Earth House, Boulder, CO 1415, 1422-1425
Sun Temple Associates, Alamogordo, NM 1310
Sunbird 2000, Wasatch Mts., UT 1733
Sunburrows Development 1802
Sun/Earth Builders, Columbus, OH 1677
sunlight see lighting: sunlight

355 Subject Index

Sunshine Farm, Columbia, MD 1503
Sunspace Designer/Builder, Burnsville, NC 1662
Suntel Design Associates, Lake Oswego, OR 307
superinsulated houses 138, 150, 300, 331, 338, 350, 394, 416, 681, 705, 710, 834, 1629, 1742, 1791
Superphenix breeder reactor, Poleyrieu, France 1360
surface bonding 507, 509, 535
surface runoff see runoff
surveys 936, 943, 947, 969-987, 1297-1299, 1312, 1317
survival shelters 669
survivalists 1731, 1734-1735, 1781
Survive Tomorrow, Inc. 1731, 1734-1735
Swanson, Fred O., owner/builder 1613
Swayze, Jay, architect 1719, 1725, 1729-1730
swimming pools 910, 1266, 1346, 1455, 1460
Symposium on Earth Architecture, Beijing, China, 1985 1177

Taisei Construction Corporation, Tokyo 451-452
tar base sealer 1690
taxation 1048, 1088 (see also solar credit program)
taxonomy 8, 217, 219, 245, 262
teleconference 83
temperate climate 243
temperature, ground see soil: temperature

terminology 122, 218, 480, 1263
Terra Dome, Inc., Independence, MO 482, 1203, 1591, 1598-1599
Terra Dome House 377
Terra Dome System see construction: Terra Dome System
Terra Domes of Australia 1211
Terra Domus, Oneida, NY 1649
Terra Grande House, Lubbock, TX 1717
Terra Therm heating and cooling system 754
Terra Vista, Frederick, MD 1502-1505
terraces 292, 429
Terraset Elementary School, Reston, VA 1116-1117, 1137, 1431
Terrasol Farms, Newton, NJ 1630
Terratech Center office-residence complex 419
La Terre Armee see construction: Reinforced Earth^R
Terrene Ark 1, La Verkin, UT 1731, 1734-1735
Terry, Karen, builder 1636
Terry Residence, Sangre de Cristo Mts., NM 1641
Texas Energy and Natural Resources Advisory Council 1723
Texas State Fair 1807
Texas Tech University, Lubbock 1721; Civil Engineering Dept. 1307
theatres 257
thermal breaks 779, 1295, 1765
thermal comfort 8, 645, 662, 703-704, 789, 810,

Earth-Sheltered Residences 356

880, 970-971, 978, 1284, 1300
thermal conductivity 758, 833
thermal convection 1470
thermal design of interiors 704, 821, 1425 (see also interior design)
Thermal Integrity Factor 352
thermal loop homes 1814
thermal mass 79, 366, 694, 774, 888, 901, 978, 1025, 1117, 1155, 1411-1412, 1445, 1474, 1511, 1617, 1669, 1711 (see also energy: storage; heat: storage; rock bed heat storage; chimney rock bins)
thermal performance see energy: performance
thermal roofs see roofs: thermal
Thermal Time Constant 758
thermally layered houses 331
thermistors 1709
Thermocurve insulation see insulation: Thermocurve
thermosiphoning 633, 1753
Thomason, Harry 1627
TIF see Thermal Integrity Factor
tiling see drainage: tiling
tilt-slab construction see construction: tilt-up
timber see construction: wood; wood
time-sharing vacation units 367
TMC Co., Woodland Hills, CA 1395
toolsheds 510
topography 839, 1005
tornado protection 1098, 1100, 1104, 1120, 1164, 1690, 1756, 1771 (see also storm protection)

tours 58, 78, 290, 1063, 1181, 1691
townhouses 1767 (see also Seward West Townhouses)
tracking equipment see computerized tracking equipment
transportation 1069; bus 1000
treated wood see wood: treated
trenching 405
trickle irrigation systems 852
Triform co-polymer binder 437
triplexes 1591 (see also duplexes)
Trombe walls see walls: Trombe
Troyer, Leroy, Architects, Mishawaka, IN 1161
truss and beam roofs 1106
Trust, Vera, architect 1326
TTC see Thermal Time Constant
tube homes 303, 408, 1773
tubes, earth see earth tubes
Tuff-N-Dri see waterproofing: Tuff-N-Dri
tunnels 212, 271, 1255
Turknett, Roy, engineer 1442
Twin Springs Estates, Poplar Bluff, MO 1605

U-value 649
UMR water jet technology 441
Underfloor plenum manual, by NAHB Research Foundation, Inc. 625
underfloor plenums 504, 625, 694, 910 (see also floors: heating)

357 Subject Index

Underground designs, by Malcolm Wells 119
Underground Developers Association 936
Underground Space Center 89, 321, 683, 728, 930, 1035, 1043, 1085, 1089, 1165, 1178, 1186; Technical Response Group 1089
underground water see ground water
Underground World Home Corp. 1651
Underhill, Enid, OK 1694
Underhill, Grand Rapids, MI 1621
Underhill, Holme, Yorkshire, Eng. 1352-1356
Under-the-Earth dealer, Bayfield, WI 1471
underwriting guidelines 1061 (see also insurance)
UNESCO 231
Uniform Building Code see building codes
Universal Design Group, Columbus, IN 1114
University of Kassel, Germany 479
University of Minnesota, Minneapolis 1149; Bookstore 1113; Civil and Mineral Engineering Building 221, 1112, 1135, 1165
University of Minnesota, St. Paul 1145
University of Missouri, Dept. of Psychology 936
University of Missouri, Kansas City, Center for Underground Space Studies 936
University of Missouri, Rolla, Mineral Engineering Building 1163

University of Washington, Dept. of Architecture 1108
urban development 988, 992, 995-996, 998-999, 1001-1004, 1006-1007
U'Ren, Corkey, builder 1106
urethane foam 1448, 1778
utility billings 163, 684, 691, 1421, 1550, 1702
UWENSOL (computer program to analyze consumption) 671-672

vacation homes see time-sharing vacation units
Vaile, Buck, builder 1678, 1681
Van Hagey, William, lawyer 1200
vapor control see humidity: water vapor
vaults, steel 419
VCS see vertical crawl space
vegetation 126, 182, 761, 791, 846, 848, 851, 853-855, 857, 859-860
ventilation 38, 104, 126, 186, 193, 396, 618, 626, 628, 632, 637, 669, 750, 774, 818, 905, 1045, 1096, 1474, 1564, 1690, 1715, 1789
Vento, Bruce, U.S. Rep., Minnesota 1072-1073
Vento Cave Amendment 1073
vents 846, 1690 (see also ventilation)
vermiculite 1456
Vermulen, E.T., architect 1521
vertical crawl space 368-370, 1522

Earth-Sheltered Residences 358

vertical wall fins 1093
vestibules 622, 1295
 (see also airlock entries)
Vetsch, Peter, architect 1372
Victorian Ministry of Housing, Australia 1079
Vidal, Henri, architect/engineer 432, 516, 1358
Village Homes, Davis, CA 1389-1390
Villis, Peter, architect 1320
Villis Tossani Architects 1334, 1337
visitor centers 1171

Wadena County Fair, MN 1578
waffle slab roof deck see roofs, waffle slab
Waffle-Crete precast panels see panels: Waffle-Crete precast
walls 410, 418, 536, 706, 1663-1664, 1671; cast-in-place concrete 1465; concrete 19, 1448, 1465; concrete block 1379, 1501; poured concrete 493, 1500, 1727; precast concrete 470-471; reinforced concrete 1296, 1406, 1448, 1501, 1814; retaining 410, 486, 597, 627; sandwich system 405, 536; subgrade 210; trombe 327, 627, 725-726, 1445, 1594
Ward House, Central Florida 462
warehouses 529, 1148
Warm-N-Dri see insulation: Warm-N-Dri
warranties 551

water jet rock cutting 441, 1135 (see also water jet technology, UMR)
water jet technology, UMR 441
water leaks see leakage
water table 53, 577, 606, 816, 1500
water tanks, ferrocement 1323
water vapor 586, 603 (see also humidity)
waterproofing 34, 38, 43, 79, 104, 175, 179-182, 186, 193, 340, 349, 375, 386, 418, 422, 430, 486, 507, 523, 571, 576-617, 866, 875, 901, 963, 1045, 1066, 1206, 1219, 1239, 1326, 1497, 1564, 1662-1665, 1673, 1686, 1690, 1705, 1753, 1798 (see also dampproofing); acrylic latex coating 1686; asbestos felt membrane 1512; asphalt coating 608, 1497; asphalt coating with bentonite 583; bentonite-based waterproofing 340, 349, 583, 608, 613, 1219, 1502, 1527, 1609, 1798; bentonite clay 608, 614, 617; Bentonize C-R-80-S 588; Bentonize C-R-80-S4 588; Bentonize C-R-80-T 588; bituthene liquid polyurethane 608; bituthene membrane 349; butyl 608; butyl rubber sheets 340, 593, 1417; cementitious coating 617; elastomeric membrane 349, 1626; ethylene propylene diene monomer 608; Hydroside 1690; Hypalon 1389-1390; Karnak elas-

Subject Index

tomeric membrane 1626;
liquid-applied 614, 617;
pitch coating 608; polyethylene 1518, 1632;
polyethylene-coated
rubberized asphalt 583;
polymers 605; polyurethane 1456; sheet rubber
membranes 617; Sure-Seal
elastomeric membrane
349; Tuff-N-Dri sprayapplied polymer 605;
Waterstop-plus 588
weather conditions 821
weather data 843
weatherproofing 422
Weber, Larry, builder 1471
Webster, Richard, architect
305, 689
Wells, Malcolm, architect
119, 194, 224, 1131, 1152,
1213, 1218, 1229, 1241,
1391, 1621, 1625, 1627,
1633, 1679-1680
wells 1777; geothermal
1803
wellwater (as source of
radon) 963
Western Industries, Cadillac,
MI 494
Western Michigan Energy
Show 1521
Whaley Condominium,
Ocean City, MD 1439
wheelchair use modifications see handicapped,
design features for
Wheeler, Elbert, architect
1683
Whittet Construction, Walnut Creek, CA 1400
Wilkes, Joseph, architect
1153
Wilkes, Faulkner, Jenkins
and Bass, Washington, DC
1153
Williams, Pat, U.S. Rep.,
Mont. 1071
wind assisted homes 1818
wind breaks 863, 1092-1093, 1685 (see also wind
protection)
wind generators 1128, 1647
(see also windmills)
wind protection 1099, 1120
(see also wind breaks)
wind towers 621, 628, 1401
wind tunnel tests 818
windcatchers see wind towers
windmills 144, 1344 (see
also wind generators)
windowless space 905-906,
918, 928-929, 935, 945,
1489, 1494, 1735
windows 552, 563, 762, 839,
920, 929, 935, 1266; clerestory 1401
wingwalls 563
Winston House, Lyme, NH
234, 1619-1620, 1623
Wisconsin Ready Mixed
Concrete Association
1775, 1822
wood (see also construction: wood): pressuretreated 338, 349, 1518,
1713; treated 456, 1296,
1400, 1410, 1713
Wood Brothers Concrete
Construction Company,
Gallatin, MO 536
wood-burning stoves see
stoves, wood-burning
Woods, Charles, designer
108-109, 338-340, 360,
373, 1243
Wood-Tech^{TM} panelized
wood system see construction: Wood-Tech^{TM}
Woodward, Howard, contractor 1433
workplaces, subsurface
1108
World of Concrete

Conferences 1184
Wright, David, architect 1228, 1393, 1405, 1636
Wright, Frank Lloyd, architect 389, 1194, 1227, 1418
Wukasch, Eugene, architect 1714

Youngblut Corp., Washburn, IA 1772

Zanetto, James, architect 1389-1390
zero lot line construction
see construction: zero lot line
zoning ordinances 179-181, 320, 986, 991-992, 1015, 1029, 1041, 1043, 1045, 1048-1049, 1057